Spain and the Great Powers in the Twentieth Century

Edited by
Sebastian Balfour and Paul Preston

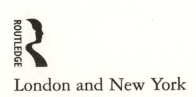

London and New York

First published 1999
by Routledge
11 New Fetter Lane, London EC4P 4EE

Simultaneously published in the USA and Canada
by Routledge
29 West 35th Street, New York, NY 10001

Typeset in Garamond by
J&L Composition Ltd, Filey, North Yorkshire
Printed and bound in Great Britain by MPG Books Limited, Bodmin

British Library Cataloguing in Publication Data
A catalogue record for this book is available from the British Library

Library of Congress Cataloging in Publication Data
Spain and the great powers in the twentieth century/edited by
    Sebastian Balfour and Paul Preston.
        p.   cm. — (Routledge/Cañada Blanch studies in
    contemporary Spain)
    Includes bibliographical references and index.
        ISBN 0–415–18077–5 (hb). — ISBN 0–415–18078–3 (pbk.)
        1. Spain—Foreign relations—20th century.   2. Spain—Politics
and government—20th century.   I. Balfour, Sebastian.
II. Preston, Paul, 1946–   .   III. Series.
DP233.8.S64   1999
327.46'009'04—dc21   98–39238
                                                           CIP

ISBN 0–415–18078–3 (Pbk)
ISBN 0–415–18077–5 (Hbk)

Spain and the Great Powers in the Twentieth Century

'An important volume . . . by the leading specialists, that will become the standard work in the field.'

Stanley Payne, *University of Wisconsin, USA*

'An impressive team of contributors . . . a work of high quality and accessibility.'

Martin Blinkhorn, *University of Lancaster, UK*

Spain and the Great Powers in the Twentieth Century examines the international context to, and influences on, Spanish history and politics from 1898 to the present day. Spanish history is necessarily international, with the significance of Spain's neutrality in the First World War and the global influences on the outcome of the Spanish Civil War.

Taking the defeat in the Spanish–American War of 1898 as a starting point, the book includes surveys on:

- the crisis of neutrality during the First World War
- foreign policy under the dictatorship of Primo de Rivera
- the Allies and the Spanish Civil War
- Nazi Germany and Franco's Spain
- Spain and the Cold War
- relations with the United States.

This book traces the important topic of modern Spanish diplomacy up to the present day.

Sebastian Balfour is Reader and **Paul Preston** is Professor at the London School of Economics and Political Science.

Routledge/Cañada Blanch Studies in Contemporary Spain

Contents

List of contributors

Sebastian Balfour is Reader in Contemporary Spanish Politics and Deputy Director of the Cañada Blanch Centre for Contemporary Spanish Studies at the London School of Economics and Political Science. His books include *Dictatorship, Workers and the City. Labour in Greater Barcelona since 1939* (Oxford: Oxford University Press, 1989), *Castro. A Profile in Power* (London: Longman, [2nd edn.], 1995) and *The End of the Spanish Empire 1898–1923* (Oxford: Oxford University Press, 1997).

Christian Leitz is Lecturer in History at the University of Auckland, New Zealand. He is the author of *Economic Relations between Nazi Germany and Franco's Spain, 1936–1945* (Oxford: Oxford University Press, 1996), he is also editor of a forthcoming book entitled *Spain in an International Context* (New York: Berghahn Books).

Boris Liedtke completed his PhD in the London School of Economics and Political Science and works for Deutsche, Morgan Grenfell in Singapore.

Enrique Moradiellos is Lecturer in History at the University of Extremadura in Cáceres, Spain. He is author of several books, including *Neutralidad benévola: el Gobierno británico y la insurrección militar española de 1936* (Oviedo: Pentalfa, 1990) and *La pérfida de Albión: el Gobierno británico y la guerra de España* (Madrid: Siglo XX1, 1996).

Florentino Portero is Lecturer at the Universidad Nacional de Educación a Distancia in Madrid. He is author of *Franco aislado. La cuestión española (1945–1950)* (Madrid: Aguilar, 1989) and co-editor with Javier Tusell of *Antonio Cánovas y el sistema politico de la Restauración* (Madrid: Biblioteca Nueva, 1998).

Paul Preston is Príncipe de Asturias Professor of Contemporary Spanish History and Director of the Cañada Blanch Centre for Contemporary Spanish Studies at the London School of Economics and Political Science. His books include *The Coming of the Spanish Civil War: Reform, Reaction and Revolution in* *the Second Spanish Republic 1931–1936* (London: Routledge [2nd edn], 1994); *The Triumph of Democracy in Spain* (London/New York: Methuen, 1986); *A Concise History of the Spanish Civil War 1936–1939* (London: Harper Collins, 1996); *Franco: A Biography* (London: Harper Collins, 1993) and *¡Comrades! Portraits from the Spanish Civil War* (London: Harper Collins, 1998).

Francisco Romero is Lecturer in Contemporary History at the London Guildhall University. He is author of *Twentieth Century Spain. Politics and Society, 1898–1998* (London: MacMillan, 1998) and a forthcoming book, *A Fatal Neutrality: Spain between War and Revolution, 1914–1918*, to be published shortly by Routledge.

Ismael Saz is Head of the Department of Contemporary History at the University of Valencia and author of *Fascistas en España: la intervención italiana en la Guerra Civil a través de los telegramas de la 'Missione Militare Italiana in Spagna' (15 diciembre 1936 – 31 marzo 1937)* (Madrid: CSIC, 1980) (in collaboration with Javier Tusell) and *Mussolini contra la 11 República: hostilidad, conspiraciones, intervención (1931–1936)* (Valencia: Edicions Alfons el Magnánim, 1986).

Denis Smyth is Professor of European History at the University of Toronto. He is author of *Diplomacy and Strategy of Survival: British Policy and Franco's Spain (1940–4)* (Cambridge: Cambridge University Press, 1986), and (with Paul Preston) of *Spain, the EEC and NATO* (London: Routledge, 1994).

Angel Viñas is Professor at the Complutense University of Madrid and was Executive Adviser to the Spanish Minister of Foreign Affairs between 1983–7 and EU Ambassador to the UN. His books include *La Alemania nazi y el 18 de julio* (Madrid: Alianza, 1974), *El oro español en la guerra civil* (Madrid: Ministerio de Hacienda, 1976) and *Los pactos secretos de Franco con Estados Unidos: bases, ayuda económica, recortes de soberanía* (Barcelona: Grijalbo, 1981).

Introduction

Spain and the Great Powers

Sebastian Balfour and Paul Preston

It is now an unquestionable assumption among historians that the history of Spain has been an integral part of a European and international process and indeed has been a regional variant of that process.[1] This new perspective represents a significant revision of traditional interpretations in which the history of Spain was seen as a deviation from a supposed European or universal model. Such was the grip of the latter view in Spain that it became common among Spaniards themselves to see their own history as a tragedy, born of a supposedly conflictive and self-destructive national character. In the aftermath of the Disaster of 1898 in which Spain lost the residue of her old empire in a war with the United States, some critical intellectuals went as far as suggesting that Spain suffered from a chronic illness.[2] The philosopher Ortega y Gasset proposed later that only through integration in Europe could Spain find a cure. 'If Spain is the problem,' he wrote, 'Europe is the solution.' From the end of the nineteenth century, almost an entire publishing industry was built around explanations for the country's supposed decadence and utopian solutions for her recovery. The myth of Spain's peculiarity among European nations was shared by many foreigners who came into contact with her. In the 1930s, W.H. Auden described the country as 'that arid square, that fragment nipped off from hot Africa, soldered so crudely to inventive Europe'.[3]

Far from being an exceptional case among European powers, however, Spain mirrored the problems of Europe even before the twentieth century. Her crises and civil wars were part of the wider crises and civil wars of Europe as a whole, though they took forms specific to Spain. Without ever having been absent or distant, Spain was drawn into even closer contact with Europe from the end of the nineteenth century. Her increasing *rapprochement* was due not only to the exigencies of strategic security in an increasingly unstable international environment but also to a growing economic, social and cultural interrelationship. This greater involvement in the affairs of the continent continued in the twentieth century. Yet Spain's minor and subaltern membership of the international relations system carried a high price. It would be a recurrent complaint of the Spanish military establishment, for example, that the indefensible frontiers of Spanish North Africa were the consequence of an Anglo-French agenda which ignored Spanish interests. At a later stage, the Spanish Second Republic of 1931–39 would be sacrificed by the Western democracies as part of their policy of appeasement of the Fascist powers. There was a major hiatus in Spain's foreign relations in the 1940s after the victory of the right in the Civil War and the unofficial alignment of the Franco dictatorship with the Axis throughout most of the Second World War. But Spain was partially reinstated in the early 1950s by becoming a partner of the United States in the Cold War, and economic relations with Europe were resumed with an accelerated burst from the early 1960s as Spain was sucked into the Western economic boom. When Spain joined the North Atlantic Treaty Organization (NATO) in 1982 and the European Union (EU) in 1986, she completed the process of integration and became an organic part of Europe. In 1998, as we write, Spain appears to fulfil the conditions for entry into the European Monetary Union.

It is with this overall perspective that the contributors to this book examine the duality of Spain's relations with the Great Powers in the one hundred years from 1898 to 1998. Collectively, this is an account of how the Great Powers have influenced the development of twentieth-century Spain, in particular in terms of dictating the course of the Spanish Civil War and thereafter helping to keep General Franco in power. It is also an account of Spanish foreign policy and of the ways in which Madrid's decision-makers have tried to steer the most advantageous path among the Great Powers. All the contributions bring new data to and an elucidation of that complex story and all serve to reveal a greater involvement of Spain in the system of international relations than has hitherto been assumed.[4]

The book begins with an analysis of Spain's foreign policy in the period following her defeat in the Spanish–American War of 1898 and the loss of the remnants of her old empire overseas. As we write, the centenary of that event is being commemorated throughout Spain, as indeed in the United States and Spain's ex-colonies, Cuba, Puerto Rico and the Philippines. Much has been done to revise the catastrophic interpretation of Spain's defeat that year which baptized it as the Disaster.[5] But the shock caused by the rout and the subsequent loss of the empire led to a profound revision by Spain's elites of her relations with the Great Powers. Having relied fatally on a foreign policy based mainly on dynastic and religious connections, Spain was now forced to seek a firmer foothold in the volatile international relations of the end of the nineteenth century. Spanish policy-makers chose to enter into close alliance with France and Britain, despite the fact that the sympathies of a section of the elites and the dynastic links of the monarchy were tied to Austria and Germany.

This realignment of Spanish foreign policy marked the beginning of a deeper implication in the affairs of the Great Powers in which Spain would remain, until the Civil War, a subordinate partner of Britain and France. It was under Britain's wing that Spain took on a new colonial role in North Africa, administering a buffer neo-colony beyond her littoral enclaves in northern Morocco between the French sphere of influence and Britain's strategically vital base in Gibraltar. Morocco became the means whereby Spain re-entered international relations in a dynamic period of neo-colonial expansion when most of the remaining uncolonized world was carved up into spheres of influence through tense negotiations and close confrontations. Yet, to the chagrin of many influential Spaniards, particularly conservative politicians and the military, Spain was invariably sidelined in Franco-British relations over the Mediterranean. France sought hegemony over all of Morocco while Britain used Spain's desire to re-establish an international presence in order to curb French expansionist ambitions. Neither bothered to include Spain, however, when they delineated the spheres of influence or bargained over the status of Tangier before taking their conclusions to an international conference. Britain signed a formal agreement with Spain in 1907, the so-called Pact of Cartagena, whereby both parties agreed to maintain the status quo in the Mediterranean, sealing the supposed *rapprochement* of the two nations upon the young Spanish King's marriage to Queen Victoria's niece. However, in the following year, without consulting Spain, Britain proceeded to build an iron fence some 400 metres within Spanish territory on the isthmus of Gibraltar.[6]

Nor was Spain consulted in the Great Power realignments prior to the First World War. Nevertheless, her neutrality in that war did not prevent the European conflict from causing internal turmoil, as Francisco Romero argues in Chapter 2. Spanish public opinion was divided between support for the Entente and the Central Powers, reflecting the divisions which arose from a complex set of political, social and economic conflicts within Spain herself. Tensions were further exacerbated by the economic effects of the war. The Spanish economy experienced an unprecedented boom as both her industry and her agriculture took advantage of intense demand from the war-torn economies to the north. Demand from both sides led both to dramatic shortages of consumer goods within Spain and dramatic price increases. The resulting inflation doubled the price of subsistence goods and intensified the class struggle. The ensuing political crisis in Spain from 1917 was part of the wider crisis of European society in the post-First World War period. The specific form it took in Spain derived in part from the progressive erosion of the legitimacy of the liberal state and in part from the unevenness of the process of modernization. The cleavages were not just political and ideological but also regional because economic growth and urbanization had taken place above all in the more developed periphery of Spain, whose elites had occupied subordinate positions in the structure of political power. The crisis of the liberal state was further deepened when the Spanish army in Morocco suffered a severe and humiliating defeat in 1921 at the hands of the Berber rebels in the Rif mountains of the northeast. The combination of military revanchism and social unrest led to the military coup by General Miguel Primo de Rivera on 13 September 1923.[7]

The new dictator's preoccupations were primarily domestic, according to Ismael Saz in Chapter 3. He sought to redeem his country, allegedly corrupted by politics, regionalism and class struggle, through a nationalist revolution from above. In this endeavour, he was deeply influenced by Mussolini. Nevertheless, the Primo de Rivera regime was authoritarian, not totalitarian, and more akin to the Salazar state in Portugal or the Piłsudski regime in Poland than to the Italian Fascist state. His foreign policy oscillated between the attractions of Italian expansionism and Spain's traditional alignment with France and especially Britain that served as the anchor of Spain's international relations. Like many military officers, he wished to raise Spain's status among the Great Powers and campaigned unsuccessfully for her incorporation into the League of Nations as a permanent member. The dictator's only achievement in foreign affairs came about unexpectedly. Despite opposition from the *Africanista* sections of the army, he determined at first to withdraw Spanish forces from the Moroccan enterprise. However, he quickly reversed his policy when the French were drawn into the war in the Rif after Abd el-Krim had been tempted by the Spanish retreat into making incursions into French territory. Drawn together, the combined Spanish and French forces defeated the rebels and Primo was able to claim the credit for solving one of Spain's most intractable problems of the early twentieth century.

It was Primo de Rivera's domestic failures that led to his resignation and the fall of the monarchy, which had been closely associated with the dictatorship. The Second Republic was launched in 1931 amid widespread popular jubilation and not a few inflated expectations of what could be achieved at home. Its foreign policy at first reflected the democratic agenda of its internal policy. Spain achieved a degree of international stature by the insistence of the new government, despite the risk of upsetting traditional allies, on championing the pacifist and interventionist role of the League of Nations, in particular over the issue of disarmament. But the domestic achievements of the Second Republic, particularly its enactment of progressive social reform, aroused the hostility of both Britain and the United States, whose establishments viewed both this policy and the radical agitation in Spain as a threat to their economic interests. The victory of the republican right in the elections of November 1933 brought to power a coalition government more in tune with international conservative opinion. However, the sympathy with Mussolini's Italy manifested by one of the parties, the Catholic authoritarian CEDA or Confederación Española de Derechas Autónomas, which composed the new government's parliamentary majority, threatened to upset Britain. Accordingly, as Ismael Saz argues in Chapter 4, the foreign policy-makers of the CEDA, while discreetly cultivating relations with Rome and Berlin, adopted a much lower profile in international affairs than had their predecessors.

The foreign policy of the Popular Front government in Spain, elected in February 1936, reflected both the experience of the first government of the Republic of 1931–33 and the deteriorating domestic and international situation. Seeking to temper the chronic hostility of Mussolini towards the progressive Republic, the government opposed the policy of international sanctions against Italy over that country's 1935 invasion of Abyssinia. Despite her deep and continued involvement in the League of Nations, Spain's greater neutrality and her passivity in the face of violations of the League pacts were part of a wider pattern of appeasement by the democracies of the ever more aggressive Fascist powers. The policy of the British government in particular was driven by the desire to avoid a confrontation that might lead to war and by the fond hope that Fascism would crush the threat of revolution without challenging the conservative bourgeois democracies. Spain would be the first to suffer the consequences of this profoundly misguided international policy.[8]

Indeed, the Civil War in Spain was fundamentally conditioned by the international context, as Chapters 5 to 7 reveal. In Chapter 5, Enrique Moradiellos argues that the Western Allies' arms embargo on the Spanish Republic during the conflict profoundly undermined both its morale and its war effort. The Soviet Union, the only active ally of the Spanish government, was so concerned to maintain good relations with Britain and France because of the threat of war with Germany that she was consistently hesitant about the provision of military aid to the Loyalists. On the other hand, the military uprising against the Republic could not have succeeded without the support of Germany and Italy. Conscious of their own weaknesses, the Nationalists sought the help of Mussolini and Hitler, both of whom instinctively identified with the insurgents' cause. They did so not just because of ideological solidarity with a potentially Fascist ally, but, much more, because of the potential of the Spanish Civil War for altering the international balance of power in their favour. The possibility of fostering the creation of a third Fascist state on France's borders augured well for the weakening of the Anglo-French hegemony to whose destruction both Fascist Italy and Nazi Germany were committed. The readiness of both the Duce and the Führer to intervene in the Spanish Civil War was based on the accurate calculation that the Allies were unlikely to spring to the defence of a sister democracy, as both Christian Leitz and Paul Preston show in Chapters 6 and 7. A Nationalist victory would also give them a foothold in the strategically crucial area of the Western Mediterranean. The bombers provided by the Fascist dictators enabled the rebels to airlift to the mainland the Army of Africa, without which the war could not have been won. The subsequent massive programme of military, financial and diplomatic aid provided by Italy and Germany proved crucial to the overwhelming victory of the Nationalists. Hitler took a close interest in developments in Spain, as Leitz demonstrates in Chapter 6, personally making the decision to intervene and ensuring that German military aid was channelled to General Franco himself, rather than to the more senior and rival leader of the insurgent cause, General Mola. According to both Leitz and Preston, Franco's efforts to flatter both dictators were rewarded by their eventual decision to support him against his competitor. Nevertheless, in both cases, Franco's determination to stand up for his own interests resulted in occasionally tense relations with his erstwhile allies. During the Spanish Civil War, Franco resisted the Duce's attempts to run the Nationalist war effort from Rome and he resisted some of the more rapacious of Germany's economic demands.

The British and French arms embargo and the isolationism of the United States in the 1930s deprived the Spanish Republic of the right to buy arms from the democratic powers. It was obliged, therefore, to acquire what it could in the murky and extortionate world of the private arms market. The efforts of British and French governments to prevent the Spanish Civil War from sparking off a continent-wide conflagration appeared to have succeeded when the European powers subscribed to a Non-Intervention Agreement in August 1936. However, Germany, Italy and Portugal violated the agreement by continuing openly to arm the Nationalist forces. The Allies' failure to respond induced Stalin to revise his policy of neutrality because a rapid Nationalist victory would have strengthened Fascism in Europe and intensified the strategic insecurity of the Soviet Union. Thus Soviet military aid, funded by Spain's gold reserves, began to reach Republican-held areas from October 1936. Soviet military aid was accompanied by intense pressure to curb the revolutionary tendencies on the Republican side. Stalin's foreign policy was driven by his search for a common defence agreement with the Allies against Fascist expansionism. To the consequent conservative agenda advocated by the Communists in Spain was added the sectarian persecution of anti-Stalinist forces. Accordingly, the revolutionary militia were starved of arms and their political organizations crushed in the civil war within the Republican camp in Barcelona in May 1937. The Socialist premier who formed the new government after the May events, Juan Negrín, shared with the Communists the logical perception that the Republic had to follow a bourgeois liberal agenda not only to preserve the allegiance of the middle classes but to encourage the support of Britain and France. It was a policy that coincided with the Soviet Union's need to woo the Allies.[9]

Nevertheless, Soviet military aid to the Republic lagged far behind that of Germany and Italy.[10] Despite desperate resistance, the Republican war effort was finally crushed at the end of March 1939. Of the causes of the defeat of the Republic, the most decisive was the readiness of the Allies to turn a blind eye to the aggression of the Fascist powers in Spain while they themselves blocked any attempt by the democratic government of Spain to purchase arms. As Moradiellos argues in Chapter 5, the Allies' betrayal of a fellow democracy hastened the formation of the Axis and undermined efforts among the Allies to create a broad diplomatic and military alliance against Fascist expansionism.

Under the dictatorship of Franco, Spain remained officially neutral throughout the Second World War. From the beginning, however, Franco sought to negotiate Spain's entry into the war on the Axis side in order to share in the spoils of victory. Leitz's account in Chapter 6 shows that Hitler was convinced that the price Franco was demanding for Spain's participation in the war, the eventual award of the French African colonies, was greater than could be justified by the limited contribution his depleted economy and war-weary armed forces could make to the Axis cause. Hitler, who was never especially interested in Spain, was not prepared to revitalize the Spanish economy and military apparatus at massive cost to the Third Reich's own war effort. The two dictators met on 23 October 1940 on the French–Spanish border at Hendaye and Franco signed a protocol undertaking to join the war without specifying any date.[11] After Germany had invaded the Soviet Union in the summer of 1941, Franco, to show his solidarity with the German war effort, sent a volunteer force, the Blue Division, to fight on the Russian front, in violation of his official policy of non-belligerence. When the tide of the Second World War turned against the Axis in the winter of 1942, Franco sought to reassure the Allies of Spain's neutrality, as Denis Smyth indicates in Chapter 8, though the Caudillo continued to provide logistical and material support for Germany.

On the eve of peace in April 1945, the Franco regime promulgated a number of purely cosmetic reforms whose main objective was to try to persuade the Allies of Spain's democratic credentials. However, his regime owed its survival in the new democratic world order mainly to the growing tensions of the incipient Cold War. In Chapter 9, Florentino Portero demonstrates how the British government, under both Churchill and Atlee, played a pivotal role in the policy adopted by the democracies in the aftermath of the war. Although London favoured a transition towards a parliamentary monarchy in Spain, successive British governments were reluctant to take action against the Franco dictatorship in case a renewal of internal strife would be to the advantage of the Soviet Union. In the context of the Greek Civil War, London was able to convince the United States to block French initiatives to break off all relations with Spain. As a result, international disapproval of the Franco regime took the form of a token gesture, the diplomatic boycott of Spain, as voted by the United Nations in December 1946.

Spain's diplomatic isolation ended in 1953 when the Vatican signed a Concordat with Spain and when the United States, in an effort to broaden her Cold War defences, signed the Madrid Pact with the regime. As Boris Liedtke shows in Chapter 10, after tortuous negotiations the agreement gave the United States the right to establish military bases in Spain in exchange for financial aid. It also marked Spain's incorporation into the Cold War Western network and the beginning of close economic ties with the West. US support for the Franco regime proved crucial to its survival. The ground for greater economic contact with the West had been prepared since the late 1940s by the Franco regime's increasing search for loans from the United States and commercial agreements with France and Great Britain. All three powers were anxious to penetrate Spain's closed economy, as Portero indicates in Chapter 9. The speed of this *rapprochement* with the West after the Pact of Madrid was such that by 1958 Spain had become part of the Organisation for European Economic Co-operation (OEEC), the International Monetary Fund and the World Bank as well as the United Nations.

Spain's relations with the Great Powers since the 1950s can be understood only in the light of the extraordinary rate of her assimilation into the European economy. This came about as a result of the failure of the semi-autarky of the 1950s. The severity of Spain's economic crisis finally persuaded a deeply reluctant Franco and his closest advisers into carrying out an immediate semi-liberalization of the economy. Many protectionist barriers were lifted, restrictions on foreign investment were withdrawn, a range of government subsidies were eliminated in order to reduce the public sector borrowing requirement and prices of many goods and services were raised. Simultaneously, in an important move to open up the economy, the peseta was devalued by 50 per cent and exchange rates were unified, giving the peseta a fixed value on the international exchange and making it a convertible currency. The immediate effect of the plan was to provoke a recession in the Spanish economy lasting until the end of 1961. Thereafter, until the energy crisis of 1973, the economy experienced an annual rate of growth of approximately 10 per cent, higher than in any other country in the West and for a period more than twice that of the European Community (EC). From being a predominantly agrarian society only partially integrated into Europe, Spain became an industrialized, urban and consumer society largely assimilated by Western economy and culture, experiencing structural and social problems similar to those of the more developed countries of northern Europe.

The motor of this growth was the economic boom of the Western economy in the 1960s and early 1970s. Foreign investment poured into Spain, drawn by a market full of potential and by the favourable conditions offered by the Spanish government. Technologically advanced industries sprang up, dominated by multinationals in sectors such as engineering, chemicals and pharmaceuticals. Spain also benefited from rising living standards in Europe. Drawn by her natural attractions, growing numbers of Europeans began to visit Spain and earnings from tourism rose from $129 million to $919 million between 1959 and 1964 alone. Tourism, foreign investment and the remittances of Spanish emigrants provided the invisible export earnings that compensated for the huge deficit in Spain's balance of trade.[12]

The regime's attempts to gain entry into the EC, however, were repeatedly denied because Spain did not fulfil Europe's democratic conditions. The Preferential Agreement of 1970, which gave Spain greater economic access to European markets, did not imply any compromise over these basic conditions. It was only after Franco's death in 1975 and the election in 1977 of the first democratic government since the Second Republic that negotiations began over Spain's incorporation into the EC. There was huge support within Spain for EC entry because it was believed it would consolidate the infant democracy. Negotiations were protracted, however, because EC members were divided over the terms of accession. France, under pressure from a powerful agrarian lobby, insisted that Spain's entry should not entail any sacrifice of French agricultural interests. Italy, though threatened with greater economic competition from Spain than was France, supported Spain's accession because it would help to create a more equitable balance between north and south in the formulation of EC policy. Britain, though in favour of incorporating Spain, was opposed to budgetary reform unless her own contributions were reduced. Other hurdles had to be crossed. The second EC enlargement towards the new democracies in the south – Spain, Portugal and Greece – involved a huge increase in the budget of the Common Agricultural Policy and a massive extension of structural funds.

Spain's membership of NATO became the crux of the issue of entry into the EC. Under the first, centre-right government of the new democracy, Spain had joined NATO. The Socialist Party had been resolutely opposed to remaining within NATO because of the latter's scant regard for the democratic complexion of regimes and because it was dominated by the United States, which had been the essential prop of the Franco dictatorship. After their electoral victory in 1982, the Socialist leaders agreed to campaign to remain in NATO in exchange for German support for entry into the EC. The deadlock over the negotiations was finally broken when France, with François Mitterrand as president of the EC Council of Ministers, modified her opposition to Spain's entry. Nevertheless, this was made conditional on a relatively slow integration of Spain's agricultural produce beyond the date of entry. Preparations for accession also involved the dismantling of protectionist walls for Spain's industry built during the dictatorship and the modification of tax and labour legislation. The treaty was finally signed in 1985 and Spain joined at the beginning of 1986. Committed to a referendum over NATO, the Socialist government and the Prime Minister, Felipe González, turned it into a confidence vote in themselves. Their espousal of the Western international defence system conflicted with the neutralist convictions of the Spanish people. Nevertheless, the wording of the ballot implied that Spain's continued membership would not involve integration into NATO's military structures, or the presence of nuclear weapons on Spanish soil. In addition, the government made clear its intention to lobby within NATO for a reduction of US military presence. After a vigorous campaign, the government won the support of a majority of the votes in March 1986. The positive vote helped to strengthen Spain's bargaining position with the United States, which had been a strong advocate of her membership of NATO because of the strategic importance of the Peninsula. Even under the first government of the new democracy, Spain had renegotiated the defence agreement with the United States in order to make it more bilateral. Further negotiations under the Socialist government led in 1988 and 1996 to the closure of the US bases and the withdrawal of US troops and armaments.

Between 1986 and 1996, Spain's relations with the Great Powers were marked by her support for denuclearization and the development of international crisis management structures. The Socialist government was a strong proponent of the European defence system, the Western European Union, as a parallel organization to NATO, and of the European Union's Common Foreign and Security Policy. Spain thus remained within the Europeanist as opposed to the Atlanticist camp. Spain also played an active part in UN peace-keeping missions, such as in ex-Yugoslavia. Her integration into international defence systems, however, did not result in any significant loss of autonomy in foreign-policy formulation. Spain continued to press for a greater flow of resources to the Maghreb countries because of the potential destabilization of the Western Mediterranean resulting from economic crisis. Under the Socialists, Spain played an independent role in relations with Latin America, promoting the spread of human rights and democracy in the continent through commercial links and international aid, in contrast to the US policy of embargo in the case of Cuba.[13]

And Spain continued to press for the return of Gibraltar to Spanish sovereignty. The Rock became a sore point of contention between Britain and Spain in the 1990s because it served as a smuggling base and a tax haven for Spanish companies. Negotiations on the future of Gibraltar stalled as a result of the refusal of its population to accept the terms of autonomy offered by the Spanish government. Despite Spain's successful integration into the EU, there has been a significant decline in popular illusions about its benefits. As the economy has now met the Maastricht criteria for monetary union, the polls are registering a large majority against Spain's inclusion because of the high cost in unemployment and the cuts in public expenditure that it has entailed. Popular scepticism about the EU has been matched by the greater reservations of the conservative Popular Party government elected in 1996. Alongside Italy, Spain has also expressed fears that EU enlargement towards Eastern Europe might divert resources from the south and create a new east–west axis that will harm the interests of the countries of the Mediterranean basin. The new government veered to the right in its foreign policy, adopting a more aggressive policy towards Cuba and moving towards closer identification with US international policy.[14] Relying on the prestige gained from her internal democratization rather than on her resources,[15] Spain's foreign policy since the end of the Franco dictatorship has scored considerable achievements. Over the twenty-one years since the new democracy began, Spain completed her integration into the economic, political and security systems of the post-Cold War world. Within the limits of her economic and political status, she has played a positive role in world affairs, using links with Arab and Spanish American countries to create bridges between continents, and encouraging trade with and aid to poorer countries. Spanish political leaders have also argued forcibly, in Spain and from within the international organizations, for greater global *détente* and dialogue. In the process, as Angel Viñas explains in Chapter 12, Spain shed from her foreign policy the last residue of the backward-looking dictatorship.

Notes

1 For a recent analysis of this kind, see Juan Pablo Fusi and Jordi Palafox, *España: 1808–1996. El desafío de la modernidad* (Madrid: Espasa Calpe, 1997).
2 Ricardo Macías Picavea, *El problema nacional: hechos, causas, remedios* (Madrid: Victoriano Suárez, 1899), pp. 368–9.
3 'Spain', in *Selected Poems* (London: Faber & Faber, 1979), p. 53.
4 A recent Spanish study also stresses this involvement: Javier Tusell *et al.*, *La política exterior de España en el siglo XX* (Madrid, 1997).
5 For example, Sebastian Balfour, *The End of the Spanish Empire, 1898–1923* (Oxford: Oxford University Press, 1997).
6 Fernando Olivié, *La herencia de un imperio roto* (Madrid: Mapfre, 1992), p. 253.
7 For a recent analysis of the Moroccan war and its repercussions in Spain, see Pablo La Porte, 'El Desastre de Annual y la crisis de la Restauración en España (1921–1923)', doctoral thesis, Universidad Complutense (Madrid, 1997).
8 Enrique Moradiellos, *La perfidia de Albión: el gobierno británico y la guerra civil española* (Madrid: Siglo XXI, 1996); Douglas Little, *Malevolent Neutrality: the United States, Great Britain, and the Origins of the Spanish Civil War* (Ithaca: Cornell University Press, 1985).
9 Paul Preston, *A Concise History of the Spanish Civil War* (London: Fontana, 1996).
10 For calculations of the balance of aviation power, see Gerald Howson, *Aircraft of the Spanish Civil War (1936–1939)* (London: Putnam, 1990).
11 For further details, see Paul Preston, *Franco: a Biography* (London: HarperCollins, 1993), pp. 374–400.
12 See, for example, J. Nadal, A. Carreras and C. Sudrià (eds), *La economía española en el siglo XX: una perspectiva histórica* (Barcelona: Ariel, 1987).
13 For further details, see R. Gillespie, F. Rodrigo and J. Story, *Democratic Spain: Reshaping External Relations in a Changing World* (London: Routledge, 1995).
14 During the Iraq crisis of 1998, Spain's Prime Minister, José María Aznar, gave unequivocal support for US military action, in contrast to the more neutralist position adopted by the Socialist leader, Joaquín Almunia: *El País*, 12 and 13 February, 1998.
15 Esther Barbé, 'European political cooperation: The Upgrading of Spanish Foreign Policy', in Gillespie *et al.*, *Democratic Spain*, pp. 106–22.

1 Spain and the Great Powers in the aftermath of the Disaster of 1898

Sebastian Balfour

In 1898, Spain lost the scattered remnants of her once great empire after a disastrous war with the United States. The war gave rise in Spain to exaggerated displays of jingoist enthusiasm, and defeat plunged public opinion into excessive gloom. The so-called Disaster severely under-mined the legitimacy of the political regime, the Restoration system, a parliamentary monarchy resting on a largely fictitious electoral contest between the two parties of the landowning and financial oligarchies. It also boosted social and economic movements opposed to the regime that had been emerging through the process of modernization.

Despite the sense of catastrophe that prevailed in Spain, however, the Disaster of 1898 was not an isolated event but part of a global process of colonial redistribution in a new era of expansionism which had begun in the 1870s. Japan, the United States and Germany had recently emerged as world powers and were not only encroaching on old spheres of influ-ence but also joining the search to colonize those parts of the globe still left untouched by colonialism. As a result, the existing balance of power began to destabilize. At the same time, empires were being challenged by a wave of anti-colonial revolts, such as the struggle for independence in Cuba and the Philippines between 1895 and 1898, the revolt against the Italian occupation of Ethiopia in 1896, and the Boer rebellion in South Africa at the turn of the century. In this process, weaker powers such as Spain, Portugal and Italy were forced to cede colonies and curtail their ambitions or redirect them elsewhere. At the same time, the older Great Powers such as France, Russia and Britain found themselves jockeying for position in areas hitherto untouched by colonial expansion that were now the object of intense competition.[1] While tensions also centred on the Far East, the Balkans and the Mediterranean, Africa was the most explosive of these new international flashpoints. Few of the powers, however, were indifferent to the outcome of the Spanish–American War. A Spanish cartoon of the period shows the

European kings and emperors observing the 1 May 1898 naval battle between Spain and the United States, standing on the shore with their fishing-rods, 'waiting for the weather to calm down', as the caption reads, 'to see if they can catch something'.

After the Disaster, Spain's role in the emerging system of international relations was shaped by another, seemingly unconnected event that took place in the same year as she lost her empire. The competition between European powers to partition Africa which had begun in the 1870s had given rise to a series of bilateral negotiations, preceded at times by great tensions, between Britain, Germany, France, Italy and Portugal. The latter two had had to retreat in face of the dynamism of the others. Britain, for her part, was seeking to consolidate control over a north–south axis from Cairo to the Cape, while France sought to establish a west–east axis from North-West Africa to the Red Sea. In September 1898, two months after the Spanish capitulation in Cuba, forces of Britain and France confronted each other in the small village of Fashoda in the Sudan. Faced by the threat of war with Britain, France was forced to withdraw. In the negotiations that followed, leading eventually to the Entente Cordiale between the two countries, France agreed to direct her colonial interests in Africa primarily towards Algeria, Tunisia and Morocco.[2] Both countries also agreed on delineating spheres of influence elsewhere in Africa. Apart from her possessions in the Gulf of Guinea, Spain had a tenuous hold on territory on the North-West African coast opposite the Canary Islands which had been recognized as her protectorate in the 1884 Treaty of Berlin. This enormous stretch of land was now subject to the scrutiny of the two powers, and Britain appeared to have little objection to the French insistence on considerably reducing the area under Spanish control.[3]

However, it was Morocco that became the focus of tension between the powers. This was partly because of her strategic situation, dominating the entrance to and exit from the Mediterranean, and partly because of the growing commercial rivalry in North-West Africa between France and Germany. French expansion in that corner of Africa posed a potential threat not only to the commercial interests of Britain and Germany but also to the strategic security of Britain. Above all, London would not accept French penetration as far as the Mediterranean shore of Morocco because of the risk this would pose to the safety of Gibraltar and the control of the Straits. Britain had observed a purely formal neutrality during the Spanish–American War. The real sympathies of the government had lain with the United States. Britain had supplied coal to American ships and at the same time had applied pressure on the Egyptian authorities to refuse to allow the Spanish Mediterranean fleet to refuel, with the result that it could not sail to the Far East theatre of action through the Suez Canal.[4]

The consequent Spanish resentment towards Britain in the aftermath of the Disaster, added to the close ties that appeared to be developing between France and Spain, fuelled British fears that France might gain some territorial advantages over Britain. In the event of a war between the two countries, France might gain control over Spain's railway system, enabling her to transport troops directly to Gibraltar. Furthermore, because of the two Spanish enclaves on the northern Moroccan coast, Ceuta and Melilla, France might threaten British control of the Straits of Gibraltar themselves. Her Majesty's ambassador in Spain warned the British Prime Minister in August 1898:

> Spain, though fallen from her station as a Great Power and unable therefore to gratify any ambition of her own, still possesses points likely to attract the ambition of others, especially France. . . . The position and influence of Spain in Morocco can be utilized, while her desire for increased territory in Africa to make up for her lost colonies may render her susceptible to the overtures of her new ally. I have more than once pointed out the dangers to Her Majesty's possessions if France obtained uncontrolled access to the Hinterland of Gibraltar.[5]

The Spanish regime, however, was reluctant to adopt any measure that might alienate Britain. In informal contacts between the British ambassador and Spanish ministers (including the Premier, Francisco Silvela), Britain was assured that Spain needed a close alliance with 'the most powerful of the Maritime states' because Spain was now 'a Maritime Power without a fleet'.[6] Britain was therefore able to take advantage of Spain's weakness to use her as a cushion against further French expansion. It was characteristic of British foreign policy in Africa to construct a sub-imperial system of alliances, such as that with Italy in the 1880s and later Portugal in Southern Africa, to compress the territorial ambitions of Britain's rivals in the area. After secret negotiations between France and Spain in 1902 in which the Spanish were offered a large area in northern Morocco as a sphere of influence in which they might gain considerable commercial advantages and international prestige, Spain's leaders got cold feet and declined the offer. Paris had sought also to use Spain's relative debility in an attempt to gain a strategic advantage over Britain in the sensitive area of North Africa and the Straits of Gibraltar,[7] but the Spanish government had feared Britain would object to a purely Franco-Spanish alliance that would further French strategic interests over those of the British.[8] The British government, however, was keen to encourage the assignation of a sphere of influence for Spain in northern Morocco as long as this worked to contain rather than encourage French expansion.

What helped to encourage a Franco-British consensus over North-West Africa that would incorporate Spain was Germany's growing commercial and military ambitions. France had been anxious to demarcate official spheres of influence in North-West Africa so that Germany could not muscle in where borders were unclear. Thus she had signed a treaty with Spain in 1900 confirming Spanish ownership of the strip of territory opposite the Canary Islands, Río Muni and part of the Sahara; this represented a strategic guarantee both for the islands and for Spain's fishing industry off the mainland coast. Concern about German expansionism also lay behind the 1904 Entente Cordiale between France and Britain. However, during the negotations leading to the treaty, France sought to reduce the Spanish sphere of influence in Morocco as much as possible while Britain, still concerned at a potential later French expansion in North Africa, insisted that France should sign a treaty with Spain allowing for Spanish presence in Morocco. Although the area subsequently conceded to Spain was much reduced in comparison to that offered to her in 1902, it was nevertheless considerable: some 22,000 square kilometres (in contrast to the 42,000 square miles of the 1902 offer), amounting to 20 per cent of Moroccan territory.[9] Yet the bulk of the area in north-west Morocco was also notorious for instability owing to the rebelliousness of its mainly Berber tribes against the domination of the Sultanate.

It should be clear, therefore, that in the unstable system of international relations at the end of the nineteenth century Spain's very weakness was seen by the European powers as potentially destabilizing. Her geographical position made Spain a strategically vital piece in the complex power game between European powers in the Mediterranean and North Africa. Spain lay astride two continents and two seas, dominating the Straits of Gibraltar from both coasts, and therefore the route towards the Far East through the Suez Canal; she also could offer coaling stations and port facilities along her north-west coast and in the Western Mediterranean.[10] Her presence in northern Morocco ensured that neither France nor Britain directly controlled the Straits of Gibraltar. This suited the interests of not only both these powers but Germany as well. From being the ugly sister, politely shunned in 1898 by other members of the European family, Spain became the potential bride of one or more of the Great Powers.[11]

Indeed, in addition to France and Britain, Germany began to woo Spain in an effort to erode the Entente Cordiale, into which Spain was being drawn as a subordinate partner. The Pan-German press was urging the German regime to play a more aggressive role in Africa. 'Morocco is a German concern,' wrote the *Rheinische-Westfälishe Zeitung*, one month after the Entente was signed, 'owing to our increasing population and our need of naval bases. If Germany does not peg out claims, she will retire empty-handed from the partition of the world.'[12] Making use of family connections between the Spanish and Austrian monarchies and the notorious sympathy of the Spanish royal family for the German state model, the Kaiser endeavoured to present himself as the protector of the interests of Spain in the new international situation. In 1904, he made a much-commented-on visit to the young and recently crowned King, Alfonso XIII, in Vigo. However, the overly assertive style of German diplomacy did not appear to go down well with many Spanish politicians. It widened the gulf between those on the right who saw Germany as an ally to be cultivated and those in the centre and left who favoured the alliance with Britain and France.[13]

In the following year, Wilhelm landed in Tangiers in an effort to internationalize the Moroccan question and force the French to the negotiating table. German pressure led to the Algeciras Conference of 1906 in which the thirteen participating nations agreed that they should enjoy equal commercial status in Morocco and that the sovereignty of the Sultan should be respected. France and Spain were given responsibility for the increasing problem of law and order in the Moroccan Empire that was partly the result of foreign penetration itself. The last stage in Spain's incorporation into the Franco-British Entente as opposed to the Triple Alliance of Germany, Austria-Hungary and Italy was completed in the Cartagena Pact of 1907. The agreement settled the tensions over Gibraltar, which had been simmering since 1898, and provided a mutual guarantee between Britain, France and Spain against German ambitions.[14] From within the pact, however, Spain was happy for Germany to act as brake on any further French expansion in Morocco. A Franco-German agreement in 1909, which temporarily removed their mutual tensions over Morocco, therefore did not suit Spanish interests. It enabled France to act more independently of Spain or indeed to oppose Spanish participation in negotiations over Morocco.[15] According to the British ambassador to Spain:

> She regarded Germany as a useful drag on the progress of France into the interior, a progress which threatened to make France the southern neighbour of Spain, as she always had been naturally her northern neighbour. By the conclusion of the Berlin agreement she was left alone, as it were, with France in Morocco to adjust their

conflicting pretensions. . . . Spain feared she would be overwhelmed by her more powerful partner with Germany no longer there to protect her.[16]

France's already low opinion of Spain as a partner in the colonizing process in Morocco was intensified by the Spanish government's handling of attacks in 1909 by rebels from the Rif mountains near Melilla on Spanish workers building a railway to carry minerals to the coast. The Spanish army became embroiled in a difficult and intermittent campaign in which it suffered heavy casualties. France's tendency to encroach on her neighbour's sphere in Morocco and ignore joint consultation, in breach of treaties, was exacerbated as a result. The French ambassador wrote disparagingly, 'Spain's ineptitude as a colonizer and her economic impotence are hindering future prospects for other countries in the area which has been reserved for her.'[17] In the rapidly disintegrating Moroccan empire, France occupied Fez and began to threaten Spain's sphere, to which the Spanish government under its premier, José Canalejas, responded by occupying Larache and Alcazarquivir. Shortly afterwards, Germany provoked a second crisis in Morocco in 1911 by sending a gunboat to the port of Agadir. She was alarmed by France's continued penetration into Morocco and by the intense competition between French and German mining interests. The crisis was resolved by the concession to Germany of an enormous slice of the French Congo in exchange for some smaller territory in Central Africa over which Germany had established control, as well as a recognition of France's hegemony in most of Morocco.

The following year, during Franco-Spanish negotiations in 1912 finally to formalize the partition of Morocco into Protectorates, France demanded a further reduction of territory in the Spanish sphere of influence in order to compensate for her loss in Equatorial Africa. London, however, anxious once again to limit French expansion, took on the role of protector of Spanish interests, insisting that Spain should not lose any significant part of her territory in the assignation of the Protectorates in Morocco.[18] In the Treaty of Fez of 1912, the issue of Morocco was finally settled at the expense of Morocco; in all but name, the old empire was now divided up into a Spanish Protectorate in the north and the far south-west and a French Protectorate that covered most of Morocco.[19] Spain was now firmly ensconced in the new system of international relations on the side of the Allies.

In order to understand the Spanish response to these international pressures, it is important to bear in mind that no other European country had experienced such an intense degree of insecurity. Spain's defeat in the Spanish–American War had cruelly exposed her military unpreparedness to defend her small, over-extended empire. It had also revealed the diplomatic isolation into which she had fallen. Spain's foreign policy in the first years of the new century was thus shaped above all by a preoccupation to ensure the defence of the Peninsula and her islands in the new volatile context of competitive imperialism. It had been traditional to see the possession of the northern coast of Morocco as strategically necessary for the defence of Spain; according to the elder statesman of the regime in the last quarter of the nineteenth century, Antonio Cánovas, Spain's natural frontier was the Atlas Mountains.[20] Similarly, the defence of the Canary Islands depended on the security of the Spanish territories on the nearby Saharan coast. Thus the driving force behind Spanish foreign policy at the beginning of the twentieth century was the search for external guarantees; that is, Spain's willingness to become involved in Morocco was rooted in the strategic insecurity that followed the Disaster of 1898. The policy was clearly stated by the Liberal ambassador in France: 'Morocco is for us not just a question of honour, but a question of frontier and national security.'[21] There were important differences over foreign policy between the Conservatives and the Liberals. The latter were keener on Spanish integration into the new system of international relations than the former, whose traditional instincts were to maintain the *status quo* in Morocco. Thus it was the change of government from Liberal to Conservative that led to Spain's withdrawal from the secret negotiations with the French in 1902, to the despair of the Liberals.[22]

Yet the Conservatives also believed that Spain's strategic security demanded her involvement in Morocco. With typical pessimism about its potential costs, the Spanish Premier, Francisco Silvela, declared shortly after the fall of his second government in 1902:

> we should banish from our thoughts the idea that the situation in Morocco . . . represents profit and wealth for us, when, on the contrary, it is the source of poverty, sterility and stagnation for Spain, and we accept it and we have to maintain it merely to avoid worse ills of a political and international nature.[23]

This view was confirmed by the two politicians and premiers who most influenced Spanish policy in Morocco, the Conservative Antonio Maura and the Liberal José Canalejas. In their private correspondence with each other in 1911, both insisted on the need to maintain a strategic and defensive presence in Morocco within the Anglo-French alliance. In a letter to Canalejas, then the Premier, Maura wrote:

The Anglo-French agreement leaves no other possible option for Spain for whom the convergent hostility of both nations would be intolerable. Like you, I continue to think that [if we had followed] any other path we would have run up against incomparably greater adversities.[24]

Other explanations for Spain's increasing involvement in Morocco advanced by international spokesmen of the time are less convincing. For example, the British ambassador in Spain in 1899 had received the impression from a conversation with the Premier, Francisco Silvela, that Spaniards saw Morocco as a compensation for the loss of Spain's colonies; that is, that Spain was seeking to restore her international prestige and her own self-esteem.[25] Always scornful of Spain's abilities as a colonizer, French colonial opinion in 1904 judged Spanish aims in Morocco to consist of 'unlimited dreams . . . vague and latent ambitions'.[26] It is true, as we shall see, that there was an array of different pressures within Spain for greater penetration into North Africa. But there was also a new and powerful body of opinion as a result of the Disaster that called for a retreat from any significant international involvement in order to concentrate on internal regeneration. What is surprising, in fact, is the degree to which Spanish foreign policy remained impervious, at least in the first years of the new century, to these different pressure groups of whatever hue. This relative impermeability derived from the peculiarity of the political system of the Restoration regime. The two dominant parties, Conservatives and Liberals, were not modern parties articulating the prevailing social and economic interests of Spain but political factions imperfectly representing the landowning and financial oligarchies whose power rested on patronage and electoral fraud administered by local bosses or *caciques*.[27] The narrowness of their constituency gave governments a certain degree of autonomy in the formulation of policy, especially that of foreign affairs because it touched on the interests of a limited range of internal interests.

At an international level, however, these political elites enjoyed little autonomy in the determination of Spain's policy. As Maura pointed out, they had no other option but to align themselves with the Entente Cordiale if they wished to defend the interests of Restoration Spain in the new expansionist era. This alignment, moreover, entailed military and financial commitments. On one hand, Spain was drawn into a process of negotiations leading to formal guarantees for the security of her territories. On the other hand, she was required progressively to take control of northern Morocco, where she found herself sucked into disastrous military campaigns against indigenous rebellions provoked largely by Spanish and French penetration. Spain's eventual integration into a network of international alliances was due not to her skilful manipulation of rivalries between France, Britain and Germany, as some orthodox Spanish historical accounts suggest,[28] but to the balance of power in the Mediterranean and to the geostrategic value of her territories.

Against the largely reactive foreign policy of the Restoration governments were pitted two groups of lobbies advocating greater intervention in North Africa. The first was a neo-colonial lobby. This was not a caucus or an organized pressure group, such as the 'colonial party' in France, but a range of interests promoting the penetration of Spanish capitalism in Africa, above all in Morocco, where it appeared that Spain's new international role might generate exciting economic opportunities. The lobby embraced not only a small number of financial, industrial and commercial interests but well-known figures such as the regenerationist intellectual Joaquín Costa, the journalist Gonzalo de Reparaz, the Liberal politician and Premier Count Romanones, and his colleague, José Canalejas.[29] Among the economic groups in this lobby were Catalan industrialists seeking new markets to compensate for the sudden fall in trade with the ex-colonies, as well as shipping companies, insurance companies and fruit merchants in the Levant and Andalusia. In addition, there were investors keen to take advantage of the mining resources of Morocco and the infrastructural works needed to open up the new market, such as road, railway and port construction.[30] These varied interests campaigned through the liberal and mercantile press, the geographical societies (a common type of lobby throughout Europe from towards the end of the nineteenth century) and the chambers of commerce. Four Africanist congresses were held between 1907 and 1910 to bring the different groups together in order to exercise pressure on government policy.

For all its vociferation, however, the neo-colonial lobby wielded only a small fraction of Spanish investment abroad.[31] Its ability to influence opinion rested less on its economic power than on the high profile of some of its members and on the lure of the wealth that it was believed could be obtained in the markets, fields and mines of Morocco. The neo-colonial lobby worked hard to convince the Spanish public of the benefits both to Spain and to Morocco of a peaceful expansion of capitalism in Africa. Grossly overestimating the potential of the Moroccan market and the realizable value of Morocco's mines, it was thought that economic penetration into Morocco would help to regenerate the Spanish economy. According to the secretary-general of the first Africanist Congress of 1907, 'In order for Spain to recover her lost well-being, there is only one path: Morocco.'[32] The new investment would bring in its train the supposed benefits of Western civilization to a backward country. Moreover, Spain was believed to have a historic responsibility towards Morocco and, according to the speeches and publications of the lobby, the planned expansion would respect the sovereignty of the Sultan and those Arab traditions judged to be progressive. In sum, it was a typically late nineteenth-century programme of positivism, imbued with the characteristic ambiguity of the period, oscillating between enlightened liberalism and social Darwinism.[33]

There was another body of opinion, on the other hand, that, explicitly or not, was beginning to advocate a colonial and military expansion in Africa. This view embraced two different currents. The first was the traditionalists, such as the Church and the Carlists, for whom Spain had an evangelical mission in Africa. As an ecclesiastical spokesman proclaimed, 'With regard to Africa and in particular to the neighbouring Moroccan empire, Spain has a supreme and providential mission to accomplish.'[34] The second current was a new conservative nationalism based above all in the army, whose agenda ranged from the policy of restricting French expansionism in a traditionally Spanish sphere of influence to an almost metaphysical belief in the creation of a new empire in Africa to compensate for the loss of the American empire. There was little sympathy between the military and the neo-colonial lobby. Officer opinion saw the military penetration of Africa as a necessary prerequisite of commercial penetration, while the neo-colonial lobby advocated a substantial cut in the military budget. The president of the Africanist Congress of 1909 was taken to task in a military newspaper for not mentioning the army in his opening address and the participants were described as '[e]xhibitionists, who go to them [the congresses] more out of desire to show off than to contribute to the enlargement of the motherland'.[35]

Nevertheless, these lobbies – the neo-colonial, the 'evangelical' and the military – were not able to exert irresistible pressure on the government, at least until 1909. The traditionalists, in particular, represented a comparatively small and politically marginal minority. The influence of these lobbies was together far weaker than that wielded for example by the French 'colonial party'. The social composition of the latter was similar to that of the Spanish neo-colonial lobby: their members were businessmen, journalists, politicians and so on. Like its Spanish equivalent, the French colonial party lacked a popular base, at least until the First World War. Yet it exerted an enormous influence over French foreign policy through the extent of its investments, the politicians who supported its programme and the sympathy it enjoyed in the French foreign ministry at the Quai d'Orsay.[36]

As the first decade of the twentieth century progressed, however, the Spanish army began to re-emerge as a powerful institution that no government could ignore. In the aftermath of the colonial and Spanish–American wars, officers were absorbed in the problems caused by defeat and the loss of the colonies: mass repatriation, early retirement and redundancy, a severe cut in pay during peacetime and an immensely complex question of professional scales and promotion.[37] In addition, they found themselves the target of much popular scorn over their defeat at the hands of the Americans. Thus, although the military press argued in favour of intervention in Africa, officers appeared too engrossed in domestic issues to push for new colonial ventures.[38] The rehabilitation of the army as an authoritative lobby was facilitated by its use, owing to the absence of an adequate police force, in the repression of the wave of social agitation that swept the country at the beginning of the century. What also renewed its standing among conservative and nationalist circles was its self-identification as the principal defender of national unity during a period when regional nationalism was gaining huge constituencies for the first time.

The *¡Cu-cut!* incident in 1905, when officers stationed in Barcelona ransacked the offfices of two Catalanist newspapers, and the consequent Law of Jurisdictions passed by the Liberal government to appease military anger against regionalism, marked the consolidation of the army as the main political force in the country. During the first twenty-five years or so of the Restoration regime, the army had withdrawn to the barracks after decades of political intervention. But in its new role in the first decade of the century as defender of law and order and centralism, it began to shed the progressive and republican tendencies of the nineteenth century to embrace an increasingly anti-democratic ideology.[39] Support among officers for a new imperialist role for the army revived when Spain was awarded a sphere of influence in Morocco by France and the other Great Powers. When the army was called into action in 1909 against the rebellious tribes of the Rif, the new pretorian enthusiasm for colonial war flourished.[40] But the doctrine typical of the Spanish military at the time was based above all on the traditional values of heroism, dash and energy rather than on military science, logistics and the study of terrain and local culture (with the exception of a small group of Arabist officers).[41]

Military intervention in Morocco, however, lacked a popular base. The experience of the wars of 1895–8 had created a strong isolationist and anti-militarist current in Spain. The defeat stimulated a wave of introspection among the middle classes whose most eloquent expression was the regenerationist movement led by the Spanish chambers of commerce.

Relentless critics of imperialist dreams, the regenerationists were staunch partisans of the modernization of Spain. Their programme for Spain's regeneration focused on infrastructural investment and education and made little reference to foreign affairs or foreign trade.[42] The organic intellectuals of the regenerationist movement set out to explore Spanish geography and popular culture in search of an autochtonous national identity. While many regenerationists favoured an intensification of Spanish investment in Africa, they totally rejected any new colonial enterprise requiring an increase in the military budget since public expenditure had to be devoted above all to the reconstruction of Spain's interior.[43]

Among many currents of opinion in Spain, even among conservatives, there was nervous apprehension that Spain's role as 'protector' of the Moroccan empire might degenerate into an uncontainable military intervention because of its increasing instability. Silvela's view on the matter has already been mentioned. Other politicians and not a few journalists echoed his fears. The Spanish ambassador in Tangiers, in a private conversation with his British equivalent, confessed, according to the latter, that 'Spain was not in a position to undertake control of any portion of the Moorish littoral: the task was beyond her strength.'[44] The Madrid paper *La Tribuna* regretted the Moroccan commitment acquired by Spain in the 1904 Treaty, describing it as a 'far from fortunate duty'. It went on to refer to 'the ever ingenuous Spain . . . acting free of charge as guardian of somebody else's estate'.[45] Catalan bourgeois opinion, as expressed in its press, warned of the difficulties of peaceful penetration into the interior of Morocco and the threat which a military campaign might pose to the security of the Spanish enclaves on the coast.[46]

Moreover, many politicians recognized that there was no popular support for any enterprise in Morocco other than that of defending the *status quo*. Nor did they make any effort either to promote the new international role of Spain. The relative lack of enthusiasm among politicians and press when the Franco-Spanish treaty was signed in 1904 was in marked contrast to the colonialist fever in many of the French media. Even before 1909, politicians gave the impression, in their speeches and private correspondence, of looking behind their shoulder, fearful of an outburst of popular anger in the event of a war in Morocco.[47] Indeed, the experience of the colonial wars and the Disaster was too recent and too overwhelming to allow politicians any hope that new military ventures in other parts of the world could reawaken popular jingoism. Antonio Maura himself, in a speech to the Senate in 1907 on the new budget he was presenting for the reconstruction of Spain's navy, admitted that 'a majority of public opinion was against this expenditure, as a result of painful experiences and disappointments in the past'.[48]

In fact, the myths and rituals of colonialism prevailing in Britain, Belgium, Germany and France – 'Third World exoticism', the 'White Man's Burden', the excitation provoked by territorial rivalry between the imperial powers, the patriotic marches and hymns and so on – hardly made inroads into popular culture in Spain. Although there had been a great deployment of such myths and ceremonies during the colonial wars and on the eve of the war with the United States, the defeat emptied them of meaning and helped to empower alternative identities, such as regionalism and left-wing ideologies. The contrast between the triumphalist send-off of the troops to the battlefields and their humiliating and poorly recompensed return home no doubt deepened latent feelings of social injustice and undermined new appeals to patriotism.[49]

Popular disenchantment with the political regime was exacerbated by the process of modernization, which began to undermine old social structures. From the 1870s, the typical features of modernization – industrialization, migration from the countryside, the massive growth of cities, the extension of the communications system – began to accelerate. Far from creating the basis for the integration of the masses into a national and expansionist polity of a social-liberal kind, as was the case to a certain extent in Britain and France, the popular experience of war, added to the growing social agitation in the cities and in some parts of the countryside, undermined the legitimacy of the established order. Consequently, popular grievances were expressed through economic demands, anti-clericalism and anti-militarism, articulated above all by republicans and anarchists. These feelings culminated in 1909 during the so-called Tragic Week in Barcelona, when the mobilization of soldiers on reserve for the new war in Morocco unleashed a violent and widespread protest which began as a general strike and ended in riots and the burning of convents.[50]

The violence in Barcelona confirmed the fears of many politicians that the regime might have to pay a high price for Spain's involvement in Morocco. But on an international level also, two related processes were beginning to undermine Spain's original policy of maintaining in the north of Morocco a mainly defensive military and administrative presence. The first was the progressive disintegration of the Moroccan empire as a result of its internal contradictions, intensified by the opening of the country to international commerce. The problem of order in the Spanish sphere was worsened by the inefficiency of and lack of coordination between military and civil administration. The military came increasingly to dominate policy-making and its implementation in the area. Using a policy of divide and rule, their relations with local Arab leaders oscillated between punishment and bribery. The long-term subversive effects of this practice were exacerbated by the lack of understanding among many officers of the different cultures in the Spanish sphere of influence and the informal boundaries dividing its tribes.[51] Colonial penetration, whether military, administrative or commercial, increasingly provoked revolts against the authority of the Sultan and later a war of liberation against the colonists themselves.

The second related process was the progressive expansion of the French beyond the boundaries of their sphere of influence in Morocco. Their motives were driven by the need to defend France's interests in Northern Africa against the continued assertiveness of Germany. But the expansion was also motivated by the apparent failure of the Spanish to maintain order in Spain's own sphere of influence. Spain faced the repeated conundrum of having to make deals with rebels against the Sultan in order to try to ensure peace. The situation became critical in 1908 and 1909 after the Rif rebels carried out a twofold attack on mines near Melilla belonging to a Franco-Spanish company and on the Spanish workers building a railway to carry iron ore to the coast. The threat of a French intervention to guarantee order in the area and to take over Spain's trade with the inland tribes obliged the Maura government unwillingly to send troops towards the interior of the Rif mountains.[52] The outcome of the campaign in Morocco was a new military disaster and the beginning of an intermittent war that would last until 1927.[53]

Thus Spain found herself drawn into a war for which she had neither the resources nor the popular support vital for such an effort. The new war in Morocco destabilized the internal situation. On the one hand, it deepened political divisions. The repression in the wake of the Tragic Week unleashed a wave of protests in Spain and abroad against Maura's government, leading to a new political alignment, a united front between liberals, republicans and socialists that threatened the political system itself. In his memoirs, Count Romanones, one of the principal investors in the Moroccan mines, frequently a Liberal minister and thrice Spanish Premier, tells an anecdote that reveals the extent to which the war had become unpopular among the people. Walking through a village near his lands in Sigüenza, where the Count had always assumed he was much appreciated as the local boss, he was stoned by a group of youths. Shortly afterwards, while he was hunting with his dog, he met a reaper with whom he had had very cordial relations for many years. The worker greeted him with the following words: 'Your lordship [Señor conde], is it true that so many people are dying in Melilla for your sake?

I have two sons there; I may not see them again and it grieves me even more to think that you are responsible.'[54]

On the other hand, the army gained a fresh momentum as a result of the Moroccan campaign. The war gave officers in the field a new sense of identity and furnished them with funds, salary rises and numerous opportunities for promotion. However, it also generated internal problems among the military. The inequality of opportunity in promotion and salary between those officers on campaign and those remaining in Spain after the government introduced a new promotion scale rewarding war service provoked disturbances in Barcelona and Madrid in 1910. It led to the creation of military committees or *juntas* outside the military framework of command.[55] These new committees were driven fundamentally by corporatist demands but their growth gave the *junteros* a sense of political power that they would use to great effect in the crisis of 1917. While the Moroccan campaign divided the army, however, it also revitalized it. One of the generals who made his reputation in the war wrote later that:

> the Spanish army died bloodily and gloriously in el Caney [in Cuba] in 1898 and revived with equal bloodiness, though with less glory, in the barranco del Lobo [in Morocco] in 1909. . . In the conflict, it is regaining its faith and the awareness of its mission, and at the same time the war is awakening magnificent qualities that were lying dormant.[56]

For revanchist officers, the Moroccan war was a means of avenging grievances that had accumulated since 1898. It also offered the opportunity of a new imperialist role.

From 1909, the influence of the military lobby in the formulation of Moroccan policy began to grow, with the discreet but decisive participation of the King, for whom the army was an important source of power and prestige.[57] The pressure it was exercising for the military occupation of the Spanish sphere of influence was strengthened in 1911 by a new wave of French expansionism near its southern frontier. French encroachment provoked the dispatch of more troops from Spain and the extension of the territory controlled by the military. When the role of the two powers in Morocco was finally settled by the division of the country in 1912 into two Protectorates, it was the Spanish army above all that took on the responsibility of administering the territory awarded to Spain. Unlike the French, the Spanish state did not have the resources to administer the necessary civil colonial administration in the territory adjudicated to Spain by the Great Powers. Instead it was the army that largely took on the role of running the Protectorate, for which it was neither prepared nor especially interested. The neo-colonial project of peaceful penetration into Morocco, respecting the integrity of her cultures, was by now a scrap of paper.

Between 1898 and the First World War, therefore, foreign and domestic policies in Spain were closely bound up with each other. The search for national security after the Disaster led Spain to accept a role in the north of Morocco as a buffer between rival powers and a policeman for the interests of international capitalism. But Spanish policy-makers over-estimated the strategic importance of the area just as they underestimated both the costs of policing it and the negative effects of Spain's inefficient and under-resourced administration. The progressive disintegration of order in Morocco led Spain into a war for which she was not qualified, in part because of the failure of any effective reform of the army. The military campaign rebounded on Spain, exacerbating the political and social divisions generated by the internal crisis and encouraging the re-emergence of the army as the main political force in the country. The over-extension of troops under the command of the ambitious and impulsive General Silvestre led to the Disaster of Annual in 1921 in which up to 14,000 Spanish soldiers were killed and almost all the Spanish-controlled area in north-east Morocco was lost to the insurgent Rif tribes. As a result, the internal divisions grew ever more intense until the army staged a *coup d'état* under General Primo de Rivera, bringing to an end the political system of the Restoration.

Notes

1 For a discussion of theories of colonial expansion into Africa, see G.N. Sanderson, 'The European Partition of Africa: Coincidence or Conjuncture?' in E.F. Penrose (ed.), *European Imperialism and the Partition of Africa* (London, 1975), pp. 1–54. For the international context of colonial redistribution, see José María Jover Zamora, '1898: teoría y práctica de la redistribución colonial', *Fundación Universitaria Española* (Madrid, 1979) and Jesús Pabón, *Días de ayer: historias e historiadores contemporáneos* (Barcelona: Alpha, 1963).

2 G.P. Gooch and Harold Temperley, *British Documents on the Origins of the World War, 1898–1914*, vol. 1, *The End of British Isolation* (London: HMSO, 1927), Documents 157–235, pp. 132–93.

3 According to a report from the Spanish ambassador in Britain to the Spanish Minister of State on 7 April 1899, Archives of the Ministerio de Asuntos Exteriores (MAE), Política Africa no. 2285.

4 Rosario de la Torre del Río, *Inglaterra y España en 1898* (Madrid: Eudema, 1988), pp. 141–53 and 178–88; for the official British position on the Suez Canal episode, see Gooch and Temperley, *Documents*, Doc. 379, 28 June 1898, p. 319.

5 Drummond-Wolf to Salisbury, 14.8.1898 Public Records Office (Foreign

Office) (henceforth PRO FO) 72.2065. See also file 2066 and *British Documents on Foreign Affairs: Reports and Papers from the Foreign Office Confidential Print* (henceforth *BD*), (1991), part 1, series F, vol. 27, Doc. 57, p. 60, 20 May 1899.

6 *BD*, Doc. 46, p. 47 (4 February 1899).

7 'Note sur la question marocaine', 15 July 1902, *Documents Diplomatiques Français (1871–1914)*, deuxième série, vol. 2, Doc. 333, pp. 398–9.

8 As the British ambassador to Spain wrote to the Marquess of Landsdowne in 1903, 'the Spaniards greatly fear us; and I think their fear has the effect not only of making some of them advocate an alliance with England but of making many others nervous about committing themselves to an alliance with the French'. Sir Maurice Durand (11.9.03) in *BD*, Doc. 103, p. 101. For details of the draft treaty between France and Spain, see Diario de las Sesiones de las Cortes for 26 November, 1912 (Apéndice), when it was first revealed in Parliament after a request for it to be made public.

9 For further details, see José María de Areilza and Fernando María Castiella, *Reivindicaciones de España* (Madrid: Instituto de Estudios Políticos, 1941).

10 *BD*, C.F. Frederick Adam to Marquess of Lansdowne, confidential report, 12 September 1902, Doc. 88, p. 88.

11 For sections of the opposition, however, Spain's new role in Morocco merely confirmed her role as a pawn in Britain's international power game: 'Espanya y Inglaterra', *La Veu de Catalunya*, 8 October 1904.

12 Quoted in Sir Charles Petrie, Bt, *King Alfonso XIII and His Age* (London: Chapman & Hall, 1963), p. 76.

13 *BD*, Cartwright to Landsdowne (26.8.1905), Doc. 133, p. 126. Confidential British diplomatic notes also suggest that, while the Spanish Queen Regent was 'very much under the spell of the Kaiser's strong personality' (*Ibid.*), the young king, Alfonso XIII, was not so impressed by the German military machine with which the Kaiser sought to dazzle him on his visit to Germany in 1905, feeling that it was 'an over-regulated body without individuality'; *Ibid.*, Nicolson to Landsdowne (28.11.1905), Doc. 144, pp. 134–5.

14 Rosario de la Torre del Río, 'Los acuerdos anglo-hispano-franceses de 1907: una larga negociación en la estela del 98', *Cuadernos de la Escuela Diplomática*, no. 1, segunda época, June 1988, pp. 81–104.

15 Manuel González Hontoria, *El protectorado francés en Marruecos y sus enseñanzas para la acción española* (Madrid: Publicaciones de la Residencia de Estudiantes, 1915), p. 239.

16 *BD*, Maurice de Bunsen to Sir Edward Grey, Annual Report, 25.1.1910, Doc. 45, pp. 87–8.

17 Quoted in Andrée Bachoud, *Los españoles ante las campañas de Marruecos* (Madrid: Espasa Calpe, 1988), p. 49.

18 *BD*, Bunsen to Grey, 11.3.1913, Doc. 102, p. 314.

19 For the text of all treaties involving Spain, see the Appendix in Servicio Histórico Militar (Ministerio del Ejército), *Acción de España en Africa* (Madrid, 1941), vol. 3.

20 Melchor Fernández Almagro, *Historia política de la España contemporánea* (Madrid: Alianza, 1956), vol. 1, p. 364.

21 Fernando León y Castillo, *Mis tiempos* (Madrid: Sucesores de Hernando, 1921), vol. 2, p. 126.

22 Thus the comments of the chief Spanish representative in the 1902 negotiations, León y Castillo, in his memoirs, *Ibid.*, vol. 2, pp. 126–97.

23 *Artículos, discursos, conferencias y cartas* (Madrid: Mateu Artes Gráficas, 1922–3), vol. 111, p. 115.

24 13 Septembre 1911, in Duque de Maura and Melchor Fernández Almagro, *Por qué cayó Alfonso XIII: evolución y disolución de los partidos históricos durante su reinado* (Madrid: Ediciones Ambos Mundos, 2nd ed., 1948), p. 193.

25 Drummond-Wolff to Lord Salisbury, 20.5.1899, *BD*, Doc. 57, p. 60.

26 *Bulletin du Comité de L'Afrique Française*, no. 4, April 1904, p. 118.

27 José Varela Ortega, *Los amigos políticos: partidos, elecciones y caciquismo en la Restauración (1875–1900)* (Madrid: Alianza, 1977).

28 For example, Enrique Rosas Ledesma, 'Las "Declaraciones de Cartagena" (1907): significación en la política exterior de España y repercusiones internacionales', *Cuadernos de historia moderna y contemporánea*, no. 2 (1981), pp. 213–29.

29 For Costa, see Joaquín Costa Martínez, *El comercio español y la cuestión de Africa* (Madrid: Imprenta de la Revista de Legislación, 1882) and 'Los intereses de España y Marruecos son armónicos', supplement to *España en Africa*, 15.1.1906; for Reparaz, see *Política de España en Africa* (Madrid: Calpe, 1907).

30 Ministerio de Fomento, *Expansión Comercial de España en Africa* (Madrid, 1906).

31 For details see María-Rosa de Madariaga, 'L'Espagne et le Rif: pénétration coloniale et résistances locales (1909–1926)', thèse de doctorat, Université de Paris 1 (1987), vol. 1.

32 *Primer Congreso africanista* (Barcelona, 1907), p. 21.

33 For a contemporary statement from the neo-colonial lobby, see 'Exposición que la Real Sociedad Geográfica de Madrid eleva al Excm. Sr. Presidente del Congreso de Ministros', in Archivo Antonio Maura, Fondo Documental, Mortera, Caja 4 (30 April 1904). For further discussion, see n.a., *Intereses de España en Marruecos* (Madrid, 1951) and Victor Morales Lezcano, *El colonialismo hispanofrancés en Marruecos (1898–1927)* (Madrid: Siglo 21, 1976).

34 Gabriel Maura Gamazo, *La cuestión de Marruecos desde el punto de vista español* (Madrid: M. Romero, 1905), p. 37.

35 'El Congreso africanista', *El Ejército Español*, 15.12.1909.

36 C.M. Andrew and A.S. Kanya-Forstner, 'The French Colonial Party: Its Composition, Aims and Influence, 1885–1914', *The Historical Journal*, vol. 14, 1 (1971), pp. 99–128.

37 For further details, see Jorge Cachinero, 'Intervencionismo y reformas militares en España a comienzos del siglo XX', *Cuadernos de Historia Contemporánea*, no. 10 (1988), pp. 155–84.

38 See, for example, 'Militares y paisanos' and 'Remedio radical' in *La Correspondencia Militar*, 15.2.1899 and 13.5.1899 and 'Ni honradas, ni patriotas', *Correo Militar*, 2.4.1899.

39 Sebastian Balfour, *The End of the Spanish Empire, 1898–1923* (Oxford: Oxford University Press, 1997).

40 'Las operaciones en el Riff', *El Ejército Español*, 20.7.1909.

41 Pablo La Porte, 'El Desastre de Annual y la crisis de la Restauración en España (1921–1923)', tesis doctoral, Complutense University of Madrid, 1997.

42 J. Moneva y Puyol, *La Asamblea Nacional de Productores (Zaragoza 1899)* (Zaragoza: Mariano Salas, 1899); *El Imparcial*, editorials and reports 16–20.2.1899 and 13.4.1899.

43 For a wider analysis of the regenerationist movement, see Balfour, *The End*, ch. 3.

44 Nicolson to Landsdowne, 22.4.1904, PRO FO 99.413.

45 Quoted in *La Vanguardia*, 6.10.1904.

46 *El Diario de Barcelona*, 14.4.1906; *La Veu de Catalunya*, 8.10.1904.

47 For example, Figueroa y Torres, Alvaro de, Conde de Romanones, *Notas de una vida (1868–1901)* (Madrid: M. Aguilar, 1934), p. 284.

48 Quoted in the *Diario de Barcelona*, 27.11.1907.

49 Sebastian Balfour, '"The Lion and the Pig": Nationalism and National Identity in *Fin-de-siècle* Spain', in Clare Mar-Molinero and Angel Smith (eds), *Nationalism and the Nation in the Iberian Peninsula* (Oxford: Berg, 1996), pp. 107–18.

50 For a further analysis of popular responses to the wars, see Balfour, *The End*, ch. 4.

51 González Hontoria, *El protectorado*, pp. 269–70; C.R. Pennell, *A Country with a Government and a Flag: The Rif War in Morocco 1921–1926* (Wisbech, Cambs: Middle East and North African Studies Press, 1986), p. 22.

52 *BD*, Bunsen to Grey, Annual Report, 25.1.1910, Doc. 45, p. 93.

53 For details of the situation leading to the 1909 disaster, see Bachoud, *Los españoles*, pp. 35–140.

54 Romanones, *Notas*, pp. 286–7.

55 The polemic over promotion can be followed from January 1910 in two military papers which took opposing positions: *La Correspondencia Militar* and *El Ejército Español*.

56 Alfredo Kindelán Duany, Teniente General, *Ejército y Política* (Madrid: M. Aguilar, 1946), pp. 179, 185.

57 For the close ties between the King and the army see the editorial of *La Correspondencia Militar*, 12.1.1912.

2 Spain and the First World War

Francisco Romero

The First World War was a watershed in modern European history. Until then the traditional governing elites had managed to preserve their political hegemony by relying on patronage, social subservience, prestige and tradition. Such a devastating conflict produced massive social distress and economic dislocation which in turn generated a process of ideological mobilization and political militancy. It heralded the arrival of a new era of mass politics in which the hitherto ruling classes would be confronted with the unwelcome prospect of democracy and the rapidly advancing threat of socialism.[1]

Spain was no exception. Paradoxically, a conflict in which the country did not intervene was to alter decisively her contemporary history as this was the moment in which the process of modernization accelerated while the burden of the country's past remained to be fought.[2] This was a time in which internal and external affairs appeared mutually intertwined. The result was not only the crisis of a political system but also the end of an era. Neutrality spared Spaniards from the human slaughter of the conflict but its ideological, social and economic impact hastened the erosion of the fragile foundations of the regime. Most dynastic politicians were determined to keep Spain out of the war but it was beyond their power to prevent the war from entering Spain.

The very same day on which hostilities broke out in the continent, Eduardo Dato, the Conservative Prime Minister, declared the official neutrality of the country. The reasons for this policy appeared in the letter that Dato wrote to the former leader of his party, Antonio Maura, on 25 August 1914:

> We would depart from neutrality only if we were directly threatened by foreign aggression or by an ultimatum. . . . Germany and Austria are delighted with our attitude as they believed us compromised with the Entente. France and Britain cannot criticize us as our pacts

with them are limited to Morocco. . . . I do not fear that the Allies would push us to take sides with or against them. . . . They must know that we lack material resources and adequate preparation for a modern war. . . . Would we not render a better service to both sides by sticking to our neutrality so that one day we could raise a white flag and organize a peace conference in our country which could put an end to the current conflict? We have moral authority for that and who knows if we shall be required to do so.[3]

A distant dispute in the Balkans was no reason to depart from Spain's neutral position between the two European camps. Furthermore, neutrality permitted the concealment of the country's economic and military weakness.[4] Finally, there was a significant amount of opportunism involved in that decision. The hope of the King and many politicians, which lasted until almost the end of the struggle, was that by playing the neutrality card, Spain could have a leading role in organizing a peace summit and thereby gain in the diplomatic arena what could never be achieved on the battlefield.

Neutrality was initially welcomed by nearly everyone in the country. From the followers of Antonio Maura or *Mauristas* on the right to the Socialists, all agreed that Spain should not get immersed in the conflict and applauded Dato when the Cortes opened after the summer recess on 30 October.[5] However, from the start, there were dissenting voices. On the one hand, the Republican Radical party, led by Alejandro Lerroux, a man with a shady reputation for demagoguery and corruption, did not hide its clear support for the Allies and even campaigned for intervention.[6] On the other, the ultra-clerical and intolerant Carlists quickly expressed their pro-German feelings. Most shocking, however, was the attitude of the leader of the other dynastic party, Count Romanones.

It has been suggested that Romanones' leadership of the Liberal party revealed the lack of morality of Spanish Liberalism and the hollowness of the politics of that age. A Spanish grandee with vast landowning, industrial and mining interests partly linked to French capital, Romanones can be described as the perfect example of the professional politician of the Restoration system.[7] A few days after the declaration of official neutrality, his newspaper, *El Diario Universal*, published an article called '*Neutralidades que matan*' ('Fatal neutralities') which openly criticized the policy of the government. The article constituted a clear appeal to Spain to cast its lot with the Entente. 'Fatal neutralities' did not advocate open intervention but argued that by moving closer to the Allied camp, Spain could seize a golden opportunity to enlarge the empire in Africa and strengthen the economy.[8] Joint economic interests with France certainly influenced the Count's pro-Allied feelings. Realizing that the article had received a bad reception, Romanones tried to deny his authorship and on 30 October he congratulated Dato effusively for his declaration of neutrality. Nevertheless, the damage to his future position as Prime Minister had already been done.[9]

During the first months, the war was followed in Spain as if it were a game, with bets even being placed on the outcome. Yet hopes that it would end before Christmas were soon dashed. The halt of the German offensive at the bank of the river Marne and the defeat of Russia in East Prussia meant the stabilization of the front and the beginning of a long war of attrition. From 1915 on, the majority of the Spanish politicians desperately tried to cling to neutrality. They continued behaving as if nothing was happening, ignoring the war and hoping in turn to be ignored in the vain belief that the conflict would soon finish and thus they could return to the profitable practices of the past. They could not prevent the break-up of the initial consensus and the division of the country into the staunchest supporters of either the Allied or the German cause.

The impact of the European struggle proved crucial at two levels: ideological polarization and radical social and economic transformation. For most of the population, especially in the countryside, the war on the continent did not have any particular meaning. Their living standards were inevitably hurt by the hardships and shortages brought about by the war but they did not understand the struggle. Yet for the cultural and political elites based in the cities, the European conflict became a question of obsessive concern. The war was almost immediately perceived as an ideological clash in which each of the warring factions came to symbolize certain transcendent ideas and values: the Allies represented democracy and freedom and the Central Powers, authority and order. The quarrel between Francophiles and Germanophiles generated a violent debate around the neutrality issue which, rather than merely reflecting contrasting opinions, revealed a deep pre-existing division within the Spanish people that the war only exacerbated. It was such a bitter polemic that it had the moral quality of a civil war – 'a civil war of words'. It represented a verbal clash between two Spains that was a portent of the real civil war that still lay a generation in the future.[10] Passions reached such a pitch that families and friends were often divided and many cinemas refused to give news of the conflict in order to prevent fights.

Although there was no clear-cut ideological and social division between the two sides, it can be affirmed that the right wanted a victory for the Central Powers and the left for the Entente. The main Germanophile voices in the country were those of the privileged social groups – the clergy, the aristocracy, the court, the upper bourgeoisie and the army – and those of right-wing parties such as the Carlists and the *Mauristas*. They regarded a German victory as a triumph for the continuity of a hierarchical social order. The Church became the ideological leader of this group. Its biased Germanophile fervour reached the extremes of condoning the German invasion of Catholic Belgium and of even spreading the bizarre rumour that the Kaiser was a Catholic prince in disguise raised up to chastise immoral France and restore the temporal power of the Pope.

Entente supporters were the professional middle classes, the petty bourgeoisie and the intellectuals. The latter, historical adversaries of the Church over the control of education and culture, considered anti-clerical France the example to follow to build a modern and democratic state. Catalan Nationalists, Republicans and Socialists were the political parties identified with that cause.[11] Historical links with France and admiration for the principles and ideals defended by the 'sister' nation made most Catalanists believe that a French victory represented the best hope for the fulfilment of their nationalist aspirations. As early as August 1914, Catalans volunteered to fight for France. One year later a magazine, *Iberia*, was created to praise and defend their cause and a formal organization, the so-called Comité de Germanor, was established in February 1916 in Barcelona to facilitate the recruitment of volunteers. In total, there were more than 2,000 Spanish soldiers, almost half of them Catalans, fighting as members of the French Foreign Legion. They took part not only in the main battles on French soil but also in the Dardanelles and Macedonia.[12]

The conflict between the partisans of both camps changed with the entry of Italy into the war in May 1915 followed a few months later by Portugal. The Francophiles began to regard official neutrality as a sham and their demands ranged from diplomatic rupture with Germany to open intervention. The Germanophiles then became the most ardent defenders of strict neutrality. That position, which they tried to disguise as a patriotic defence of the independence of the fatherland or *Españolismo*, in reality responded to the perception that it was the best way to support the Central Powers. Even the most rabid Germanophiles realized that with the country surrounded by the Allies, intervention in favour of Germany would be military suicide.

At the same time, Spain underwent radical demographic, economic and social changes during the conflict. She took advantage of her neutral status to supply both camps. Foreign intervention was eliminated in the internal market and new outlets abandoned by the belligerent nations were taken over. The explosion in the volume and prices of exports and the drastic curtailment of imports were reflected in the balance of trade, which from a position of chronic deficit now registered fabulous profits. This was a period of unexpected economic growth, an era of continuous inflow of capital and gold. Yet the spectacular development of the econ-omy neither served to consolidate the industrial infrastructure of the nation nor benefited society as a whole. The war provided a kind of artificial protection to the economy that vanished as soon as the conflict concluded. Those who amassed huge fortunes preferred to squander them on ostentation and luxury rather than use them for investment. Furthermore, the massive profits of a privileged few did not produce a state of general prosperity. On the contrary, they benefited only certain areas and certain social classes. External demand produced an astonishing expansion of Spanish industry concentrated in the north and east of the country. By contrast, the agrarian regions of the centre and south went through a stage of endemic depression. Thus, simultaneously, scenes of feverish activity in the Catalan factories and unemployment and misery in the Andalusian countryside could be observed in the same nation. In fact, for a majority of the population, these were years of hardship, pri-vation and worsening living standards which were known as *crisis de subsistencias* (shortage of basic commodities). The old-fashioned railway network virtually collapsed under the new pressures. Internal migratory currents intensified from the countryside to the cities, with emigrants having to survive in appalling living conditions. The increase of money in circulation, the explosion in external demand and the drop in imports caused a previously unknown galloping inflation. Speculators and profiteers flourished and with them shortages, hunger and desperation.[13]

The moral bankruptcy of the Restoration governments was now amply confirmed. They were unable or unwilling to fight those benefiting from the *crisis de subsistencias.* This was scarcely surprising, as the profiteers were often the very same *caciques* to whom the political class owed its votes. In 1915 the first signs of popular discontent appeared, turning soon into food riots and assaults on shops. The *crisis de subsistencias* caused the fall of Dato, who, under heavy attack for his lack of a coherent eco-nomic policy, left office in December 1915, to be replaced by the other dynastic party, led by Romanones.

By 1916, the impact of the war could be clearly observed in Spain. The divorce between state and society became more pronounced than at any time since 1875. The rapid ideological polarization and economic changes brought about by the European conflict meant that the regime's artificial foundations in a period of mass mobilization could no longer be concealed. This was the moment in which the Catalan industrial bourgeoisie, the labour movement and the army began to revolt against the regime.

Aware of its recently gained economic strength, the Catalan bourgeoisie, represented politically by the *Lliga Regionalista,* sought to translate the new reality into political terms. The *Lliga* was a socially conservative but eminently pragmatist group. The objective was to put an end to the political monopoly enjoyed by the financial and landowning oligarchy in Madrid and to establish a new decentralized system which favoured the growth of a modern capitalist economy based on the Catalan model.[14]

In July 1916, the unchecked rise of the cost of living, the food shortages and the lack of a positive response from the government led to a historical alliance between the two main workers' organizations in Spain: the Socialist *Unión General de Trabajadores* (UGT) and the anarchosyndicalist *Confederación Nacional del Trabajo* (CNT). The larger membership and solid organization of the UGT meant that the moderate and prudent Socialists were in charge of the partnership. Yet the failure to obtain redress from the Liberal cabinet prompted them to harden their position and even threaten in March 1917 to overthrow the existing system by means of a general strike.[15]

Inflation and economic hardship hurt army officers as much as other classes. Furthermore, the proximity of the conflict encouraged the government to break the traditional policy of non-intervention in military affairs. In 1916 a Bill of Military Reform was introduced in an attempt to professionalize the services and deal with the always sensitive question of reducing the overmanned officer corps by introducing tests of intellectual and physical ability. The incensed officers had been observing how the workers at least could fight back by joining trade unions and declaring strikes. From mid-1916, they began to join military trade unions known as *juntas de defensa* from which they denounced the corruption of the political system and the favouritism enjoyed by certain generals, and demanded that the promotion system be based on strict seniority and pay increases.[16]

However, international factors were what finally initiated the chain reaction of events leading to the collapse of Restoration politics. During Romanones' cabinet, polarization around the neutrality issue reached an active phase. The Count's imperialist ambition and the brutality of German foreign policy placed Spain close to intervention in the war. Despite all his declarations, the Liberal Prime Minister never abandoned his pro-Allied convictions or the ideas expressed in 'Fatal neutralities'. Romanones endeavoured to hide this fact from the public. While he proclaimed in Parliament his adherence to neutrality, he resorted to secret diplomatic channels to carry out his foreign policy.[17] In order to accomplish his purpose, he appointed his friend León y Castillo, a Francophile with good connections among French political elites, as new ambassador to Paris.

In exchange for his sympathy, the Count expected to obtain the concession of Tangiers from the French government. In January 1916, Romanones wrote to León y Castillo:

> Our fate is inevitably linked to that of France and Britain. . . .
> Tangiers still remains my greater concern. . . . We cannot pacify our
> zone without that city. . . . Tangiers is not only the key to the
> control of the Mediterranean but also to the pacification of our
> Protectorate in Morocco.[18]

All hopes of acquiring Tangiers soon vanished. The Allies were certainly not prepared to award any territory in exchange merely for promises of eternal platonic friendship. Moreover, Spain was regarded by the French as a Germanophile country. The fact that the government was temporarily in friendly hands did not mean a thing as long as important institutions such as the Church, army and court made no effort to conceal their support for the cause of the Central Powers.[19]

An immediate departure from the official neutrality was something that Romanones, in a country polarized by the issue, could not offer. After December 1916, however, the evolution of the war in Europe and the brutality of German diplomacy persuaded the Count to take a firmer step towards the Entente.

In December 1916, first the Central Powers and then the American President, Woodrow Wilson, launched a series of abortive initiatives to seek an end to the war. Alfonso even felt confident that his moment as peace arbiter had finally arrived.[20] The negative response of the Allies, confirmed in a meeting between Romanones and the French ambassador, persuaded the Spanish Prime Minister that it was naive to expect that Spain could obtain anything in a negotiated peace which was utterly rejected by at least one of the two camps.[21]

There is no evidence that the Allies exerted any kind of pressure to achieve the entry of Spain into the war. It would not have been difficult to force Spain's hand since they controlled the sea routes and the traffic of coal, cotton and oil vital for her economy. At the outbreak of the war, Britain, fearing that Italy might throw in her lot with the Central Powers, wished for Spanish involvement. Portugal and Spain were regarded as the ideal counterbalance to Italy in the Mediterranean.[22] The alignment of Italy with the Western powers in May 1915, followed a few months later by that of Portugal, diminished the value of an alliance with Spain. Certainly, France and Britain were eager to have Spain on their side. Yet they were not prepared to pay an excessive price for an ally that they did not consider indispensable for the course of the war. Hence the strategy adopted by the Allies was to wait and negotiate from a position of strength in case Spain decided on her own to enter the war.

In contrast, the Central Powers followed an aggressive diplomacy which sought to ensure by any means the maintenance of Spanish neutrality and, simultaneously, to damage the interests of the Entente in the Iberian Peninsula. Germany, and to a lesser extent Austria, pursued those objectives through different means: their intelligence services set up a vast and impressive spy network which extended from the Canary Islands to the French border. Bribes were generously lavished to win the favour of the local authorities, and anarchist groups were infiltrated and financed in order to direct their activities against those industrial concerns producing material for the Allies.[23] At the same time, relying on the often scandalous complicity of the Spanish colonial authorities, Germany organized and supplied Moorish rebel bands to create trouble in French Morocco.[24]

Both warring sides, but above all the Central Powers, took advantage of the exorbitant rise in the price of paper to win control of a substantial number of Spanish publications. By early 1917, not only the best-known national right-wing journals but also some anarcho-syndicalist and Republican newspapers were under their control. Thus an intelligent and well-planned campaign seeking to influence and manipulate public opinion was carried out. With editorials in which either neutrality was equated to *Españolismo* or intervention to involvement in an imperialist war in which workers would be slaughtered, these journals managed to conceal their pro-German feelings. Any criticism of the outrages committed by Germany – be it of innocent lives lost in a submarine attack or atrocities in the occupied territories – was depicted as warmongering and an open invitation to intervention.[25] Finally, German submarines carried out a vicious campaign against the Spanish merchant fleet trading with the Allies.[26]

Events reached a head after December 1916. The fight between the Prime Minister and his Germanophile enemies was, metaphorically speaking, to the death. The outcome could only be either the end of Romanones' premiership or Spain's total breach with the Central Powers. The Count refused to endorse Wilson's peace initiative and instead published a statement protesting against Germany's contempt for the rules of international law. Romanones even clashed with Alfonso XIII when he opposed the latter's attendance at the funeral of the late Austrian

Emperor, Franz Joseph, in Vienna and at his wearing an Austrian uni-
form at the private service held subsequently in Madrid.[27] Convinced
that the Liberal Prime Minister was the main enemy of their cause in
Spain, the Central Powers orchestrated a vicious offensive with the objective of removing him from office. The signal was given by the Austrian
ambassador, the Prince of Furstenberg, who declared on 26 December
that Romanones was behind contraband interests.[28] A few days later, the
French secret services intercepted a radiogram in which the German
ambassador, Prince Ratibor, asked Berlin for more funds with which to
increase the campaign against the Count.[29] For the next four months, the
Germanophile press singled out the Prime Minister as a warmonger sur-
reptitiously seeking to embroil the nation in the European conflagration
and accused him of placing Allied interests above those of Spain and of
using his position to make profits by smuggling war contraband.[30]

At the same time, from late 1916 the number of submarine actions,
sabotage and spying activities shot up dramatically.[31] The result was the
growing polarization of the country between those who were prepared to
defend neutrality at any price and thus willing to condone any German
outrage and those who argued that such contempt for Spain's neutral
status should be answered by the immediate rupture of diplomatic relations. In his quest for an approach to the Western powers, Romanones
had to face formidable odds. He was confronted by a very resourceful
German intelligence network which could act at will with the complicity of a large section of the authorities and was backed by a powerful
press lobby. Furthermore, the fact that, ironically, the most ardent supporters of the Count's foreign policy were Republicans and Socialists persuaded the bulk of the dynastic forces that his downfall was a price worth
paying.

In February 1917, Spain's polarization increased dramatically when
the Central Powers announced the intensification of their submarine
campaign. Henceforth any neutral vessel navigating in the forbidden
areas off the Allied coasts would be sunk. The Germanophiles insisted
that Germany and Austria were within their rights to adopt any strategy
to survive. The Francophiles demanded to follow the American example
and break off diplomatic relations with Germany. Romanones declared in
Parliament that his government was determined to take the necessary
steps to face the alarming situation and avoid the disruption of the economic life of the country.[32] He wrote to León y Castillo that were public
opinion not so divided he would immediately adopt the American policy.
He added that for the present he could not do so but had to wait for the
right psychological moment and encouraged the ambassador in Paris to
initiate contacts with the French government.[33]

In the most absolute secrecy, Spanish diplomacy sought for the next two months to clinch a favourable deal with the Allies. Thus León y Castillo met the French Foreign Minister and asked that, in exchange for diplomatic rupture with Germany and a more active contribution to the Allied war effort, Spain should obtain Tangiers, Gibraltar and a free hand in Portugal. The French government was prepared to reach an agreement although for internal reasons said that a settlement in Morocco should be postponed until the end of the war. For the French, Spain's collaboration could represent the end of the nightmare which Morocco had become, the free access of their fleet to the Spanish ports and the possible reinforcement of the front with thousands of fresh troops.[34]

The British government proved more cautious. The entry of Spain into the war was considered a mixed blessing. To a large extent, the disadvantages of her cooperation outweighed the advantages. The state of the Spanish army was pitiful. It lacked modern equipment, heavy artillery and aeroplanes, and the senior officers were utterly incompetent. However, Spain had some of the largest mineral resources in Europe and her intervention would represent for the Entente an increase of half a million troops and four million in the reserve. There was no opposition in principle to a treaty linking Portugal to Spain in some form, for Portuguese misgovernment was a persistent source of anxiety. Yet it was feared that the announcement of such a treaty at that stage of the war would be a bad exercise in public relations since the Entente claimed to fight for the rights of small nations. Britain refused to make any promises with regard to the question of Gibraltar but a committee was formed by members of different departments to study the subject. In turn, there were proposals to restore Spanish control of the Caroline Islands and to extend the Spanish colony of Guinea northwards.[35]

In April, the psychological moment awaited by Romanones seemed to have arrived when the Spanish steamer *San Fulgencio* was sunk. The incident went beyond the long list of outrages committed by Germany: the ship was in possession of a German permit of free circulation and when torpedoed was navigating outside the forbidden waters and heading towards Spain with a much-needed cargo of Welsh coal. Romanones confided his plan to his friend León y Castillo:

> The crucial moment has arrived. The sinking of the *San Fulgencio* has been the final straw. The route I will take is already determined in the direction that you know. . . . The note to Germany will be the first and fundamental step.[36]

Romanones' plan was thus to send a harsh note of protest to Germany amounting almost to an ultimatum. The sinking of another vessel would mean the immediate rupture of diplomatic relations and the final alignment with the Entente.[37] Yet the Liberal leader lost the game. On 19 April his resignation was made public before he could send his note. The Germanophiles had obtained their greatest success, the head of the Prime Minister. One of their journals even pictured the Count in a cartoon with his heart pierced by a sword called neutrality.[38]

In fact, the frail structures of the regime did not permit the implementation of the adventurist foreign policy defended by Romanones. In his farewell statement, the Count mentioned the opposition of important members of his party and of public opinion as main reasons for his fall.[39] Certainly, several notables of the Liberal party used the neutrality issue as an excuse to oust him from office and replace him with the weak and malleable Marquis of Alhucemas. Four of the ministers of the Romanones cabinet resigned with him and the other four remained in the new Liberal cabinet led by Alhucemas. It is impossible, however, to argue that public opinion removed Romanones. He did not resign but was dismissed by Alfonso. The King, and the King alone, could appoint and sack Prime Ministers according to the rules of the Restoration system.[40]

If the court had always adopted a Germanophile position, this feeling only increased after the revolution and subsequent fall of the Tsar in Russia in March 1917. This event sent waves of panic among the Spanish ruling classes and represented one of the greatest propaganda successes for the German cause. The end of tsarism was received with jubilation by the Spanish left. The nature of the Russian regime had always been a source of embarrassment, but now the establishment of a progressive system in Russia, added to the entry of the United States into the war in early April, was regarded as confirmation that the war in Europe was a worldwide ideological struggle between democracy and autocracy. Additionally, the attitude of the Allies, abandoning the Russian monarch to his fate and supporting the new provisional government, meant that more than ever the Spanish elites identified with the cause of the Central Powers. Hence, paradoxically, at the same time that Romanones was considering aligning the country with the Allies, events in Russia were confirming the commitment to absolute neutrality of Spain's leading circles. They concluded that with a radicalized proletariat, a restless bourgeoisie and an unhappy officer class, it was madness even to consider entry into a war for which, after all, Spain was neither militarily nor economically prepared. Henceforth strict neutrality would be maintained regardless of the price in terms of human lives and national honour.

Neutrality, however, was not enough to save an oligarchic order that based its hegemony on the apathy of the population. Political awakening and mass ideological mobilization were not exclusive to Russia but spread like wildfire across the continent. The divorce between state and society had reached a point of no return in Spain. The two Restoration parties were thoroughly discredited and the country was divided by the war and restless because of the *crisis de subsistencias*. Yet the final crisis unexpectedly began in the military garrisons.

The existence of the *juntas de defensa*, which constantly spoke out against royal favouritism, and the corruption of the regime were continuous sources of alarm for Alfonso. He feared that the Russian events could be repeated in Spain.[41] On 27 May, at a pro-Allied gathering at the bullring of Madrid attended by over 20,000 people, the King was accused of being both the main friend of the German cause and the greatest obstacle to the democratic modernization of the country. He was warned that he might soon be following the fate of the monarchs in Greece and Russia.[42] Alfonso took the threat seriously and ordered the new War Minister, General Aguilera, to dissolve the *juntas*. Neither the King nor the government had foreseen the strength and resolution of the officers. The leading *junteros* refused to disband their unions and when they were arrested a new provisional central *junta* was immediately created. On 1 June 1917, the officers submitted an ultimatum demanding the release of their leaders and the official recognition of the *juntas*. This event marked the return of the army to active politics and effectively initiated the subordination of public life to military exigencies. The bewildered and overwhelmed Alhucemas cabinet resigned after less than two months in office.[43]

The successful insurrection of the officers initiated a process of expectation and hope in the country. The editorials published in the *juntas'* mouthpiece, *La Correspondencia Militar,* by playing down their economic and corporative demands and increasing the attacks on the ruling oligarchy, consolidated the belief that the time for change and reform had finally arrived.[44] The decision of the monarch to cling scrupulously to the two-party system and entrust Dato with the formation of a new government infuriated the whole nation. The return of Dato with practically the same Conservative cabinet as had failed miserably two years earlier appeared to be a blatant challenge to public opinion.[45] All the political groups, from *Mauristas* to Socialists and Catalan Regionalists, announced their opposition to the *status quo*. The fall of the monarchy in Greece, the revolution in Russia and the democratic influence created by the entry of the United States into the war seemed to herald the end of the regime in Spain.

In this context, a possible alliance of army, bourgeoisie and proletariat presented a formidable threat. It was the Catalan bourgeoisie that tried to organize a coalition of forces with which to lead the offensive against the *turno*. The *Lliga Regionalista* sought to take advantage of the existing chaotic situation to end the monopoly of power enjoyed by the land-owning oligarchy. The *Lliga* was anything but revolutionary. In fact, its objective was to carry out a political revolution in order to pre-empt a deeper social revolt.[46] With this goal in mind, the Catalan Regionalists summoned an assembly of parliamentarians in Barcelona for 19 July at which to discuss a thorough constitutional reform. The Catalan offensive rapidly obtained the enthusiastic support of Republicans and Socialists, basically moderate groups that were delighted to let the Regionalists lead the offensive, but all the attempts to win over the *juntas* failed. Antonio Maura, the veteran Conservative leader, who might have become the link between parliamentarians and officers, refused to play that role.[47] Since early June, lacking political contacts the *juntas* had turned to him for guidance. Equally, Catalan leaders and even some outstanding *Mauristas* tried to persuade Maura to throw his support behind the assembly and join forces with those seeking the renovation of the country. Nevertheless, nobody changed his mind. Maura recognized the artificial character of the political system but declined to take part in any initiative that could lead to the fall of the dynasty.[48]

The lack of coordination between the opposition forces played into the hands of the government. The outbreak of a transport strike in Valencia, coinciding with the celebration of the assembly in Barcelona, provided the government with a golden opportunity to take the initiative and present itself as the ultimate guarantor of the social order.[49] The plan was to provoke the proletariat into an ill-timed and unprepared general strike, whose pending threat had existed since March, compromise the army with the task of putting it down and force the bourgeoisie to break with the labour movement.[50] In the short term, the governmental manoeuvre was a success.

August 1917 illustrates a turning point in the history of the Spanish labour movement. It represented its baptism of fire, leading the offensive for the first time in a vain attempt to carry out a political revolution.[51] The Spanish proletariat paid dearly for its inexperience and excessive optimism. Events developed according to the plan devised by the Conservative cabinet. The stoppage was total only in the largest cities. By contrast, it had little if any impact on the countryside. The conflict remained a purely urban revolt in a few city centres, thus facilitating the task of the authorities, who crushed it in less than a week. The bourgeoisie limited its role to awaiting the outcome of the events.

Furthermore, hopes that the army would refuse to defend the regime quickly disappeared. Unlike in Petrograd, there was no fraternization between workers and troops. On the contrary, the officers ignored all the reformist rhetoric of the previous two months and behaved once more as the ultimate guarantor of public order, suppressing the strike with unexpected brutality. Undoubtedly, rumours spread by the government that the movement was financed by the Allies, to impose a change of regime and force the entry of the country into the war, influenced the attitude of the officers. Most of them agreed that it was better to shoot their working-class compatriots in Spain than to dig trenches in France.[52]

The crushing of the revolutionary movement ended the hopes of bringing democracy. Yet the victory of the Conservative administration proved short-lived. The threat presented by the proletariat had been eliminated, but the bourgeoisie continued its political campaign against the system, and the *juntas*, soon realizing that they had been manipulated, turned their hostility on Dato.[53] The officers were incensed when they intercepted a cable sent by José Sánchez Guerra, the Minister of the Interior, advising the civil governors to limit their role to finding out the names and political leanings of the leading *junteros* until the moment arrived to turn against them.[54] Their deadly blow arrived on the night of 26 October 1917 when a message signed by all the corps of the army was submitted to the King, giving him seventy-two hours to appoint a new cabinet 'more in tune with the wishes of the nation'.[55]

For the second time in a few months, the army overthrew a government. The Liberal regime never recovered. The solution to the crisis of October 1917 revealed fully the defeat of the Restoration groups and the emergence of new decision-making centres. After a record eight days without a government, a coalition cabinet was formed. The new administration represented the beginning of the end of an era. The so-called *turno pacífico* or the rotation in power of the two monarchist parties, the basic foundation of the political system for more than forty years, was destroyed. The coalition was still packed with Restoration politicians but the real winners from the crisis were the Crown, the *juntas* and the Catalan industrial bourgeoisie. The King preserved his privileged position as all the demands for constitutional reform were abandoned. The officers abandoned their reformist pretensions but ensured the satisfaction of their economic interests and the security of having veto powers over any cabinet. Finally, the Catalan Regionalists, in a clear exercise of political opportunism, broke with the anti-dynastic front and joined the power bloc. The *Lliga Regionalista* had achieved its immediate objectives: the monopoly of power of the two monarchist parties had been shattered, as Catalan Regionalists now had portfolios in Madrid for the first time, including control of the economy. The Catalan bourgeoisie showed by its behaviour that class interests counted for more than nationalist and reformist ambitions.[56]

In March 1918, a new coalition government, the most impressive cabinet ever in the Restoration era, was created. Among the members of this government there were three former Prime Ministers (Dato, Romanones and Alhucemas) and the leader of the *Lliga*, Cambó, and it was presided over by none other than the veteran Maura. The so-called *Ministerio de Primates* (Cabinet of Titans) was received with popular enthusiasm. One of the sceptics was Antonio Maura himself. Time proved him right. On his very first morning in office he confided to his son, Gabriel, 'They kept me away for ten years, years which could have been the most useful of my life, and now I am seized on to preside over the whole lot. Let us see how long the charade lasts.'[57]

The Maura cabinet lasted just long enough to see the end of the war. Yet it always remained a ramshackle affair. Its short life was marked by internal squabbles and rivalries among its members that made it impossible to undertake any enterprise with success. A good example was its mishandling of the international situation. In fact, after being obscured by the domestic events, the neutrality question re-emerged with great intensity in 1918. The position finally adopted by such a flamboyant cabinet, despite all the glaring evidence of German aggression, looked like impotence, surrender and humiliation. Spain was held up to ridicule in the eyes of the world.

The year 1918 saw the final great effort undertaken by the Central Powers to win the war before the arrival of hundreds of thousands of American troops tilted the balance against them. In Spain, this campaign meant a considerable increase in the number of attacks on industrialists and factories producing for the Allies, and sinkings of her merchant fleet. There were frequent revelations in the press of Germany financing anarchist groups and bribing local authorities. For instance, *El Sol*, a highly influential newspaper, published a document in March exposing the collusion between the German Embassy and anarchists and, in June, *Solidaridad Obrera*, the CNT's mouthpiece, provided conclusive evidence that Manuel Bravo Portillo, the Chief of Police in Barcelona, was supplying vital information which helped German submarines sink Spanish vessels. Faced with this proof, the response of the government was pathetic: *El Sol* was temporarily banned in March and a Law of Espionage was hurriedly passed in July, which effectively represented a gag on the press.[58] *El Sol*, judging the new law, commented, 'Henceforth spies in Spain might be fined 20,000 pesetas, and those who expose them will have to pay 100,000 pesetas.'[59]

The lack of a firm and resolute foreign policy was a consequence of the very fragility and weakness of the regime. Not even in the summer of 1918, when the conflict was reaching its conclusion, was Spain's strict neutrality abandoned, though it was proving to be fatal and humiliating. By that date, the German submarine campaign had caused the sinking of more than sixty Spanish vessels, representing a quarter of Spain's merchant fleet, and the death of a hundred Spanish sailors. On 10 August, the government, in an unexpected act of defence of the national honour, sent a note of protest to Germany warning that from then onwards, in the event of any fresh torpedoing, the tonnage sunk would automatically be replaced by an equal amount from the forty German and Austrian vessels which had sought refuge in Spanish ports at the outbreak of the war.[60]

The government was devastated when Germany responded that the seizure of any of her ships would constitute *causa belli*, and within one month her submarines torpedoed five other Spanish vessels. Its impotence was amply illustrated when in the council of ministers of 31 August the Marine Minister expressed the opposition of King and army to any hasty decision that might endanger the country's neutrality. The spectre of the Russian revolution and the awareness of military incapacity determined the veto of monarch and officers on foreign policy.[61] Finally, the government announced in October that Spain was soon to seize seven German vessels. The impression was one of sadness, if not ridicule, when it emerged that this almost amounted to an act of charity on Germany's part. In fact, the ships would not be confiscated by Spain but borrowed as soon as the German Embassy decided which ones to lend.[62] Ironically, a few days later the armistice was signed. One of its clauses was the surrender of the Central Powers' fleet in neutral ports to the Allies. It was the just reward for a bankrupt regime that had mortgaged its foreign policy to a shameful neutrality.

The collapse of the Maura cabinet in November 1918, which practically coincided with the end of the war, revealed in full the authority crisis in which the Liberal monarchy was plunged. The following years were marked by the agony and decline of a regime unable to meet the growing demands generated by the mobilization and political consciousness brought about by the war. With officers and the King intervening actively in politics, making and toppling cabinets, the result was social turmoil, political instability and, in the end, the destruction of the ruling system.[63]

In the international field, Spain paid the penalty for her neutrality. Isolated and scorned by the Allies, she had to struggle alone in the unpopular and grossly underfunded adventure of Morocco that led to the

Disaster at Annual in the summer of 1921. At the same time, the domestic situation turned chaotic. The Restoration parties, increasingly divided into rival factions, could not solve the political deadlock. Furthermore, the post-war economic recession, the Allied victory and the Bolshevik triumph in Russia intensified the social struggle, but with the difference that now the offensive was no longer led by the moderate Socialists but by the more intransigent anarcho-syndicalists. It was amid that climate of colonial disasters, social warfare and political vacuum that the same groups which had played a crucial role in the crisis of October 1917 – Crown, army and industrial bourgeoisie – decided to end the constitutional facade and throw their support behind an authoritarian solution in September 1923. Yet that year Primo de Rivera did not overthrow the last dynastic government; he merely limited himself to filling a vacuum that had existed largely as a consequence of the impact of the First World War.

Notes

1 Martin Blinkhorn (ed.), *Fascists and Conservatives* (Cambridge: Unwin Hyman, 1990), p. 4.
2 Manuel Tuñón de Lara, *Poder y sociedad en España, 1900-1931* (Madrid: Espasa-Calpe, 1992), p. 187.
3 Gabriel Maura and Melchor Fernández Almagro, *Por qué cayó Alfonso XIII* (Madrid, 1948), pp. 472–3.
4 This was the main reason, according to the Socialist, Manuel Cordero, as stated in his *Los socialistas y la revolución* (Madrid: Impresa Torrent, 1932), p. 26.
5 *Parliamentary Records* (hereafter DSC), 30.10.1914. Also see Public Record Office, *Foreign Office Records* (hereafter FO) 371–2104, 72,750. Dispatch from Ambassador Hardinge to Foreign Minister Grey, 18.11.1914.
6 Joan B. Culla i Clara, *El republicanisme lerrouxista a Catalunya, 1901–1923* (Barcelona: Curial, 1986), pp. 311–15; David Martínez Fiol, 'Lerrouxistas en pie de guerra' in *Historia 16*, no. 174 (October 1990), pp. 24–6.
7 Javier Tusell, *Alfonso XIII y los políticos de su época* (Madrid: Planeta, 1976), p. 61; Salvador Forner, *Canalejas y el partido liberal democrático* (Madrid, 1993), p. 38.
8 Romanones, *Las responsabilidades del antiguo régimen, 1875–1923* (Madrid: Renacimiento, 1924), p. 77.
9 Romanones' new-found commitment to neutrality was first expressed in an article written in *El Imparcial*, 4.9.1914.
10 Gerald Meaker, 'A Civil War of Words', in Hans Schmitt (ed.), *Neutral Europe between War and Revolution* (Charlottesville: University of Virginia Press, 1988), pp. 1–65; see pp. 2, 6–7.
11 There is abundant literature on the division between Germanophiles and Francophiles during the war. See, among others, Adolfo Posada, *Actitud ética entre la guerra y la paz* (Madrid: Caro Reggio, 1923); Hermógenes Cenamor Val, *Los españoles y la guerra: neutralidad o intervención* (Madrid: Sociedad

Española de la Librería, 1916); Lorenzo Ballesteros, *La guerra europea y la neutralidad española* (Madrid: Rates, 1917); Fernando de la Reguera, *España neutral* (Madrid: Planeta, 1967); Fernando Díaz Plaja, *Francófilos y Germanófilos* (Barcelona: Dopesa, 1973). Also see FO371–2471, 73,963 and FO371–2760, 20.756. Secret Reports, 29.7.1915 and 17.4.1916.

12 The best information about the Spanish Volunteers can be found in Arxiu Nacional de Catalunya, *Dr Joan Solé i Pla's Papers*. The thorough work by David Martínez Fiol, *Els Voluntaris Catalans a la Gran Guerra, 1914–1918* (Barcelona: Biblioteca Serra D'Or, 1991), pp. 105–28, destroys the myth of the existence of 15,000 Spanish Volunteers, 12,000 of them Catalans. This author proves that there were 2,118 Volunteers, 935 of them Catalans. Also see Albert Balcells, 'Los Voluntarios Catalanes en la Gran Guerra (1914–1918)', in *Historia 16*, no. 121 (May 1986); FO371–2471/73.963. Memo on Catalans, 29.7.1915.

13 On the impact of the war on the economy see J.L. García Delgado, S. Roldán and J. Muñoz, *La formación de la sociedad capitalista en España* (Madrid: Ceca, 1973); J.A. Vandellós, 'La balanza comercial y el cambio de la peseta', in *Revista Nacional de la Economía* (1931); Ignacio Bernís, *Consecuencias económicas de la guerra* (Madrid: Imprenta Stanislao Maestre, 1923); Instituto de Reformas Sociales, *Movimientos de los precios al por menor durante la guerra y la posguerra, 1914–1922* (Madrid: IRS, 1923).

14 See Francesc Cambó, *Memorias, 1876–1936* (Madrid: Alianza, 1987), pp. 224–9; Jesús Pabón, *Cambó* (Barcelona: Alpha, 1952), vol. 1, pp. 448–9.

15 *El Socialista*, 28.3.1917.

16 Benito Márquez and J.M. Capó, *Las juntas militares de defensa* (La Habana: Biblioteca Porvenir, 1923), pp. 23–4; Carolyn Boyd, *Praetorian Politics in Liberal Spain* (Chapel Hill: University of North Carolina Press, 1979), pp. 52–5.

17 Romanones declared four times in Parliament in 1916 his commitment to strict neutrality. See DSC, 10.5, 6.6, 13.10 and 4.11.1916.

18 Real Academia de la Historia, *Romanones' Papers* (hereafter AR). Correspondence with Ambassadors (II I A). Letter from Romanones to León y Castillo, 25.1.1916.

19 AR II I A. Correspondence from León y Castillo to Romanones, 5.2 and 17.4.1916. See also FO371–2762, 189,921. Dispatch from Hardinge to Grey, 16.9.1916.

20 The expectations of the King are reported in Real Academia de la Historia, *Natalio Rivas' Papers* (hereafter ANR), File 89,303, 5.12.1916. Also see FO371–2762, 256,871. Dispatch from Hardinge to Balfour, 12.12.1916.

21 AR II I A. Two letters from Romanones to Fermín Calbetón, 26.12 and 28.12.1916. Also see FO371–2762, 256,871, dispatch from Hardinge to Balfour, 16.12.1916.

22 FO371–2472, 159,874, secret report by War Admiralty staff, 31.8.1914.

23 A summary of German subversive activities between 1915 and 1917 can be found in AR File 63, 46, April 1917. Also see FO371–3372, 118,736, dispatch from Hardinge to Balfour, 6.7.1918.

24 Archivo General de la Administración, *Foreign Office* (hereafter AGA), French section, Box 5960 (Morocco 1917–18).

25 A full account of German activities to control the Spanish press can be found in Archivo Histórico Nacional, *Home Office*, File 48A, no. 13, 2.2.1929. Also

see FO 195–117, 237,928, report on German activities in regards to the press, October 1917.

26 A full list of Spanish vessels sunk by German submarines until April 1917 (a total of 31 vessels or over 60,000 tons) can be found in AR File 63, no. 46, April 1917. Also see *Algunos datos sobre la guerra submarina* (Madrid: Tipografía de los Hijos de Tello, 1918).

27 For Romanones' statement, see *El Liberal*, 28.12.1916. Romanones' opposition to the King's wishes to please the Austrians can be found in AR II I A, letters from Romanones to Calbetón, 26.12 and 28.12.1916.

28 It was published by the Austrian-financed newspaper *La Nación*, 26.12.1916.

29 FO 371–3033, 23,605. Dispatch from Hardinge to Balfour, 23.1.1917.

30 The most noteworthy newspapers taking part in that campaign were *La Tribuna, La Acción, El ABC, Solidaridad Obrera, España Nueva, El Debate, El Día, El Correo Español* and *La Nación*.

31 See French protests about the increase in the number of illegal activities in Spain in AGA, French Section, Box 5946, September–December 1916.

32 DSC, 1.2.1917.

33 AR II I A, letters from Romanones to León y Castillo, 3.2 and 6.2.1917.

34 AR II I A, letter from León y Castillo to Romanones, 10.2.1917. Also see Public Record Office, *Cabinet Papers* (hereafter CAB), 23/2, War Cabinet, Discussion of Spain's approaches to France, 8.3.1917; FO371–3035, 75,548, dispatch from Vaughan, Secretary at the British Embassy in Madrid, to Balfour informing that Romanones had told the French Ambassador that Spain could no longer remain neutral, otherwise she would sink to the level of an insignificant power such as the Netherlands, 12.4.1917.

35 For discussion over the possible entry of Spain into the war see CAB 24/7, GT 161, 14.3.1917; FO 371–3033, 76,696 and 77,736, 13.4 and 14.4.1917.

36 See AR II I A. Letter from Romanones to Castillo, 14.4.1917. The same day the Spanish Ambassador in Paris wrote to the Prime Minister, 'We must act now otherwise it will be too late.'

37 A draft version of the note which should have been delivered to Germany and a complete list of some of the most infamous outrages committed by Germany on Spanish soil can be found in AR File 63, 46, April 1917.

38 *La Acción*, 21.4.1917.

39 *La Epoca*, 19.4.1917.

40 This opinion was shared by the British military attaché, Jocelyn Grant, in FO371–3033, 96,857, 5.5.1917.

41 For the King's fear of the Russian events see Romanones, *Notas de una vida, 1912-1931* (Madrid: Espasa-Calpe, 1947), pp. 135–7; also see FO85–1344, 268, dispatch from Hardinge to Balfour, 19.5.1917.

42 *El País*, 28.5.1917.

43 On the events surrounding the *juntas*' rebellion, see Márquez & Capó, *Las juntas militares*, pp. 35–7; Boyd, *Praetorian Politics*, pp. 53–63; Juan Antonio Lacomba, *La crisis española de 1917* (Málaga: Ciencia Nueva, 1970), pp. 112–35; José Buxadé, *España en crisis: la bullanga misteriosa de 1917* (Barcelona: Imprenta Bauzá, 1917), pp. 41–63

44 *La Correspondencia Militar* published between 1.6 and 15.6.1917 a series of articles called 'Against the existing empire of oligarchy and *caciquismo*'.

45 Even the moderate and loyal monarchist Catholic newspaper *El Debate* called the King's solution 'royal blindness'.

46 According to Manuel Burgos y Mazo, *Páginas históricas de 1917* (Madrid: Núñez Samper, 1918), p. 59, the Catalan leader, Francesc Cambó, declared, 'The most conservative thing to do was to be a revolutionary.' On the *Lliga*'s initiative see Lacomba, *La crisis española*, pp. 174–8, and Pabón, *Cambó*, pp. 501–7.

47 Francisco J. Romero Salvadó, 'Maura, Maurismo and the Crisis of 1917', *Journal for the Association of Contemporary Iberian Studies*, 7: 1 (Spring 1994), p. 22.

48 On different approaches to Maura, see Fundación Antonio Maura, *Maura's Papers* (hereafter AM), File 402, 22, several officers from the regiment of *Cazadores de Estella* to Maura, 6.6.1917; File 389, 10, the Catalan *Maurista* Gustavo Peyrá to Maura, 22.6, 25.6 and 28.6.1917; File 80, the leading *Maurista* Angel Ossorio to Maura, 7.7.1917; File 19, Cambó to Gabriel Maura, 10.7 and 11.7.1917. On Maura's refusal, see AM, File 389, 10, Maura to Peyrá, 23.6.1917; File 397, 7, Maura to Ossorio, 12.7.1917.

49 Francisco J. Romero Salvadó, 'Spain and the First World War: The Structural Crisis of the Liberal Monarchy', *European History Quarterly*, 25: 4 (1995), p. 543.

50 Most historians agree that the government provoked the workers into an unwanted general strike. See, for instance, Albert Balcells, *El sindicalism en Barcelona, 1916–1923* (Barcelona: Nova Terra, 1965), p. 31; Gerald Meaker, *The Revolutionary Left in Spain, 1914–1923* (Palo Alto: Stanford University Press, 1974), pp. 83–4; Andrés Saborit, *Julián Besteiro* (Mexico City: Losada, 1961), p. 99; Manuel Tuñón de Lara, *El movimiento obrero en la historia de España* (Madrid: Taurus, 1972), p. 589; Melchor Fernández Almagro, *Historia del Reinado de Alfonso XIII* (Barcelona: Montaner & Simón, 1977), p. 245; Buxadé, *op. cit.*, pp. 218–19; Pabón, *Cambó*, p. 537; Lacomba, *La crisis española*, pp. 238–40.

51 Francisco J. Romero Salvadó, 'The Organized Labour Movement in Spain: The Long Road to Its Baptism of Fire, 1868–1917', *Tesserae (Journal of Iberian and Latin-American Studies)*, 2: 1 (1996), pp. 14–17.

52 On the events of August 1917, see Joan Serrallonga, 'Motines y revolución: España en 1917', Francesc Bonamusa (ed.), *La huelga general*, vol. 4 (Madrid: Ayer, 1991), pp. 169–94; Fernando Soldevilla, *El año político de 1917* (Madrid: Imprenta Julio Cosano, 1918), pp. 363–404; Lacomba, *La crisis española*, pp. 213–84. They can also be followed in the national press. For instance, see *El Imparcial*, *La Epoca*, *El Heraldo de Madrid* and *El Liberal*, 13–21.8.1917.

53 See in Soldevilla, *El año político*, pp. 437–40, a statement published by the *juntas* on 7 September accusing the government of having turned a peaceful strike into a revolutionary movement.

54 Márquez and Capó, *Las juntas militares*, p. 68.

55 *Ibid.*, pp. 216–22.

56 The *Lliga*'s intention to abandon its reformist partners and join a monarchist coalition can be seen in Arxiu Nacional de Catalunya, *Lluis Duran i Ventosa's Papers*, mail exchanged between Cambó and Ventosa, 27 and 30 October 1917. Also see *España*, 22.11 and 13.12.1917.

57 Maura and Fernández Almagro, *Por qué cayó Alfonso XIII*, p. 311.

58   *El Sol*, 4.3.1918; *Solidaridad Obrera,* 9.6.1918.

59   *El Sol*, 4.7.1918. According to the new Law of Espionage, the penalty for those in Spain furnishing the agents of a foreign power with information would be imprisonment or a fine of between 500 and 20,000 pesetas; and the penalty for those spreading news 'contrary to the respect due to the neutrality or security of Spain' would be imprisonment or a fine of between 500 and 100,000 pesetas.

60   The decision of the government was caused by the brutal sinking on 25 July of the steamer *Ramón de Larriñaga*. That ship, bringing oil from New York, was torpedoed when entering Spanish waters. Eight members of the crew were killed, some of them machine-gunned in the water. Maura wrote, 'The limits of Spanish patience have been reached. A resolution has to be adopted without further delay.' In Real Academia de la Historia, *Dato's Papers*, letter from Maura to Dato, 28.7.1918. The note of protest to Germany can be found in Soldevilla, *El año político* de 1918 (Madrid, 1919), pp. 226–8.

61   The ex-minister and Liberal politician Natalio Rivas wrote that in order to defend neutrality the King was prepared to sack all his ministers. ANR File 8906, 31.8.1918. Also see AM, letter from Dato to Maura, 3.9.1918.

62   Manuel Burgos y Mazo, *El verano de 1919 en gobernación* (Cuenca: Tipografía E. Pinos, 1921), p. 50.

63   Teresa Carnero, 'Modernització, desenvolupament politic i canvi social', *Recerques*, 23 (1990), p. 79.

3 Foreign policy under the dictatorship of Primo de Rivera

Ismael Saz

Translated by Susan Edith Núñez

The dictatorship of Miguel Primo de Rivera constitutes a crossroads in the history of Spain in the twentieth century. Neither fascist nor democratic, Primo de Rivera's regime was anchored in the powerful Liberal tradition of Spain, but in its aimless drift towards nowhere it also looked to Fascism for inspiration.[1] If we compare it to the Franco dictatorship, the differences are enormous; but as a result of the *limitations* of Primo's dictatorship, the Spanish extreme right constructed a programme that would be carried out, in its fundamental aspects, under Francoism.[2] In the same way, the foreign policy of the dictatorship oscillated between following the traditional patterns of Spanish diplomacy and revising them. While they were based on an acceptance of the international *status quo* and the policy of collaboration with France and the United Kingdom as a subordinate partner, their revision entailed challenging this *status quo* to some extent as well as favouring a new actor: Fascist Italy.

In practice, both directions were pursued incoherently, as policy moved abruptly from one to the other. One of them implied respect for the accepted norms of diplomacy, while the other meant a new type of foreign policy, in which revisionist whims plus a policy of bold statements and gestures seemed to gain ground. One of the paths headed towards a policy of peace and cooperation within the privileged framework of the League of Nations, while the other led to a policy of power and a distancing from the League. This essentially contradictory character found its proper reflection in the absence of an even minimally defined project or programme.[3] Without such a plan, the dictator nearly always acted intuitively, adopting *ad hoc* responses according to circumstances and setting goals which were often improvised and not infrequently incompatible.

A good example of the above is the reform of the administration of foreign affairs undertaken by the dictatorship – one of the aspects with which historiography has been relatively benevolent. It is true, for example, that an important effort was made to rationalize diplomatic careers by improving the system of entrance and increasing the number of Spanish embassies abroad, especially in Latin America.[4] However, the reform – belated, halting and often contradictory – was characterized above all by a lack of ministerial continuity. The Ministry of State (which dealt with foreign policy), like the rest, was suspended during the Military Directory. With the reintroduction of civil government at the end of 1925, a civilian member of Primo's *Unión Patriótica* party, José María de Yanguas Messía, was named Minister. But just at that time, Primo removed everything related to Morocco from the Ministry, and one year later he would do likewise with all colonial affairs. Immediately after, he would undertake negotiations over Tangier, turning his back on his own Minister of State. After the latter's inevitable resignation, the dictator himself took over the portfolio until, at the end of 1928, he decided to abolish the Ministry, converting it into an office of the *Presidencia del Gobierno* (Presidency of the Government).[5] It was then that he embarked on the administrative reform mentioned earlier; that is, in the final period of his dictatorship and after the great battles of foreign policy had already been fought. In the midst of the almost chaotic administrative discontinuity, the only constant element was Primo de Rivera himself.[6]

Nonetheless, the absence of a firm ideology, the lack of a carefully thought out and coherent programme, and the erratic character of the administrative reform do not imply in any way that the dictator was without two basic ideas that fundamentally defined his foreign policy. The first, implicit in his confused regenerationist ideal, was that the domestic restructuring of Spain and the idea that Spain should once again play a central role among the Great Powers were two sides of the same coin. The second was so to speak the reverse of the first. It was based on his firm conviction that his regenerationist programme, indeed the regime itself, depended to a great degree on the achievement of continuous success abroad. For both reasons – his longing for grandeur in foreign policy and its link with internal affairs – the dictatorship of Primo de Rivera constitutes the first expression of conservative regenerationism in the sphere of international politics.

Morocco: a grand . . . and unique . . . success

On his accession to power, Primo de Rivera encountered three open questions in Spanish foreign policy, all interrelated. On the one hand there was the problem of Morocco, where the consequences of the terrible defeat in Annual by the Rif rebels still lingered. On the other hand there were the negotiations concerning the Tangier Statute. The third question was the proposed royal visit to Italy. The first issue had become a genuine national problem, which burdened the budget, took a high toll in human lives and profoundly divided national opinion. The fact that Primo de Rivera's *coup d'état* has always been associated with the attempt to stop the parliamentary inquest on Annual gives the best evidence of this.[7] The second matter, concerning the internationalized enclave in Tangier, pitched Spanish aspirations to increase the country's quota of influence there against the same, though more solidly supported, French hopes. The third responded in great measure to the wishes, in the first place, of King Alfonso XIII himself, together with the latest constitutional cabinets, to play the Italian card against French hegemony.

In November 1923, Primo de Rivera accompanied Alfonso XIII on his trip to Rome.[8] It was the first visit by a Spanish monarch since the unification of Italy. However, the special significance of this trip lay in the fact that it took place shortly after the establishment of a dictatorship that, by its very nature, bore similarities with the Italian regime. This circumstance, together with the chronological coincidence of the renewal of the talks over Tangier and the wave of Francophobia sweeping Spanish public opinion, surrounded the visit with extraordinary and justified expectations. From the moment the *coup* occurred, signs of cordiality between the two regimes had multiplied. Only days before the trip, a commercial treaty, which had proved long, difficult and ultimately quite favourable to Italy, had been signed.[9] Once in Rome, Alfonso XIII did not hesitate to introduce Primo as 'my Mussolini'. But above all, the two dictators negotiated a treaty, of which a first draft was drawn up. No documentary evidence remains but indirect references to it suggest that it was far from limited. Of evident anti-French slant, although not anti-British, it included clauses concerning benevolent neutrality and the Mediterranean question, as well as references to Latin American republics, which Primo finally considered counterproductive.[10] Be that as it may, the truth is that he thought better of it, and soon informed Mussolini that it was best to forget about the agreement. According to the Spanish dictator, the 'intimate and sincere union' which existed between the two countries and governments made it useless, 'if not detrimental', to pursue it further.[11]

The key reasons for the Spanish government's change of mind lay in the fear over the likely international response, the lack of sympathy shown by Britain toward this type of initiative and, above all, in the Tangier issue, the cause of the initial *rapprochement* with Italy. In the earlier talks held throughout the summer of 1923, the Spanish representatives had already given up their main demand – the incorporation of Tangier into their zone in the Protectorate of Morocco – in favour of the British proposal of a complete and effective internationalization of the enclave.[12] This is the situation that Primo encountered and to which he gave his approval. Italy, for her part, strove for her own admission, seeking equal conditions in the negotiations, to the extent that she was willing to support the Hispano-British ideas. However, when the talks were renewed, Spain was disagreeably surprised to find that Britain's position had changed in favour of France. The Italian card was worth little if the French and British played in unison. Consequently, the Spanish government was left with little alternative other than to sign an agreement clearly unfavourable to itself; not only did it recognize the sovereignty of the Sultan, which amounted to French hegemony, but it also deprived Spain of a Spanish Tabor, or chief of police. For these reasons, the agreement was signed *ad referendum* with express reservations. Only after France made some minimal concessions and showed an interest in increasing collaboration in Morocco did the Spanish government decide to ratify the agreement in February of 1924. It is possible that the spectre of the Spanish–Italian *rapprochement* had some influence in the French concessions. But if this was the case, Italy did not gain a great deal.[13] She was excluded from the negotiations and Mussolini was forced to limit himself to showing surprise at the ease with which Spain had agreed to sign. For Primo de Rivera, who had not yet made Tangier one of the decisive axes of his foreign policy, the promises, vague though they might be, of French collaboration in Morocco appeared more promising.

In fact, while the claim over Tangier was part revisionist, part irredentist, the Moroccan war was a national problem of the greatest concern.[14] Primo had promised a 'prompt, dignified and sensible' solution, but he did not seem to be quite sure what was meant by that. The dictator's abandonist tendencies over the Moroccan question were well known, as was his old and utopian plan to negotiate with Great Britain an exchange of Gibraltar for Ceuta. His position was therefore nationalist and not in the slightest bit militarist or imperialist. Once in power, he could not defend policies which clashed outwardly with those established in international treaties or with the pro-African factions of the country, but he was not prepared completely to abandon these positions either.[15] In practice, he maintained substantial continuity with the last constitutional cabinet. The concern was, on one hand, to maintain a policy of negotiation with the Rif people and, on the other, to withdraw Spanish forces to a security zone on the coast, centred on the sovereign areas of Ceuta and Melilla.

The announced withdrawal began in the spring of 1924. It was an operation that had to be undertaken in the face of powerful national and international constraints in addition to essentially military pressures. Among the former were the pressures of the Spanish military in Morocco itself. Among the latter were the French, who feared the military vacuum that Spanish withdrawal would create. Predictably, the leader of the Rif rebellion, Abd el-Krim, perceived the Spanish retreat as a clear-cut victory and, emboldened, made the mistake of launching a powerful and efficient offensive against the French zone. This fact in the end proved decisive. France for once felt under considerable pressure and, not without contradictions, opted for complete cooperation with Spain. From this would come the successful Spanish landing at Alhucemas (al-Hoceima) in September 1925 and the subsequent offensive leading to the surrender of Abd el-Krim in May of the following year.

This sudden and overwhelming success contributed to the rebirth of the myth that it had all been due to the general's ingenious strategy, who had supposedly organized the retreat with the ultimate goal of forcing the French to intervene.[16] This is far removed from the truth. Primo had conceived the withdrawal as an end in itself. His first plans for the landing at Alhucemas had been part of the strategy of retreat, and it was not until much later that he contemplated the possibility of a general offensive. He was finally convinced by the turn of military events as well as by Pétain's willingness to maintain the collaboration until a total victory had been achieved and by the far-sightedness of the former High Commissioner in Morocco, General Francisco Gómez Jordana.[17] But while Primo lagged behind events to a great extent, he also revealed his ability to adapt to these events, and, above all, his unswerving decision to carry out the withdrawal. But in addition, his thoughts about the whole question also changed radically during the process. In the final phase of the conflict, he no longer wanted to hold even minimal negotiations with the Rif people, nor did he consider any solution other than a purely military one. He considered himself strong, as well as his regime and his country. He no longer contemplated simply revising the treaties delegating responsibilities in the Protectorate but wanted to force the Great Powers to make revisions which would seal Spain's victory, with Tangier as the final finishing touch.

The revisionist outburst

With the dramatic Moroccan conflict almost resolved and his regime consolidated, Primo considered the time appropriate to break ties with the Liberal past. On the domestic level, he began to prepare for the institutionalization of the dictatorship on a corporative basis; abroad, it seemed the moment had arrived to challenge the *status quo* to the extent of including Spain among the Great Powers. Tangier and Spain's role in the League of Nations would constitute the nuclei of Primo's frenetic foreign policy over the next two years.

From the moment the League of Nations had been constituted, Spain had formed a part of the council, which had meant recognition of the prestige she had gained by being the largest neutral country in the First World War.[18] But it was a non-permanent place, which implied, in the first instance, that Spain was not recognized as one of the Great Powers, and second, that it had to be subject to an annual re-election. From the beginning, Spain's claim to a permanent place became a focus of her activity in Geneva. This, however, did not prevent her from playing an active and prestigious role at the centre of the League. A sign of this recognition was, for example, that the League council met in San Sebastián in 1920, or that some of the most delicate tasks of the council were entrusted to the Spanish representative in the League – as well as ambassador in Paris – José María Quiñones de León. In the first renewal of the council held after the establishment of the dictatorship, Spain was re-elected, albeit with a slight decrease in support. Primo merely gave Quiñones de León instructions to continue to present the question of permanence, although he did not make it an essential issue.

When the question of Germany's accession to the League of Nations was raised at the beginning of 1926, Spanish diplomacy considered it the ideal moment to win its long-standing claim. At first, the circumstances seemed favourable, as France, Britain and Italy, among others, appeared willing to support the Spanish request. However, Spain was not the only applicant; Poland and Brazil also hoped to gain admission. Some of the neutral countries felt that the number of permanent members on the council should not increase, and, above all, Germany turned the question of its unique accession into one of principle. It was soon clear that both Britain and France would place Germany's incorporation, and with it the 'spirit of Locarno', before any other consideration or previous commitment. Thus, when the assembly of the League met in March, the matter was already well on track, but following a direction quite unfavourable to Spanish aspirations. In any case, a commission was formed to study the problem before a definitive decision would be taken in the September assembly.

In this context, those responsible for Spanish foreign policy made it clear that failure to obtain a permanent place could mean Spain's withdrawal from the League itself. Although the threat was a double-edged sword and demonstrated a utilitarian position that said little for the

Spanish government's convictions about the League, it was nonetheless a relatively normal form of exerting pressure. But Primo de Rivera decided to go even further. Against his Minister of State's views, he and the King proposed a *quid pro quo* to the British, French and Italians whereby Spain would renounce a permanent place on the council without withdrawing from the League in exchange for the incorporation of Tangier in its Protectorate. It is true that the agreement of 1923 had proved to be impracticable in more than one aspect. It was also the case that Spain still considered the enclave a source of instability in its Protectorate and that in the negotiations prior to the landing at Alhucemas which had led to the victory over the Rif rebels, the Spanish had already attempted to reopen the question.[19] But by combining the two issues, Spain's negotiating position in Geneva was weakened when it announced that what she was seeking was not a central issue in her foreign policy. The proposal could be considered, as the British saw it, vulgar haggling, almost blackmail. Finally, Primo de Rivera initiated a parallel policy that did not always coincide with that of his own Minister of State, Yanguas.[20]

In May, the committee set up in Geneva to study the question found an escape route in the creation of a new, intermediate category: that of semi-permanent member of the council. The proposal was based on the possibility that some countries could be re-elected every three years, as long as they obtained two-thirds of the assembly votes. Conceived in great measure for Spain's benefit, it would imply the *de facto*, if not *de jure*, consideration of Spain's permanence in the council.[21] But the Spanish government had clearly bet on all or nothing – for either absolute permanence or for Tangier – and it affirmed this position to all who suggested that it moderate its attitude. In a meeting with Alfonso XIII in London in June, Chamberlain characterized Spain's claim as 'asking for the moon', although he said he was willing to consider the possibility of conceding a mandate to Spain for a certain period, provided that the principles of the neutralization and internationalization of the zone were not infringed.[22]

In fact, the position of the British was much less favourable. They expressed acceptance of the idea of the mandate, but were convinced that the French and the Italians would reject it. And above all, they seemed willing to play the Italian card against Spain. With this aim in mind, they intensified efforts to gain Italy's adherence to the agreement of 1923, demonstrating furthermore, as did France, a favourable predisposition to make the necessary concessions. It goes without saying that had Italy accepted the agreement on the given dates, Primo de Rivera's strategy would have been brought to a screeching halt. Thus, Italy's position suddenly acquired an unexpected importance. Initially opposed to the

Spanish aspirations, Italy soon realized that the Spanish claims offered her the opportunity to make her own. So for the moment, Italy simply shielded herself behind the British refusal and postponed her response to the invitations from London. At the end of July, the Italians made these dilatory intentions public.[23]

Collaboration with Italy was another of the great and indispensable elements of the Spanish diplomatic offensive. Relations between the two countries had been relatively low-key since the Italian monarch had visited Spain in June 1924, although at the level of domestic policy the displays of friendship and solidarity between the two regimes were still frequent.[24] These displays were used to prestigious effect at home by both dictatorships, but they also laid the basis for the rekindling of mutual relations at the foreign-policy level whenever the circumstances arose. At times of the highest tension in Morocco, Primo had played the bluff of relinquishing his obligations in the Protectorate to Italy; Mussolini had gone as far as offering his (scarcely disinterested) services for an eventual negotiation with Abd el-Krim.[25]

Now that the question of Tangier was once again reactivated, the Italian factor was immediately brought into play. As early as March, Alfonso XIII had expressed to the Italian ambassador, Raniero Paulucci de' Calboli, his weariness and disgust with that 'Masonic business' that the League of Nations was turning into, as well as the Spanish intentions to link the Geneva question with the Tangier issue. In April, the Labour Minister, Eduardo Aunós, travelled to Italy, where he raised the possibility of signing a treaty of friendship, and in June the head of Mussolini's cabinet visited Madrid. It was agreed then that the treaty would include a clause of neutrality with the explicit purpose of differentiating it clearly from the others that Spain had signed or was negotiating.[26] Two months later, on 7 August 1926, the Treaty of Friendship, Conciliation and Judicial Arbitration was signed. It did not contain anything particularly alarming; it was much more modest than the draft of two years earlier, and the only significant aspect was the clause of neutrality referred to above. What was most striking was the secrecy of the negotiations, the fact that the text was published belatedly and the timing of the signing. Such an accumulation of circumstances together with the apparent inanity of the content of the treaty caused speculation in the international press about the possible existence of secret clauses of military significance; for example, about the cession of bases in the Balearic Islands to Italy in the event of war.[27]

None of this was true.[28] But that does not diminish the political importance of the treaty. If Spain was now in favour of signing, it was evidently because she felt that it would contribute to an improvement of her negotiating capacity with the British and, especially, with the French. Of course, lurking behind the signing of the treaty as well as the Spanish–Italian *rapprochement*, there was also an element of mutual profit. But this did not make it less effective. On the basis of her utilitarian policy, Italy had decided to protract negotiations over the British proposals concerning the 1923 agreement. But this alone had done Spain a great service, though it had not been previously agreed. Now that the possibility of a common front of the other three powers had been removed, and strengthened by the signature of the pact, Primo felt able to raise the tone of his diplomatic offensive.

This is exactly what he did. One week after the signing, the Spanish dictator announced with great ceremony that Spain would not accept anything less than a permanent place on the League of Nations council and the integration of Tangier into her Protectorate. Spain must be recognized as a Great Power. As such, she could not attend the world stage seated in the stalls or the amphitheatre, but must 'take a seat in a box'.[29] That same day Italian support of the Spanish demands was requested, and a week later the powers concerned were officially informed of the Spanish petition to open negotiations.[30] To what was already an unorthodox link between the Geneva questions and the claim to Tangier was now added what Chamberlain would define as an 'ultimatum given in a press conference'.[31] European public opinion felt that the Spanish government had gone past all imaginable limits. Of course, both Britain and France deemed the Spanish proposal unacceptable. Italy was willing to consider the Spanish petitions 'in a friendly way', but maintained that if talks were to be opened on this matter, they should be held outside the framework of Geneva and after the League Assembly.[32]

In that Assembly, held at the beginning of September, the Spanish withdrawal from the League of Nations was consummated. Once the alternative of creating a semi-permanent place in the council had been offered, the majority of the committee members had considered the matter resolved. Spain had been left isolated. Not even the two Spanish American countries represented on the commission, Argentina and Uruguay, supported Spain.[33] Nor, for the moment, had any compensation in Tangier been obtained. Primo de Rivera had no other option than to do what he had so vociferously said that he would. He had compromised Spain's prestige, or rather, that of his own regime, and he was obliged to carry out his threat.

Meanwhile, the idea of opening talks on Tangier had made headway. Convinced that everything possible should be done to return Spain to the League of Nations, Austen Chamberlain showed his willingness to open talks on Tangier between Spain, France and his own country.[34] For her part, France accepted negotiations with Spain, provided that they were held within the framework of the 1923 agreement. Italy exerted pressure in order not to be excluded from the process. In the end, everyone obtained something: there would be an initial phase of negotiations between two countries, France and Spain, and a later one among four, with Italy and Britain. This was the solution finally adopted. The Spanish–Italian *rapprochement* seemed to have reached some of its objectives, though not all, and not solely by those countries' own efforts. Spain had obtained the reopening of the question of Tangier, and Italy her participation in the conference on equal terms with Britain, something she had sought in vain in 1923. It is not surprising that Italy considered this a first success.[35]

No sooner had it achieved its initial objectives than the Spanish government began to water down the treaty. It was ratified in October, and, specifically at Spain's request, as discreetly as possible. In his explanations to Paulucci, Primo referred to the innumerable 'speculations about war' aroused by the mere announcement of the treaty, and emphasized Spain's weakness against the Western powers, against which it would be 'bound to lose'. It was, as Paulucci affirmed, a confession of impotence. But it was also, as the ambassador equally indicated, directly related to the talks with France about Tangier.[36]

From February, a new *rapprochement* in Spanish–Italian relations began. The Spanish delegation presented itself in Paris that month with claims that implied the *de facto*, if not *de jure*, incorporation of Tangier into Spanish Morocco, which was completely unacceptable to both France and Britain. Chamberlain in particular considered the Spanish memorandum inappropriate, and invited Spain to present a more practical and acceptable formula.[37] Mussolini, on the contrary, was delighted with the firmness of Spain and stated that, once Italy's interests were recognized, Italy would support a *'predominantly'* Spanish solution.[38] Though appreciative of Italian support, Primo de Rivera preferred to avail himself, for the moment, of Chamberlain's suggestions, and hence by April he had noticeably toned down his claims. He wrote to his ambassador in Paris, Quiñones de León, 'For the possible exercise of our Protectorate, it will be enough for us that it remain in Spanish hands and that the composition of the police and the organization of public order organism be Spanish.'[39] But French persistence in opposing this, and other issues, led to a new phase of tension in the negotiations. Primo once again threatened to withdraw the Spanish delegation and the personnel of the embassy itself in Paris, abandon Tangier and do likewise with the Protectorate.[40] The good offices of Chamberlain and his suggestion that immediate negotiations between the four countries should take place –

a means of putting pressure on France – succeeded in preventing a breakdown.[41]

Under these conditions, the summer of 1927 proved to be particularly intense. Although disappointed by the Spanish concessions, Mussolini perceived in the new period of tension the opportunity to increase his pressure on Spain to return to the initial extremist position. It was then that the Duce accepted for the first time a plan that had been outlined a while before by his consul in Tangier, Luigi Vanuttelli Rey.[42] According to this plan, Spain's maximum claims would be supported with the aim of vitiating the negotiations, and hence forcing a general reassessment of the question of French Morocco. In that context, the problem of free commerce and the non-denationalization of Spanish and Italian subjects in the French Protectorate could be raised. But there was no duplicity on Mussolini's part. As soon as he adopted the plan, he made it known to Primo, together with the suggestion that they should form a 'united front', capable of inducing even Britain to make the appropriate concessions.[43]

By August, Primo appeared to be more in agreement with the Italian position. He would wait for the French response in October and, if it were unsatisfactory, break off the bilateral negotiations, accept the quadrilateral ones, once again pose the maximum claims and present a common front with Italy, provided that were possible.[44] At the same time, the demonstrations of Spanish–Italian friendship multiplied. In August, an agreement over air navigation was signed. In October, an Italian flotilla visited Tangier, where it was rapturously received by the Spanish authorities. In November, Alfonso XIII visited Naples for a dynastic wedding and made profuse declarations of friendship. That same month, the Italian Minister of Corporations, Giuseppe Bottai, visited Spain.[45]

But Primo had misgivings about the Italian proposals. 'I'll only go through this madness while very much in agreement with and on the arm of England,' he had written to his ambassador in London. Thus, in some way, he reformulated the Italian proposal in order to include the Portuguese and the British.[46] Naturally, not only was Chamberlain opposed to the whole fanciful idea of forming a bloc with anti-French overtones, but in addition he was working on quite different lines. In mid-September, he met with Aristide Briand, then French Foreign Minister, with whom he agreed it would be appropriate to make some concessions to Spain. At the end of that month, he informed Primo in Majorca that France was favourably disposed. That was all the Spanish dictator needed to hear. He immediately stated that he was ready to rejoin the League of Nations, implicitly acknowledged he had been wrong to withdraw and justified his actions in terms of domestic policy: 'the extralegal origin [of the regime] forced him to live on continuous success'.[47]

The meeting in Majorca proved decisive. Soon the issues headed in the direction envisaged by Chamberlain. In November, the Hispano-French agreement was practically within reach, and in February 1928 a joint text was agreed. The second phase of the negotiations would then begin, which would now bring together the four powers. The decisive aspect of the British intervention should not, however, lead to an underestimation of the scope of the Italian factor.[48] For one reason, the British leader's action in itself is not comprehensible unless seen within the global framework of the relations between the four powers. Furthermore, during the critical moment in November, the French ambassador in Madrid, Peretti, suggested to Briand – who concurred – that in order to keep the Spanish–Italian *rapprochement* from getting out of hand, it was advisable that some concessions be made to Spain on the question of Tangier.[49]

As was to be expected, the Spanish position disappointed Mussolini, who stated that he had, at any rate, not been exceedingly hopeful, given the 'constitutional weakness' of the Spanish policy regarding France.[50] The truth of the matter is that, just as had occurred and would continue to occur on other occasions, Primo de Rivera cooled his relations with Italy as soon as he obtained minimum satisfaction from France. The Spanish dictator was willing to consider the quite 'attractive' Italian policy, but he was also conscious of the hazards that could derive from an excessive solidarity. When informed of the Italian attitude, Primo had told his ambassador in Paris, 'I reciprocate only half-heartedly.' In summary, what was occurring was a shift in Spain's game of special relationships. Italy would still be important, but less so, and Britain too, but more so. As Primo explained to Quiñones, Britain constituted the basis of Spain's international relations.[51]

Although the negotiations among the four countries stretched out over several months until the final signing of the agreement in Paris at the end of July, the matter had practically been resolved in March. That same month, Spain was officially invited by the League council to rejoin. His prestige salvaged, Primo accepted the invitation, although he did so under the same conditions that he had rejected two years earlier; that is, with a semi-permanent place on the council.[52]

What conclusions are to be drawn, on balance, from the accomplishments of those two years of revisionist frenzy in Primo de Rivera's foreign policy? As far as the League of Nations was concerned, the result could not be more negative. Primo had squandered the political capital that Spain had accumulated since the time of her neutral status in the

First World War. He had shown the world that he was more concerned with using the League to bolster the prestige of the nation and his own regime than with fulfilling the purposes of the League itself. Despite all his Spanish American rhetoric, he had been willing to disregard one of the best and most fertile grounds for relations with the Spanish-speaking American republics. Finally, he had managed definitively to close what had been, until 1925, an open issue: *permanence*.[53] In Tangier, the longed-for control of the police had been achieved. It was not, of course, a trivial matter, and the Spanish government was right to attribute many of the security problems in the Protectorate to the issue. So, in a way, Primo had put the icing on the cake of the pacification of Morocco, though he had not gained the incorporation of Tangier into his zone. 'The game is postponed, but not over,' he said at the conclusion of the agreement.

The extent of the Spanish *rapprochement* with Italy during the dictatorship has been, and continues to be, widely debated by historians.[54] The problem of the presumed secret clauses in the 1926 treaty has distorted the assessment of the process. The non-existence of secret clauses of a military nature does not mean that the treaty did not fulfil the function for which it had been conceived. Like most treaties, it was not a treaty of military alliance, although the value of the neutrality clause could not in any way be dismissed. Nor was it a treaty *about* Tangier, and hence both countries kept their freedom of action regarding Tangier at all times. At a more generic level, as a treaty of friendship, it was a way of telling the world that the sole points of reference of Spain's foreign policy were no longer the two traditional ones, London and Paris; there was also now a third, Rome. At a more concrete level, it meant an effective, though limited, improvement in the negotiating capacity of both in relation to the problem of Tangier.

In any case, the limitations of any revisionist action were clearly demarcated for both Spain and Italy by the British attitude. A point of reference for all, the leadership of Britain in the conditions of the relative stability of the 1920s could not be questioned. Britain was willing to allow Spain and Italy to exert a certain amount of pressure on France but she also clearly marked the limits beyond which no one could venture. For this reason, Chamberlain's attitude proved decisive in Spain's achievement of something, but also in her failure to attain everything. But if Britain could use her function as intermediary, it was because the revisionist challenge existed and, as in the case discussed in this chapter, because the Spanish–Italian conjunction helped to give it credibility. In this sense, the parallel interests of Spain and Italy, with the exception of the obvious differences, are revealing. Chamberlain applied the same benevolent mediation with both countries. Like Spain, Italy saw Great

Britain as the basic and positive reference point in her foreign policy. Like Spain also, Mussolini's few gains during the decade were achieved only where and to the degree to which the United Kingdom consented.[55] Under these conditions, the Spanish–Italian *rapprochement* moved within the limits that the international system of the 1920s permitted, but it also constituted a potential promise in a more fluid international framework. It was not, nor could it be, a revolution, but it was much more than simple 'circumstantial flirtation'.[56]

A policy of prestige by other means

His revisionist challenge over, Primo de Rivera would promote some of the issues of his foreign policy that had to a certain degree remained in the background. This was the case in Spain's relations with Portugal and especially Latin America, marked by an increasingly ideological policy.[57] The case of Italy is also significant in this regard. With all possibilities of active collaboration on the issue of Tangier closed, the Spanish–Italian *rapprochement* was structured almost exclusively in terms of domestic policy. Personalities as important in both regimes as Bottai and General Martínez Anido, Primo's tough Minister of the Interior, visited Spain and Italy respectively in 1928 and 1929, and during that time Primo de Rivera's declarations indicating his desire to emulate the Fascist dictatorship increased in number. In July 1929, he went so far as to ask Mussolini to study his constitutional projects and offer him advice on them. The Duce avoided such an unusual request through a courteous manifestation of solidarity, but he first commissioned a report entitled 'Promemoria', the contents of which were highly revealing. According to this report, the Spanish regime was not comparable to the Fascist revolution because it lacked three basic elements of the latter: 'a war ending in victory, a *condottiero*, and a myth'. In the constitution that was submitted to examination, there was an excess of elective elements, and above all, it constituted a 'mosaic of partial imitations and uncertain intentions, *halfway* between the principles of fascism and the principles of liberal democracy'.[58] There has never been a more accurate characterization of Primo de Rivera's dictatorship.

Another of the areas in which domestic and foreign policy were closely connected is that of economic nationalism. The largest problems here were generated by the nationalization of the oil industry. Although the decision was adopted in the middle of 1927, the negotiations with the companies concerned carried on to the beginning of 1929. Unlike the British, the governments of France and the United States intervened in the negotiating process, to the point that Briand and Frank Kellogg, US

Secretary of State, coordinated a common response to the Spanish government. More sensitive to this type of problem than the French government, the Americans maintained a wary attitude towards the Spanish regime as a result of the incident.[59] This was not, of course, the best situation from which to face what would be the last, although the smallest, diplomatic battle of the dictatorship; that is, the one relating to the signing of the Kellogg–Briand Pact, which excluded war as an instrument of national policy. Marginalized by Kellogg among the countries invited to the initial signature of the pact, Spain did her best to be included on the list of first signatories, now with the clear support of France and Britain. Since the problem had been seen once more in terms of prestige, the failure was again due to the appearance of more aspirants as well as to the indiscretions of Spanish diplomacy. But above all, it was due to Kellogg's opposition, under pressure by the American oil companies, if we are to believe Quiñones de León. This time at least, there was no Spanish reaction other than that typical of Primo, who first denied the importance of the pact and then hailed it after signing in February 1929.[60]

After this small but significant blunder, Primo de Rivera had his last moments of glory with the League of Nations Assembly held in Madrid, and the exhibitions in Barcelona and Seville. Yet these achievements were not very noteworthy. As far as the League of Nations was concerned, they amounted to what had already been achieved in 1920, when the council was held in San Sebastián. The other achievements did not prevent his prestige and popularity from plummeting close to the eve of the fall of his own dictatorship. Things were not going much better abroad. The internal difficulties of the regime evoked a widespread response in the international press. And it is not insignificant that Primo ended his foreign action spending, in vain, enormous sums of money in order to obtain better treatment of himself and his regime in the European media.[61]

In general terms, the foreign policy of the dictatorship could be summarized as one great success – Morocco – plus a series of failures and some minor successes. The offensive against the League of Nations ended up eventually in absolute failure, and the result obtained in Tangier must be qualified as a relative failure at least. Regarding the Great Powers, Spain had to return to where she had usually stood, that is, to a relationship as privileged as it was subordinate to the great Western powers. If Britain was the positive pole of reference, France was, at the same time, both positive and negative; the object of Spanish claims and discontent, she was, at the same time, the country from whose orbit there was no escape.[62] Issues over Portugal and Spanish America stood better, although the best results began to be gained with regimes of clear authoritarian or conservative character, which to a certain degree enabled them to be a projection more of a regime than of a state. In short, Primo de Rivera had failed in his attempt to elevate Spain to the category of a Great Power.

Nonetheless, it would be inexact to present the foreign policy of the dictatorship as a simple continuation of the previous dynamics, an aberration or a mere parenthesis. Since the end of the First World War, all the political and intellectual classes in Spain had come to terms with the fact that international society had changed and that Spain should play a much more dynamic and active role in it. The Spanish monarchy was beginning to emerge from that spirit of 'smallness and seclusion' for which the Republicans had so reproached it.[63] It remained to be decided if this would be done in terms of power politics or full participation in the new international order symbolized by the League of Nations. The last constitutional cabinets had, in part, followed both policies. Primo de Rivera did likewise, but in such a way that he ended up making them ineffective – treating them as sacred, at times; frivolously mixing them, at others; abandoning them halfway, frequently; subordinating them to his politics of prestige, almost always. His own concept of international relations explains his oscillations. He sought a revision of treaties, but from a local viewpoint: irredentist, if you like, incapable of seeing beyond the problem of Tangier. He had a utilitarian vision of international organizations and multilateral diplomacy, but he was substantially pacifist and always in favour of solutions based on the reconciliation and arbitration of conflicts between nations.[64] He was willing to challenge the traditional allies of Spain, the Western powers, but he knew that in the last analysis, he could not do without them, nor did he wish to. If at the level of domestic politics he stood halfway between the liberal tradition and the influence of fascism, on the level of foreign policy his revisionism can only be expressed as half-hearted in comparison with the Italians'.

However, the experience of the dictatorship constituted a potential legacy for posterity. One of these legacies was the link made between foreign and domestic policies, both because the latter became an instrument of legitimization of the former, and because priority in his foreign relations was given to those countries with similar regimes. Another was the eventual extension of the Tangier issue to all of French Morocco. Primo's foreign policy towards Spanish America also created the basis of a rhetorical pseudo-imperialism, the foundations of a profoundly reactionary ideology.[65] As far as his methods were concerned, he could have pursued his utilitarian position towards the League of Nations to the extent of simply abandoning it and identified with the country or countries which led the open challenge to the *status quo*. We do not know if he would have followed this direction nor to what extent. Nevertheless, we do know that this would be the path that another dictatorship would attempt to follow more boldly and resolutely: the regime of General Franco.

Notes

1 S. Ben Ami, *Fascism from above: The Dictatorship of Primo de Rivera in Spain, 1923–1930* (Oxford: Oxford University Press, 1983); J.L. Gómez Navarro, *El regimen de Primo de Rivera: reyes, dictadores y dictadura* (Madrid: Cátedra, 1991); M.T. González Calvet, *La dictadura de Primo de Rivera: el directorio militar* (Madrid: El Arquero, 1987); J. Tusell, 'La dictadura de Primo de Rivera (1923–1930)', in *Historia de España. Ramón Menéndez Pidal. La España de Alfonso XIII. El estado y la política*, T. XXXVIII, V. 2 (Madrid: Espasa-Calpe, 1995).

2 R. Morodo, *Acción española. Los orígenes ideológicos del franquismo* (Madrid: Tucar, 1980).

3 G. Palomares, 'La política exterior española: de la dictadura de Primo de Rivera a la Guerra Civil', in R. Calduch (coord.), *La política exterior española en el siglo XX* (Madrid: Ediciones Ciencias Sociales, 1994), pp. 47–70.

4 A. Martínez de Velasco, 'La reforma del cuerpo diplomático por Primo de Rivera', *Revista Internacional de Sociología*, no. 35 (1980), pp. 409–42.

5 *Ibid.*; F.Mª. Castiella, *Una batalla diplomática* (Barcelona: Planeta, 1976), pp. 199–201; N. Tabanera, *Ilusiones y desencuentros: la acción diplomática republicana en Hispanoamérica (1931–1939)* (Madrid: CEDEAL, 1996), pp. 39ff.

6 Tusell, 'La dictadura', p. 540.

7 For a recent questioning of this thesis, see Tusell, 'La dictadura', p. 268.

8 J. Tusell and I. Saz, 'Mussolini y Primo de Rivera: las relaciones políticas y diplomáticas de dos dictaduras mediterráneas', *Boletín de la Real Academia de la Historia* 169, (1982), pp. 413–83; G. Palomares, *Mussolini y Primo de Rivera: política exterior de dos dictaduras* (Madrid: EUDEMA, 1989), pp. 147ff.; S. Sueiro, 'Primo de Rivera y Mussolini: las relaciones diplomáticas entre dos dictaduras', *Proserpina* 1 (1984), pp. 23–33.

9 I. Saz, *Mussolini contra la II República* (Valencia: IVEI, 1986), pp. 25–6.

10 *Ibid.*, pp. 428ff.

11 Paulucci to Mussolini, 19.2.1924, Documenti Diplomatici Italiani (hereafter DDI), 7, II, no. 654.

12 For the entire question of the negotiations about Tangier, see especially S. Sueiro, *España en el Mediterráneo: Primo de Rivera y la 'Cuestión Marroquí', 1923–1930* (Madrid: UNED, 1992). Also, J.C. Pereira, 'El contencioso de Tánger en las relaciones hispano-francesas (1923–1924)', in *Españoles y franceses en la primera mitad del siglo XX* (Madrid: CSIC, 1986), pp. 303–22.

13 Palomares, *Mussolini*, pp. 163–4.

14 For the Moroccan question, see especially Sueiro, *España en el Mediterráneo*, and Tusell, 'La dictadura'. Also, S. and A. Fleming, 'Primo de Rivera and Spain's Moroccan Problem, 1923–1927', *Journal of Contemporary History*, 12 (1977); and G. Ayache, 'Les relations franco-espagnoles pendant la guerre du Rif', in *Españoles y franceses*, pp. 287–93. For an overall view of Spanish

interests in Morocco, see V. Morales, *El colonialismo hispanofrancés en Marruecos (1898–1927)* (Madrid: Siglo XXI, 1976).

15 In 1925 he still pursued the pipedream of a proposal to the British of an exchange with predictable and total lack of success. See J. Tusell and G. García y Queipo de Llano, *El dictador y el mediador: España–Gran Bretaña, 1923–1930* (Madrid: CSIC, 1986), pp. 30, 38–9.

16 In this sense, see F. Gómez Jordana, *La tramoya de nuestra actuación en Marruecos* (Madrid: Editora Nacional, 1976).

17 Sueiro, *España en el Mediterráneo,* pp. 187–327.

18 Castiella, *Una batalla diplomática*; G.B. Bledsoe, 'The Quest for *Permanencia*: Spain's Role in the League Crisis of 1926', *Iberian Studies,* 4 (1975), pp. 14–21; J.L. Neila, 'España y el modelo de integración en la Sociedad de Naciones (1919–1939): una aproximación historiográfica', *Hispania,* 176 (1990), pp. 1373–91.

19 Sueiro, *España en el Mediterráneo,* pp. 226–41.

20 Castiella, *Una batalla,* pp. 167ff; Tusell, 'La dictadura', pp. 441–6; Sueiro, *España en el Mediterráneo,* pp. 348–9.

21 S. Madariaga, *España: ensayo de historia contemporánea* (Madrid: Espasa-Calpe, 1979), pp. 279–80.

22 Tusell and García, *El dictador,* pp. 56–7.

23 Relazione dell'ufficio V Europa e Levante, 31.3.1927, DDI, 7, V, n. 106 (as the editors of DDI indicate, the report was probably compiled some days after 15 August. 1926); Promemoria, May 1927, DDI, 7, V, n. 230; Palomares, *Mussolini,* pp. 107–8.

24 Tusell and Saz, 'Mussolini', pp. 435ff.

25 Sueiro, *España en el Mediterráneo,* pp. 311–12 and 342–3.

26 Paulucci to Mussolini, 3.VI, 26, Archivio Storico del Ministero degli Affari Esteri (hereafter ASMAE), Gabinetto, 1919–29, busta 158.

27 Tusell and Saz, 'Mussolini', pp. 439ff.; Palomares, *Mussolini,* pp. 178ff, 213ff.

28 The existence of a secret pact was taken up almost unanimously by post-Second World War historiography, which furthermore was associated with future Italian aid to Franco. See especially p. van der Esch, *Prelude to War: The International Repercussions of the Spanish Civil War* (The Hague: Martinus Nijhoff, 1951), p. 26; D. Puzzo, *Spain and the Great Powers* (New York and London: Columbia University Press, 1962), p. 43. Subsequent historiography demonstrated the non-existence of these clauses and the considerably more limited scope of the treaty. See J.F. Coverdale, *Italian Intervention in the Spanish Civil War* (Princeton: Princeton University Press, 1975) and Tusell and Saz, 'Mussolini'. The single recent attempt to give credibility to the existence of the infamous secret clauses is unconvincing. Cf. Palomares, *Mussolini.*

29 *ABC,* 15.8.1926; *El Debate,* 19.8.1926.

30 Relazione dell'ufficio V Europa e Levante.

31 Tusell and García, *El dictador,* p. 59.

32 Mussolini, 21 and 26.8.1926, ASMAE, Gabinetto, b. 157.

33 Castiella, *Una batalla,* pp. 160, 230–2.

34 Tusell and García, *El dictador,* p. 60.

35 Promemoria, May 1927.

36 Paulucci, 29.10.1926, ASMAE, Gabinetto, b. 158; Tusell and Saz, 'Mussolini', p. 445.

37 Merry to Primo, 21 and 23.2.1927, in Tusell and García, *El dictador*, pp. 117 and 119–20.

38 Appunto del Capo del Governo e Ministro degli Esteri, Mussolini, sul collo-quio con l'ambasciatore spagnolo a Roma della Viñaza, 2.3.1927; Primo de Rivera to Mussolini, 4.3.1927; Mussolini to Primo de Rivera, 21.3.1927. All in DDI, 7, V, nn. 39, 48 and 87, respectively.

39 Primo, 7.4.1927. In Tusell and García, *El dictador*, pp. 107–9.

40 Primo to Merry, 25.6.1927, in Tusell and García, *El dictador*, pp. 121–2.

41 Merry to Primo, 7.7.1927, in Tusell and García, *El dictador*, pp. 123–4.

42 Vannutelli, 18.12.1926, DDI, 7, V, n. 550; Promemoria, May 1927.

43 Mussolini to Medici (ambassador in Madrid), 11.7.1927, DDI, 7, V, n. 320. The thesis concerning Mussolini's duplicity and Machiavellian pursuit of extremist objectives which he hid from Primo de Rivera has had a practically unanimous consensus in the historiography. The root of the confusion lies in the fact that the postures maintained by the consular agent in Tangier, Vannutelli, have frequently been taken as the official position of the Italian government, especially those of the winter of 1926–7. However, as explicitly stated in a document dated May 1927, the government had not accepted, 'at least not until now', any plan like the one suggested by Vannutelli. Promemoria, May 1927.

44 Primo de Rivera to Merry, 2.8.1927, in Tusell and García, *El dictador*, pp. 124–6. Medici to Mussolini, 16.8.1927, DDI, 7, V, n. 357. As Primo de Rivera would tell the Italian ambassador, not only he himself, but Chamberlain as well, would be 'notably influenced' by Mussolini.

45 Tusell and Saz, 'Mussolini', pp. 450ff.

46 Primo to Merry, 2.8.1927, in Tusell and García, *El dictador*, p. 124.

47 *Ibid.*, pp. 66ff.

48 For a different opinion, see Tusell, 'La dictadura', pp. 446ff, and Sueiro, *España en el Mediterráneo*, pp. 379 ff.

49 Peretti, 6.11.1927, in Palomares, *Mussolini,* pp. 234, 238–9.

50 Mussolini, 10.2.1928, DDI, 7, V, n. 94.

51 Primo to Quiñones, 22.10.1927, in Tusell and García, *El dictador*, pp. 109–12.

52 Castiella, *Una batalla*, pp. 252ff; Tusell and García, *El dictador*, pp. 76ff.

53 Tusell and García, *El dictador*, p. 257.

54 Among recent contributions, the thesis that Spain's friendship with Italy was virtual folly has been put forward by G.B. Bledsoe, 'Spanish Foreign Policy, 1898–1936', in J.A. Cortada (ed.), *Spain in the Twentieth Century World: Essays on Spanish Diplomacy, 1898–1978* (London: Greenwood Press, 1980), pp. 3–40; Coverdale, *Italian Intervention*; Sueiro, *España en el Mediterráneo*; and, most recently, Tusell, 'La dictadura'. Palomares, *Mussolini*, on the contrary, besides returning to the idea of secret military and naval agree-ments, casts over the whole of the Spanish–Italian relationship elements of coordination and planning which are, by any reckoning, unreasonable.

55 Carocci, *La politica estera*, p. 240; Di Nolfo, *Mussolini*, p. 240; R. De Felice, *Mussolini il duce. I. Gli anni del consenso, 1929–1936* (Turin, 1974), pp. 348–9.

56 Tusell, 'La dictadura', pp. 446, 454.

57 H. de la Torre, 'Portugal frente al "peligro español"', *Proserpina,* 1 (1984), pp. 59–79. For Peninsular relations especially, see, by the same author, *Del*

'*peligro español*' *a la amistad peninsular: España–Portugal 1919–1930* (Madrid: UNED, 1984). For Latin America, see F. Pike, *Hispanismo, 1898–1936* (Notre Dame, IN: University of Notre Dame Press, 1971); I. Sepúlveda, *Comunidad cultural e hispanoamericanismo, 1885–1936* (Madrid: UNED, 1994). Tabanera, *Ilusiones*.

58 Tusell and Saz, 'Mussolini', pp. 467–70.

59 A. Shubert, 'Oil Companies and Governments: International Reaction to the Nationalization of the Petroleum Industry in Spain: 1927–1930', *Journal of Contemporary History*, 15 (1980), pp. 701–20; J.A. Cortada, *Two nations over Time: Spain and the United States 1776–1977* (London: Greenwood Press, 1978), pp. 172–3.

60 A.Mª. Tamayo, 'España ante el Pacto Briand–Kellogg', *Cuadernos de Historia Moderna y Contemporánea*, 5 (1984), pp. 187–213.

61 Tusell, 'La dictadura', p. 550.

62 Sueiro, *España en el Mediterráneo*, p. 390.

63 M. Azaña, 'La discordia republicana' (speech in the bullring of Bilbao, 9.4.1933), in *Obras completas*, vol. II (Mexico City, 1966), pp. 689–90.

64 J.C. Pereira, 'De una guerra a otra: la actitud española ante el desarme y el pacifismo (1914–1936)', in *Comité International des Sciences Historiques* (Madrid: Comité Español de Ciencias Históricas, 1992), I, pp. 452–70; Bledsoe, 'Spanish Foreign Policy', p. 22.

65 L. Delgado, *Imperio de papel: acción cultural y política exterior durante el primer franquismo* (Madrid: CSIC, 1992).

4   The Second Republic in the international arena

Ismael Saz

Translated by Susan Edith Núñez

Both in its circumstances and in its ideas, Republican foreign policy was the exact opposite of that of Primo de Rivera. In a largely stable international context, Primo de Rivera carried out a policy that, for all its bombast, entailed a timid challenge to the international status quo. In a much more fluid and problematic international situation, the Republican government relied on a policy of collaboration in order to maintain this *status quo*. Nevertheless, there was one aspect in which the two converged and diverged at the same time. In both cases, an attempt was made to raise Spain from the alleged prostration in which she lay, projecting the country outwards and aspiring to play a significant role in international relations. But while the Dictatorship constituted a first and contradictory expression of conservative regenerationism, the Republic did likewise, but of progressive democracy.[1]

From this coincidence/antagonism arose the most radical and negative visions – according to their source – of each of these experiences. For the Republicans the monarchy in itself had a negative connotation. For over a century, according to the Republican Minister of War and later President, Manuel Azaña, the 'foreign [policy] of Spain consisted in not having one'. Enclosed in a spirit of 'smallness and seclusion', the monarchy had led the country into absolute international indigence. The pretentious, grandiloquent policy of the Dictatorship, far from improving the situation, had left Spain in a state of greater weakness and subordination with regard to France and Great Britain.[2] In a certain sense, the victorious Francoists transferred these judgements to the Republic. In their opinion, while Spanish liberalism had plunged Spain into a state of prostration before the Western powers, the Republic, after the parenthesis of the Dictatorship, would have led the process to its culmination. Slavishly yielding to France and England, to the point of falling into the 'most shameless vassalage', the Republic, according to them, lacked any 'authentic national foreign policy' whatsoever.[3]

What is surprising is that the same overall judgement was adopted by the democratic, anti-Franco left, itself. The lack of a foreign policy worthy of the name could be explained by in this case because of the inability of the Republicans to forge a solid alliance with France, which would have saved Spain from the coming Fascist intervention in the Civil War, and, in a wider sense, because of their absurd relapse into a policy of neutrality.[4] As a whole, this thesis proved to be completely appropriate in that it perfectly suited what we knew, or thought we knew, about contemporary Spain. On one hand, it assumed a straightforward and simple explanation for Republican isolation during the Civil War. On the other, it linked in with the image of a backward, immobile, peripheral and inward-looking Spain. It is therefore not strange that a deeply negative image of Republican foreign policy should have almost entirely dominated historiography.[5]

Yet this created a sort of vicious circle: as there appeared to be no foreign policy, it was not studied, and, since it was not studied, it did not exist. As new research began to be carried out, that thesis began to crumble. This does not mean, of course, that deficiencies in the foreign action of the Republic have been ignored. These include the inexperience of the new people in charge of Republican diplomacy, the discontinuity resulting from the existence of fourteen governments and ten ministers of state in only five years, the inadequacies of the infrastructure, the inertia of the bureaucracy, the lack of programmes and the absence of mechanisms of coordination. To these should be added the budgetary consequences of the economic crisis and the resulting priority given in government expenditure to the Republican policy of domestic reform. Above all, the violence of the internal conflict weighed like a millstone on the foreign policy of the Republic. It absorbed nearly all the available time and energy, encouraging international problems to become a vehicle of national politics, thus reinforcing the traditional tendency of Spaniards to look inwards and distance themselves from European problems.[6]

Nonetheless, many of these problems were less important than has frequently been suggested. Some were merely temporary, others weighed differently in the successive phases of the Republic, and others were, in short, not confined to Spanish diplomacy. Although the first Minister of State of the Republic, Alejandro Lerroux, was probably the least suited for the post, his successors, Luis de Zulueta and Fernando de los Ríos, were recognized at home and abroad as excellent ministers.[7] Neither Azaña nor of course Salvador de Madariaga, a former official in the League of Nations, were unaware of the ins and outs of international politics. Some of the new political ambassadors surpassed their predecessors in talent, efficiency and results.[8] Ministerial discontinuity was quite normal in the first phase of the Republic, and at its most intense between September 1933 and February 1936. Each in his own way and from different positions – Azaña, Madariaga, Alcalá Zamora and again Azaña covered almost the entire Republican experience.[9]

Moreover, Azaña had a clear vision of the interdependence of military and defence policies, and whenever it was necessary, something – although not much – was done to improve coordination.[10] Although Spanish dealings in foreign affairs were light-years behind those of Britain's Foreign Office, they do not seem to compare badly with those of France, about which it has been written that nothing was done to integrate her foreign and defence policies.[11] Of course, the differences in tradition, experience and resources that divided these diplomatic corps were still enormous. We only have to note that Spanish expenditure for cultural propaganda abroad was roughly 10 per cent of that spent by countries such as France, Italy or Germany.[12] Despite all this, it is revealing that a government forced to set aside a major portion of its exiguous state funds for domestic reform decided to quadruple expenditure in this field between 1932 and 1933.[13]

However, the fundamental problem lies in the fact that to confine the discussion merely to the foreign policy of the Republic as a whole is undoubtedly to fall into abstraction. In foreign policy as in domestic policy, there were different phases in the Republican period. As I will attempt to demonstrate, some of the characteristics generally attributed to the foreign policy of the Republic are mere blatant generalizations; though frequently valid for one phase or another, they are not true for all of them.

A hopeful and coherent project

Above any other consideration, Republican leaders had a clear, coherent, modern and progressive concept of what Spanish foreign policy should be. This does not necessarily mean that successive governments were able to construct upon this base a well-defined or articulated programme. The nucleus of this concept was their conviction that the foreign policy of the Republic could be nothing other than an outward projection of the democratic principles that inspired domestic policy; this would endow it with coherence, credibility and prestige. And because of its location, bridging two continents and two seas, as well as its history and culture and the size of its population, Spain could and should occupy a privileged position among nations.[14]

Consequently, Republican foreign policy had to be democratic, pacifist, devoid of any territorial or colonial ambitions, based on principles of publicity and universality, and ready to participate – by right, but also out of obligation – in the destinies of Europe and the world. The fundamental reference point was the League of Nations, which was perceived as the equivalent on the international level of what the Republic represented on the domestic level. At the level of bilateral relations, a policy of good relations with all countries – especially with the democracies – would be maintained. Through tradition and political culture, agreement with Britain and France would constitute another of the fundamental pivots of foreign policy, although it was firmly intended to maintain autonomy in relation to these countries. Portugal and the Latin American republics would also be special areas of concern, though there was no intention of superiority or hegemony.[15]

As the Republic's officials repeatedly declared, this policy based on principle would strictly correspond with the national interest. The existence of a peaceful world was perceived as a vital necessity in order for the new regime to be able to consolidate and carry out its reformist policy. The League of Nations guaranteed that peace, and would make a costly arms policy unnecessary. In this great world tribunal, Spain could carry out an active policy that would make its 'moral authority' felt and would enhance its presence and prestige.

Such a clear reliance on the Geneva institution did not mean that Spain excluded other aspects of foreign policy. Spain's very location, apart from the advantages it gave which have already been mentioned, was also inconvenient in that it constituted an area of great strategic interest for the Great Powers. Furthermore, the League of Nations might fail in its attempt to ensure world peace. Hence, from the very first moment, two complementary paths of action were considered. One was the possibility of an agreement over the Mediterranean that would guarantee the *status quo* there. The other was to adopt the necessary measures to modernize and rationalize the Spanish army and reinforce Spain's defences, especially in the Balearic Islands. Azaña's military reform was not unconnected with these kinds of concerns. As he stated, the crucial question was to guarantee Spain's freedom of action.[16]

Of course, within this common framework of policy, there was a range of different sensibilities. Alcalá Zamora, for example, had a more conservative vision that led him to try to distance the Republic as far as possible from the problems of Europe. At the other end of the spectrum, Madariaga tended to address the problems of Spanish foreign policy almost exclusively from a League standpoint. Finally, Azaña had a more realistic view, in which a genuine policy based on the League of Nations was balanced by the concerns of a military and strategic nature.[17] But all were agreed on the substance of foreign policy, and in practice their differences were minor.

What was more problematic and unorthodox was Azaña's attempt to carry out a 'high-profile foreign policy' which went so far as to intervene directly in the internal affairs of other countries. Thus he actively collaborated with Portuguese revolutionaries by providing them with arms and he gave financial support to a presidential candidate in Cuba. This was not merely a marginal issue. As Azaña himself wrote in his diary, an issue like the Portuguese one could 'fulfil all my ambitions'. Nor was it a question simply of solidarity or democratic idealism. In fact, these initiatives appear explicitly linked to the military, Peninsular and Spanish American policies of the Republic. And his statement to one of the Portuguese conspirators, 'Together we would be great in the world', is highly reminiscent of another delivered by Alfonso XIII a decade earlier. In short, Azaña's realism had a hyperrealistic side to it, or shared certain characteristics of nineteenth-century democratic nationalism, or had both at the same time.[18]

In the course of events and as international contradictions deepened, the Republican leaders were forced to reconsider their optimism, and even their grand pretensions. The world was not going to move over the next few years towards the affirmation of democratic principles and regimes, nor was the League of Nations going to fulfil in any way the objectives for which it had been conceived. But this was not so clear in 1931, a year of transition in both Spanish and international terms. Arnold Toynbee himself, who characterized it as an *annus terribilis*, could still hail the proclamation of the Spanish Republic as a sign of hope.[19] And the expectations raised by the disarmament conference had still not been dashed. In this context, the Republic could incorporate into its constitution the principle of the Kellogg–Briand Pact, which excluded war as 'an instrument of national policy'.

Development of Republican foreign policy

In September 1931, at almost the same time that Lerroux made a flamboyant presentation of the principles of the Republic's foreign policy in the Geneva forum, Japanese aggression began in Manchuria. The conference on disarmament began its sessions five months later. These would be the two great tests to which the League of Nations would be put, and they would also constitute the first great challenges that the new Republican diplomatic corps would have to face.

As far as the conflict in the Far East was concerned, the Spanish position constituted a sound defence of the League's principles, led principally by the man who would be the Spanish representative in Geneva during the greatest part of the Republican period, Salvador de Madariaga. He adopted a position of passionate defence of the League's principles and collaborated with small democratic powers in demanding that the League faithfully comply with its obligations. This attitude marked at times a contrast with the more dilatory and passive attitudes of the Great Powers towards Japan. As a result of all this, Madariaga's prestige rose to spectacular heights, and he soon began to be known as 'Don Quijote de la Manchuria'.[20]

It was on this issue that the differences between Madariaga and the government he represented arose. The Minister of State, Zulueta, sensed that perhaps this policy of 'ultra-Leaguism' was going too far. Madariaga seemed to forget at times that he represented a country, not his own personal opinion, and all this could have unfavourable consequences for Spanish relations, both with Japan and with Britain or other countries. But the underlying question, the condemnation of Japan, was never discussed. In his speeches in Geneva, Zulueta too followed the policy of the strict defence of the Pact, and the government showed its solidarity with Madariaga in Parliament whenever it was necessary. Thus the differences did not go beyond mere nuance. The government possibly sought only to achieve slightly more prudence of action and a toning down of Madariaga's willingness to march with the minority and in the vanguard of the 'international Left'.[21]

In the disarmament conference, the Spanish position followed the same script. The demand was made for the greatest possible disarmament compatible with a guarantee of internal public order and the fulfilment of international obligations. As a 'minimum programme', a drastic and efficiently controlled reduction in arms was advocated. In the defence of these proposals, the Spanish diplomatic corps was again especially active. Madariaga chaired one of the committees set up to consider disarmament, that of aerial disarmament, and took the initiative in the process that would lead to the creation of the Group of Eight, consisting of the Scandinavian countries, Belgium, the Netherlands, Czechoslovakia and Switzerland. As democratic powers without great military capacity, all of them shared with Spain the resolute desire to go down the path of disarmament and support every initiative to reinforce the principle of collective security. For that same reason, they were especially concerned that the negotiations take place with the greatest clarity and transparency, without their being hijacked by the tendency of the Great Powers to solve their differences in parallel meetings.[22]

The truth was that the Group of Eight could not do much in the face of the initiatives of the Great Powers, nor did the latter seem able to reach a minimum basis of agreement. Trapped between the French insistence on security issues, the German concentration on equal rights and the more flexible British position, the conference on disarmament dragged on throughout 1932 without any positive progress. In this context, an increasingly isolated French diplomacy tried hard to win the support of the intermediary powers, including Spain, for what would be its final attempt to retain a certain initiative: Édouard Herriot's so-called *plan constructif*. Although somewhat encumbered by commercial problems and the presence of the exiled monarchs, Spanish–French relations were excellent at that time. And the prestige Spain had gained in Geneva made her collaboration even more desirable.[23] This was the background to Herriot's visit to Spain in November 1932. The trip generated widespread expectations and the customary speculations about the possibility of reaching secret agreements about the eventual passage of French colonial troops through Spanish territory in the event of war. The fact that there was absolutely no basis to such speculations was stressed repeatedly by the Spanish and French authorities, and the British, French and Italian diplomats in Spain were soon convinced by the denials.[24]

The issue would not have had any major significance if Madariaga had not later implied the existence of these or similar aspirations on Herriot's part. However, not only is there no documentary evidence whatsoever of this, but a close reading of Madariaga's own writings leads to a similar conclusion: Azaña could hardly have assumed an alliance that no politician or diplomat, either French or Spanish, nor even Madariaga himself, had ever suggested.[25] Moreover, an alliance would have been in flagrant contradiction with one of the basic tenets of Republican foreign policy, about which, furthermore, there was not the slightest disagreement. Similarly, it makes no sense to attribute to Azaña's actions any of the terrible consequences that would have arisen from this attitude.[26]

It is true, on the other hand, that Azaña had felt little enthusiasm about the visit of the French minister and that he had even been somewhat elusive during its course. But this did not indicate a lack of interest in international affairs. On the contrary, it stemmed from Azaña's concern over the hegemonic plans of Spain's northern neighbour as much as his determination to safeguard the principle of autonomy and the non-subordination of Republican foreign policy.[27]

The truth is that the visit fulfilled the objectives that had been set. It meant a certain international backing for the Republican regime, it led to the signing of some agreements on social services, and the monarchist refugees in French territory began to receive a less benevolent treatment from the authorities. But above all, the visit served to show that Spain and France had a similar perception of the great international problems of the time. That, and nothing else, had been the principal objective behind the trip, and, to judge by subsequent events, the goal had been met to a reasonable degree. This much can be interpreted, at least, from the conditional support which Spanish diplomacy gave to the French plan of disarmament when it was discussed in February 1933.[28]

Hitler's rise to power introduced a new factor, to which the foreign ministries reacted differently. Britain took the initiative in March with the MacDonald plan, and Roosevelt did the same in April with a declaration of support. Mussolini took advantage of the German challenge to launch an initiative, the Pact of the Four, designed to constitute a type of 'directory' or hierarchy of the British, French, Italians and Germans in Europe. Although none of these initiatives obtained the desired results, it was evident that the international situation had undergone a change of such magnitude that it required important readjustments in the attitude of the other countries.

During this process, Spanish diplomacy was not at all passive. Believing that it was necessary to save the disarmament conference at all costs, it conditionally supported the MacDonald and Roosevelt initiatives. Faced with the challenge of Hitler's rise to power, the Spanish diplomacy proposed the constitution of a common front. Reacting against Mussolini's proposal of a 'European directory', its diplomats carried out a full-blooded offensive in Madrid, Paris and Geneva to thwart it. But at the same time, an attempt was made to take advantage of the new atmosphere created by the Italian initiative in order to put the idea of a Mediterranean or Locarno Pact on the table. Given France's inconsistencies and oscillations in this and other matters, a strategy of *rapprochement* with Britain began to be designed.[29]

The change in Spanish foreign policy did not represent a suspension of collaboration with France, but it did constitute a clear reaffirmation of Spanish autonomy with regard to Paris. It was perceived as such in Rome, where, moreover, the dispelling of the doubts raised by Herriot's trip had contributed to a relaxation of the atmosphere of mutual distrust. Even as regards domestic policy, Mussolini's long hostility towards the Spanish Republic began to be softened by the impression caused by Azaña's energetic action over the attempted *coup* of August 1932. A result of the new, more relaxed atmosphere was the Italian offer of the early renewal of the 1926 treaty of friendship, and the favourable response that it received in Madrid.

Taking advantage of this complex series of relatively favourable circumstances, the new Minister of State, Fernando de los Ríos, decided to seize the initiative in the perennial question of the Mediterranean Pact. There was full agreement with France on this matter, while the British were well known to be little inclined towards this type of agreement. As for Italy, the Rome offer was taken up, a move not initially ill received by the Italians. Neither of the proposals prospered in the end, partly because the fall of the Republican-Socialist government occurred at that moment. After this, nobody seemed to remember the initiative any longer: neither the new Republican governments, nor France, nor Mussolini, who considered that now that Spain had entered a new period of instability, it was better to forget the matter. It is possible that even without these governmental changes the Spanish initiative would ultimately have failed. But the significant fact is that it existed and that Republican diplomacy was gaining a degree of prestige and credibility.[30]

A marked improvement in relations was also taking place with those democratic powers that had most coldly greeted the proclamation of the Republic: Britain and, especially, the United States. In both cases, more weight seemed initially to be given to the risk that the Republic would constitute the threshold of a socialist revolution – the 'Kerensky syndrome' – than to its democratic character. Moreover, the conservative nature of the businesses with interests in Spain and of the consulates meant that they did everything in their power to portray the reformist and labour legislation of the first two years of the Republic as clearly anti-capitalist. Such attempts were especially acute in the case of the United States. As if that were not enough, the timid attempt to nationalize the telephone company controlled by ITT had led to overreaction on the part of the Americans.[31]

Yet by 1933, Britain had begun to evaluate much more realistically the scope of the Republican reforms, as well as Azaña himself. Moreover, Spanish offers of friendship were well received in London, where Spanish collaboration was perceived as possibly 'of some worth' in international forums, and where, at the same time, it was feared that a cold welcome might result in a Spanish relapse into the French orbit.[32] Something similar was happening in the White House. Worried about the retreat of democracy in Europe, Roosevelt showed his willingness to value Spanish democracy as well as the advisability of having 'Spain on our side of the table with us'. The new ambassador, the Jeffersonian Democrat Claude Bowers, did all he could to dispel the prejudices surrounding the evolution of the Spanish Republic. However, the new climate did not have much time to develop. Azaña's progressive loss of control of the situation contributed to the fact that once again the perceptions of instability gained ground – to the point that the constitution of Lerroux's first government could be judged as a sign of greater stability and moderation, albeit only for a short time.[33] Something similar would occur, on another level, with the process of recognition of the Soviet Union, in which the agreed exchange of ambassadors was paralysed by the new turn in Spanish politics.[34]

Downhill

By the summer of 1933, Spanish diplomacy had gained well-deserved prestige in the League of Nations. A semi-permanent member of the council, the Spaniard Pablo de Azcárate occupied one of the two posts of general sub-secretaries of the organization. Madariaga chaired one of the committees of the disarmament conference, and Spanish participation in the tasks of League mediation in Latin America was notable. The relations with the countries of that region were generally good, and in some cases excellent. At the same time, innovative plans for cultural activities were being elaborated. The small democratic powers in Europe gave Spain credit for its leadership. Without burning bridges with France, Spain was improving her relations with Britain and the United States, and something similar was happening with Italy and the USSR. Although the initial hopes of the League had been watered down, the policy of collaboration with large and small democratic powers was maintained, as well as an active commitment to the tasks of the League. It was not, after all, a bad balance sheet.

Some of these things would change radically in the years that followed – so much so that if at any time Republican foreign policy lived up to its stereotype of non-existence, it was in the period between September 1933 and February 1936. Of course, such a characterization would still be exaggerated, and hence unfair. But it was then that the ministerial discontinuity reached a dizzying rhythm – eight ministers of state in twenty-nine months, compared to four in the remaining thirty-four. It was during this period that the political ambassadors who were nominated were in general not notable for their competence, as revealed by the appointment of the Radical politician Emiliano Iglesias – universally and rightly notorious for his corruption – to the embassy in Mexico.[35] The differences of approach between the various government agencies and within the governments themselves were never so sharp as at that time. It was also during these years that the weight of domestic policy on foreign policy became suffocating.

But the most notable feature was the continuous descent of Spanish foreign policy down a slope leading from the former commitment to the League and to a search for collective security towards a hesitant and frequently shameful neutrality. This cannot be attributed entirely to the swing to the right; the international situation was going down a similar slope.[36] But even here, the shift in Spanish foreign policy was as abrupt as it was striking, even before the victory of the right in the November elections. After Germany withdrew from the conference and the League itself, Spanish diplomacy showed opposition to any anti-German front, such as the one that France and Britain seemed to be jointly encouraging. At this time, José María Doussinague, a young diplomat who was clearly a Germanophile, began his ascent. Under his direction, a plan was drawn up to create a sort of alliance of neutral countries; because of its grandiloquence, almost intrinsic rigidity and controversial nature, it was received with strong reservations by the countries to which it was addressed. After it had been reformulated in more flexible terms, a new group – that of the neutral countries or Group of the Six – was able to take shape, but it was in large measure due to Spanish diplomacy that the 'Francophiles', Belgium and Czechoslovakia, were marginalized from the group.[37]

It cannot be said that the action of this group, nor that of Spain within it, was particularly brilliant. The first joint act of the group was the April 1934 memorandum on disarmament, which ran up against French opposition. Other similar initiatives undertaken throughout the year had similar results. When in the early months of 1935 Sweden proposed mediation regarding Germany, with British acquiescence, the proposal was not seconded by the other neutral countries, nor by Spain, which was frightened that the measure might have a 'counterproductive effect'. After obligatory military service was reinstated in Germany, the Spanish delegation in Geneva participated in the elaboration of a motion of condemnation that was rejected by France and Britain because of its excessive mildness. By then, the unity of action of the neutral countries had evaporated.[38]

It cannot be said that Spain's prestige in Geneva suffered seriously during 1934. Doussinague's removal from the ministry, and a greater prudence in neutralist declarations, contributed to a normalization of Spanish foreign policy. A Spanish representative took part in the League committee formed to supervise the Sarre referendum. The option of neutrality was common to other small and middle-sized democratic powers. However, behind the Spanish position lay a conservative component that was not completely comparable to that in the rest of the neutral countries. Spain, unlike the others, was not a neighbour of Germany, and hence what was for the other members of the group a logical precaution in the face of a powerful neighbour was for Spain a relapse into its old isolationist tendencies. The incorporation of CEDA, or *Confederación Española de Derechas Autónomas* (Spanish Confederation of Autonomous Right-wing Parties), in the government in the autumn of 1934 would mark a further shift to the right of Republican foreign policy.

In fact, such was the composition of the new government that the different inclinations of its members did not contradict one another. The Radicals acted within the League principles of the Republic, but they were willing to interpret them minimally. Catholic circles, hardly supportive of the League and in favour of strict neutrality, knew that there were certain limits beyond which they could not venture. CEDA had an anti-French tendency; the Radicals clearly placed London before Paris. The former openly sympathized with the two Romes: the Vatican and the Fascist state. The Radicals, in their desire to improve relations with the Vatican, had gone so far as having the Minister of State, Leandro Pita Romero, proclaim himself ambassador to the Holy See. In short, London and Rome were the two points of reference for the governmental coalition.[39] Within this context, the conflict in Abyssinia would bring about a radical change in the situation – first, because the challenge would now come from nearby Italy and not from distant Germany, and second, because Rome and London would now appear in opposing camps.

The first symptom of a shift of the European problems toward the Mediterranean was marked in the January 1935 Rome agreements between Mussolini and Laval. In reaction to it, Spanish diplomacy responded in its traditional way; that is, after undergoing a certain self-imposed isolation from European issues, it became alarmed when faced with the possibility that the Mediterranean issue might be addressed in its absence. But the agreements in Rome looked more towards Ethiopia than to the Western Mediterranean, so the government could soon stop worrying. For a moment, Spanish diplomacy seemed to regain a certain dynamism. But it did not last long, and no European chancellery took it very seriously; indeed, Rome and London coincided in judging that it was motivated by domestic policy concerns.[40]

While the Franco-British positions were geared to making maximum concessions to Italy within the framework of the League, Spanish diplomacy could be in step with London without arousing the enmity of Italy. But when Britain began to adopt a tougher line in the summer of 1935 and Anglo-Italian tensions heightened considerably in the Mediterranean, the situation grew complicated for the Spanish government. The problems lay both abroad, where the two principal poles of attraction of the allied forces in the government now found themselves in opposing positions, and at home, where public opinion became involved in the conflict as never before. The left was against the imperialist ambitions of Italy and for the strict defence of the Covenant, and the extreme right was for out-and-out neutrality, the logical corollary of its overt sympathies towards Italy.[41]

Towards the end of August, the dissension within the government came out in the open in the speeches of Lerroux, Prime Minister of the right-wing coalition government, and José María Gil Robles, leader of CEDA. Both favoured neutrality, but while the former turned implicitly to London, the latter advocated strict neutrality and the primacy of national interests over international obligations. For the moment, all of this was reflected in an unusual silence of the Spanish delegation in the League Assembly in September. Despite this, or precisely because of it, Madariaga was elected as president of the Committee of the Five, in charge of exploring all possibilities for seeking a negotiated end to the conflict. But Madariaga was no longer the brilliant spokesperson of neutral countries, which, except for Switzerland, now openly opposed Italy, but rather the representative of a government that Rome as well as London and Paris considered ill-defined and easily influenced. The favourable disposition towards Italy of the committee presided over by Madariaga would show that those powers had not made a wrong choice.[42]

After the Italian aggression in Ethiopia began, Spain had no option other than to abandon to some extent her ambiguous position. The delegation in Geneva voted silently for the sanctions, but later did everything in its power to minimize enforcement. Even the President of the Republic had to exert every effort in order to prevent the Spanish government from breaching its League obligations. In mid-October, Madariaga lost a vote in which he had supported those countries which, like Austria and Hungary, had refused to apply the sanctions. When the British government solicited guarantees of support from the Mediterranean countries against possible Italian aggression, the Spanish government decided to ignore the British suggestion. Hence, pressures from London were necessary in order that finally, in mid-January 1936, Spain made public her willingness to comply with the commitments derived from the compliance of article 16. By striving not to make enemies with either London or Rome, the Spanish government had ended up arousing the distrust of both.[43]

In contrast to its relations in Europe, Republican foreign policy reaped significant success in its colonies around this time. In April 1934, the occupation of Sidi Ifni had been carried out, with the complete agreement of France, in a final move to pacify Morocco. In 1935 three circumstances coincided which would bring the problem of Tangier and Morocco to the fore. In the first place were the fears aroused by the agreements in Rome. In the second place was the desire to make up for the complete absence of demands in the colonial policy of the first two-year period. The final circumstance was the proximity of the revision of the Tangier Statute scheduled for November 1935. Thus, a kind of 'moderate revisionism' was established which led to some improvements in the Spanish position in Tangier and a certain rectification of the frontiers between the Spanish and French zones of the Moroccan Protectorate. But what undoubtedly proved decisive was that this event coincided with the critical phase of the Abyssinian conflict. In this sense, British willingness to intercede with Paris and the latter's surprising speed in agreeing to concede most of the Spanish demands were the price that had to be paid for helping a reluctant Spain to comply with her obligations in the League. Despite this, the revision of the statute was without doubt a diplomatic success, although in practice it would fail, at first largely because of the resistance of the French colonialists, and later because of the internal upheavals in Spain.[44]

In fact, there was no contradiction whatsoever between the nearly total paralysis of the European policy of the Republic and the minor African successes. In both cases, it was an almost logical consequence of the swing to the right. The increasing conservatism of the Radicals led to an overestimation of the problems of domestic policy. This went along well with the retreat from European affairs and the achievement of certain improvements in Africa that could be used to bolster prestige. From the point of view of CEDA, the traditional Africanism and the minimal Europeanism of the Spanish right heightened the tendency to subordinate foreign policy to domestic problems. As a German report stated, Gil Robles's reorganization of the army was caused by the international situation, but it was also used as a pretext to pursue internal objectives. It could not be otherwise if we bear in mind that the negotiations to obtain arms accompanied those aiming to establish police collaboration with the Gestapo. It was suggested to the Italians that Spanish support over Abyssinia would be greater if Rome ceased to back the monarchists.[45]

But the swing to the right in the domestic policy of the two-year period of the government did not strengthen its foreign policy. Relations with Portugal improved extraordinarily, of course, although not to the extent that traditional Portuguese reservations disappeared.[46] The improvement with Rome and Berlin was also appreciable. And the swing to the right met with the approval of those sectors of the British and American establishment who had shown hostility towards the former Republican radicalism.[47] But while the benefits accruing from this improvement in international status could not be total because of the increasing disintegration of the domestic political situation, the perspective of an improvement in relations with these countries was undermined by the erratic and vacillating nature of Spanish foreign policy.

The end of an illusion

On the surface, the foreign policy of the Popular Front governments followed the same path of refuge in neutrality as in the preceding period.[48] On the one hand, the confluence of the German and Italian challenges in the first months of 1936 brought about an extraordinary deterioration of the situation in Europe. On the other hand, the domestic conflict in Spain grew in intensity until it broke out into the Civil War. An international situation filled with dangers and a growing internal conflict would seem to be two powerful reasons for the Spanish to take refuge, turning inwards to seek the solution to their domestic problems.

In their formulation of foreign policy, the new Spanish leaders adopted perspectives of this kind. While still in opposition, Azaña had implicitly warned against the risks of imbuing the condemnation of the Italian aggression in Ethiopia with excessive sentimentality.[49] Once in power, he reaffirmed the desire to cooperate with the League of Nations but also the need for reciprocity in the fulfilment of its obligations; he defended complete loyalty to the League, but without taking on obligations which 'we should not accept'.[50] Simultaneously, he abandoned his former airs of grandeur, accepted that his country carried little weight in European affairs and gave up any attempt to interfere in the affairs of the neighbouring Portuguese Republic. The perception about the influence of domestic on foreign policy was now more conservative. As Azaña and Augusto Barcia Trelles, the Minister of State, reiterated on more than one occasion, it was imperative to avoid an international conflict because this would no doubt provoke a revolution – either communist or anarchist.[51] The revolutionary democratic optimism of 1931 had changed into pessimism and precaution in the face of revolution. Within the framework of the League of Nations, Spain objected to sanctions against Germany for the remilitarization of the Rhineland and soon backed the lifting of the sanctions against Italy. Spanish diplomacy even became involved in a confused project for a regressive reform of the League of Nations. Clearly traditional formulas were frequently reiterated, such as the allusion to the need always to march in step with France and Britain. Barcia did not even attempt to hide the fact that Spanish international policy was conducted on a day-to-day basis, without any possibility of introducing the minimum elements of programming or planning.[52]

There is some truth in all of this. But this was where the continuity with the foreign policy of former governments ended. It can be argued that Spanish foreign policy took a new and clearly distinct direction, opposed to that of the preceding two-year period. This is for three fundamental reasons: first, because Republican diplomacy regained its voice; second, because it became active once again on the international scene; and third, because whatever the policy was, it was carried out on the basis of collaboration with and commitment to the rest of the countries in the League of Nations.

This was clear in the Spanish attitude towards the remilitarization of the Rhineland. As was mentioned above, Spanish diplomacy was not in favour of imposing sanctions and was especially concerned about a difference of opinion between France and Britain, which would make the Spanish option more difficult. But on this occasion it was willing to intervene between the two powers. Moreover, Spain strove to find a compromise, arguing, in tune with French desires, for the explicit condemnation of the German violation of the Treaty of Versailles and of Locarno, but ruling out the imposition of sanctions, as Britain wished. The speech given by Barcia in Geneva went along these lines. According to him, the League of Nations should rule only on whether or not the Germans had violated the treaty, while the possible imposition of sanctions was a question for the Locarno powers, since it was in this treaty and not in the Covenant that the remilitarization of the Rhineland had been compared to an act of aggression. These formulations contained a strong dose of political realism, of course, but the legal argument was nonetheless irreproachable. After all, that was the line that was approved by the Assembly, and the speech was very well received in France.[53]

The chronological coincidence between the problem of the Rhineland and that of Abyssinia reinforced Spanish determination to distance the arena of conflict from the Mediterranean. As Barcia told Herbette, the French ambassador in Madrid, Spain was less concerned about the existence of an Anglo-French-Italian coalition against Germany than about the increase of tensions in the Mediterranean. Hence Spain opposed any stiffening of sanctions. This was also coherent with Madariaga's acceptance of the presidency of the Committee of the Thirteen, which allowed him to lead the last and fruitless attempts at mediation by the League of Nations. When, after the conquest of Abyssinia had ended, the question of lifting sanctions was faced, Spain openly advocated it. And its diplomats then showed distinct signs of impatience with the apparent rigidity of the British. But this was not at all an isolated position. Practically all the European countries had turned in the same direction and Neville Chamberlain himself stated at the beginning of June 1936 that keeping the sanctions would constitute 'a summer madness'. When the Assembly met at the end of the month, it was to sign the lifting of the sanctions in an atmosphere of open frustration and general silence.[54]

The reason why the Spanish government had supported this option since the beginning of May was consonant with its overall policy. The sanctions had been adopted in order to achieve an objective, and once the attempt had failed, it made no sense to maintain them indefinitely. From the European standpoint, the problems over peace emanated from the centre, not from the south. From the point of view of the League, the degree of compliance with article 16 concerning the sanctions should develop in parallel with what was done with article 8, which related to disarmament. From a specifically Spanish perspective, there was also the Italian factor. Azaña did not think that the growth of Italian power in the Mediterranean was necessarily harmful to Spain, and since this rise in power was occurring anyway, it was better to nurture relations with the neighbouring Peninsula. Finally, this course of action was also connected with domestic policy; cordial, even friendly relations with Italy could help to some extent to defuse Mussolini's old hostility towards the Spanish Republic.[55]

While Republican diplomacy was able to pass the two great tests it faced in the spring of 1936 relatively well, it almost failed in a much smaller test in which it had become unnecessarily involved. The multiplication of conflicts and the proven failure of the sanctions renewed the debate about whether or not the League of Nations should be reformed. The Spanish position on this was clear: open to the idea of reform, and opposed to changing the Covenant, and in favour of working towards universalizing the League and establishing a clear connection between the requirements of articles 8 and 16. On the other hand, it was considered advisable to exchange opinions over this matter with the neutral countries. At the meeting between these countries held at the beginning of May, Madariaga committed himself to drawing up the memorandum; it was this that would spark off the controversy.

The conflictive core of Madariaga's project was his proposal to submit article 16 to a 'general reserve' which would affect those states that were geographically and politically far from the areas of conflict, thus freeing them from compliance. In addition, when the note was leaked to the press, the Spanish government suddenly became associated with the idea of a clearly restrictive reform of the League of Nations. Thus it had no choice but to deny not only that it had drawn up the document, which was strictly true, but even that it had had the slightest knowledge of the text, which was not so true.[56] In any case, the Spanish government was taken by surprise by the devastating scope of the document drawn up by Madariaga.[57] The final outcome of the episode was Barcia's reassertion, both in the meeting of the neutral countries on 1 July and in the League Assembly two days later, of the general principles of the Spanish position, which were as previously outlined but without any 'general reserve' concerning compliance with article 16. But the episode had an added cost: Madariaga's resignation.[58] It was certainly not a very successful ending, nor probably a fair one. But one must surely agree that Madariaga, who had thought he had moved even further 'left' than the League convictions of his government in 1931, had ended up overtaking it on the 'right' five years later.

The fact that Madariaga went much further than his government intended does not mean that it did not lean more and more towards neutrality, as attested by its signature of the declaration of the neutral countries on 1 July.[59] Scarcely two weeks later, and four days after the Spanish government decreed the lifting of sanctions against Italy, the Civil War broke out, a war in which Italy would have an especially important role. The great and age-old problems of Spanish foreign policy seemed to have combined to hasten the collapse of the Republic: the worsening of the internal conflict, leading to the Civil War, and a policy of neutrality that, by isolating Spain from the democratic powers, threatened to leave it at the mercy of Fascist aggression.

But was it really like this? Actually, the Spanish Republic was destroyed by everything except its foreign policy, essentially by the magnitude of an internal conflict that furthermore contributed to reducing force and credibility in its foreign policy. But this did not distract Spain from what was happening in Europe. On the contrary, the perception of the degree and nature of the political confrontation that was developing in Europe contributed to intensifying the internal conflict in Spain. If Azaña can be criticized for anything, it is not for ignoring the problems in Europe but rather for having considered them more serious than, for example, the rumours about a *coup*, which made him laugh.[60]

In July 1936, relations with France were excellent, without any serious disagreement over foreign policy or over regimes and governments that shared similar policies. The Spanish Republic's policy in Geneva no longer generated the discord with Britain that had dominated the preceding period.[61] As for Latin America, traditional rivalry with the United States had not prevented Spain from gaining wide support in her efforts to be invited to the Pan-American conference due to be held in Buenos Aires.[62] Moves towards an exchange of ambassadors with the Soviet Union were resumed. And relations with the neutral countries, soon to be known as the Oslo Group, were excellent.

The problem lay in the fact that whatever the Republic's foreign policy, some countries were willing to subordinate it to something that concerned them much more. Despite the extraordinary tact with which the Republican authorities dealt with Portugal, this country added to its old fear of the 'Spanish threat' a new and not less terrible dread about the 'revolutionary danger' posed by Spain.[63] This obsession was shared by the Americans and the British. For both, the conflictive situation within Spain appeared to threaten their investments while at the same time Spanish commercial policy was seen as essentially hostile to their interests. Above all, everyone seemed to be obsessed with the risk of the triumph of a social revolution in Spain.[64] As soon as the opportunity of

rebuilding bridges with Italy arose, between June and July, Spain's foreign policy became less important for Britain than the dangers posed by
Spain's internal situation. Some of the problems that arose with the
French, British and Italians over the implementation of the Tangier
agreements were generated by these perceptions rather than by strictly
foreign policy motives.[65] Despite this, the French ambassador in Madrid
repeatedly advised his government to make the appropriate concessions
to Spain in this area.[66]

As for the two powers that were to intervene so decisively in the
Spanish Civil War, Italy and Germany, the situation was relatively different. It does not seem that the latter was especially interested in what
Spanish diplomats did or did not do.[67] With Italy the situation was even
more paradoxical. Italy's earlier agreement to collaborate with the Spanish
conspirators was made in the preceding two-year period. Throughout the
spring of 1936, Mussolini ignored all their requests for help. Once their
rebellion began, his initial response was equally negative. It is true that
the centrality of the operation in Abyssinia had something to do with
this. But it was also related to Mussolini's conviction that, with Azaña in
power, the probabilities of success of a *coup* were minimal. The Italian
government was aware that Spain was favourably disposed towards Italy
on the question of sanctions. In April 1936, the 1926 Friendship, Arbitration and Conciliation Treaty was deliberately left untouched, which
meant that it was automatically extended.[68]

If the Spanish Republic was finally isolated in July–August 1936, it
was because of the profound political and international contradictions of
the time. France displayed an initial willingness to help the neighbouring
republic, but in the end she 'could not' help, fearing internal upheavals
and international isolation. Britain soon adopted a position of benevolent
neutrality towards the rebels because for her government the risk of war
carried with it the risk of revolution, and the situation in Spain seemed
to embody both dangers. Italy and Germany intervened because unexpectedly they were offered a unique opportunity.[69]

Of course, none of this exonerates the Republican leaders from all
responsibility for the subsequent events. By 1936, they had tended
increasingly to take refuge in neutrality and they had played their part in
ensuring that the great violations of the agreements and the Covenant of
the League of Nations had gone unpunished. But there was nothing
exceptional about this. If the Republican diplomacy 'lived from hand to
mouth', it was because of the extraordinary instability of the international situation and because the other governments were doing likewise.
Fearful of war, of revolution and internal tensions, or of all of these at
the same time, the small and great democratic powers sought to appease

the dictators simultaneously or alternately. The Spanish Republic did likewise, although it ended up being the first European victim of this policy. Nevertheless, it must be agreed overall that, for better or for worse, the Spanish Republic had been in and with Europe as it had not been for decades, constructively and optimistically in 1931, and with pessimism in 1936. The history of the isolation of Spain belongs to an earlier and, above all, a later period. But it is not the history of the foreign policy of the Second Republic.

Notes

1   For the regenerationist contents of the foreign policy of the Republic, see M.A. Egido, *La concepción de la política exterior española durante la 2ª república* (Madrid: UNED, 1987), pp. 51–60.

2   M. Azaña, *Obras completas* (hereafter *OC*) (Madrid: Giner, 1990), II, pp. 41, 224, 689.

3   J.Mª. Areilza and F.Mª. Castiella, *Reivindicaciones de España* (Madrid: Instituto de Estudios Políticas, 1941), pp. 7–11.

4   J. Maurín, *Revolución y contrarrevolución en España*, (Paris: Ruedo Ibérico, 1966 [1935]); S. De Madariaga, *Memorias (1921–1936): amanecer sin mediodía* (Madrid: Espasa-Calpe, 1977); *España: ensayo de historia contemporánea* (Madrid: Espasa-Calpe, 1979) and *Españoles de mi tiempo*, (Barcelona: Planeta, 1974).

5   Cf. R. Tamames, *La república: la era de Franco* (Madrid: Alianza Editorial– Alfaguara, 1977), pp. 193–7; G.B. Bledsoe, 'Spanish Foreign Policy, 1898– 1936', in J.W. Cortada, *Spain in the Twentieth-Century World: Essays on Spanish Diplomacy* (London: Greenwood Press, 1980), pp. 3–40; J.J. Carreras, 'El marco internacional de la Segunda República', *Arbor* 426–7 (1981), pp. 37–50; J.C. Pereira, *Introducción al estudio de la política exterior de España (siglos XIX y XX)* (Madrid: Akal, 1983), pp. 161–8.

6   For one state of the question about the foreign policy of the Second Republic, see J.C. Pereira and J.L. Neila, 'La política exterior durante la II República: un debate y una respuesta', in J.B. Vilar (ed.), *Las relaciones internacionales en la España contemporánea* (Murcia: Universidad de Murcia, 1989), pp. 101–14; J.L. Neila, 'España y el modelo de integración de España en la Sociedad de Naciones (1919–1939)', *Hispania*, 176, (1990), pp. 1373–91; G. Palomares, 'La política exterior española: de la Dictadura de Primo de Rivera a la Guerra Civil', in R. Calduch (ed.), *La política exterior española en el Siglo XX* (Madrid: Ediciones Ciencias Sociales, 1994), pp. 47–70.

7   N. Tabanera, *Ilusiones y desencuentros: la acción diplomática republicana en Hispanoamérica (1931–1939)* (Madrid: CEDEAL, 1996), pp. 884–5; J.L. Neila 'España república mediterránea: seguridad colectiva y defensa nacional (1931–1936)', PhD thesis (Madrid, 1993), I, pp. 204ff.

8   Tabanera, *Ilusiones*, pp. 150ff.

9   I. Saz, 'La política exterior de la II República en el primer bienio (1931–1933): una valoración', *Revista de Estudios Internacionales*, 4 (1985), pp. 843–58.

10 Neila, 'España república mediterránea', I, pp. 110ff.

11 A. Adamthwaite, *Grandeur and Misery: France's Bid for Power in Europe 1914–1940* (London: Arnold, 1995), p. 157.

12 Tabanera, *Ilusiones*, p. 216.

13 *Ibid.*, p. 207; A. Niño, 'La II República y la expansión cultural en Hispanoamérica', *Hispania*, 181 (1992), p. 639. However, it should be noted that these expenditures were reduced with the budgetary restrictions of following years.

14 Azaña, *OC*, II, pp. 41, 224.

15 *Ibid.*, pp. 41–2, 89, 499–500; Madariaga, 'Nota sobre política exterior de España', 27.5.1932, in Madariaga, *Memorias*, pp. 606–15; Respuesta del ministro Zulueta a la interpelación del diputado Eduardo Ortega y Gasset. Diario de Sesiones de las Cortes Constituyentes, n. 246, 25.10.1932, pp. 912ff.

16 Madariaga, 'Nota sobre política exterior'. Azaña, *OC*, II, pp. 41, 212–13, 498–500, 689–90.

17 F. Quintana, *España en Europa, 1931–1936: del compromiso por la paz a la huida de la guerra* (Madrid: Nerea, 1993), pp. 43–4, 140, and 'Salvador de Madariaga, diplomático en Ginebra (1931–1936): la película de la política exterior de la II República', *Historia Contemporánea*, 15 (1996), pp. 125–45; A. Egido, 'La proyección exterior de España en el pensamiento de Manuel Azaña', in *Manuel Azaña, pensamiento y acción* (Madrid: Alianza Editorial, 1996), pp. 75–100; I. Saz, 'La política exterior', pp. 845–9.

18 M. Azaña, *Memorias política y de guerra* (Barcelona: Crítica, 1978), pp. 84–5, 135, 261–2, 386, 578–9.

19 *Survey of International Affairs 1931*, pp. 29–30.

20 Madariaga, *Memorias*, pp. 285ff, 574ff.

21 'Respuesta del ministro Zulueta . . .'; Quintana, *España en Europa*, pp. 66ff; Azaña, *Memorias*, II, pp. 413–14, 437, 458.

22 Quintana, *España en Europa*, pp. 92ff.

23 For Hispano-French relations, see C. Páez-Camino, 'La significación de Francia en el contexto internacional de la Segunda República española (1931–1936)', PhD thesis Madrid, 1990.

24 Quintana, *España en Europa*, pp. 133ff; Saz, 'La política exterior', pp. 849–54.

25 Madariaga, *Memorias*, pp. 3676–73, and *España*, pp. 395–6; Quintana, *España en Europa*, p. 134; Saz, 'La política exterior', pp. 851–2.

26 'Spain came out losing, and even more so did the Republic.' This memorable comment by Madariaga and the line of argument preceding it constitute one of the fundamental bases on which the myth of the non-existent Republican foreign policy has been supported. Cf. Madariaga, *Memorias*, p. 373, and *España*, p. 396.

27 Cf. C. Rivas Cherif, *Retrato de un desconocido: vida de Manuel Azaña* (Barcelona: Grijalbo), 1980, pp. 277–8; Páez-Camino, *La significación*, pp. 704ff; Saz, 'La política exterior', pp. 852–3.

28 Quintana, *España en Europa*, pp. 143ff.

29 *Ibid.*, pp. 150ff; Saz, 'La política exterior', pp. 855ff.

30 *Ibid.*, pp. 856–8.

31 D. Little, *Malevolent Neutrality: The United States, Great Britain, and the Origins of the Spanish Civil War* (Ithaca: Cornell University Press, 1985), pp. 58–130; J.A. Cortada, *Two Nations over Time: Spain and the U.S. 1776–1977* (London: Greenwood Press, 1978), pp. 175–8; E. Moradiellos, *Neutralidad benévola: el*

gobierno británico y la insurrección militar española de 1936 (Oviedo: Pentalfa, 1990), pp. 70–1, 102–3.

32 Little, *Malevolent Neutrality*, p. 134; J.F. Pertierra, *Las relaciones hispano-británicas durante la Segunda República española (1931–1936)* (Madrid: Fundación Juan March, 1984), pp. 13–14.

33 Little, *Malevolent Neutrality*, pp. 131–4.

34 Madariaga, *España*, pp. 394–5.

35 Tabanera, *Ilusiones*, pp. 151–3, 160–1.

36 Quintana, *España en Europa*, pp. 185–6.

37 *Ibid.*, pp. 176–7, 190ff.; Madariaga, *Memorias*, p. 415.

38 Madariaga, *Memorias*, pp. 231 and 239–45.

39 Cf. Egido, *La concepción*, pp. 217ff.; I. Saz, 'Acerca de la política exterior de la 2ª República', *Italica*, 16 (1982), pp. 267–9.

40 I. Saz, *Mussolini contra la II República* (Valencia: IVEI, 1986), p. 83; Quintana, *España en Europa*, p. 254.

41 Saz, 'Acerca de la política exterior', pp. 270–6.

42 *Ibid.*; F. P. Walters, *Historias de la Sociedad de Naciones* (Madrid: Tecnos, 1971), p. 626; Quintana, *España en Europa*, p. 277.

43 N. Alcalá-Zamora, *Memorias (Segundo texto de mis memorias)* (Barcelona, 1977), p. 331; Quintana, *España en Europa*, pp. 293, 311.

44 Egido, *La concepción*, pp. 270–7; J.L. Neila, 'Revisionismo y reajustes en el Mediterráneo: Tánger en las expectativas de la II República Española', *Hispania*, 181 (1992), pp. 655–85; Quintana, *España en Europa*, pp. 289–90; Pertierra, *Las relaciones hispano-británicas*, pp. 26–30.

45 A. Viñas, *La Alemania nazi y el 18 de julio* (Madrid: Alianza Editorial, 1977), pp. 99, 246–9; Saz, 'Acerca de la política exterior', p. 277.

46 Torre, *La relación peninsular*, pp. 71–93.

47 Little, *Malevolent Neutrality*, pp. 148–51.

48 Cf. Quintana, *España en Europa*, pp. 316–17.

49 Azaña, *OC*, III, p. 278.

50 *Ibid.*, p. 316.

51 Torre, *La relación peninsular*, pp. 108–9; Quintana, *España en Europa*, p. 318; Herbette to Flandin, 10.3.1936, Documents Diplomatiques Français (DDF), 2nd s., I, nos. 362 and 404.

52 Quintana, *España en Europa*, p. 316.

53 *Ibid.*, pp. 325–6; Herbette to Flandin, 10.3.1936 and 12.3.1936.

54 *Ibid.*, pp. 330ff; Walters, *Historia*, pp. 658–9; Herbette to Flandin, 10.7.1936, DDF, 2nd s., II, n. 423.

55 Saz, *Mussolini*, pp. 154–6.

56 Cf., Madariaga, *Memorias*, pp. 555–7, 706–17; Quintana, *España en Europa*, pp. 346–59.

57 Madariaga insinuated the existence of a type of order from Azaña along this line: 'The first thing you must do is get rid of that article 16. I don't want to have anything to do with it.' There is no way to verify the truth of such an expression. However, Madariaga's own story hints that these were not the 'instructions' which were received. Azaña would have liked the plan that Madariaga forwarded, although without 'going into details'. Barcia would not have known what 'I was looking for', although, given Azaña's receptive attitude, he would have given his 'general blessing'. Cf. Madariaga, *Memorias*, pp. 554–5.

58 Actually, Madariaga never officially represented Spain in Geneva. While he was the ambassador in Paris, until April 1934 he combined both occupations, so from that time onwards, he did not hold any official office. Near the dates we are discussing, the Frente Popular government was planning to establish a permanent delegation in Geneva. Cf. Madariaga, *Memorias*, pp. 730–1.

59 Quintana, *España en Europa*, p. 361.

60 Herbette to Flandin, 10.4.1936, DDF, 2nd s., II, n. 54.

61 Moradiellos, *Neutralidad benévola*, p. 118.

62 Tabanera, *Ilusiones*, pp. 190–1.

63 Torre, *La relación peninsular*, pp. 110–20.

64 Moradiellos, *Neutralidad benévola*, pp. 117ff; Little, *Malevolent Neutrality*, pp. 205ff.

65 Little, *Malevolent Neutrality*, pp. 128–30.

66 Herbette to Flandin, 14.5.1936 and 10.7.1936, Documents Diplomatiques Français (DDF), 2nd s., II, nos. 213 and 423.

67 Viñas, *La Alemania nazi*, pp. 255ff.

68 Saz, *Mussolini*, pp. 156, 163ff, 178ff.

69 See the following chapters of this volume.

5   The Allies and the Spanish Civil War

Enrique Moradiellos

The origins and causes of the Civil War were internal to Spain: the severe social tensions and the violent political polarization that had arisen in the country within the context of a profound economic crisis. Nevertheless, the effective course and the final outcome of this internal conflict were significantly conditioned by the contemporary European context. The most obvious expression of this conditioning was the intervention (or non-intervention) in the Spanish war of various continental powers which provided (or denied) their help to one or other of the contenders. The internationalization process resulting from this foreign intervention gave the Spanish crisis a decisive importance in the diplomatic scene preceding the Second World War and led to a passionate debate which convulsed European and international public opinion of the time. It was no coincidence that for almost three years Spain became the bloody setting of a miniature and small-scale European civil war, a forewarning of the war that would break out in September 1939.

The rapid internationalization of the Spanish conflict gave rise to a system of support and inhibition whose effects were very unequal and disparate on either side. On the one hand, the insurgent army led by General Francisco Franco was able to rely at the beginning and during the rest of the conflict on the vital military and financial support of two great powers, Nazi Germany and Fascist Italy, as well as on important logistical support from Portugal led by Oliveira Salazar. On the other, the Republican government saw its efforts to acquire the necessary military assistance from France and Great Britain frustrated and was able to secure only the unavoidable but insufficient support of the Soviet Union.

This configuration of forces gave a decisive military advantage to the Francoist side and lethally damaged the defensive capacity of the Republican government. It also meant a diplomatic realignment of enormous importance for relations among the European powers at a critical juncture. On the one hand it reinforced the growing alliance between the two fascist regimes engaged in a violent revision of the continental *status quo*, and on the other, it confirmed the mutual lack of understanding between the Western democracies and the Soviet Union over how to face up to this shared danger. In fact, the Spanish Civil War would clearly reveal the very different perceptions of the European situation and its dangers held in the official circles of the Soviet Union and within the governments of the Franco-British entente. Over a period of almost three years, the prickly 'Spanish problem' would reveal the profound cleavage between the 'policy of collective security' as it was understood by Soviet diplomacy and the 'appeasement policy' as it was practised by the French and British governments.

The European and international context of the 1930s

The crisis of the European order which would be so vividly manifested from 1936 onwards originated in the frailty of the international relations system which had emerged after the narrow victory of the Allied coalition in November 1918. The symbol of this system was the League of Nations, the institution responsible for collective peace-keeping and security through regular intergovernmental consultations, mediation and economic or military sanctions against an 'aggressive' state. The profound economic crisis of late 1929 destroyed its precarious stability since it had engendered severe imbalances in inter-state relations and in the socio-political internal dynamics of various European and extra-European powers.[1]

The main threat to the dominant international order in inter-war Europe came from the new counter-revolutionary and totalitarian regimes imposed by Benito Mussolini in Italy (1922) and Adolf Hitler in Germany (1933). Along with their shared policies of iron social discipline, economic autarky and nationalist exaltation, both the Fascist and the Nazi dictatorships practised a belligerent foreign policy, revisionist in the territorial *status quo*, searching for a solution across their boundaries for the grave tensions and latent difficulties within their own.

In the Italian case, the pragmatism displayed by the Duce was accompanied by a notable programmatic coherence, the purpose of which was to convert Italy into a hegemonic power in the Mediterranean, reviving Imperial Rome's *Mare Nostrum*. Mussolini's cautious activities in Corfu, Albania and Libya during the 1920s were a prior step towards greater initiatives only conceivable were Italy to become a sufficient economic and military power and thereby ensure more propitious diplomatic support.[2] In the case of the Third Reich, the tactical opportunism of the Führer was also accompanied by a programme of German expansion in

gradual phases: (1) the recovery of full military capacity and of those territories lost by the Treaty of Versailles in 1919; (2) the transformation of
Germany into a hegemonic power in Central Europe, annexing or
neutralizing rivals such as Austria, Czechoslovakia or Poland; and (3) the
conquest of European Russia in order to become an impregnable continental power and a world power without parallel. This territorial
expansion would be accompanied by a process of biological purification
of the German and European populations involving the extermination of
those races considered inferior from the racist Nazi perspective.[3]

The revisionist plans of Fascist Italy and Nazi Germany were in direct
contrast to the interests and objectives of the two principal powers which
benefited from and guaranteed the *status quo* in Europe: the democratic
regimes of France and Great Britain. In both countries, the territorial
revisionism of the Nazis and Fascist imperial irredentism were perceived
with apprehension. For this reason, the Franco-British entente remained
unchanged during the entire inter-war period despite occasional tensions
which had led France to develop a complex system of bilateral alliances
with Poland, Czechoslovakia, Romania and Yugoslavia in order to prevent German aggression. Nevertheless, a hostile combination of both
dictatorships was considered very improbable because there was a clear
antagonism in their respective foreign policies. The German aim to
annex Austria and to achieve hegemony in the Balkans came up against
the Italian aspiration to guarantee Austrian independence (as a 'cushion
state' in the north) and to exercise a *de facto* protectorate over the
Balkans.[4]

On the other hand, the Franco-British fear of a problematic Italo-
German agreement was eclipsed by another fundamental concern in the
diplomatic arena of the period: the substitution of Russia by the Soviet
Union after the triumph of the Bolshevik Revolution in October 1917.
Through its social revolutionary and anti-capitalist nature as well as its
rising influence within the politics of other states through Communist
parties, the Soviet Union provoked strong reactions in the British and
French governing circles whether they were conservative, liberal, social
democratic or labour. In addition, these political circles were convinced
that the eruption of another European war would only serve to unleash
new social revolutions and extend communism, as had occurred in Russia
itself and in Central Europe between 1917 and 1920.

In the meantime, the iron dictatorship of Stalin had generated a
remarkable change in the direction of the Soviet Union's foreign policy
after the establishment in Germany of the Nazi regime and its declared
programme of anti-Communist expansion towards the East. Until this
moment and through the Comintern, the Soviet leaders had pushed for a

programme of global revolution that would bring the revolutionary regime out of its isolation and facilitate the difficult process of the 'construction of socialism within one country' through industrialization and agrarian collectivization. Once this hope had been destroyed, the acute realization of the Soviet Union's strategic vulnerability and military unpreparedness had been aggravated by the almost simultaneous emergence of a Japanese expansionist threat in East Asia and the German threat in Central Europe. The fear of a combined aggression on both of its remote and exposed frontiers with the possible complicity of the rest of the capitalist powers had forced Stalin to withdraw his support for a world revolution and search for a diplomatic and military understanding with the democratic powers to contain the German threat and avoid the nightmare of a coalition of capitalist states against the Soviet Union. This was the firm resolve of the new Soviet foreign policy, based upon the defence of collective security and the *status quo* embraced in 1934 with its accession to the League of Nations. It was necessarily accompanied by a new Communist strategy favouring the establishment of popular inter-class fronts defending democracy and opposing fascism. The most valued outcome of this new political orientation was the signing of a Franco-Soviet treaty in May 1935 which reflected strong French apprehension in the face of a revived German threat and prescribed mutual assistance by both powers in the case of third-party aggression.[5]

Within this unstable diplomatic context, the first blow to the precarious international system was Japan's occupation in 1931 of the Chinese province of Manchuria despite the protests and condemnation of the League of Nations. Two years later, Hitler showed his defiance by withdrawing Germany from the League of Nations and initiating an intense rearmament programme which openly violated the terms dictated by the Treaty of Versailles. In 1935, it was Mussolini's turn once again to breach the policy of collective security by violently occupying Abyssinia and resisting economic sanctions imposed by the League of Nations against Italy. Finally, in March 1936, Hitler seized the opportunity created by the division between Italy and the democratic powers generated by the crisis over Abyssinia and ordered the remilitarization of the Rhineland, the strategic province bordering France that had been demilitarized in 1919.

None of these revisionist acts, invariably carried out *manu militari*, had been contained effectively by either France or Britain, which continued to rely on the possibility of avoiding a new armed confrontation and of achieving a modification of Italian and German ambitions within the European and international arenas. Accordingly, British leaders, followed by the French authorities with varying degrees of enthusiasm, had initiated the so-called 'appeasement policy' towards the two dictatorships from the beginning of the crisis. This policy was essentially an emergency diplomatic strategy designed to avoid another war by means of explicit negotiation (or implicit acceptance) of reasonable changes within the territorial *status quo* (especially in all of Eastern Europe) which would substantially satisfy the Italo-German revisionists without endangering vital Franco-British interests.[6] One of the first indications of this policy had been the signing of an Anglo-German naval agreement in June 1935 which unilaterally condoned the Nazi military rearmament in return for the promise of strict limits in the size of its war fleet. The logic behind this agreement was exactly the opposite of that behind the Franco-Soviet agreement signed the previous month and revealed the progressive abandonment of collective security policy by the British in favour of a more pragmatic and realistic bilateral diplomacy.

The core of this appeasement policy was based upon the conviction that the two democracies did not possess sufficient military strength on the one hand or human or economic resources on the other to enter into a possible conflict with the three revisionist powers simultaneously. This was for a number of reasons. The first was the economic weakness of both countries as a result of the severe economic crisis, a weakness that had affected France much more than Britain, giving the latter a dominant position in the bilateral Franco-British alliance. Second, the French and British would be militarily vulnerable in the event of a simultaneous conflict with Japan in the Far East, Germany in Europe, and Italy in the Mediterranean. In fact, the First World War had demonstrated the intense difficulty of containing the German war effort on one front without allies. Third, the diplomatic situation of the 1930s was unfavourable. Unlike the 1914–18 period, Britain and France could not rely on the vital support of the United States (which had withdrawn into a position of complete isolationism), or of Russia (now a dangerous country because of its social doctrines, suspect political motives and uncertain military strength). The fourth and last reason was the political frailty of both states. The expectation of a military confrontation generated great opposition in the British and French public, whose pacifism sought to avoid wherever possible and at whatever cost another human bloodbath such as that of the Great War.

These strong reasons lay behind the belief that the appeasement policy was the most appropriate strategy to avoid a new European conflict and to seek the possibility of a realignment of Italian and German demands without resorting to total confrontation. Indeed, the Anglo-French response in view of the outbreak of the Spanish Civil War and its international implications would be at all times subordinated to the basic objectives of this policy of general appeasement. Equally, the Soviet reaction to the Spanish crisis would be within the parameters of its collective security policy and its search for Western allies to counter German expansionism.

The internationalization of the conflict: Republican failures and insurgent successes

In this international context, a powerful military insurrection against the Republican government began on 17 July 1936 in Spanish Morocco which would extend in the following days to the Peninsula, the Balearic Islands and the Canary Islands. This was the final act of a broad conspiracy, the formation of which had begun with the electoral victory of the Popular Front in February 1936. The generals who designed the operation had anticipated a simultaneous uprising of the armed forces in the entire country which would be able to secure the apparatus of the state without encountering too much resistance within a short period of time, as had happened on other occasions (most recently in 1923). Nevertheless, the political fragmentation of the armed forces themselves, the loyalty of broad sectors of the security forces and the navy, together with the decisive resistance of the organized urban proletariat, led to the failure of the uprising in the most populated, urban and industrialized areas of the country. This unexpected setback left the insurgents with the need militarily to conquer the area controlled by the Republican government while the latter set about preparing for defence despite the serious social and institutional damage of its defensive capabilities due to the vast defection of its armed and security forces. Essentially, the partial failure of the military uprising made civil war inevitable.[7]

Both sides instantly realized that the material means and military equipment necessary to sustain a considerable and prolonged war did not exist or were not available in Spain. For this reason, on 19 July 1936, both the leader of the new Republican government, José Giral, and General Francisco Franco, commander of the forces which had participated in the uprising in Morocco, sought aid from the European powers from which they could expect some aid and support. The Republic secretly requested that France, where a government similar to that of the Popular Front had risen to power under the leadership of the Socialist Léon Blum, send aeroplanes and ammunition to crush the uprising. General Franco sent his personal emissaries to Rome and Berlin to request aircraft and arms to transport his experienced troops to Seville, thereby enabling them to begin the march on Madrid, whose conquest was necessary to secure international recognition. The simultaneous requests for foreign aid formulated by both sides indicated the explicit recognition of the international dimension of the Spanish conflict and a deliberate attempt to plunge it into the severe tensions which fragmented Europe in the 1930s. In effect, both requests, in the critical context of the summer of 1936, would initiate a rapid process of the internationalization of the Civil War that would have very different results for the insurgent armed forces and for the Republican authorities respectively.[8]

Shortly after the wave of strikes which had preceded the electoral victory of the Popular Front in France, Blum decided on 21 July secretly to accept the Republican request for support after consulting with his government coalition partners, the Radical party ministers Édouard Daladier (War) and Yvon Delbos (Foreign Affairs). Sound political and strategic reasons independent of ideological preference lay behind this measure. The Spanish Republic was led by a recognized and friendly government, whose indulgence and collaboration would be vital in the event of a European war so that peace on the Pyrenees border could be ensured as well as free circulation (commercial and military) between France and its vital North African colonies (where a third of the French army was stationed). Nevertheless, immediately following the news of this decision, leaked by a Francoist agent in the Spanish embassy in Paris, French public opinion and political circles became deeply divided over the issue.[9] The left as a whole, both Socialists and Communists as well as sectors of the Radical party, approved the measure. The right, Catholic public opinion, and broad sectors of the state and military administration, on the other hand, vociferously rejected the sending of aid and proposed neutrality for two reasons: the hostility towards the revolutionary characteristics they perceived among supporters of the Spanish government and the fear that French aid would unleash a European war. Even the President of the French Republic crudely advised Blum that 'What is being planned, this delivery of arms to Spain, may mean war or revolution in France.'[10] In addition to this fierce internal opposition, which soon swayed influential radical ministers (particularly Daladier and Delbos), Blum was also confronted with another equally firm and decisive opposition: the position of strict neutrality adopted from the beginning by the British government, its vital and indispensable ally in Europe.

Indeed, for the Conservative-dominated British cabinet, in power since 1931 and led by Stanley Baldwin, the Spanish war was seen above all as a serious obstacle to its appeasement policy and the potential source of a new European war. In addition, on the basis of the Spanish situation during the first six months of 1936 and the news about what was happening on the Republican rearguard, British leaders were convinced that within Spain, under the helpless gaze of the Republican government, a conflict was evolving between a counter-revolutionary army and abominable Republican militia dominated by militant communists and anarchists.[11] This was the warning repeatedly made by British diplomatic and consular representatives: 'The fact about Spain was that no government existed today. There were military forces in operation on the one hand, opposed by a virtual Soviet on the other' (telephone call by the Commercial Attaché on 21 July); 'If the government are successful in suppressing the military rebellion, Spain will be plunged into the chaos of some form of Bolshevism' (dispatch of the Consul in Barcelona on 29 July). This dual concern was evident in the only political directive given by Baldwin to his Foreign Secretary, Anthony Eden, on 26 July 1936: 'On no account, French or other, must [you] bring us into the fight on the side of the Russians.'[12]

On the basis of this dual concern and in order to guarantee the security of the naval base of Gibraltar (of key strategic importance in the imperial route to India) and the substantial British economic interests in Spain (40 per cent of total foreign investments in Spain were British), the Baldwin government immediately resolved to adopt strictly neutrality between the two contending sides. This neutrality signified the imposition of an embargo of all arms and munitions to Spain, thus reducing to the same level in one key aspect the legally recognized government (which retained the sole legal capacity to import this *matériel*) and the military insurgents. This was therefore benevolent neutrality towards the insurgent faction and notorious malevolence towards the Republican government. The private comments of the First Lord of the Admiralty clearly indicated the differential character of this policy:

> For the present it seems clear that we should continue our existing policy of neutrality. . . . When I speak of 'neutrality' I mean strict neutrality, that is to say, a situation in which the Russians neither officially or unofficially give help to the Communists. On no account must we do anything to bolster up Communism in Spain, particularly when it is remembered that Communism in Portugal, to which it would probably spread and particularly to Lisbon, would be a great danger to the British Empire.[13]

The situation created by the profound internal cleavage in France and by the uncompromisingly neutral British position deeply worried the French government and led it to overturn its initial decision to provide aid to the Republic. On 25 July 1936, following an intense debate in the cabinet, Léon Blum announced the decision not to intervene in the Spanish conflict and the cancellation of any shipment of arms and munitions. The French leaders believed that in this way they could contribute to appeasing the domestic situation, reinforcing their alliance with Britain, and confining the conflict to Spain to avoid the threat of its transformation into a European war. Nevertheless, the French retraction did nothing to prevent the rapid internationalization of the conflict.

The first appeals for aid sent by the insurgents to Germany and Italy had not obtained an immediate positive response. On 25 July, however, after receiving two personal emissaries sent by Franco from Morocco, Hitler decided to send secretly 20 transport planes and 6 fighter-planes with their crew and technical personnel.[14] Two days later, following repeated appeals for help conveyed by Franco through the Italian consul in Tangier, Mussolini also decided to secretly send 12 transport planes.[15] With the help of this equipment, Franco was able to transport troops to Seville from 29 July, thereby evading the naval blockade imposed in the Straits of Gibraltar by the Republican navy, and begin the march on Madrid.

The decision of both dictators to intervene in support of Franco (decisions taken without mutual consultation) lay in very similar political and strategic considerations. Above all, if the dispatch of modest and covert aid favoured the triumph of the military insurrection, this would allow for a low-cost and low-risk adjustment of the balance of forces in the Western Mediterranean, depriving France of a dependable ally on her southern flank and ensuring an allied or at the very least neutral regime in the Iberian Peninsula. In addition, in view of French retraction and British inhibition, both Hitler and Mussolini appreciated the opportunity to reassure both governments with the pretext that, with no ulterior motive, they were providing disinterested support to an anti-communist counter-revolution. The unexpected prolongation of the war and the quantitative increase of Italo-German support to Franco would reinforce these first motives with other, secondary reasons: the German aims of ensuring the supply of Spanish steel and pyrites (essential to Germany's accelerated rearmament programme), of transforming the Spanish war into a military laboratory where Germany's armed forces could try out techniques and acquire war experience for future use, of orchestrating the conflict to accentuate the differences between the French and British governments and public opinion within both countries, etc. Towards the end of December 1936, the German ambassador in Rome accurately outlined these priorities and justified the agreement that Italy should take precedence in the policy of aid to the Spanish insurgents, in a confidential memorandum sent to his superiors:

The interests of Germany and Italy in the Spanish troubles coincide to the extent that both countries are seeking to prevent a victory of Bolshevism in Spain or Catalonia. However, while Germany is not pursuing any immediate diplomatic interests in Spain beyond this, the efforts of Rome undoubtedly extend towards having Spain fall in line with its Mediterranean policy, or at least towards preventing political co-operation between Spain on the one hand and France and/or England on the other. . . . We must deem it desirable if there is created south of France a factor which, freed from Bolshevism and removed from the hegemony of the Western powers but on the other hand allied with Italy, makes the French and British stop to think – a factor opposing the transit of French troops from Africa and one which in the economic field takes our needs fully into consideration.[16]

The origin and significance of the policy of non-intervention

The beginning of the Italo-German intervention in favour of Franco (immediately discovered because two of the planes sent by Italy accidentally landed in French Algeria on 30 July) forced the French government to reconsider its decision not to intervene in support of the Republic. Nevertheless, the deep internal division within the country and the total opposition of its British ally prevented the adoption of any effective measure that would favour the Republicans. Faced with this situation, following a fierce discussion in the cabinet and establishing as a minimum objective the isolation of the Spanish war, the French government proposed on 1 August 1936 that the main European powers subscribe to an Agreement of Non-Intervention in Spain and prohibit the sale, shipment or transfer of arms and munitions intended for either side. Essentially, the French authorities endeavoured, in the words of Blum's *chef de cabinet* 'to prevent others from doing what we were incapable of accomplishing'.[17] Since they were incapable of assisting the Republic, the French authorities were at the very least attempting to ensure that Italy and Germany should not support the rebels. A year later, Louis de Brouckère, president of the Socialist International and a close collaborator of Blum, confessed to the President of the Republic, Manuel Azaña, that it was impossible to adopt any other policy, as the latter noted revealingly in his diary:

Last year, on his return from Spain [De Brouckère had visited the country in early August 1936], he arrived in Paris when the non-intervention policy was implemented. He spoke about the matter with Blum one afternoon. Blum was unable to take any other course. If he had given arms to Spain, the civil war in France would have erupted soon after. Blum told him that he did not have the security of the armed forces. The General Staff was opposed to supporting Spain. Opinion would have turned against Blum, accusing him of answering to Moscow. England would not have supported him in case of a foreign conflict. De Brouckère speaks of a 'fear of England' as one of the motives for the particular policy.[18]

The French proposal to secure a non-intervention pact and a collective arms embargo was immediately taken on board by the British authorities, who saw in this an ideal mechanism to maintain their neutrality and to mitigate the criticism of a Labour Opposition which stood by the Republic (it was fortunate that the initiative originated from the Socialist Blum).[19] In addition, the proposal would equally guarantee three basic diplomatic objectives established by the Foreign Office in the Spanish crisis: confine the conflict to Spain and, at the same time, restrain Britain's French ally's support for the Republic; avoid alignment with the Soviet Union in Spain; and evade a confrontation with Italy and Germany for their support for Franco. Hence, for the British authorities, the multilateral policy of non-intervention contained a hint of deceptiveness, in that its real end was not the one declared (the avoidance of foreign participation in the war) but rather the safeguarding of those established objectives by its mere existence and apparent efficacy. That is to say, it was 'the best if not the only means' to carry out a policy, as drawn up by Winston Churchill in the following terms in a private letter to Eden on 7 August:

> This Spanish business cuts across my thoughts. It seems to me most important to make Blum stay with us strictly neutral, even if Germany and Italy continue to back the rebels and Russia sends money to the Government. If the French government takes sides against the rebels it will be a god-send to the Germans and pro-Germans.[20]

In these circumstances, the tenacious Franco-British diplomatic effort enabled all European states (with the exception of Switzerland, neutral by constitutional decree) towards the end of August 1936 to subscribe officially to the Agreement of Non-Intervention in Spain. In addition, these countries agreed to form part of a committee, based in London and composed of their respective diplomatic representatives in the capital, charged with overseeing the application of this agreement of the collective arms embargo. From the very beginning, however, the triumph of this multilateral non-intervention policy sponsored by France and Britain was more apparent than real. Italy, Germany and the Salazar dictatorship in Portugal, the three states that had been the most sympathetic towards the insurgents, had consented to sign the agreement to ease international tension and not provoke a forceful Franco-British reaction. However, they had no intention of respecting the compromise, and in fact Italy and Germany continued to send Franco arms and ammunition while Portugal continued to provide him with vital logistical and diplomatic support.[21] In addition, while Rome and Berlin subscribed to the Non-Intervention Pact, they also began to coordinate their military activities in Spain in a way that would lead to the formal establishment in October of that year of their diplomatic alliance, the so-called 'Rome–Berlin Axis'. Consequently, the continual Italo-German sabotage, along with the weakness of the Franco-British response, dictated the clear failure of the non-intervention policy in Spain from the very beginning.

In effect, during September 1936, while the first discussions were taking place in the Non-Intervention Committee, the process of the internationalization of the war had led to a support network which favoured the insurgents' war effort and damaged the Republican government's defensive capacities. On one hand, General Franco's side had succeeded in preserving the vital passage of military supplies from Italy and Germany (granted, moreover, by credit) and the logistical support of Portugal, despite the principles of the agreement and the presence of representatives from these countries in the London Committee. On the other hand, the Republican authorities had seen their military supplies from France, Britain and other states cut off as a result of their respective governments' strict adherence to the pact. Since this policy had been seconded by the Democratic administration of President Roosevelt in the United States by means of the establishment of a unilateral arms embargo, the Republic could count only on the open but limited support of Mexico and the dubious opportunities offered by the shadowy world of arms dealers.[22]

The crystallization of such an asymmetrical structure of international support and inhibition in the autumn of 1936 was reflected immediately in the course of the Spanish conflict with the insurgent military triumphs and resounding Republican defeats during the months of September and October 1936. As a result, on 5 September, with the rebels' conquest of Irún and occupation of the entire border between the Basque Country and France, the narrow and isolated Republican pocket in the north had been completely cut off from the rest of the area still loyal to the government. For their part, the troops of General Franco on the central front liberated the fortress of the Toledo Alcázar on 28 September, clearing the way for a frontal and arguably definitive assault on Madrid.

The Soviet shift and its implications

In her support for the Franco-British initiative, the Soviet Union had also subscribed to the non-intervention treaty and had joined the supervision committee in London without delay.[23] Soviet leaders had perceived the outbreak of war as a serious and untimely disturbance since the revolutionary threats unleashed in the Republican zone could ruin its efforts at *rapprochement* with France and Britain and could even strengthen the links of these powers with the Fascist dictatorships because of a shared fear of the threat of a new revolution in Europe. For this reason, Stalin had decided to distance himself from the conflict, proclaiming Soviet 'platonic sympathy' for the Republican cause and allowing funds to be collected for humanitarian aid (food, clothes and medicines), but without intervening in its favour by supplying arms or munitions. As the Italian representative in Moscow accurately described the situation at the beginning of the war, 'In no circumstances would the Soviet Government get itself mixed up in the internal events of the Peninsula where it has everything to lose and nothing to gain.' In addition, Stalin, like the French leaders, had also relied on the possibility of localizing the war and avoiding the threat of rebel triumph by the cancellation of all foreign supplies. As the same diplomat stated soon thereafter, 'French initiative for a non-intervention agreement on Spain has thus been received with intense relief.'[24]

Nevertheless, the initial Soviet position would progressively be modified from the end of August 1936 once it was clear that the non-intervention policy had failed in practice to stop the Italo-German aid to Franco. The first step in this gradual shift was the establishment of diplomatic relations with the Republic: on 31 August the Soviet ambassador, Marcel Rozenberg, presented his diplomatic credentials, arriving in Madrid accompanied by numerous military advisers. The process was accelerated with the establishment at the beginning of September of a new Popular Front government led by Francisco Largo Caballero, leader of the Socialist left, and in which two Communist leaders had been included. Finally, towards the beginning of October, at a critical moment in the war, the Soviet Union began to give military support to the Republic without officially abandoning the non-intervention policy, thereby following the steps of the Axis powers.

The motives for this shift were essentially both political and strategic. Everything seems to indicate that Stalin had decided to confront the Fascist powers in Spain to avoid the deterioration of the strategic position of his reluctant French ally and to put to the test the viability of his strategy of collaboration with the European powers in face of the Nazi expansionist threat. Spain would have to be the touchstone of this great anti-fascist coalition project: the arena where the willingness or reluctance of the democracies to collaborate with the Soviet Union in the containment of German aggressive plans would be tested. The British ambassador in Moscow had understood from the beginning this omnipresent strategic concern in Soviet calculations. In his judgement, the 'correct and neutral attitude' of the Kremlin would have persisted, 'but for the growing weight of evidence that the two principal "Fascist" States were actively assisting the insurgents'. He also underlined what he saw as 'the kernel of the Soviet Government problem' by suggesting that 'Spain and the world revolution can wait; meanwhile, any danger to France is a danger to the Soviet Union'.[25] The Republican ambassador in Moscow, Marcelino Pascua, was repeatedly informed by Stalin himself of the temporary nature of Soviet aid (awaiting Franco-British support) and the insuperable limitations placed on the aid (the possible confrontation with the Franco-British bloc and the eruption of a general war). Pascua would tell the President of the Republic, Manuel Azaña, in the summer of 1937 that:

> [Stalin] repeats categorically that here [in Moscow] they are not pursing any specific political objective. According to them, Spain is not inclined towards communism, nor prepared to adopt it and even less prepared to impose it, and even if it did adopt or impose it, it would never last, given that it is surrounded by hostile and bourgeois nations. They propose to prevent the weakening of power and the military situation in France by opposing the triumph of Italy and Germany. . . . The Russian government has a fundamental interest in maintaining peace. It knows full well that the war would gravely endanger the communist regime. It still needs years to consolidate. Even in the military sphere, they are far from having achieved their objectives. They barely have a fleet and they are proposing to construct one. The territorial army is numerous, disciplined and seems to be well trained. But it lacks all kinds of matériel. . . . Considerable concern not to clash with England.[26]

In these circumstances, the Soviet authorities decided to establish two parallel means of facilitating Republican resistance to what seemed to be the uncontainable military advance of Franco's troops, at least until the hypothetical Franco-British support arrived, by means of: (1) the formation of the International Brigades; and (2) the direct consignment of Soviet war *matériel*.

From the end of September 1936, Communist parties around the world (under the leadership of the Comintern and with Moscow's prior authorization) had initiated the recruitment of volunteers to fight on the Republican side in Spain. Owing to the enormous impact of the war on international anti-fascist public opinion, the campaign enjoyed a resounding and immediate success. Towards the middle of October, the first troops arrived at the Spanish base in Albacete and on 8 November, in the midst of the battle for Madrid, the first of the International Brigades went into battle (the IX Brigade, made up of approximately 1,900 men, the majority Germans). A total of between 35,000 and 60,000 volunteers (the lack of central archives makes the calculation of a precise figure difficult), originating from more than fifty countries from all continents, fought in the International Brigades on the Republican side. Working-class volunteers predominated among them, although there were many volunteers from the middle classes and intellectual circles. The International Brigades would fight as shock-troops in almost all of the great battles of the war until September 1938, when the Republican government, led by Dr Juan Negrín, decided on their unilateral evacuation in a vain attempt to force the Francoist side to imitate this measure. Their contribution to the Republicans' capacity to resist was essential not so much for their military value as the example of international solidarity which they demonstrated and the model of discipline they offered to the Republican forces being trained.[27]

The first shipment of war materials sent from the Soviet Union was received in the harbour of Cartagena on 4 October 1936. From then on and until the end of the war, the Soviet supply of planes, tanks, machine guns and artillery did not cease to flow into Republican Spain, albeit intermittently, and depending on the facilities or obstacles encountered in Mediterranean maritime routes and on the French border with Republican Catalonia. Along with war *matériel*, the Soviets also sent a group of approximately 2,000 military advisers and experts to Spain, who tried to help the creation of the Popular Army of the Republic and who would be discreetly withdrawn in the summer of 1938. There is no doubt that the Soviet military aid signified a vital strengthening of Republican defensive capabilities. Indeed, it would be the essential contribution of war *matériel* to the Republic throughout the war, greatly exceeding the amount received from France or elsewhere. According to reliable calculations, of the total number of aircraft imported by the

Republic during the war (between 1,124 and 1,272 planes), approximately 60 per cent came from the Soviet Union (between 680 and 757, all of which were military aircraft), 20 per cent from France (between 237 and 287, of which only 60 to 69 were military) and 4 per cent from Czechoslovakia (between 43 and 53, all of which were military).[28]

Just as the Italo-German aid towards the end of July 1936 had saved the insurgents from a critical situation (since this allowed them to transport troops from Africa to the Peninsula and initiate the march on Madrid), Soviet aid also contributed decisively to the unexpected Republican resistance in Madrid in November 1936 (preventing the expected final defeat of the Republic at this critical juncture).

The link between the Republic and the Soviet Union was strengthened in October 1936 with the controversial decision of the Republican government to deposit in Moscow three-quarters of the Bank of Spain's total gold reserves (totalling approximately 635 tons of fine gold). The Bank of Spain had been mobilized from the beginning to meet the costs incurred over the purchase of various arms and supplies abroad. The reasons for these measures varied: to guarantee the security of the reserves against possible enemy attack within the country and against its legal actions in foreign banks; to put a stop to acts of sabotage and boycott against Republican financial transactions in Western banks; and to ensure the availability and convertibility of funds confidentially and efficiently thanks to the Soviet banking system.

According to the detailed studies of Professor Angel Viñas, a total of some 510 tons of composite gold was sent to Moscow and was used as credit towards the purchase of military supplies for the Republic from the Soviet Union and other European states. The funds generated by the sale of the gold (approximately US$518 million) were spent in their entirety on the purchase of war *matériel* and payment for various services (imports of food, petrol, medicine, etc.). Thus the myth disseminated by Francoist propaganda about the 'Moscow gold' stolen by the Republicans and given to Stalin without compensation must be refuted. The same use was found for a small quantity of gold reserves (totalling one quarter; that is, 174 tons of fine gold) which was sold to the Bank of France and the exchange value of which (approximately US$195 million) helped to finance supplies from this country. For obvious political reasons, the same degree of propaganda and accusation was not employed concerning 'French gold'.[29]

The military and financial support of the Soviet Union to the Republic from October 1936 had two distinct but equally negative consequences for her global diplomatic objectives. On the one hand, Soviet intervention on the opposite end of the European continent deeply accentuated the apprehension and distrust of the French and British governments towards the Soviet Union's true intentions. On the other hand, it served as an ideal pretext to justify the quantitative and qualitative increase of support given by the Axis powers to General Franco (the former officially recognizing the Francoist government as the *de jure* government of Spain on 18 November 1936 while the frontal offensive on Madrid was taking place). Within this process of the escalation of German and Italian military, diplomatic and financial support, the collective non-intervention policy sponsored by France and Britain failed outright.

British government circles, to a greater degree than their French counterparts, had always suspected that the Soviet policy of supporting the collective security concealed less honourable intentions. They had therefore observed the signing of the Franco-Soviet pact in 1935 with trepidation and had refused to echo calls in favour of a great anti-Nazi alliance. One month before the outbreak of the Spanish Civil War, an influential analyst in the Foreign Office had noted on this issue that:

> I am quite prepared to believe that M. Litvinov [Soviet Commissar for Foreign Affairs] wishes for the sake of his immediate policy that France should be strong and anti-German at this moment. But the Third International may well be still pursuing the old and fundamental Bolshevist policy, which is to sow trouble in Europe generally in the hope of being able to reap a harvest of communism.[30]

The rapid ideological polarization caused in Europe by the Civil War had revived these latent fears in both London and Paris, which reached their maximum degree of intensity with the Soviet decision to support the Republic militarily. The British interpretation of this measure, similar to the French interpretation, was expressed in a memorandum written towards the end of October 1936 by Sir Robert Vansittart, Permanent Under-Secretary at the Foreign Office:

> It would seem that the Russians were prepared to go to the limit. Without going quite so far, I think they are probably prepared to go to great lengths, and this letter illustrates again this point, on which I have so often dwelt of late, that the urge to world revolution must be much stronger in Russia than anybody has believed in the last two or three years; so strong in fact that not even Stalin can stand against it. It is rather a surprising development seeing that the growth of the German danger in Europe had, since 1933, been until this summer steadily tending to cause Russia to make friends so far as possible with the western democracies and to go slower on the

revolutionary doctrines. Not only has the slowing down been changed, but an enormously increased tempo has been adopted.[31]

The result of this interpretation of Soviet action was to reassert the desire, in the British and French governments, not to become involved in the Spanish conflict and to preserve a multilateral non-intervention policy as the only way to avoid the feared general war. Faced with this firm attitude, the explanations given on the matter by the Soviet ambassadors in London and Paris proved useless. On 3 November, the Soviet ambassador in London offered Eden 'an exposition of the motives which had actuated the Soviet Government in the Spanish Conflict':

> The Soviet Government's admitted sympathy with the Government in Spain was not due to their desire to set up a Communist regime in that country. . . . And the Soviet Government's purpose in attempting to assist the Spanish Government was far more immediate. . . . The Soviet Government were convinced that if General Franco were to win the encouragement given to Germany and Italy would be such as to bring nearer the day when another active aggression would be committed – this time perhaps in Central or Eastern Europe. That was a state of affairs that Russia wished at all costs to avoid and that was her main reason for wishing the Spanish Government to win in this civil strife.[32]

Taking advantage of this auspicious situation, the Axis powers decided to respond to Soviet intervention by substantially increasing the material support given to Franco. In November 1936, Hitler decided to send an exclusively German military unit to Spain, the Condor Legion, which had at its disposal approximately 100 planes and a total of 5,000 men which rotated periodically. In total, approximately 19,000 German soldiers would fight in the Francoist rank and file, participating as an independent unit in almost all the operations carried out throughout the course of the war. Mussolini for his part reinforced Italy's military presence by sending Franco a veritable expeditionary army between December 1936 and January 1937. The *Corpo Truppe Volontarie* grouped together 40,000 Italian soldiers on a permanent basis and its total number increased throughout the war to 73,000 men (79,000 if one includes the Italian air force contingent).

Thus between October 1936 and February 1937 a fundamental change took place in the international arena of the Spanish war. The Soviet commitment to the Republic and the escalation of the Axis powers' support to General Franco marked the climax of the long-drawn-out process of internationalization of the Civil War. From February 1937 onwards, the framework of military and diplomatic support for each side became clearly established and remained intact until the end of the war. On the one hand, the Francoist side could continue to rely on the vital support of Fascist Italy, Nazi Germany and (to a lesser extent) Salazar's Portugal. For its part, the Republic was essentially supported by the Soviet Union and received some covert, hesitant and intermittent aid from France, which would be described by Blum as 'relaxed non-intervention' (occasional surreptitious provision of small quantities of arms to the Republic and a blind eye to the transit of foreign arms supplies across the Franco-Spanish border). Meanwhile, the rest of the European states, led by Britain, continued to adhere to the Non-Intervention Treaty and strictly respected the arms and munitions embargo.

A victory in stages and a defeat in instalments

Following a British initiative and French agreement, throughout the first half of 1937 the Non-Intervention Committee made various efforts to halt the dangerous escalation of massive intervention by imposing a difficult naval and terrestrial control of the Spanish borders. Its objective was to make the containment of the Civil War implicit in the agreement an effective reality, preventing the arrival of foreign war *matériel* by land or sea, at least where it was on a grand scale and without camouflage (the possibility of air control was ruled out from the beginning because of its technical unfeasibility). To this end, from March to June 1937, the Spanish coasts were patrolled by the fleets of four of the signatory countries of the agreement (France, Britain, Germany and Italy) which possessed the right to detain and register European mercantile ships bound for Spanish ports. Similarly, international observers and inspectors had been deployed to various parts of the Spanish borders with French and Portugal with the same purposes *vis-à-vis* terrestrial circulation. The British government, the driving force behind the measure, was aware from the beginning of the relative uselessness of the measure if it could not rely on the loyal collaboration of the interventionist powers. A confidential memorandum drafted by British military intelligence at the beginning of May 1937 had pointed out that:

> The Non Intervention Committee's Supervision Scheme came into force on 20th April, 1937. It may deter mass movement but it is unlikely to prevent the steady infiltration of arms and volunteers (e.g. technical personnel) into Spain. It does not cover movement by air, or in Spanish or American vessels, or to Portuguese ports. It is

therefore not surprising to find, since 20th April, aircraft flown to Spain, normal arms traffic continuing in Spanish and 'Panamanian' ships, and an apparent increase in the movement of disguised consignments to Lisbon. In any case, the supervision staff have no power of control, only of observation.[33]

Nevertheless, from the crucial summer of 1937, even these timid efforts at control were abandoned by the Italo-German withdrawal of the maritime patrol in June and their demands for the recognition of General Franco's rights of belligerence. Despite Soviet protests, the predictable Franco-British retreat was manifested in their common acceptance of the end of the system of controls and simultaneous insistence that the Non-Intervention Committee should remain in place. Henceforth, the idea of the restoration of the control, combined with the supervised withdrawal of foreign troops and the recognition of the belligerent rights of the insurgents, would remain as a mere theoretical possibility and pretext to justify the application of the agreement and the existence of the committee. The non-intervention policy had essentially become an institutionalized and mutually accepted farce. The German and Italian authorities understood this well during the summer crisis and attempted to adjust their military and diplomatic support to Franco without exceeding the established formal limits to what they perceived as being tacit British tolerance. As Germany's influential ambassador in London and the Committee's German delegate, Joachim von Ribbentrop, wrote to Hitler in July 1937:

> No serious complications for the general European situation are to be expected from the present tension in non-intervention policy. England desires peace, as does France also; in spite of the sharp line followed at present, neither of them will push things to the limit. We can continue to count on this as an absolutely certain factor and can make our future decisions without being influenced or disturbed. [. . .] The British will try in the next few days, covertly or through calling a new session of the subcommittee [of Non-Intervention] to find a compromise solution.[34]

From the crisis of summer 1937, the delicate balance of military force between the two Spanish sides began to swing towards General Franco and against the Republic. The main reason for this process was the strong renewal of military support to the nationalist side by the Axis powers, to a degree that could not be met by the Soviet military shipments or arms contraband from elsewhere.

At the time, the Soviet Union was not a great military power and her shipments of war *matériel* encountered various logistical obstacles in reaching Republican territory. Above all, the distance between the two required a long and costly transport by sea. The voyage across the Mediterranean from Crimea was threatened by the blockade of the Francoist navy and the support of the Italian fleet to the blockade from its strategic bases in Sicily. On the other hand, the crossing from the Soviet Arctic through the Atlantic required the unloading of the *matérial* in France and waiting for the unpredictable decisions of the authorities to allow or prohibit the transfer through the Pyrenees border to Republican Catalonia. In both cases, the uncertainty and irregularity in the shipments seriously affected Republican military planning. In clear contrast to the Soviet difficulties, shipments of war *matériel* from Italy and Germany were much easier to import in geographical terms and could be more constant and regular, and suited to Franco's needs. In these conditions, the Francoist diplomatic strategy emphasized the preservation of the existing international network. To win his localized war, Franco needed the continued rejection of the Republic by the democratic powers without the undermining of his own ability to receive Italian and German support. As a high-ranking Francoist diplomat would subsequently recognize:

> Our principal and almost exclusive task had to be to localize the war in Spanish territory, avoiding in this way by all means an international war out of which we would have little to gain and much to lose. At the same time, however, we had to ensure that we would still be able to obtain the aid we needed from our foreign friends while ensuring at all costs that our enemy received no aid or at least that this aid was minimized.[35]

The new government led by the Socialist Dr Negrín from May 1937 tried to hold back the gradual disintegration of the Republican military situation. Alongside his domestic policy of eliminating revolutionary remnants and strengthening state power, Negrín's efforts in foreign policy aimed at securing the support of Western democracies and ending the non-intervention policy, which was being applied only against the Republic and was highly damaging to its war effort. Until this objective was achieved, Soviet military support continued to be a 'lifeline to a drowning man', something which had allowed it to resist temporarily and avoid total defeat. This is what the Republican head of government would privately and bitterly confess at the end of 1937:

Germany, Italy and Portugal will brazenly continue to help Franco and the Republic will last as long as the Russians want us to last, since our defence depends on the armaments they send us. Only if the inevitable encounter of Germany with Russia and the Western powers occurs, would we have the possibility of winning. If this does not occur, we will only be able to fight to achieve an honourable peace.[36]

Nevertheless, Negrín's tireless efforts to secure the support of the democracies proved fruitless because both Britain and France continued to maintain the facade of the non-intervention policy as the best means of confining the Spanish conflict, avoiding its transformation into a European war, and limiting its negative effects on the appeasement policy. In July 1937, the French Foreign Minister, Yvon Delbos, confessed to the American ambassador in Paris that France's position was subordinated to that of the British and the 'Spanish problem' to that of the appeasement policy:

In so far as he could foresee the future the position that France would take would depend entirely on the position of England. France would not undertake alone to fight Germany and Italy. The position of France would be the same as her position in the Spanish affair. If England should wish to stand firmly by the side of France against Germany and Italy, France would act. If England should continue to hold aloof France could not act. France would never be caught in the position of having the Soviet Union as her only ally. [. . .] The British in his opinion would like to see Franco win provided they could feel sure his victory would not mean Fascist domination of the Mediterranean. They were trying to get sufficient assurances from Mussolini and Franco to convince themselves that Franco's victory would not mean loss of their route through the Mediterranean.[37]

The British leaders, with French support, only once showed firmness: in September 1937, when the indiscriminate attacks of Italian planes and submarines on merchant ships trading with the Republic had gone beyond acceptable limits, spreading throughout the Mediterranean basin and endangering international navigation through these waters. It was no coincidence that between 6 August and 2 September, 30 merchant ships of various nationalities (11 British, 6 Republican, 3 Russian, 3 French, etc.) had been attacked and often sunk without prior warning. Through a Franco-British initiative and with Soviet support, a conference of Mediterranean and Black Sea powers then took place in Nyon (near Geneva) with the purpose of guaranteeing free trade in the area and ending the attacks of 'pirate submarines' (a euphemism used to avoid a direct accusation against the Italian fleet). With the Republic excluded and in the absence of Italy (which refused to participate), the Nyon conference entrusted to the powerful British navy and the French navy the task of watching over the commercial routes of the Mediterranean, with the authority to sink any submarine or vessel that attacked international merchant traffic.[38]

The energetic Franco-British response in Nyon, supported by all Mediterranean states, put precise limits to the Italian support of Franco, something which Mussolini subsequently understood and respected. Thereafter, the Spanish war was transformed into a stable and marginalized arena of continental political tension. Nevertheless, European and international attention and concern began to focus on the growing problems generated by German expansion in Central Europe.

On 12 March 1938, Hitler proceeded to annex Austria to the Third Reich, without a military response from the democratic powers and with Italian consent (the Duce had agreed to cede Austria to the Führer in exchange for his support for Italian hegemony in the Mediterranean). The only response to the Nazis' action was the establishment in Paris of a new Popular Front government led by Blum which seemed to be prepared to reconsider its Spanish policy and provide direct support to the Republic. Nevertheless, in the meeting of the *Comité Permanent de la Défense Nationale* of 15 March, Blum's proposal clashed with the opposition of the General Chiefs of Staff and the War Minister: 'intervention in Spain will unleash a general war' and 'England would distance itself from us if we abandon Non-Intervention'. As a result, the only measure taken by Blum consisted of a *de facto* opening of the French border with Catalonia to allow for the free passage of Soviet war *matériel* and other supplies bound for the Republic.[39] With the closure of the Mediterranean maritime passage by the Francoist naval blockade with Italian support, this terrestrial route became the only safe channel for war imports for the besieged Republic and would remain open until June 1938. The secret decision by the French government allowed for the entry through Catalonia of enough military supplies to deter the great offensive staged by Franco at the beginning of March on the eastern front which had divided Republican-controlled territory into two by the middle of April 1938.

Nevertheless, strong pressure from the British cabinet succeeded in appeasing the fears of the new French government led by Daladier (formed in April without Socialist participation) and it agreed once again to close the Pyrenees border on 13 June 1938. The British leadership had decided some time previously that, for various reasons, Franco's victory would not pose a serious political or strategic problem for the Franco-British entente. The first reason was that the human exhaustion and the material destruction caused by the devastating Civil War would make it impossible for Franco to participate in a European conflict even if he wished to do so. Second, the Francoist government would need to resort to British credit and capital to finance the process of post-war economic reconstruction in Spain. Finally, the Franco-British naval power was so superior and Spanish military vulnerability so evident that this would be sufficient to dissuade a military man like Franco from engaging in any provocative or hostile action. Next to these factors that militated against the fear of a Francoist victory, the continuation of the Spanish Civil War, in the opinion of the British authorities, was very dangerous in that it divided democratic public opinion at home and hindered efforts to separate Italy from Germany and weaken the latter in its objectives in Czechoslovakia and Central Europe. In short, from May 1937 the Conservative British government led by Neville Chamberlain believed that the Spanish Republic could be sacrificed without excessive danger, to the benefit of Italian cooperation in Europe and the preservation of continental peace.

Indeed, from the moment that the French border was closed, the Republic saw its last vital channels of foreign military supplies cut off. The *coup de grâce* that destroyed its hopes of receiving support from the democracies occurred during the severe crisis of September 1938 caused by Hitler's pressure on Czechoslovakia to cede the Sudetenland. During this critical month, the risk of war erupting between Germany and the Western powers (France was the guarantor of Czech integrity, as was the Soviet Union) seemed so evident that Franco himself was forced to adopt an extreme measure with undisguised regret. On September 27, after informing Rome and Berlin, he officially communicated to the British and French governments his decision to remain neutral in the event of a conflict over the Czech question. According to the pragmatic analysis of the Francoist authorities, shared with varying degrees of distaste by their international protectors, there remained no other solution but to attempt to isolate the Spanish war from the general European crisis to avoid the contingency of a total defeat:

> It is enough to open an atlas to convince oneself of this. In a war against the Franco-English group one can say, without exaggerating at all, that we would be surrounded by enemies. From the first moment they would be surrounding us, on all our coasts and all our borders. We could contain them in the Pyrenees, but it would be

highly impossible to prevent an invasion across the Portuguese border. [. . .] Germany and Italy would only be able to offer insufficient aid to a weak Spain, and nothing they could offer us would make up for the risk of fighting on their side.[40]

In the end, the German–Czech crisis did not result in war but in a new diplomatic and strategic triumph for Hitler. On 29 September 1938, Daladier and Chamberlain signed, along with Hitler and Mussolini, the Munich Agreement, which accepted the break-up of Czechoslovakia according to German demands and in exchange for a German assurance of peace and the future negotiation of any territorial changes. In fact, the Agreement seemed to establish the Four-Powers Pact (with the exclusion of the Soviet Union) which Britain had always pursued and meant the (apparently triumphal) climax of the appeasement policy of the Western democracies.

The resolution of the Czech crisis in September 1938 with the Munich Agreement destroyed Republican expectations because it clearly indicated that if the Western powers did not struggle for Czechoslovakia, they would not do so for Spain. This gloomy international horizon radically accelerated the political disintegration of the Republic, accentuating the latent confrontation between those supporting a continuation of the resistance and those enticed by the possibility of negotiating surrender with Franco and with the support of the Western powers. This situation enabled the triumphant Francoist advance on Catalonia, initiated in December 1938, and led to the complete collapse of Republican military resistance. Towards the end of March 1939, following brief scenes of internal struggle within the government's own ranks, Franco's troops occupied all Spain without encountering resistance and thus ended the Civil War with total and unconditional victory.

At the time, European tension had shifted directly towards the outbreak of the Second World War in September 1939. During March, in violation of his Munich commitments, Hitler occupied what remained of Czechoslovakian territory under the astonished and powerless gaze of France and Britain; a month later, Italy annexed Albania, clearly violating her guarantees to Britain over the *status quo* in the Mediterranean; in the meantime, the Soviet Union had withdrawn into distrustful isolationism, sizing up the possibility of an alternative to the Franco–British entente through a non-aggression pact with Germany. In this sense, one simple chronological fact is very revealing: scarcely five months after the end of the Civil War in Spain, the European war broke out, an event which had been so laboriously avoided (or rather, postponed) by the collective non-intervention policy.

Conclusion

There is no doubt that the international context essentially determined, directly and crucially, both the course of the war in Spain and its final outcome. Without the consistent military, diplomatic and financial support given by Hitler and Mussolini, it is highly unlikely that the side led by Franco would have been able to achieve such an absolute and unconditional victory. Without the suffocating embargo imposed by the non-intervention policy and the inhibition of the Western powers, with its serious effect on military capacity and moral strength, it is highly unlikely that the Republic would have suffered an internal collapse and a military defeat of such proportions. In that respect, it is revealing to see the judgement contained in a confidential memorandum drafted by the British military attaché in Spain:

> It has become almost superfluous to recapitulate the reasons [for Franco's victory]. They are, firstly, the material superiority throughout the war of the Nationalist forces on land and in the air, and, secondly, the qualitative superiority of all their cadres up to nine months or possibly a year ago. . . . This material inferiority [of the Republican forces] is not only quantitative but qualitative as well, being also the result of multiplicity of types. However impartial and benevolent the aims of the Non-Intervention Agreement, its repercussions on the armament problem of the Republican forces have been, to say the least of it, unfortunate and, no doubt, hardly what they were intended to be. The material aid of Russia, Mexico and Czechoslovakia has never equalled in quantity or quality that of Germany and Italy. Other nations, whatever their sympathies, have been restrained by the attitude of Great Britain.[41]

That this international context was crucial to the outcome of the Civil War is not subject to doubt, but what is also certain is that the influence of the struggle itself within the European crisis of the second half of the 1930s was limited by the partial success of the collective non-intervention policy. The localized Spanish conflict did not need to become the catalyst for the European war, which broke out subsequently for other reasons. Nevertheless, although this policy cauterized the worst effects of the Spanish conflict on the European scenario, it could not avoid at least three serious consequences that would later be of enormous importance: the final crystallization of the Italo-German Axis; a crippling division within the Franco-British entente; and the growing inclination of the Soviet Union towards a policy of expectant isolationism. Indeed, the war in Spain had repeatedly shown the practical incompatibility between the Franco-British policy of appeasement and the Soviet policy of collective security. The former required absolute support for the policy of non-intervention, while the latter implied a defence of the Republican cause. Everything seemed to indicate that the Republic would not be the only victim of this tragic incompatibility and the resulting failure of the creation of a broad diplomatic and military front against the expansionism of the Axis powers.

Notes

1 For useful information on this period, see Anthony Adamthwaite, *The Lost Peace: International Relations in Europe, 1918–1939* (London: Edward Arnold, 1980) and P. M.H. Bell, *The Origins of the Second World War in Europe* (London: Longman, 1993).

2 MacGregor Knox, *Mussolini Unleashed, 1939–1941: Politics and Strategy in Fascist Italy's Last War* (Cambridge: Cambridge University Press, 1986), ch. 1; Renzo de Felice, *Mussolini il fascista* (Torino Einaudi, 1966, 1968), 2 vols; Esmonde M. Robertson, *Mussolini as Empire-Builder: Europe and Africa, 1932–1936* (London: Macmillan, 1977).

3 Gerhard L. Weinberg, *The Foreign Policy of Hitler's Germany: Diplomatic Revolution in Europe, 1933–1936* (Chicago: University of Chicago Press, 1970). Klaus Hildebrand, *The Foreign Policy of the Third Reich* (London: Batsford, 1973); Andreas Hillgruber, *Germany and the Two World Wars* (Cambridge, Mass: Harvard University Press, 1981).

4 Anthony Adamthwaite, *France and the Coming of the Second World War* (London, Frank Cass, 1977); Jean-Baptiste Duroselle, *Politique étrangère de la France: la décadence (1932–1939)* (Paris: Imprimerie Nationale, 1979); R.A.C. Parker, *Chamberlain and Appeasement: British Policy and the Coming of the Second World War* (London: Macmillan, 1993); Gustav Schmidt, *The Politics and Economics of Appeasement: British Foreign Policy in the 1930s* (Leamington Spa: Berg, 1984).

5 Jonathan Haslam, *The Soviet Union and the Struggle for Collective Security in Europe, 1933–1939* (London: Macmillan, 1984); Fernando Claudín, *The Communist Movement: From Comintern to Cominform* (Harmondsworth: Penguin, 1975); Geoffrey Roberts, *Unholy Alliance: Stalin's Pact with Hitler* (Bloomington: Indiana University Press, 1989).

6 In addition to those works cited in note 4, see Martin Thomas, *Britain, France and Appeasement: Anglo-French Relations in the Popular Front Era* (Oxford: Berg, 1997); Robert J. Young, *In Command of France: French Foreign Policy and Military Planning, 1933–1940* (Cambridge, Mass: Harvard University Press, 1978); Paul Kennedy, *The Realities behind Diplomacy: Background Influences on British External Policy, 1865–1980* (London, Fontana, 1981), ch. 3; Corelli Barnett, *The Collapse of British Power* (Gloucester: Alan Sutton, 1987).

7 Hugh Thomas, *The Spanish Civil War* (Harmondsworth: Penguin, 1977); Paul Preston, *A Concise History of the Spanish Civil War* (London: Fontana, 1996); Sheelagh Ellwood, *The Spanish Civil War* (Oxford: Blackwell, 1991).

8 Michael Alpert, *A New International History of the Spanish Civil War* (London: Macmillan, 1994); P.A.M. van der Esch, *Prelude to War: The International*

Repercussions of the Spanish Civil War (The Hague: Martinus Nijhoff, 1951); Glyn Stone, 'The European Great Powers and the Spanish Civil War', in R. Boyce and E.M. Robertson (eds), *Paths to War: New Essays on the Origins of the Second World War* (London: Macmillan, 1989), pp. 199–232.

9 Pierre Renouvin, 'La politique extérieure du premier gouvernement de Léon Blum', in *Léon Blum, chef de gouvernement, 1936–1937* (Paris: Fondation Nationale des Sciences Politiques, 1967), pp. 329–53; David W. Pike, *Les Français et la guerre d'Espagne* (Paris: Presses Universitaires de France, 1975); John E. Dreifort, *Yvon Delbos at the Quai d'Orsay: French Foreign Policy during the Popular Front, 1936–1938* (Lawrence: University Press of Kansas, 1973); testimony of Léon Blum in 1947 collected in Assemblée Nationale. *Rapport fait au nom de la Commission chargée d'enquêter sur les événements survenus en France de 1933 à 1945* (Paris: Assemblée Nationale, 1951), *Annexes*, I, pp. 215–20.

10 Quoted in Geoffrey Warner, 'France and Non-Intervention in Spain, July–August 1936', *International Affairs*, 38: 2 (1962), pp. 203–20.

11 Jill Edwards, *The British Government and the Spanish Civil War* (London: Macmillan, 1979); Douglas Little, *Malevolent Neutrality: The United States, Great Britain, and the Origins of the Spanish Civil War* (Ithaca: Cornell University Press, 1985); Enrique Moradiellos, 'The Origins of British Non-Intervention in the Spanish Civil War: Anglo-Spanish Relations in Early 1936', *European History Quarterly*, 21: 3 (1991), pp. 339–64.

12 Quoted in Thomas Jones, *A Diary with Letters, 1931–1950* (Oxford: Oxford University Press, 1954). The author, friend and confidant of Baldwin, had been Secretary in the British Cabinet between 1916 and 1930. Previous quotes are from Enrique Moradiellos, *La perfidia de Albión: El gobierno británico y la guerra civil española* (Madrid: Siglo XXI, 1996) pp. 43, 61.

13 Minute by Sir Samuel Hoare, 5 August 1936. Quoted in Enrique Moradiellos, 'British Political Strategy in the Face of the Military Rising of 1936 in Spain', *Contemporary European History*, 1: 2 (1992), pp. 123–37 (quotation on p. 130).

14 Robert Whealey, *Hitler and Spain: The Nazi Role in the Spanish Civil War* (Lexington: University Press of Kentucky, 1989); Raymond Proctor, *Hitler's Luftwaffe in the Spanish Civil War* (Westport, Conn: Greenwood Press, 1983); Denis Smyth, 'A Reflex Reaction: Germany and the Onset of the Spanish Civil War', in Paul Preston (ed.), *Revolution and War in Spain, 1931–1939* (London: Methuen, 1984), pp. 243–65; Angel Viñas, *La Alemania nazi y el 18 de julio: antecedentes de la intervención alemana en la guerra civil española* (Madrid: Alianza, 1977).

15 Paul Preston, 'Mussolini's Spanish Adventure: From Limited Risk to War', in P. Preston and A.L. Mackenzie (eds), *The Republic Besieged: Civil War in Spain* (Edinburgh: Edinburgh University Press, 1996), pp. 21–51; John Coverdale, *Italian Intervention in the Spanish Civil War* (Princeton: Princeton University Press, 1975); Ismael Saz, *Mussolini contra la Segunda República (1931–1936)* (Valencia: Institució Valenciana d'Estudis i Investigació, 1986); Ismael Saz y Javier Tusell (eds), *Fascistas en España: la intervención italiana en la guerra civil a través de los telegramas de la 'Missione Militare Italiana in Spagna'* (Madrid: CSIC, 1981).

16 Report by the German ambassador to Italy, 18 December 1936. *Documents on German Foreign Policy, 1918–1945*, ser. D (1937–45), vol. III, *Germany and*

the Spanish Civil War (London: HMSO, 1951, document number 157), pp. 170–3. Hereafter *DGFP* and number.

17 Quoted in Martin Thomas, *Britain, France and Appeasement*, p. 96. The text of the proposal is in *Documents Diplomatiques Français*, 1932–1939, série 2 (1936–1939), vol. III (Paris: Ministère des Affaires Étrangères, 1966, n. 56). Hereafter *DDF*, volume and number.

18 Diary entry of 19 September 1937 regarding his interview with De Brouckère. Manuel Azaña, *Memorias de guerra, 1936–1939* (Barcelona: Grijalbo, 1996), p. 263.

19 For more on the Labour position, see Tom Buchanan, *The Spanish Civil War and the British Labour Movement* (Oxford: Oxford University Press, 1991); and John Francis Naylor, *Labour's International Policy: The Labour Party in the 1930s* (London: Weidenfeld & Nicolson, 1969).

20 Public Record Office (Kew), Foreign Office Records, Eden Papers (FO 954), file 27. Hereafter, FO 954/27. Cf. E. Moradiellos, 'British Political Strategy', pp. 129–30 (see note 7 for full details).

21 For more on Portuguese support for Franco, see the works of César Oliveira, *Salazar e a guerra civil de Espanha* (Lisbon: O Jornal, 1987); and Glyn Stone, *The Oldest Ally: Britain and the Portuguese Connection, 1936–1941* (Rochester, NY: Boydell Press, 1994).

22 Richard P. Traina, *American Diplomacy and the Spanish Civil War* (Bloomington: Indiana University Press, 1968); T.G. Powell, *Mexico and the Spanish Civil War* (Albuquerque: University of New Mexico Press, 1981); M. Falcoff and F. Pike (eds), *The Spanish Civil War: American Hemispheric Perspectives* (Lincoln: University of Nebraska Press, 1982).

23 David T. Cattell, *Soviet Diplomacy and the Spanish Civil War* (Berkeley: University of California Press, 1955). Edward H. Carr, *The Comintern and the Spanish Civil War* (London: Macmillan, 1984); Jonathan Haslam, *The Soviet Union* ch. 7; Denis Smyth, 'We Are with You: Solidarity and Self-Interest in Soviet Policy towards Republican Spain, 1936–1939', in P. Preston and A. L. Mackenzie (eds), *The Republic Besieged*, pp. 87–105; Geoffrey Roberts, *Unholy Alliance*, pp. 75–83.

24 Dispatches dated 23 July and 6 August. Cited in D. Smyth, 'We Are with You' pp. 90–1 (see note 23 for full details).

25 Dispatch dated 10 August. *Documents on British Foreign Policy, 1919–1939*, ser. 2, vol. XVII, *Western Pact Negotiations: Outbreak of the Spanish Civil War, June 23, 1936 en January 2, 1937* (London: HMSO, 1979, n. 78). Hereafter *DBFP*, volume and number.

26 Diary entry made by the President regarding his interview with Pascua, 12 June 1937. Manuel Azaña, *Memorias de guerra, 1936–1939* (Barcelona: Grijalbo, 1978), pp. 74–5. On 13 August, following another interview with the Ambassador, Azaña noted in his diary that 'Russian cooperation has a limit which is not a possible obstacle but the official English friendship. I believe that the USSR will not do anything in our favour which could gravely jeopardize its relations with England or compromise its position in its friendship with Western powers,' *op. cit.*, p. 216.

27 The minimum figure, 35,000, is supported by Jacques Delperrie de Bayac, *Las Brigadas Internacionales* (Gijón: Júcar, 1980), and Robert Rosentone ('International Brigades', in James Cortada (ed.), *Historical Dictionary of the Spanish Civil War* (Westport, Conn: Greenwood Press, 1982). The figure of

60,000 originates from Andreu Castells, *Las Brigadas Internacionales de la guerra de España* (Barcelona: Ariel, 1974). By nationality, the majority of volunteers were French (between 10,000 and 15,000), Germans (5,000), Poles (5,000), Italians (3,400), North Americans (3,000) and British (2,400). cf. R. Dan Richardson, *Comintern Army. The International Brigades in the Spanish Civil War* (Lexington: University Press of Kentucky, 1982), and Michael Jackson, *Fallen Sparrows: The International Brigades in the Spanish Civil War* (Philadelphia: American Philosophical Society, 1994).

28 Gerald Howson, *Aircraft of the Spanish Civil War* (London: Putnam, 1990), pp. 303–5. According to official Soviet figures collected by Geoffrey Roberts (*Unholy Alliance*, p. 78), Soviet military aid to the Republic included 648 planes, 347 tanks, 120 armoured cars, 1,186 artillery pieces, 20,486 machine guns, 497,813 rifles, 340 mortars, 826 m. bullets and 3.4 m. shells.

29 Angel Viñas, *El oro de Moscú: alfa y omega de un mito franquista* (Barcelona: Grijalbo, 1979). From the same author, 'The financing of the Spanish Civil War', in P. Preston (ed.), *Revolution and War*, pp. 266–83. According to Viñas, 'If my calculations are correct, there is only an accounting gap of 0.4 tonnes of fine gold, equivalent to some 450,000 dollars. The official history of the Bank of Spain, as written by Juan Sardá while Franco was still alive, also reached this same conclusion: the Spanish treasure handed over to the USSR was indeed spent in its entirety by the Government of the Republic during the war.' *El Banco de España: una historia económica* (Madrid: Banco de España, 1970), p. 436.

30 Minutes of Sir Orme Sargent, Assistant Under-Secretary at the Foreign Office, 15 June 1936. Foreign Office Records, General Correspondence (FO371), File 19857, Document number C4319. Hereafter, FO371/19857 C4319.

31 Memorandum, 27 October 1936. FO371/20583 W14793. Vansittart's French counterpart, Alexis Léger, had conveyed similar impressions to the British embassy in Paris the day before. *DBFP*, XVII, n. 333 (see note 25 above for full details).

32 *DBFP*, XVII, n. 348 (see note 25 above).

33 *Note by the War Office on the supply of arms to Spain during the month of April*, 7 May 1937. FO 371/21395 W9144. Indeed, the majority of German shipments were consigned on ships carrying fictitious Panamanian flags and, in many cases, they arrived in Lisbon to continue by land to Franco's Spain. Michael Alpert, *La guerra civil española en el mar* (Madrid: Siglo XXI, 1987), pp. 153–6.

34 Dispatch, 4 July 1937. *DGFP*, Num. 376 (see note 16 above).

35 Memorandum by Ginés Vidal (Director of the European Section, Ministry of Foreign Affairs), 28 January 1939. Archivo del Ministerio de Asuntos Exteriores (Madrid), serie Archivo Renovado, file 834, box 31. Hereafter, AMAE R834/31.

36 Confidential remark made by Negrín to his colleague and confidante Juan Simeón Vidarte, Subsecretary of the Ministerio de Gobernación. Recalled in his memoirs *Todos fuimos culpables* (Mexico City: Fondo de Cultura Económica, 1973), pp. 764–5.

37 Telegram of the American ambassador in Paris, 30 July 1937. *For the President: Personal and Secret. Correspondence between Franklin D. Roosevelt and William C. Bullitt* (Boston: Houghton Mifflin, 1972), p. 222.

38 Michael Alpert, *La guerra civil española en el mar*, (Madrid: Siglo XXI, 1987), pp. 288–9.

39 DDF, vol. VIII, n. 446 (see note 17 above for full details). Testimony by Blum and Paul-Boncour (briefly Minister for Foreign Affairs in March 1938), in *Assemblée Nationale: rapport fait ... sur les événements survenus en France de 1933 à 1945. Annexes*, vol. 1, p. 253 (Blum) and vol. 3, pp. 801–4 (Paul-Boncour).

40 Memorandum of the Count of Torrellano, 'Consideraciones sobre la futura política internacional de España', 20 May 1938. AMAE R834/31 (see note 35 above for full details).

41 *Report by Major E.C. Richards on Offensive Strategy in the Spanish War*, 25 November 1938. FO 371/22631 W16269. The material superiority of the Francoist side is confirmed by the calculations of military air support from Gerald Howson: 'The Republicans can therefore be said to have had between 950 and 1,060 effective combat aircraft at their disposal during the civil war, of which 676 (or at most 753) came from the Soviet Union. Over the same period, the Nationalists disposed of 1,429–1,539 effective combat aircraft, of which 1,321–1,431 came from Germany and Italy.' *Aircraft of the Spanish Civil War*, p. 305.

6   Nazi Germany and Francoist Spain, 1936–1945

Christian Leitz

In Febuary 1945 Adolf Hitler fumed over his mistake in having entertained relations with a regime of 'plutocratic exploiters led by the nose by priests!'. The Führer's criticism came on top of a series of negative comments he had been making about Franco throughout the Second World War. In October 1940 Hitler had raved that in Germany the Caudillo would not even have made it to the position of Nazi Party district leader while on 19 January 1941 he described Franco as an 'inferior character'.[1] Using these and other harsh comments about Franco and his regime, Rainer Zitelmann attempted to emphasize that there was a clear ideological gap between the radical 'revolutionary' Führer and the clerico-reactionary Caudillo. The dubious line of argument of Zitelmann's book aside, the cited comments nonetheless help us to understand Hitler's obvious disenchantment with the Spanish dictator. Yet, as far as Hitler's reasons are concerned, the emphasis needs to be not so much on the ideological differences, which undeniably distinguished the two dictatorships,[2] but rather more on the development of the relationship between the two regimes.

During the Second World War, and particularly once the fortunes of war had turned against Nazi Germany, Hitler's views about Franco were increasingly guided by his conviction that the Caudillo had not sufficiently repaid Germany's services during the Spanish Civil War. Put in simple terms, the Nazi regime had become one of the two 'midwives' (Fascist Italy being the other) of the Franco regime[3] while Franco subsequently denied Hitler the ultimate repayment of services rendered by not fully committing himself to the Axis.

This very brief interpretation serves as a framework for the course of the following chapter. As there is not much of a pre-history and, owing to the total demise of the Nazi regime, even less of a post-history to the Hitler–Franco relationship, clear-cut first and last 'markers' can be determined, namely the outbreak of Spanish Civil War and the end of the

Second World War. In between, four phases can be distinguished: first, the Spanish Civil War and Nazi Germany's intervention in the conflict (July 1936 to March 1939); second, the very brief period of peace between Civil War and Germany's attack on Poland followed by the 'Phoney War' (April 1939 to May 1940); third, the period of Spanish non-belligerency and German domination of the war (from June 1940); and ultimately, Francoist Spain's gradual return to neutrality and the growing superiority of the Allies (from November 1942).

Civil War

Much has been made of the role the Nazi regime supposedly played in the preparations for the uprising or *pronunciamiento* that took place on 17/18 July 1936.[4] The final verdict, however, has to be that it was much ado about very little. It has been clearly demonstrated that, until the outbreak of the conflict, Spain rarely figured in Hitler's speeches and publications. Moreover, there is no indication that he intended to get involved in right-wing subversive activities in the country.[5] Convincing evidence implicating the Nazi regime in the preparatory activities of the rebels has not emerged. This is not to say that contacts between individual Germans and the conspirators did not exist. However, such contacts are not sufficient evidence to indicate some sinister involvement of the Nazi regime.[6]

The Nazi regime may not have behaved with any sinister intention towards the Spanish Republic in the months leading up to the *coup*, yet it took the opportunity to live up to its usual image very soon after. On 23 July 1936, the German Foreign Ministry (AA) rejected a request for support from the rebels or self-styled Nationalists. Two days later, Hitler demonstrated who really had ultimate control over foreign policy decision-making in the Third Reich.[7] Without consulting any other members of his government, in particular neither Foreign Minister Constantin von Neurath nor War Minister Werner von Blomberg, Hitler opted for Germany's intervention in favour of the Nationalists.[8]

In view of the future course of Germany's intervention, two aspects stand out about the Führer's decision of the night of 25/26 July 1936.[9] First, Germany's aid, consisting of 20 Junkers-52 transport aircraft, 6 Heinkel-51 fighter planes and various other supplies,[10] was granted exclusively to General Franco, joint leader of the rebellion and in charge of the troops in Spanish Morocco. A pattern was thus established which was to give Franco a clear advantage over his fellow rebel officers and helped him in his rise to become sole leader of the Nationalists and eventually of Spain.[11] Second, the process which led to Hitler's decision involved only members of the Nazi Party, beginning with Johannes Bernhardt and Adolf Langenheim, Franco's envoys to Berlin, on to Ernst Bohle, as chief of the *Auslandsorganisation* (AO), first contact of Bernhardt and Langenheim, then to Rudolf Hess, deputy Führer and Bohle's direct superior, and finally to Hitler. This process predetermined the initial direction of Germany's intervention, subordinating those ministries which traditionally guided Germany's foreign policy – the Foreign, Economics and War Ministries – to the authority of new National Socialist organizations.

However, it was not Hitler, the initiator of Germany's intervention, who was to ensure continued National Socialist control over it, but the Führer's 'First Paladin', Hermann Göring. Among the first to be consulted by Hitler after his meeting with Bernhardt and Langenheim, Göring almost instantly discarded his initial opposition to involvement in Spain and proceeded to push himself into the centre of all organizational aspects of Germany's intervention. On 26 July 1936, Göring code-named the whole supply operation *Unternehmen Feuerzauber* (Operation Magic Fire) and made arrangements for the foundation of *Sonderstab W*, which was to organize, supervise and control all supply operations of Germany's intervention.[12] While 'intervention' may give the impression of some profound and prolonged process, this is not at all what Hitler intended with his initial decision. Although Hitler was aware that the situation of the rebels was not favourable and that therefore a single act of support for Franco would not be sufficient to ensure victory, an extended intervention was not his intention.[13]

With the first consignment for Franco on its way, Göring was already busy with preparations to permit further 'acts of support' for the rebel general. The crucial decision which turned such individual acts into full-scale intervention was, however, taken not by Göring, but again by Hitler, one of the rare occasions after July 1936 that he was to involve himself in the decision-making process over Germany's intervention.[14] On 24 August Germany's dictator decided to support General Franco with further supplies, and militarily, as much as possible.[15] Only weeks later, on 9 October, General Georg Thomas officially confirmed that 'the Spanish issue . . . had been taken over by General Göring and his staff', followed by the interesting observation that Germany's intervention 'is now to be treated as an economic matter of the Reich over which, on the basis of his orders, General Göring alone has the right to decide'.[16]

To treat Germany's intervention 'as an economic matter' was not Hitler's original intention. After all, a small gesture of support would not have had economic implications. Although soon to be plagued by financial problems, Franco would have been able to raise sufficient funds to pay for small quantities of German equipment. Yet the Nationalists were certainly not prepared for a longer conflict, either militarily or financially. Growing quantities of military supplies meant growing debts to Germany (and Italy). This emerging Nationalist malaise gave Göring the opportunity to adopt a dual role *vis-à-vis* Franco. On the one hand, as Air Minister, he had control over the supply of urgently needed aircraft to Franco; on the other hand, as a key player in the running of the German economy,[17] Göring was interested in the possible economic and financial benefits of Germany's intervention. Further developments only helped to strengthen Göring's grip over Nazi Germany's interventionist campaign.

In October, Germany's involvement in the conflict experienced a dramatic expansion. From the less than 100 troops who had arrived in Spain together with the first supplies of German equipment, Germany's military contingent in Spain was to grow into a proper force, the Condor Legion, which, at any one time during the Civil War, never consisted of more than about 5,600 military advisers, technicians, pilots and soldiers. All in all, a total of 16,800 Germans were to serve on the Nationalist side while about 5,000 Germans fought in the International Brigades in defence of the Spanish Republic.[18] Although the Legion contained contingents from the German army (e.g. tanks, communication and radio units), the majority of its members belonged to the *Luftwaffe*.[19] Not surprisingly, therefore, it was Göring and not von Blomberg who had decisive control over the Legion.

With hindsight, it is clear that German aircraft made a crucial impact on the course of the Spanish Civil War. It is revealing that, of the few comments Göring made at the Nuremberg Trials about the Spanish Civil War, he emphasized the need to test 'his' *Luftwaffe* as a motive for Germany's intervention. Although neither this comment nor his claim that he urged Hitler to intervene in Spain can be substantiated from the available evidence, a kernel of truth emerges from Göring's boastful statement. *Luftwaffe* planes and pilots were undoubtedly trained in Spain. Bombing raids on Spanish cities such as Madrid and Barcelona were often undertaken without any military targets in mind, but simply to frighten the Republican population into submission. Such raids were the first examples of the suffering that many European cities were to experience after 1 September 1939. The major Republican cities, however, are not usually remembered alongside Warsaw, Rotterdam or Coventry. This sad fate was reserved for a small Basque market town previously known only to Basque nationalists. Guernica, of which barely anything was left after the annihilation raid of 26 April 1937, became a foretaste of things to come. Although Pablo Picasso's famous painting has undoubtedly helped to make the tragedy known world-wide, it is the debate about whom to blame for the raid which kept Guernica in the limelight for years to come. Even today the matter is not finally put *ad acta*, though the evidence is overwhelming that 21 German planes of the Condor Legion and 3 Italian aircraft were responsible for the destruction.[20]

Thus, the deployment of the Condor Legion had terrifying consequences for civilians and armed forces of the Spanish Republic alike. Initially, however, not all went according to plan for the Nazi leadership. Technically, some of the German equipment, including the Panzer Mark I, proved to be inferior to Soviet military hardware,[21] which the Republic started to receive in growing quantities from October 1936. More importantly, during November 1936, the month of the Legion's deployment, Soviet supplies in conjunction with the arrival of the International Brigades prevented a rapid conclusion of the Civil War. Most annoying for the Nazi regime was, however, the observation that Franco – since 28 September sole leader of Nationalist forces and territory – was partly to blame for not fulfilling his own boastful promise: to take Madrid, the capital of Spain. In anticipation of this potentially decisive conquest Hitler had promised to recognize Franco's provisional administration as the rightful government of Spain. This the German government did do on 18 November despite the Republic's successful defence of Madrid.[22] At the same time both Hitler and Mussolini considered ways of accelerating Franco's military progress.

Of central importance was the question of whether to lift intervention onto a higher plane by sending substantial numbers of troops to fight on the Nationalist side. With the arrival of the Condor Legion, German troop strength in Spain exceeded that of Italy. Yet when Wilhelm Faupel, German chargé d'affaires in Nationalist Spain since 28 November,[23] tried to persuade Hitler to increase Germany's interventionist force to divisional strength, the request was rejected.[24] If we are to believe Walter Warlimont, who, in August, had been ordered to Spain to represent Germany's armed forces at Franco's headquarters and who later acted as Faupel's first military adviser, Hitler opposed Faupel's proposal by arguing that while 'Franco should not lose ... he should [not] finish it quickly. With the continued conflict in Spain, Europe will be interested in events there and be less concerned with Germany and [Hitler's] objectives.'[25] Mussolini's almost simultaneous decision to opt for a massive increase of Italian troops undoubtedly helped this diversionary strategy.[26]

Berlin and Rome had not taken these crucial decisions altogether independently of each other. In a crucial meeting between Göring and the Duce on 14 January 1937, it was agreed to go for 'a last major supportive effort' that would 'form the absolutely secure foundation for Franco's victory'. This 'effort' was to terminate on 31 January and would provide Franco with Italian soldiers and both German and Italian *matériel*. In addition, major pressure was to be put on Franco to accelerate his operations (presumably against Madrid) with all available Nationalist forces. In their overly optimistic assessment of the potentially decisive nature of their supplies, Mussolini and Göring even agreed to 'enter into the particulars of proposals made by other parties to seal off Spain', though with the caveat that this should not impinge on Franco's chances for victory.[27] Yet, owing to continued uncertainty about the outcome of the Civil War, German and Italian aid obviously did not cease after the set date.

The 'other parties' referred to were members of the Non-Intervention Committee (NIC) in London, most likely the British and French representatives. On 8 August 1936, France had been the original proponent of a Non-Intervention Agreement (NIA) on Spain, a proposal eagerly accepted by Britain. Only weeks later, Germany and Italy became signatories of the agreement and, when the NIC first met on 6 September, they were represented by their ambassadors in London. Little needs to be said about the extent to which both regimes adhered to the NIA. Nazi Germany's attitude is clearly revealed by the fact that adherence to the NIA on 24 August 'coincided' with Hitler's decision to prolong and expand Germany's intervention. Throughout the Civil War, both Italy and Germany reacted in an almost identical fashion to the efforts of the NIC, namely by rarely letting it disturb their interventionist activities.[28]

Despite frequent meetings between German and Italian representatives, it would be wrong to overestimate the level to which the two sides coordinated their policies. Militarily, the Spanish Civil War was a reflection of the general relationship between the German and Italian military leadership. As Gerhard Schreiber has outlined so clearly, much was discussed in the second half of the 1930s but little of substance was agreed.[29] While at least some coordination took place in politico-military matters, coordination was almost totally absent in the economic field. Indeed, the Nazi regime viewed Italy as a very dangerous competitor in its attempt to achieve economic hegemony over the emerging 'new' Spain. On 28 November 1936, for instance, the signing of an economic agreement between Italy and Nationalist Spain set German alarm bells ringing.[30] By then, Göring had already set his heart upon an economic exploitation of the conflict in Spain.[31]

Again, Göring was largely responsible for the creation of the apparatus that enabled him to control the economic relationship between Germany and Nationalist Spain. From the end of September 1936, HISMA, founded in Spanish Morocco on 31 July 1936 and run by Johannes Bernhardt, acted as 'representative of Germany's economic interests in

Nationalist Spain'. In early October, HISMA's role was strengthened further by Göring's foundation of ROWAK as HISMA's German counterpart.[32] Through HISMA/ROWAK Göring pursued a radical reorientation of the pattern of Hispano-German trade away from the import of Spanish agricultural products towards a massive increase in supplies of vital raw materials such as iron ore and pyrites. Göring's interest in the Spanish economy did not end there. Worried about the possibly temporary nature of the new trade pattern, he employed HISMA to establish a more permanent foothold in Spain, in particular by buying up mining rights. During 1937, HISMA/ROWAK's employees were therefore increasingly occupied with MONTANA, as Göring's purchasing project was code-named.

The project was intended to be an undercover operation, hidden from the eyes of the Nationalist authorities and from the co-interventionist Italy. In January 1937, for instance, while HISMA/ROWAK was already engaged in initial geological explorations in Spain, Göring coolly announced to Mussolini that 'Germany's economic interests in Spain had already been sufficiently satisfied in the past.'[33] That the opposite was true became quickly apparent to the Nationalists. The response was understandably ambiguous. On the one hand, Franco could not risk losing vital supplies from Germany; on the other, he could not risk being seen as a weak leader who was giving away control over Spain to a foreign power. Even though the Nazi regime did not appear to have any territorial ambitions in Spain, the obvious longing for increased economic control was a threat in itself.[34]

During the course of 1937 and 1938, MONTANA proved to be a major element of disruption in the relationship between Nationalist Spain and Nazi Germany.[35] It was, however, neither the first nor the only instance that demonstrated that the views and objectives of the two sides were occasionally at odds with each other. One aspect that gave the Nazis frequent cause for dissatisfaction was Franco's conduct of the war. The unsuccessful siege of Madrid continued into the winter of 1936–7, but again without much progress.[36] It openly revealed that the *Generalísimo*'s tactical approach differed from German (and Italian) notions.

Further friction arose from the attitude of the German chargé d'affaires. Faupel's appointment had been a triumph for the AO. Rather than follow the wishes of the AA, Hitler gave preference to Faupel after Bohle and Hess had convinced him of the suitability of the retired general. Very quickly, however, the triumph turned sour. Faupel was eventually withdrawn and replaced by the AA's original choice, Eberhard von Stohrer.[37] Bernhardt aside – the HISMA manager developed a very good working relationship with the ambassador – Faupel had managed to antagonize not only the Nationalist leadership, but even members of Germany's interventionist forces, most notably General Hugo Sperrle, the first commander of the Condor Legion. Both clashed particularly because they had, in competition with each other, tried constantly to intervene in Franco's conduct of the war. The advice was clearly not welcome, especially as it was given in a very patronizing manner. Ultimately, and despite his continued dependency on German supplies, Franco forced both men out of Nationalist Spain.[38] While Göring was able to replace Sperrle with another *Luftwaffe* general, Hellmuth Volkmann, the political influence of the AO over Germany's intervention was, apart from Bernhardt's important role, reduced to conducting propaganda activities via the German embassy.

With Faupel gone, more stability entered the diplomatic relations between Nationalist Spain and Nazi Germany. Stohrer's style was much more suited to the attitude and expectations of Franco and his regime. Although committed to his government in Berlin, Stohrer's dispatches reveal on many occasions a very understanding approach *vis-à-vis* the Franco regime. This became particularly apparent during the Sudeten crisis of summer 1938. In anticipation of a potential military conflict between Germany and an alliance of Britain, France and possibly even the Soviet Union, Franco decided to declare neutrality, knowing full well that any participation in such a war would sound the death-knell of his regime. The initial response of the Nazi regime was obviously rather hostile. Göring, in particular, regarded Franco's decision as an affront in view of the extent of Germany's contribution to the *Generalísimo*'s war effort and the obstinacy with which his administration was trying to prevent the successful completion of MONTANA. Stohrer's reaction was distinctly milder.[39] In fact, even Hitler had to admit that Franco had good reason to distance himself from the conflict at hand. Nonetheless, both the reaction of the Franco regime to the Sudeten crisis, but even more so the difference of opinion over MONTANA, led the Nazi regime to withhold vital supplies of war *matériel* – just at a time when the equipment level of Franco's forces desperately needed replenishment.

In a last desperate effort, Republican Spain had commenced a major offensive across the river Ebro on 25 July 1938. Franco reacted immediately by throwing his troops against the Republican forces. Until mid-November a major battle of attrition ensued which nearly resulted in a stalemate. Such a development suited the Nazi regime and allowed it to score an ambivalent success. By linking further supplies of war *matériel* to the MONTANA issue it forced Franco's administration grudgingly to accept the latter. Replenished with arms, the Nationalists managed to unleash a decisive offensive against Catalonia on 23 December 1938. Just over three months later the Civil War was decided in Franco's favour. Yet despite Nazi Germany's vital contribution to this outcome, MONTANA had demonstrated to the new regime in Spain that it should not make itself wholly dependent on Germany. The Treaty of Friendship with Germany of 31 March 1939 and public admission of adhesion to the Anti-Comintern Pact on 6 April indicated both the ideological direction of the Franco regime and recognition of its debt to the Axis powers.[40] Yet at the same time, to the chagrin of the Nazi regime, Franco did not reject the political and especially the economic overtures of Britain and France.[41]

Peace and 'Phoney War'

The end of the Civil War had thus liberated Franco from almost total dependency on Germany and Italy. Faced with a devastated economy, factors such as gratitude and ideological proximity were not enough for Nationalist Spain to throw in its lot exclusively with the Axis and break off relations with the Western democracies. During the brief period of peace, which ended with Germany's attack on Poland, diplomatic relations between the Reich and Spain were cordial, though, as far as the Nazi regime was concerned, largely insignificant. Even Franco's 'outmanoeuvring' of Göring, whom in May 1939 he avoided having to meet, resulted in little more than a temporary bout of anger of Germany's then second most powerful man. Hitler and his fellow leaders were heavily engaged in preparations for a war in which Spain figured only very marginally. While Franco and other members of his regime frequently expressed their commitment to the Axis in the event of war, other comments in which they referred to the need for peace to reconstruct the country were much more realistic.[42] German assessments ran along the same lines. Spain was expected to keep herself out of any conflict for economic and military reasons, but also as long as France continued to be a threat to both Spain and her possessions in North-West Africa.

While relations on a political level were thus fairly low-key, more activity could be detected in the economic field. Franco and his regime had high hopes that Germany would continue to take up a supportive role shifting from supplier of military equipment to provider of vital economic goods. It was anticipated that the German government and German companies would play a very active role in the reconstruction of Spain. Such hopes were not at all ill-founded. Both Nazi regime and German private industry were not disinclined to adopt a leading role in the reconstruction of Spain – though clearly not simply to help Spain back on her feet.[43] German participation in the reconstruction of

Spain was intended to serve as an extension of the MONTANA project. Germany's foothold in Spain's economy was to be strengthened; indeed, further steps should be taken to achieve economic hegemony over Spain. Luckily for Spain the war upset these plans. Grandiose schemes of Spain as an economic colony never materialized. Yet even without the war it would have been very difficult for the Nazis to implement such plans. In 1939 Germany simply did not have the resources to play a leading role in the reconstruction of Spain. For financial support, Franco eventually had to turn to the Western democracies, most notably Britain.[44] In many other areas, Franco was also faced with Germany's inability to alleviate Spain's needs. The Nazi regime could simply not fulfil Spain's immense requirements of foodstuffs, fuel, cotton and other vital products, not during the few months of peace, even less so after the outbreak of war on 1 September.

If German–Spanish relations had become fairly low-key in the aftermath of the Civil War, they entered a stage close to hibernation during the so-called Phoney War. On 23 August 1939, the Franco regime had been temporarily taken aback by the news that Hitler had signed an agreement with the arch-enemy, the Soviet Union. Germany's subsequent invasion of Catholic Poland was also viewed with a certain detachment. Not surprisingly, British and French declarations of war on Germany were followed by Spain's declaration of 'strictest' neutrality on 4 September. Yet beneath this official veneer, sympathies were clearly with Nazi Germany. On a number of occasions, neutral Spain tolerated or even provided help for activities in support of the German war effort. The best-known example is the resupplying of German submarines and ships in Spanish territorial waters, indeed Spanish ports.[45] In addition, the Spanish government saw to it that German intelligence-gathering proceeded fairly undisturbed in both Spain and Spanish Morocco. For logistical reasons, however, with France controlling the land and Britain the sea routes to Spain, even such acts of assistance did not lift German–Spanish relations out of their quasi-dormant state.

The Second World War: Germany's ascendancy

'Hitler's startling conquest of France . . . drastically altered the foreign policy of the Spanish regime. . . . Germany's sudden ascendancy [opened] a new period of temptation combined with danger for both Spain and its government.'[46] The temptation referred to is, of course, the lure exerted by the Axis upon Franco to enter the war. Yet for some writers, not surprisingly those of a right-wing, pro-Francoist hue, the use of the word 'temptation' smacks of slander. To them, German–Spanish relations after the fall of France are characterized by Franco's skill and his successful struggle against Nazi Germany's insistent demands that Spain should enter the war. Apologists[47] generally portray Franco as the glorious defender of Spain's sovereignty, as the leader possessed of *hábil prudencia* (skilful prudence). They cannot, indeed do not, deny the fact that German–Spanish negotiations took place during the second half of 1940, including, on 23 October, the only meeting between the two dictators at Hendaye. In fact, Hendaye is turned into the 'central plank in the construction' of Franco 'as the man who held back the Nazi hordes'.[48] There is also no denying that Serrano Suñer, Spain's Foreign Minister, visited Germany in September and again in November for extensive meetings with the Führer and his Foreign Minister, Joachim von Ribbentrop.[49] These meetings, however, are simply explained away. After all, it is being argued, with German troops stationed on the Spanish border an invasion of the country was always possible, necessitating some kind of delaying action.

Although there are still some pieces of the puzzle missing – in particular a complete record of the conversations at Hendaye[50] – the available evidence paints quite a different picture. In the first instance, on or before 12 June 1940, the Nazis did not put any pressure on Franco to change Spain's status from neutrality to (Axis-friendly) non-belligerency. Spain's occupation of the international zone of Tangier two days later was also implemented on Franco's own initiative. Most importantly, however, it was the Spanish dictator who attempted to jump onto the Axis bandwagon when, on 19 June, he offered Spain's entry into the war under certain conditions. Hitler's reply was disappointing. While it did not amount to an outright rejection, it demonstrated a noticeable lack of interest. From Hitler's point of view Spain's entry into the war was superfluous. At that point in the war, Germany's enemies in Europe had been whittled down to one, Britain, which, according to Hitler's expectations, would either surrender or be forced into submission in little time. Very probably this was exactly the reason for Franco's offer. To take a share of the spoils of victory, namely Gibraltar and much of French North-West Africa, without getting too heavily involved in the fighting seemed to be an appealing prospect.

In the event, owing to Britain's continued resistance, neither Hitler nor Franco were to see their hopes fulfilled. With Britain proving to be more resilient than expected, Franco became slightly more cautious about a potential entry into the war. Not cautious enough, however, to reject German invitations to discuss the matter. In July and August 1940 Hitler clearly changed his tack *vis-à-vis* Franco's initial offer. As German preparations for an invasion of Britain ran into increasing difficulties, alternative strategies against the isles were considered. In these considerations, Gibraltar emerged as a natural target. A successful assault could 'strip the Royal Navy of its key Western Mediterranean base and thus imperil British communications with the Western Hemisphere and the Middle East'.[51] While this traditional interpretation of such planning (part of Germany's peripheral strategy against Britain) has recently been partly challenged,[52] it remains a fact that, by late summer 1940, Gibraltar had become a target and Spain's immediate entry into the war a necessity.

During August, preparations for the whole operation, code-named Felix, were under way. In the end, however, Felix never developed beyond the preparatory stage. On 7 December 1940, in conversation with Admiral Wilhelm Canaris, Franco rejected German demands for an entry into the war on 10 January 1941. Economic problems were given as the official reason. While the intervening months had, indeed, revealed an ever-growing gap between Spain's economic and military demands and Germany's offers,[53] the central stumbling-block consisted of Franco's territorial 'dreams'. Particularly after 23 September, when Vichy France successfully repelled the Anglo-Gaullist landing attempt at Dakar, Hitler became increasingly convinced that the Vichy government would, for the time being, be a safe guarantor of France's North African possessions. In contrast, a transfer of French Morocco into Spanish hands was judged a risky venture which could make an Anglo-Gaullist take-over more likely.[54]

Hitler could not be brought to give the definite promises that Franco was so keen on. If we are to believe Serrano Suñer, by doing so Hitler gave away the decisive opportunity to bring Franco into the war. For Franco the temptation of having his imperial aspirations fulfilled would have outweighed all other considerations, including those referring to Spain's parlous economic state.[55] Ultimately, we are faced not with a cunning Franco who, as the apologist literature wants us to believe, had managed to keep Spain out of the war, but with a disappointed Franco whose hopes of imperial expansion were disappearing into the distance. This is not to say that Franco was unconcerned about certain worrying aspects of the negotiations with Nazi Germany.[56] The approach of the Nazi regime, most notably that of Ribbentrop in his talks with Serrano, often lacked the necessary diplomatic tact. Yet even the toughness of the negotiations did not prepare Hitler for Franco's negative reply of December.

Despite the Führer's growing preoccupation with preparations for Operation Barbarossa, he did not accept Franco's rejection of Felix as the Caudillo's final word. In early February 1941, Hitler again attempted to put pressure on Franco. Yet even his Axis partner Mussolini failed to persuade Franco to enter the war when the two met in Italy on 12 February.[57] Despite further impressive German victories in the spring of 1941 the whole issue of Spain's entry into the war remained inconclusive until the summer, when Germany's invasion of the Soviet Union brought about a dramatic change. On 25 July Spain moved from non-belligerency to, in Serrano Suñer's words, 'moral belligerency'. Without much hesitation, the Spanish government decided to support the German war effort in the East by organizing the Blue Division, *División Azul*. Much has been written about the military role of the more than 18,000 Spanish troops who, over the next few years, were deployed in the environs of Leningrad.[58] In the context of this synthesis of German–Spanish relations it is, however, more valuable to examine 'reasons and repercussions', the object of the most recent scholarly contribution to the history of the Blue Division.[59]

Denis Smyth correctly opposes the notion that some 'popular upsurge of anti-communism inside Spain' was responsible for the decision to send the Blue Division. Yet he seemingly underestimates the importance for Franco himself of this central component of his 'ideology'.[60] In addition, Smyth is only partly correct when he dismisses the argument that the Blue Division was sent in 'reciprocation for the Condor Legion'. At least in financial terms this was the arrangement both sides eventually arrived at. In spring 1944 it was decided to cancel the expenses of the Condor Legion (RM 115 million) against those of the Blue Division (RM 81.5 million + RM 20 million for indemnification of Spanish dead and wounded).[61] Smyth's main conclusion, however, is undoubtedly correct. In his words, by sending the Blue Division Franco

> strove to tie Spain to the Axis via a pact that was binding enough to ensure the eventual achievement of his territorial desiderata in North Africa but loose enough to assure him the freedom of action to join, or abstain from the fray, as might seem appropriate in the developing circumstances.[62]

Again, however, both Hitler and Franco grossly miscalculated the resilience of the enemy. Rather than overcome the Soviet Union in six weeks, the *Wehrmacht* was brought to a halt after its initial furious advance. The campaign dragged on into an early Russian winter and into 1942. In the meantime, the whole course of the war again experienced a dramatic change when, in December, the United States entered it. German–Spanish relations were not unaffected by these developments. According to Preston, American involvement in the war made even

Franco realize that the war 'would be a long and titanic struggle' which forced him 'to postpone Spanish entry into the war indefinitely'.[63] The temptation, however, did not vanish.

The Second World War: Germany's decline

Gradually, German–Spanish relations shifted in favour of Spain. Franco's resounding speech against the Allies on the occasion of the fifth anniversary of the outbreak of the Civil War should not deceive us about the extent of his commitment to the Axis. Admittedly, the attack against the Soviet Union made a German victory more important than ever. In view of Stalin's attitude during the Civil War and Franco's contribution to Operation Barbarossa, victory for the Allies would undoubtedly entail serious consequences. Yet with no foreseeable end to the war on the horizon, Franco was increasingly less inclined to bring Spain into the conflict. With the *Wehrmacht* rapidly engaged beyond the limits of its capabilities, the use of military force against Spain also became less and less likely. Political options, on the other hand – most notably replacing Franco with a more pliable leader – entered the discussions within the Nazi regime during the course of 1942 (see below). Initially, however, the reversal of fortunes Germany experienced during the winter of 1941–2 had its most pronounced effect on the economic dimension of her relations to Spain.

By 31 December 1941, Nazi Germany had accumulated a deficit of RM 122.1 million in the German–Spanish clearing. Thereafter, Nazi Germany remained in the red.[64] To put the matter very simply, Germany imported more from Spain than it was able to export – on top of which Spain charged inflated prices for certain products. The development is directly linked to the German invasion of the Soviet Union. Deprived of the vital Trans-Siberian rail link to the Far East, which, since the autumn of 1939, had enabled the Nazi regime to transport goods from and to the Japanese sphere of influence, other routes for products vital to the German war economy had to be found. Such products included wolfram, or tungsten ore, tungsten being a non-ferrous metal of great importance to Germany's arms production. After Portugal, Spain emerged as the most important source, a development that the Franco regime used to its advantage until summer 1944.[65]

Spain also played a role in remedying other problems affecting the German war effort. During the first winter in Russia the *Wehrmacht* was faced with a catastrophic lack of adequate clothing. Subsequently, 35 per cent of the clothing hides used by Germany's armed forces originated in Spain.[66] Finally, Spain also made a minor contribution towards alleviating Germany's labour shortage. In summer 1943 about 8,000 Spanish workers were employed in Germany, the highest point the number reached. In addition, the Nazi regime also forced Spanish exiles in France to work in Germany and for the German occupation forces.[67]

Overall during the period 1941–4, Spanish exports contributed only an average of 2 per cent to Germany's total importation but, as the two examples of wolfram and hides have shown, a limited number of products proved to be greatly important to the German war effort. In reaction to Germany's purchasing efforts, and Anglo-American campaigns to pre-empt these purchases, the Franco regime exploited the situation and charged higher prices and taxes. Not surprisingly, this led to tensions in Spain's relationship with both belligerent camps. The annoyance of the Allies increased considerably in autumn 1943 when Spain provided Germany with a credit of RM 100 million, officially declared as a down-payment on Franco's Civil War debt.[68]

Discordances in the economic relationship between the two regimes undoubtedly affected Hitler's perception of Franco. The question of the Civil War debt, never fully repaid by the Spanish government, left a particularly bad impression. As early as 28 September 1940, Hitler complained to Ciano that when his regime demanded payment of the debt, 'this is often interpreted by the Spanish as a tactless confusing of economic and idealistic considerations, and as a German, one feels towards the Spanish almost like a Jew, who wants to make business out of the holiest possessions of mankind'.[69] In view of Hitler's other deprecatory comments about the Caudillo it may not come as a surprise that Franco's elimination was considered by the Nazi regime.

In early 1940 dissident Falangists made plans for the overthrow of Franco in order to carry out the 'Falangist revolution'. The extent of German involvement is not clear, though with the Germanophile Air Force Minister General Juan Yagüe Blanco playing a leading role some benefit might have accrued for the Nazi regime. As with many future machinations and plots,[70] the Caudillo proved to be master in his house when, on 27 June, he sacked Yagüe and had him exiled from Madrid. Nazi officials were involved in, or at least informed about, most of the subsequent plotting. In early April 1941, the AA was even approached by a representative of Don Juan who had decided to try the German road towards the restoration of the monarchy in Spain. Despite a friendly reception, the mission ended in failure. In the interest of calm German–Spanish relations Ribbentrop decided to have Serrano Suñer informed about the meeting. A few weeks later, Gerardo Salvador Merino, in charge of the Spanish syndicates, sought assistance from Germany in his attempt to force Franco to change the regime, including the removal of Serrano Suñer. Again, however, Franco – and Serrano – managed to rid themselves of the danger.[71]

By spring 1942, only one group possessed the necessary means to undertake radical (and Germanophile) changes to the regime: the Blue Division. This was recognized by a number of Nazis, most notably Stohrer's predecessor, General Faupel. Now director of the Ibero-American Institute in Berlin and still very keen to meddle in Spanish affairs, Faupel acted as an intermediary between *camisas viejas* in Spain and in the Blue Division. To Franco and Serrano, who were acutely aware of these contacts, the objective of such activities was obvious – as shown by their reaction. From late 1941 onwards attempts were made to convince the Nazi regime of the importance of having certain members of the Falange sent back to Spain. In February 1942 Serrano even pleaded for a temporary complete withdrawal of the Blue Division, though ultimately all the OKW agreed to was a regular exchange of troops.[72]

Increasingly, General Agustín Muñoz Grandes, as commander of the Blue Division, advanced into a key position. This was clearly recognized by Franco, who, in mid-May 1942, recalled Muñoz Grandes from his post, albeit unsuccessfully. In talks with Admiral Canaris, Franco was persuaded to leave the general at his post, a decision that might have had serious consequences for his regime. Yet despite a secret meeting between Hitler and Muñoz Grandes on 12 July, in which the general promised to 'bring about the necessary order in Spain',[73] this potential threat to Franco's regime ultimately produced no effect. Surprisingly enough, it was Franco's removal of Serrano Suñer on 3 September that largely extinguished Hitler's interest in using Muñoz Grandes as a political weapon. Long gone were the days when the Nazi regime had regarded the Franco's brother-in-law's (cunadísimo) presence in the Spanish government as being of advantage to the Axis. In fact, on 1 August 1942, Hitler complained: 'The most evil spirit is undoubtedly S[errano] S[uñer]: he has the task to prepare the Latin Union; he is the gravedigger of the new Spain!'[74]

For the Nazi leadership in Berlin, the removal of Serrano meant hope for improved German–Spanish relations; for Stohrer, who had developed a very good relationship with the Foreign Minister, it meant the beginning of the end of his ambassadorship. The success of Operation Torch, the Allied landings in Algeria and French Morocco on 8 November 1942, further undermined Stohrer's position. Finally, only hours after the signing of the German–Spanish economic agreement of 17 December, Ribbentrop withdrew Stohrer from his post. During the second half of 1942, Spain had regained a crucial role in German planning. In the

efforts of the Nazi regime to make Spain move closer to the Axis, the his-
panophile Stohrer, it appears, had become a potential liability.[75]

By spring 1943, German plans for a transformation of the Spanish
government, including possibly Franco's overthrow, had been abandoned. Although the secret German–Spanish protocol of 10 February
1943 provided some reassurance about Spain's continued proximity to
the Axis,[76] political relations were becoming gradually more detached.
While the Spanish press featured incessant pro-Axis reports, in some
cases right up to Germany's capitulation, the Franco regime could not
fail to notice – and react to – the military decline of the Axis. Defeated
at Stalingrad in the winter of 1942–3, thrown out of North Africa in the
spring of 1943, the Axis would not find any relief in the summer. With
the failure of Operation Citadel the initiative on the Eastern Front was
lost completely to the Red Army, while the Allied invasion of Italy led to
the fall of Mussolini on 25 July. Yet Franco did not react hastily to the
growing Allied superiority. On 26 September, he was finally convinced
of the prudent need to eliminate one blatant symbol of the regime's pro-
Axis leaning, the Blue Division. What could have become a positive sign
to the Allies was tempered, however, by Franco's acceptance of José Luis
de Arrese's suggestion that volunteers should be permitted to remain in
German units.[77]

Even when, on 1 October 1943, Franco referred to Spain's status as one
of 'vigilant neutrality', the Allies, and in particular the US government,
suspected Franco of duplicity. The RM 100 million credit and the 'Laurel
incident'[78] served as blatant reminders that Franco had not become a convert to a position of true neutrality. As a result, the pressure on the
Franco regime to distance itself from Nazi Germany increased. Its most
notable expression was the imposition of the US oil embargo on Spain,
made public on 28 January 1944. The Spanish government was informed
that only a complete cessation of wolfram exports to Germany would
lead to a lifting of the embargo. Although Franco reacted almost
immediately with the announcement of a temporary ban on all wolfram
exports, secretly exports to Germany continued.[79]

Such seemingly pro-German activities had little to do with pressure
exerted by the Nazi regime. Neither strong verbal and written protests
nor the threat of military action would have been sufficient to influence
the Franco regime markedly. Bribes and other incentives were used to
boost the decreasing level of Germanophilia in government circles –
though only with limited success. Other factors, however, worked to the
advantage of the Nazi regime. Although Franco had to tread more carefully, his nationalist pride made him condone pro-German activities in
deliberate defiance of Allied demands. Franco also considered the

continuation of lively economic relations with Germany of vital importance to Spain. Nazi Germany, after all, remained the only major source of
war *matériel* which Franco and his military longed for.[80]

While German–Spanish relations were undeniably affected by growing Allied pressure, no radical caesura took place until after the Allied
invasion of France. The curtain for the final act opened on the morning
of 21 August 1944 when the last German officers left Hendaye.[81] For
Nazi Germany and Franco Spain four years of 'neighbourly' relations had
come to an end. Although German officials continued to be active in
Spain, either in diplomatic or economic functions, or for espionage and
sabotage undertakings, the country as a whole very rapidly receded into
the background of the frantic deliberations in Berlin. Yet neither side
seriously considered a total cessation of relations. In fact, even though it
could only negatively affect her present and future position *vis-à-vis* the
Allies, Francoist Spain continued to contribute to the German war effort
in a minor way.[82] Franco thus did not take the opportunity to put a decisive end to official contacts to Nazi Germany. In the end, it needed
Germany's capitulation to do the job for him.[83]

Conclusion

Relations between Nazi Germany and Franco's Spain during the Spanish
Civil War and the first half of the Second World War were characterized
by an imbalance in favour of the former. From the undeniable recognition that, without substantial German help, Franco would not have
been able to gain power first over the Nationalist camp, and eventually
over the whole of Spain, the Nazi regime derived the right to seek influence over Spanish affairs. While outright control of Spain was not discussed until after the failure in 1940 to persuade Franco to enter the war,
throughout much of the period the Nazi leadership tried to make use of
Spain in those areas which were seen as beneficial to Germany. While
political interference was largely avoided during the Civil War and of
little effect during the Second World War, the economic exploitation of
Spain was pushed extensively. Militarily, Spain (and Spanish Morocco)
was 'developed' into a stronghold of German intelligence-gathering and
military support activities, frequently with the full knowledge and cooperation of Spanish officials. Spain's total military dependence on
Germany was, however, avoided when Hitler failed to bring the country
into the war on the Axis side. In fact, had Franco taken the plunge, Spain
would have become little more than a vassal of Nazi Germany comparable to Antonescu's Romania or possibly even Mussolini's Republic of
Salò. Very probably, General Franco would have shared the fate of both,

and indeed that of Hitler. On the other hand, if we are to believe Hitler and his military advisers, a Spanish entry into the war would have tipped the balance against Britain. So much for the theory. In practice, however, by Spain's staying out of the conflict, the balance in her relations with Germany was gradually tipped towards the Iberian dictatorship. With the *Wehrmacht* increasingly engaged on various fronts – the Soviet Union, North Africa and eventually Italy – Germany's means to put pressure on the Franco regime gave way to the growing need to placate Franco, whether in an effort to continue clandestine military activities or to ensure vital economic supplies. The brutal way of conviction – inciting a pro-German coup or even invading Spain – was considered, but never applied. Franco survived because neither Hitler nor the Allies took the necessary steps to remove him.

Notes

1 Cited in Rainer Zitelmann, *Hitler: Selbstverständnis eines Revolutionärs* (3rd edn, Darmstadt, 1990), pp. 486–7.
2 On the ideological views of the two dictators, see, *inter alia*, Stanley G. Payne, *A History of Fascism 1914–45* (London, 1995); Roger Griffin, *The Nature of Fascism* (London, 1991).
3 Succinctly put by Hitler on 28 September 1940 'without the help of both the countries [Germany and Italy] there would today be no Franco'.
4 See, for example, Marion Einhorn, *Die ökonomischen Hintergründe der faschistischen deutschen Intervention in Spanien, 1936–1939* (Berlin, 1962), pp. 87, 89; Dante A. Puzzo, *Spain and the Great Powers, 1936–1941* (New York, 1962).
5 Wolfgang Schieder, 'Spanischer Bürgerkrieg und Vierjahresplan: Zur Struktur nationalsozialistischer Außenpolitik', in W. Schieder and C. Dipper (eds), *Der spanische Bürgerkrieg in der internationalen Politik, 1936–1939* (Munich, 1976), pp. 165–6.
6 Angel Viñas, *La Alemania nazi y el 18 de Julio* (1st edn, Madrid, 1974; 2nd edn, 1976).
7 On the frequently examined and debated subject of Hitler's role in the making of foreign policy, see, in the context of the Spanish Civil War, Schieder, 'Spanischer Bürgerkrieg' (see note 5), and Hans-Henning Abendroth, 'Die deutsche Intervention im spanischen Bürgerkrieg: Ein Diskussionsbeitrag', *Vierteljahreshefte für Zeitgeschichte*, 1 (1982), pp. 117–29.
8 Despite the testimony provided by Franco's envoy Johannes Bernhardt (see Hans-Henning Abendroth, *Mittelsmann zwischen Franco und Hitler: Johannes Bernhardt erinnert 1936* (Marktheidenfeld, 1978), pp. 31–2) some authors still assume that Göring and Blomberg were present during the discussions which led to Hitler's decision. For the most recent example, see Walther L. Bernecker, 'Alemania y la guerra civil española', in Walther L. Bernecker (ed.), *España y Alemania en la edad contemporánea* (Frankfurt am Main, 1992), pp. 147, 149.
9 Detailed information on the events of 25 and 26 July 1936 can be found in Hans-Henning Abendroth, *Hitler in der spanischen Arena: Die deutsch–spanischen*

Beziehungen im Spannungsfeld der europäischen Interessenpolitik vom Ausbruch des Bürgerkrieges bis zum Ausbruch des Weltkrieges, 1936–1939 (Paderborn, 1973); Abendroth, *Mittelsmann*; Viñas, *La Alemania nazi*.

10 For the complete list, see Viñas, *La Alemania nazi* (1st edn), p. 460.

11 Paul Preston, *Franco: A Biography* (London, 1995), pp. 176–8.

12 *Sonderstab W* continued to operate until the end of the Civil War under the aegis of Göring's permanent secretary Erhard Milch.

13 Both Manfred Merkes and Wolfgang Schieder have insisted that Hitler expected Franco's quick victory. Abendroth, on the other hand, has asserted that Hitler viewed Franco's position with pessimism; see Peter Monteath, 'German Historiography and the Spanish Civil War: A Critical Survey', *European History Quarterly* 20 (1990), pp. 263–5 for a summary of the debate among the three German historians. See Viñas, *La Alemania nazi* (1st edn), p. 447, for confirmation of Abendroth's assessment.

14 One of the few occasions after August 1936 on which Hitler again directly intervened in events in Spain was in late May 1937. After a Republican air raid on the German pocket battleship *Deutschland* which killed and wounded part of the ship's crew, Hitler – who, according to Goebbels, fumed with rage – immediately ordered a retaliatory attack. Almería was subsequently shelled by the *Admiral Scheer*. See Willard C. Frank Jr, 'The Spanish Civil War and the Coming of the Second World War', *International History Review* 9 (1987), pp. 380–1 on both the *Deutschland* and the *Leipzig* incidents.

15 Abendroth, *Hitler*, p. 53.

16 For the full text of Thomas's memorandum, see German Federal Archive/Military Archive (BA/MA) RW19/991.

17 In April 1936, Göring had been ordered by Hitler to examine all possible ways to improve Germany's raw material and foreign currency position. Shortly after the outbreak of the Spanish Civil War he took charge of the newly created Four-Year Plan Office. On Göring's role in the German economy and its implications for Germany's intervention, see Christian Leitz, 'Hermann Göring and Nazi Germany's Exploitation of Nationalist Spain, 1936–1939', *German History* 14 (1996), pp. 24, 26.

18 See Robert H. Whealey, *Hitler and Spain: The Nazi Role in the Spanish Civil War, 1936–1939* (Lexington, 1989), pp. 24, 101–2, on Condor Legion figures; see Bernecker, 'Alemania', pp. 154–7 for a summary of German involvement on the side of the Spanish Republic.

19 An additional German training unit which arrived in Spain in December eventually trained 56,000 Nationalist officers and non-commissioned officers; Robert H. Whealey, 'Foreign Intervention in the Spanish Civil War', in Raymond Carr (ed.), *The Republic and the Civil War in Spain* (London and Basingstoke, 1971), p. 219.

20 Both Abendroth and (particularly) Klaus Maier used diary entries of the Legion's Chief of Staff, Wolfram von Richthofen, Italian records, and the records of *Sonderstab W* to provide a detailed picture of the events of 26 July. Subsequently, both Herbert R. Southworth and Angel Viñas attacked Maier and Abendroth for their central conclusion that a 'terror attack' against Guernica had not been planned in advance by the Condor Legion; Hans-Henning Abendroth, 'Guernica: Ein fragwürdiges Symbol', *Militärgeschichtliche Mitteilungen* 41 (1987), pp. 111–26; Klaus Maier, 'Guernica, Fakten und Mythen', *German Studies Review* 18 (1995), pp.

465–70. See also Abendroth, *Hitler*, pp. 162ff, and Klaus Maier, *Guernica, 26.4. 1937: Die deutsche Intervention in Spanien und der 'Fall Guernica'* (Freiburg, 1975).

21 Of a total of 150 Mark I which arrived during the war nearly two-thirds were destroyed; José Luis Alcofar Nassaes, 'Las armas de ambos bandos', *Historia 16*, La Guerra Civil, 10 (n.d.), pp. 97–8.

22 By that time 92 German aircraft and more than 3,800 troops of the Condor Legion as well as tanks, anti-aircraft guns and signal equipment had reached Spain.

23 Hitler appointed Faupel on 18 November. He was eventually made ambassador on 11 February 1937.

24 Akten zur deutschen Auswärtigen Politik (ADAP), D, III, doc. 144, 133–4, Faupel to AA, 5.12.1936. Both Blomberg and Admiral Erich Raeder were opposed to any further expansion of Germany's military commitment in Spain. On 21 December, Hitler informed his generals of his decision not to send major contingents of troops to Spain; Frank, 'The Spanish Civil War', p. 377.

25 Warlimont's evidence in Raymond L. Proctor, *Hitler's Luftwaffe in the Spanish Civil War* (Westport and London, 1983), p. 77. According to Warlimont, Faupel proposed sending three full infantry divisions (at least 60,000 men) to Spain; *ibid.*, p. 75.

26 By 18 February 1937 nearly 50,000 Italian troops had arrived in Spain; John F. Coverdale, *Italian Intervention in the Spanish Civil War* (Princeton, 1975), p. 175.

27 German Federal Archive/Abteilungen Potsdam (BA/Pots) 09.01/60960, summary by Schmidt of Goering–Mussolini meeting, Palazzo Venezia, Rome, 14 January 1937. On 23 January a joint Italo-German note was sent to Franco making it known that after a last major effort to ensure victory all aid would cease; Coverdale, *Italian Intervention*, p. 174.

28 According to a German post-Civil War report Nazi Germany violated the agreement at least 180 times – this being the number of shipments sent to Franco; Whealey, 'Foreign Intervention', p. 221 (see note 19).

29 Gerhard Schreiber, *Revisionismus und Weltmachtstreben: Marineführung und deutsch–italienische Beziehungen 1919–1944* (Stuttgart, 1978).

30 Aktenzur deutschen Auswärtigen Politik (ADAP), D, III, doc. 142, 132, telegram, von Neurath to German embassy in Rome, 5 December 1936.

31 See Leitz, 'Hermann Göring', p. 24 (see note 17 for details).

32 Ibid., pp. 25–6; Christian Leitz, 'Nazi Germany's Intervention in the Spanish Civil War and the Foundation of HISMA/ROWAK', in Paul Preston and Ann L. Mackenzie (eds), *The Republic Besieged: Civil War in Spain 1936–1939* (Edinburgh, 1996), pp. 53–85.

33 BA/Pots 09.01/60960, declarations by Göring during conversation with Mussolini, 15 January 1937.

34 It is revealing that, during the second half of 1940, when both sides discussed a possible Spanish entry into the war, Ramón Serrano Suñer referred to the Rio Tinto company – which the Nazi regime demanded to have transferred from British into German ownership – as an 'economic Gibraltar'.

35 On MONTANA see Leitz, *Economic Relations*, pp. 77–90; on the legal debate over MONTANA which occupied both sides particularly during 1938, see Abendroth, *Hitler*, pp. 242ff.

36 Goebbels's diary entries reveal strikingly the unsatisfactory nature of Franco's progress in December and January; see Hilari Raguer, 'La guerra civil vista por Goebbels', *Historia 16* 14 (1989), pp. 28–9.

37 Stohrer's ambassadorial appointment was announced on 30 August 1937. Biographical details on Stohrer can be found in Klaus-Jörg Ruhl, *Spanien im Zweiten Weltkrieg: Franco, die Falange und das 'Dritte Reich'* (Hamburg, 1975), pp. 51–2.

38 For more details about Faupel's behaviour, see Abendroth, *Hitler*, pp. 113ff; Proctor, *Hitler's Luftwaffe*, pp. 71–3; and Whealey, *Hitler and Spain*, pp. 64–5.

39 Aktenzur deutschen Auswärtigen Politil (ADAP), D, III, doc. 672, 638, letter, Stohrer to Weizsäcker, 2 October 1938.

40 On 8 May Franco also ended Spain's membership of the League of Nations.

41 See Glyn Stone, 'Britain, France and Franco's Spain in the Aftermath of the Spanish Civil War', *Diplomacy and Statecraft* 6 (1995), pp. 373–407.

42 Various comments are summarized in Paul Preston, 'Franco and the Axis Temptation', in Paul Preston, *The Politics of Revenge: Fascism and the Military in Twentieth-Century Spain* (London, 1995), pp. 52–3.

43 On plans for Germany's role in the reconstruction of Spain, see Bundesarchiv Koblenz (BA) R7/3412, Reich Economics Ministry report on Spain, end of 1938; US National Archives II (NA II) T83, roll 229, folder 894, IG Farben report 'Spaniens Wirtschaftskräfte', pp. 66ff, end of 1939.

44 On Anglo–Spanish relations during the first years of the war, see Denis Smyth, *Diplomacy and Strategy of Survival: British Policy and Franco's Spain, 1940–1941* (Cambridge: Cambridge University Press, 1986).

45 See Charles B. Burdick, '"Moro": The Resupply of German Submarines in Spain, 1939–1942', *Central European History* 3 (1970), pp. 265–84.

46 Stanley G. Payne, *The Franco Regime 1936–1975* (Madison, 1987), p. 266.

47 See, for example, José María Doussinague, *España tenía razón (1939–1945)* (Madrid, 1949); H.G. Dahms, *Francisco Franco, Soldat und Staatschef* (Göttingen, 1972); Brian Crozier, *Franco: A Biographical History* (London, 1967).

48 Paul Preston, 'Franco and Hitler: The Myth of Hendaye 1940', *Contemporary European History* 1 (1992), p. 3. Preston's article is an excellent settling of accounts with Franco's propagandists and their untenable claims.

49 On the negotiations in the second half of 1940 over a Spanish entry into the war, see Donald S. Detwiler, *Hitler, Franco und Gibraltar: Die Frage des spanischen Kriegseintritts in den Zweiten Weltkrieg* (Wiesbaden, 1962); Mathias Ruiz Holst, *Neutralität oder Kriegsbeteiligung? Die deutsch–spanischen Verhandlungen im Jahre 1940* (Pfaffenweiler, 1986); Preston, 'Franco and Hitler', pp. 1–16; Preston, 'Franco and the Axis Temptation', pp. 60–71; Walther L. Bernecker, 'Neutralität wider Willen: Spaniens verhinderter Kriegseintritt', in H. Altrichter and J. Becker (eds), *Kriegsausbruch 1939: Beteiligte, Betroffene, Neutrale* (Munich, 1989), pp. 153–77.

50 See Preston, 'Franco and Hitler', *passim*, for the most up-to-date reconstruction. We also lack more precise information of the discussions during Heinrich Himmler's visit to Spain just prior to the Hendaye meeting. It appears, however, that they were not linked to German–Spanish negotiations over Spain's entry into the war; David W. Pike, 'Franco and the Axis Stigma', *Journal of Contemporary History* 17 (1982), p. 369; Payne, *The Franco Regime*, pp. 272–3 n. 21.

51 Norman J.W. Goda, 'The Riddle of the Rock: A Reassessment of German Motives for the Capture of Gibraltar in the Second World War', *Journal of Contemporary History* 28 (1993), p. 297.

52 Goda emphasizes that for Hitler Gibraltar 'was the linch-pin to a scheme for a network of forward Atlantic naval and air bases in North-west Africa – bases intended . . . for a future struggle with the United States'; ibid., pp. 298ff; for additional information on Goda's thesis, see Goda, 'Hitler's Demand for Casablanca in 1940: Incident or Policy?', *International History Review* 16 (1994), pp. 491–510.

53 On Germany's failure to supply Spain with food, see Leitz, *Economic Relations*, p. 127.

54 Franco's claims to the opposite (in US Department of State (ed.), *The Spanish Government and the Axis: Documents* (Washington, DC, 1946), p. 15, Franco to Hitler, 22 September 1940), namely that Spanish control of Morocco would prevent the danger of Gaullist rebellions in Algeria and Tunisia, fell on deaf ears.

55 Heleno Saña, *El franquismo sin mitos: conversaciones con Serrano Suñer* (Barcelona, 1982), pp. 192–3.

56 For example Germany's economic claims including demands for British and French companies; see Leitz, *Economic Relations*, pp. 133–5.

57 On Italo-Spanish relations during the Second World War, see Javier Tusell and Genoveva García Queipo de Llano, *Franco y Mussolini: la política española durante la segunda guerra mundial* (Barcelona, 1985).

58 See Gerald Kleinfeld and Lewis Tambs, *Hitler's Spanish Legion: The Blue Division in Russia* (Carbondale and Edwardsville, 1979); Raymond L. Proctor, *Agonía de un neutral* (Madrid, 1972) and 'La Division Azul', *Guerres Mondiales et Conflits Contemporaines* 162 (1991). *In toto*, 47,000 Spaniards fought on the Eastern Front between October 1941 and January 1944.

59 Denis Smyth, 'The Dispatch of the Spanish Blue Division to the Russian Front: Reasons and Repercussions', *European History Quarterly* 24 (1994), pp. 537–53.

60 On Franco's obsessive anti-Communism, see Preston, *Franco*, p. 61. In the context of the events of late June 1941 it can be assumed that Serrano Suñer's 'Russia is guilty' speech was fully endorsed by Franco.

61 Leitz, *Economic Relations*, p. 134.

62 Smyth, 'Dispatch', p. 543. Preston, 'Franco and the Axis temptation', p. 76, arrives at the same conclusion.

63 Preston, 'Franco and the Axis temptation', p. 78.

64 By 30 June 1943 the deficit was to reach a level of RM 248.8 million; Leitz, *Economic Relations*, p. 137.

65 For a detailed examination of the role of wolfram in German–Spanish relations, see Christian Leitz, 'Nazi Germany's Struggle for Spanish Wolfram during the Second World War', *European History Quarterly* 25 (1995), pp. 71–92, and Leitz, *Economic Relations*, pp. 170–99.

66 BA/MA RW19/435, Appendix 25 of *War Diary No. 4* of OKW WiAmt, Wi Ausl IVa to OKM/M Rü IIb, 30.1.1943.

67 Rafael García Pérez, 'El envío de trabajadores españoles a Alemania durante la segunda guerra mundial', *Hispania* 170 (1988), pp. 1031–65.

68 Leitz, *Economic Relations*, pp. 183–4; Rafael García Pérez, *Franquismo y Tercer Reich: las relaciones económicas hispano-alemanas durante la segunda guerra*

mundial (Madrid, 1994), pp. 429–30; Angel Viñas, *Política comercial exterior en España, 1931–1975* (Madrid, 1979), vol.1, p. 409.

69 US Department of State (ed.), *The Spanish Government*, p. 19.

70 See Paul Preston, 'Franco and His Generals, 1939–1945', in *Politics of Revenge*, pp. 85–108, on oppositional activities by the Spanish military. See also Ruhl, *Spanien*, pp. 63–4.

71 Ruhl, *Spanien*, pp. 65–71.

72 *Ibid.*, pp. 100–2.

73 *Ibid.*, p. 114.

74 Werner Jochmann (ed.), *Adolf Hitler: Monologe im Führerhauptquartier 1941–1944* (Bindlach, 1988), p. 323; see also *ibid.*, p. 389.

75 In early September Hitler had already intimated to Ribbentrop that it was about time to recall the ambassador as quickly as possible; Ruhl, *Spanien*, p. 175; see also *ibid.*, p. 191. Stohrer was replaced by Hans Adolf von Moltke. When the latter died within less than three months, he was succeeded by Ribbentrop's brother-in-law, Hans Heinrich Dieckhoff.

76 US Department of State (ed.), *The Spanish Government*, p. 35, secret protocol between the German and Spanish governments, 10 February 1943.

77 Preston, *Franco: a Biography* (London, 1995), p. 499. From November 1943 until its withdrawal in March/April 1944 a 'Spanish Legion' of about 1,500 troops remained on the Eastern Front. Some Spanish volunteers continued to fight for Nazi Germany until the last days of the war.

78 On the Laurel incident, see J.W. Cortada, 'Spain and the Second World War', *Journal of Contemporary History* 5 (1971), pp. 66–7.

79 See Leitz, *Economic Relations*, p. 189.

80 See C. Leitz, '*Programm Bär*: the Supply of German War Material to Spain, 1943–44', in C. Leitz and D.J. Dunthorn (eds), *Spain in an International Context: From Civil War to Early Cold War* (Oxford and Providence, R.I., forthcoming).

81 Dieckhoff himself left Spain for Berlin on 2 September 1944, ostensibly to report on developments in Spain. He was not to return to his post and the German embassy was run by Chargé d'Affaires Sigismund von Bibra until the end of the war.

82 See Leitz, *Economic Relations*, pp. 200–18.

83 On the fate of Germans in Spain after Germany's capitulation, see Carlos Collado Seidel, 'Zufluchtsstätte für Nationalsozialisten? Deutsche Agenten in Spanien 1944–1947', *Vierteljahreshefte für Zeitgeschichte* 43 (1995), pp. 131–57. On Spanish–German relations after Germany's capitulation, see Petra-Maria Weber, 'Política española hacia Alemania, 1945–1958: el impacto político y económico de las relaciones hispano-alemanas', in Bernecker (ed.), *España y Alemania*, pp. 209–30.

7 Italy and Spain in Civil War and World War, 1936–1943

Paul Preston

Mussolini and Spain: 1936–43

Italy became involved in the Spanish Civil War largely because the military rebels had dramatically miscalculated the scale of the task facing them on 17–18 July 1936. However, the Italian interest in Spain predated the military uprising. Mussolini had given financial and other support to parties of the extreme right during the Second Republic, subsidizing the Falange, providing funds for conspiratorial activities for both the extreme monarchist organization *Renovación Española* and the Carlist *Comunión Tradicionalista*, as well as providing training facilities in Italy for Carlist *requetés* (militias).[1] He did so partly out of ideological imperialism and partly out of a sense that anything that he could do to help create a sympathetic regime in Spain would weaken France. By meddling in Spain, therefore, he was seeking to make a significant contribution to his plans to undermine the Anglo-French hegemony of international relations which he believed kept Italy imprisoned in the Mediterranean. However, his pre-1936 interference had little connection with the uprising of 17–18 July.[2]

The military rebels had not anticipated the scale of working-class resistance on the Spanish mainland nor that a naval mutiny would lead to the blockade in Morocco of the most powerful rebel force, the ruthless mercenary Army of Africa, commanded by General Franco. In the days immediately following the uprising, the insurrectionary generals desperately sought help from Fascist Italy and Nazi Germany.[3] After initial hesitation, Mussolini's involvement would escalate from the provision of transport aircraft to a point at which Italy was, in everything short of a formal declaration of hostilities, at war with the Spanish Republic. In consequence, his contribution to Franco's victory would be decisive. In the process of collaborating with Hitler in support of Franco, Mussolini enthusiastically tied his foreign policy to that of the Third

Reich. He also squandered financial and physical resources in Spain on a scale which severely diminished Italian military effectiveness in the Second World War. The precise calculation of the financial and military costs to Italy of the Duce's Spanish entanglement is a difficult subject which has only recently started to receive the treatment which it demands.[4] That Mussolini would get so embroiled in Spain was partly the consequence of the euphoria that followed upon his success in Abyssinia. His first steps in the direction of the Axis were significantly aided by the fact that on 9 June 1936 he had appointed as Foreign Minister his son-in-law, Galeazzo Ciano, who came to the post determined to give Italy a totally Fascist foreign policy. Relying on an inner cabinet of like-minded Fascists, Ciano dispensed with the wiser heads of experienced functionaries and thereby ensured that the Duce's tendency to wild and whimsical leaps would be unrestrained.[5] However, while Ciano reacted enthusiastically to the first emissaries from the Spanish military rebels, Mussolini himself was initially very cautious.

On 19 July, Franco had sent the right-wing journalist Luis Bolín to Rome to ask Mussolini for transport planes for an airlift of his troops across the Straits of Gibraltar. While Bolín was still travelling, the Italian Minister Plenipotenitary in Tangier, Pier Filippo De Rossi del Lion Nero, had – in response to the first news of the uprising – sent his military attaché, Major Giuseppe Luccardi, to Tetuán to assess the situation. In Tetuán on 20 and 21 July, Franco saw Luccardi several times and repeated the request already sent via Bolín. Franco made a cunning appeal to Mussolini, offering flattery, certain success, future subservience and a bargain price. Presenting himself as sole leader of the military uprising – which he was not, yet – Franco declared that his objective was to establish 'a republican government in the fascist style adapted for the Spanish people'. He claimed success would be assured if the limited request for eight Italian transport aircraft was granted. Finally, he promised that if Italy smiled on his cause, 'future relations will be more than friendly' (*più che amichevoli*).[6] The future Caudillo was apparently offering Mussolini the tempting prospect of a client state which could clearly tip the Mediterranean balance in his favour and against both Britain and France. However, the situation was far too confused to tempt the Duce into a precipitate response. Franco was told that no aircraft were available.[7]

Over the course of the next week, Franco continued to insist, describing the failure to send aircraft as '*miopia politica*' and that Italian help 'would have permitted the influence of Rome to prevail over that of Berlin in the future politics of Spain'.[8] Although he was too cautious to take the risk of war with either France or Britain, the Duce's interest in

the Spanish situation and in the role of General Franco was being maintained by the stream of telegrams from Tangier. The Duce's reticence
derived from his reading of reports that the French had decided to grant
Spanish government requests for military aid.[9] Mussolini began gradually to incline towards support for Franco between 25 and 27 July as a
result of several factors. He was much impressed by reports from Paris
which showed that the French were reversing their original decision to
send aid to the Republic. This was in reaction to the massive right-wing
press campaign mounted after leaks about French military assistance by
the military attaché at the Spanish Republican Embassy in Paris, Major
Antonio Barroso. Ironically, the French *volte-face* had also been made
partly as a consequence of rumours and press speculation in Paris about
possible German and Italian intervention.[10] These events were followed
closely in Rome through detailed reports from the Italian embassy,
which was liberally supplied with information from rebel sympathizers
within the Spanish embassy. By 25 July, Mussolini was fully informed of
how pressure from London was paralysing the Blum cabinet and making
it think again about help for Spain. He knew for certain by 25 July that
the French had decided definitively not to help the Spanish Republic.[11]

For a variety of reasons, Mussolini also came to the conclusion that the
British establishment supported the Spanish military rebels. Sir Samuel
Hoare, as First Lord of the Admiralty, and Admiral Sir A. Ernle
Chatfield, the First Sea Lord and Chief of the Naval Staff, were enthusi-
asts for the Nationalist cause.[12] Information reaching Rome as Mussolini
and Ciano considered granting Franco's insistent requests strongly
inclined them to believe that their action would enjoy the covert
approval of Britain.[13] Both the Duce and his Foreign Minister were convinced, for instance, that Portuguese support for the rebels would not
have been possible without the tacit permission of the British.[14] The
clinching factor in favour of Franco was the arrival in Rome on 27 July
of a detailed report that the Kremlin was deeply embarrassed by events
in Spain and had no intention of helping the Spanish Republic. The
Duce boasted later that he participated in the Civil War because he
wanted to fight communism.[15] In fact, for all his sincere anti-communism, the Duce could not contemplate a military conflict with the Soviet
Union. What emboldened him to intervene in Spain was the knowledge
that originally the Kremlin wanted no part of the events in Spain.
Believing that a rebel victory would seriously undermine Franco-Soviet
collaboration and a left-wing victory by 'armed workers' would inspire a
wave of international anti-communism, the Soviet position would be one
of 'prudent neutrality' since, according to a highly placed Soviet source,
'in no circumstances would the Soviet government let itself get involved

in the internal events of the peninsula where there was nothing to gain and everything to lose'.[16] Along with indications of French weakness, reports on Russian embarrassment convinced Mussolini and Ciano that any Italian aid to Franco would be all the more decisive. Eventually, Moscow would intervene, but the decision to do so came about well after Mussolini had committed himself to meeting Franco's first pleas for help.

Accordingly, arrangements were made during the night of 27 July and the early morning of 28 July for help to be sent to Franco. A squadron of 12 Savoia-Marchetti S.81 bombers was assembled in Sardinia on 29 July prior to flying to Spanish Morocco on the following day and a cargo ship was loaded with munitions and aviation fuel.[17] Commanded by Lieutenant-Colonel Ruggero Bonomi, Head of the School of Aerial Navigation at Orbetello, the squadron was symbolically escorted by General Giuseppe Valle, the Chief of Staff of the Regia Aeronautica and Under-Secretary of the Ministry of Aviation. General Valle instructed the crews that, on arrival in Morocco, they should join the Spanish Foreign Legion as a cover. At dawn on 30 July, they took off to fly to Nador in Spanish Morocco. They were followed by 12 sea-borne Fiat C.R.32 fighters.[18]

From the Spanish side, the decisive contact had not been the various emissaries to Rome but Franco, who, in persuading Luccardi and De Rossi that he controlled the rebel forces and that he was going to win, secured Mussolini's early support for himself. Of equal importance for the Duce were the reports from his diplomats in Paris and Moscow. After the point of no return, all the feedback from London reinforced the assumption that the British would do nothing to impede Italian help for Franco. Even as the first Italian aircraft were on their way to Morocco, the Italian chargé d'affaires in London, Leonardo Vitetti, reported on the widespread sympathy to be found within the highest reaches of the Conservative Party for the Spanish rebels and for Italian Fascism. Vitetti's conclusions derived from conversations with Conservative MPs, Captain David Margesson, the Conservative Leader of the House, with senior Tories at the Carlton Club and with representatives of the Rothermere press. Tory Members of Parliament told him of their conviction that the events in Spain were the direct consequence of 'subversive Soviet propaganda' and of their anxiety to see the Spanish left crushed. The right-wing Leo Amery, who had been First Lord of the Admiralty in the early 1920s, had told him that the Spanish war raised 'the problem of the defence of Europe against the threat of bolshevism'. Ciano was delighted and encouraged further contacts.[19] Vitetti reported that British support for French proposals for non-intervention was based entirely on the belief that it was a useful device for preventing French help to the Spanish Republic.[20]

The Italian decision to intervene in the Spanish Civil War was taken without any serious investigation into Franco's possibilities of ultimate success. On the basis of Luccardi's onward transmission of assertions from Franco, it was concluded that a small quantity of Italian equipment could be decisive for the military rebellion in Spain and provide massive rewards in terms of extended influence in the Western Mediterranean. After being provided with overwhelming evidence that its provision was not likely to provoke a dangerous reaction from London, Paris or Moscow, Mussolini decided to help Franco. In late July, both the Duce and Ciano accepted Franco's claims that a limited – but still substantial – amount of help, the Savoia-Marchetti bombers and the Fiat C.R.32 fighter sent from Sardinia, would rapidly tip the balance in favour of the rebels.[21]

Strong headwinds had reduced the speed of the Savoia-Marchetti S.81s. Only nine of the original twelve arrived. With fuel running low, one came down in the sea, one landed and one crashed in French Morocco.[22] News of their dramatic arrival was telegraphed to Paris, where it was then decisive in the French decision to push for non intervention. The initiative for an agreement emanated from the French.[23] After the crash-landings, the official Italian line was to claim disingenuously that some kind of private venture was afoot.[24] In meetings with British and French diplomatic representatives, Ciano denied any intervention in Spain by the Fascist government.[25] Despite the embarrassment of the crash-landing in French North Africa, there had been no negative repercussions to their risk-taking. Not only had they got away with it, but the return on their investment seemed to be rapid and it took the form of an intensification of the relations with Nazi Germany.

The first official communication from Germany that Hitler was committed to helping Franco came at a meeting in Bolzano on 4 August between the head of German Military Intelligence, Admiral Wilhelm Canaris, and his Italian counterpart, General Mario Roatta, the Chief of the *Servizio Informazioni Militari* (SIM). The meeting had been requested on 1 August by Canaris. Roatta agreed without knowing what the agenda might be. However, since the Lufthansa Junkers Ju 52 which had taken Franco's emissaries to Hitler had returned to Spanish Morocco via the Italian mainland and Sardinia on 28 July, it is inconceivable that the SIM was unaware of German aid to Franco. At Bolzano, Canaris requested that Italy supply, at German expense, aviation fuel to the Spanish rebels and also allow the German aircraft promised to Franco to refuel in Italy *en route* to Spain. Roatta and Canaris agreed to set up a daily exchange of telegrams to permit coordination on Spain which brought nearer the broader Italo-German cooperation in Spain which Ciano sought. On 7 August, Roatta telephoned Canaris to inform him that Mussolini had agreed to his requests.[26]

The seeds of the later escalation of Italian aid can be seen in a desperate telegram from De Rossi to Ciano of 19 August. When Canaris and Roatta met at Bolzano, it seemed as if the war would be over quickly. Franco's first columns had set off northwards from Seville two days earlier and the rest of the Army of Africa was in the process of being transported across the Straits. In the first eight days, the African columns advanced 200 kilometres and the first important town in their path, Mérida, fell on 10 August. It would take them more than two weeks to traverse the next 100 kilometres. They would not reach Talavera de la Reina in the province of Toledo until 27 August. To reach Talavera, the last major town before Madrid, 300 kilometres from their starting point, in twenty-five days was a remarkable achievement. However, Franco was shaken by the perceptible slowdown of their progress as the Republicans began to organize better defences. Accordingly, he had approached De Rossi for more Italian assistance. In his telegram to Ciano, De Rossi urged that risks be taken on Franco's behalf. Underlining the rebel general's achievements to date, he then made a comparison with the situation a month previously:

> Speedy Italian commitment to ample assistance then permitted Franco to turn around his difficult predicament and gave him the freedom of movement to become master of Western Spain and occupy the Sierra de Guadarrama before the capital. But, from such positions, solid and important that they are, he can only with difficulty go forward and secure above all possession of the capital if he does not have new resources to make up the deficiencies in his armament and to balance the help constantly sent by the forces of international subversion, especially the French Popular Front.

The telegram was seen by Mussolini.[27] Two days later, Franco now requested motor torpedo boats (presumably to neutralize the continuing blockade of Morocco), a squadron of light bombers, 24 armoured cars, 200 light machine guns with 1 million cartridges, 20,000 gas masks and poison gas bombs.[28]

Franco's request was largely successful – although, despite serious consideration in Rome of the use of poison gas in Spain, none was ever sent.[29] Soon there would be an Italian force in Majorca. Then, as Franco encountered ever greater difficulties in his march on Madrid, he turned to Italy as a matter of course. And the more that Mussolini said 'yes', the more difficult it would become for him to say 'no' since, for all that the democracies turned a blind eye, the world knew that the cause of Franco was the cause of the Duce. In the course of barely one month, Mussolini had moved imperceptibly but catastrophically from his initial cautiously reached decision in favour of limited aid towards the open-ended commitment that, within five months, would see Italy effectively at war with the Spanish Republic.

Franco's insistent requests via De Rossi – and the evidence that the African columns were finding the going ever more difficult – pushed both the Italians and the Germans to increase their involvement in Spain. In the late morning of 26 August, Ciano informed Roatta that the Duce had decided to place him in command of a full-scale *Missione Militare Italiana in Spagna* (MMIS) alongside a German mission to aid Franco. The task of the two missions would be fourfold:

> 1) to examine the possibilities and the proposals for support for the Nationalists from the Italian armed forces (provision of war material and personnel); 2) to advise the Spanish High Command on the development of military operations against the reds; 3) to guarantee the political, military and economic interests of the two respective nations; 4) to collaborate in a spirit of harmonious accord between the two missions in the implementation of decisions consequent on the three first points.

Two days later, accompanied by Lieutenant-Colonel Walter Warlimont of the War Ministry Staff, Admiral Canaris met Roatta in Rome to work out the details. It was agreed that, despite the non-intervention agreement, Franco's requests for war *matériel* would be met, possibly in equal parts by Germany and Italy. Information was exchanged on the scale of assistance delivered so far. It was also decided, at Canaris's suggestion, that material would be sent only to Franco on the grounds that he was the supreme commander and thus the competent person to decide on the division of equipment among his forces. Supplies from both countries would come through their respective armed forces and not from private companies. Each would supply the appropriate fuel for the equipment it had sent and provide technical aid in the form of drivers, engineers and mechanics. They would also each send an officer for liaison with Franco to guarantee the political-military and economic-military interests of their own country, to advise him, to arrange agreements for the payment for the equipment either in cash or raw materials, to report on the situation to their respective intelligence services and to transmit Franco's requests. For this post, the Germans had already named Warlimont. Both liaison officers were to meet at SIM offices in Rome on the evening of 3 September and then proceed to Franco's headquarters, with false passports, as soon as possible, where they would be introduced by Luccardi. They were to be under Spanish command. It was agreed not to seek any political advantages or recompense from Franco but to ensure immediate or deferred payment. Canaris raised the issue of the desirability of assistance being given to Franco's naval forces and asked if Italy might supply some motor torpedo boats (which, in the light of De Rossi's telegram of 19 August, suggested that the Admiral had recently been in touch with Franco). They each provided a list of the material supplied to date which suggested that the Italians had already gone along with much of Franco's request of the previous week.[30]

Canaris saw Ciano later in the day to discuss the ten points drafted at the earlier meeting. Ciano told him about the Italian expedition to the Balearic Islands under the '"console" della Milizia, Sig. Bonaccorsi' and also that nine heavy bombers would be sent to Burgos.[31] They agreed future cooperation in the friendliest and most flexible manner possible. Ciano raised the point that German airmen in Spain were under orders to limit themselves to maintaining equipment and training Spaniards in its use and to abstain from intervention in military operations whereas their Italian counterparts had been given total freedom to take part in military operations. He requested that German airmen be given the same freedom, and Canaris undertook to raise the matter in Berlin. On the question of political advantages to be derived from aid to Franco, Ciano categorically assured Canaris that 'the Italian Government has not requested and will not request anything from General Franco'. In an interesting sidelight on his continuing fears of Britain and France, Ciano said that he thought that any naval assistance would be altogether too dangerous since ships could not be hidden. 'Even simple motor torpedo boats would constitute too serious material proof of intervention,' he said. He proposed instead great Italian participation in bombing operations.[32]

Warlimont and Roatta, accompanied by his second-in-command, Colonel Emilio Faldella, went by boat to Ceuta on 5 September. On the following day, they flew to Seville and then drove to Cáceres where, in presenting his credentials to Franco, Roatta conveyed Mussolini's *de facto* recognition of his leadership and his confidence in an extremely quick victory.[33] That was not to be. In the days preceding the arrival of the MMIS staff, Franco had complained, via De Rossi and Major Luccardi, of an alleged superiority of Republican forces and again requested motor torpedo boats, light bombers and 24 fighter aircraft. The Deputy Chief of the General Staff, General Alberto Pariani, wrote on one telegram from Luccardi, 'Franco is always thirty short of thirty-one. It's obvious that he has just not organized enough. Why didn't he negotiate a deal first?'[34] That, of course, was not Franco's way. Franco's requests were interspersed with slavish messages of devotion to Mussolini.[35] It had taken Franco's troops six days to capture Talavera de la Reina and a further two weeks to get to the strategically important town of Maqueda on 21 September. It was hardly surprising then, that, once the MMIS had arrived, Franco's requests should have escalated. Fears of international vigilance ensured that his calls for coastal artillery and substantial naval equipment were rejected by Rome.[36] Nonetheless, Roatta's initial impression of Franco was extremely favourable and he did nothing to diminish the tendency towards ever greater Italian involvement.[37] In mid-October, Franco particularly impressed Roatta with reports of the arrival of Soviet aid. The MMIS commander, in agreement with Warlimont, advocated that Rome accede to Franco's requests.[38]

The question of whether Mussolini was manipulated by the Germans into ever greater Spanish commitments is complex. The Counsellor of the Soviet embassy in Rome was convinced that all overtures for a better Italo-German understanding emanated from Rome.[39] Mussolini wanted an immediate and spectacular victory; Hitler was happy merely to have the opportunity to try out equipment, secure strategic raw materials and to cause maximum instability in international relations. There can be little doubt, as he himself explicitly admitted at the famous Hossbach conference of 5 November 1937, that Hitler was delighted by Mussolini's acceptance of the more active role in Spain. By that time, he could contemplate encouraging the Duce to be more ambitious in the Mediterranean in order to intensify tension between Italy and the Western allies. However, it is difficult to sustain the view that, in the late summer of 1936, the Führer actively connived at getting the Italians bogged down, bearing the bulk of the risks and the costs, in conflict with the democracies and more dependent on the Third Reich.[40]

Ciano had been fishing for an invitation to Germany and one came in late September. He accepted, making it clear that he wanted a major publicity offensive for his trip to the Third Reich in October. In pursuit of the closer alignment that would become the Axis, the Germans duly obliged. Ciano was thrilled by a gala performance of *Don Giovanni* in Munich and a favourable crowd reception, in the orchestration of which Hitler himself had taken an interest. He met von Neurath in Berlin on 21 October and the Führer at Berchtesgaden on 24 October. The main public consequence of the visit was the announcement of German recognition of the Italian Empire of Ethiopia. In private, however, enthused by the 'warmth and cordiality' of his reception, Ciano waxed lyrical about the 'intimacy and community of sentiments' which now characterized Italo-German relations.[41]

Ciano and von Neurath encouraged each other in anti-British fervour but the lead was clearly taken by the Italian. On the instructions of Mussolini, he passed on to Hitler intercepted British assessments of the dangers of Nazi ambitions. It is clear that Ciano and Hitler discussed a common approach to support for Franco. There was a secret protocol whose details were kept secret in order to maintain the fiction of German and Italian respect for non-intervention. However, the proceedings did not sustain Grandi's later claim that it was as a result of this meeting that Italian intervention in Spain began to go beyond the initial limited help. That had already happened two months earlier. Now, without encouragement, Ciano was ready for immediate recognition of Franco – an astonishingly frivolous position – while von Neurath urged caution until his victory was certain. It was therefore agreed that recognition of Franco's government would follow the anticipated fall of Madrid.[42] Moreover, without pressure from von Neurath, Ciano told him:

> the Duce has encharged me to tell the Führer that he intends to make a decisive military effort to bring about the collapse of the Madrid Government. He wishes to know if the Führer is ready to associate himself with this action. For our part, over and above the new airforces which we will send, we can also provide two submarines capable of clearing the sea of the Red forces.

In consequence, Ciano and von Neurath agreed on 'an immediate joint military effort, recognition after the occupation of Madrid and joint action to prevent the creation of a Catalan State'.[43]

There is little doubt that the inexperienced Ciano, on his first official visit abroad, indulged in some irresponsible posturing. However, that does not mean that he was the victim of clever German manipulation. What he said did not exceed his instructions from Mussolini. At their Berchtesgaden meeting, Ciano and Hitler tried to incite each other's anti-British feelings. However, the initiative came from Ciano. In response to a question from Hitler, he boasted, 'Should England aim at forging a ring around Italy in order to suffocate her, our reaction would be immediate and most violent.' Infuriated by the British documents supplied to him by Ciano, Hitler stated that 'the Mediterranean is an Italian sea. Any future modifications of the Mediterranean balance of power must work in Italy's favour.' The counterpart to this consideration was that 'Germany must have liberty of action towards the East and the

Baltic'. Ciano informed Hitler of Italian determination to destroy the Madrid government and of 'the Duce's intention of sending another 50 aeroplanes and two submarines'. Without apparent subterfuge, Hitler, while expressing his approval, made it clear that the Germans would send substantial units only if a Republican victory were imminent.[44]

On 1 November in a speech at the Piazza del Duomo in Milan, Mussolini publicly gave the name Axis to the growing collaboration set in train by Ciano's visit.[45] In real terms, Italo-German cooperation in Spain was a localized operational coordination. The long-term advantages to the Third Reich of the disproportionate distribution of labour were perceived only *after* Italy had irrevocably committed herself to securing victory for Franco. One of the bases for the widespread assumption that Mussolini was Hitler's dupe in Spain is an assessment of the situation written by the German ambassador in Italy, Ulrich von Hassell. He wrote to the Wilhelmstrasse on 18 December 1936:

> Germany has in my opinion every reason to be gratified if Italy continues to interest herself in the Spanish affair. The role played by the Spanish conflict as regards Italy's relations with France and England could be similar to that of the Abyssinian conflict, bringing out clearly the actual, opposing interests of the powers and thus preventing Italy from being drawn into the net of the Western powers and used for their machinations. The struggle for dominant political influence in Spain lays bare the natural opposition between Italy and France; at the same time the position of Italy as a power in the Western Mediterranean comes into competition with that of Britain. All the more clearly will Italy recognize the advisability of confronting the Western powers shoulder to shoulder with Germany. . . . In my opinion the guiding principle for us arising out of this situation is that we should let Italy take the lead in her Spanish policy.

The report was shown to Hitler by von Neurath and copies were sent to other German embassies.[46] In fact, it is clear that Mussolini assumed risks in Spain without needing persuasion on the part of the Germans. The scale of Italian participation was decided upon autonomously by the Duce. There was no Machiavellian agenda to be read into the contrast between Mussolini's anxiety for a swift victory and frustration with Franco's slowness and the Germans' readiness to let Franco run the war at his own pace.

A salutary indication of Franco's dilatory agenda had been provided in the aftermath of the capture of Maqueda on 21 September by the

politically motivated decision to divert his troops to Toledo and the
time taken to consolidate his political supremacy.[47] The consequence was
that the assault on Madrid did not begin again until 7 October and was
eventually to reach stalemate in late November. That assault was amply
supported by Italian artillery and light tanks manned by Italian regular
army gunners.[48] Despite the fact that, by now, he had little respect for
Franco's military prowess, Mussolini formally bestowed recognition
on the Caudillo on 18 November. The Duce was totally optimistic about
the prospects when he addressed the Gran Consiglio on 18 November:

> The Balearics are in our hands. The Spaniards are cowardly and
> cruel. For them the numbers of dead in battle are irrelevant, the
> numbers in the massacres are enormous. In the veins of Spaniards
> there are ninety-nine drops of negro blood. Catalonia will not be
> difficult to overcome. It's a land of shopkeepers and shopkeepers
> don't fight.[49]

The recognition of the Caudillo was a rash gesture given that Franco's
columns were on the verge of defeat as they pounded against the defences
of Madrid now reinforced by Soviet tanks and aircraft and the
International Brigades. A theoretical price was exacted from Franco in
the form of the Italo-Spanish agreement on military and economic cooperation. Signed on 28 November, it was negotiated by Filippo Anfuso,
deputy head of Ciano's cabinet and his special emissary to Salamanca,
with Franco's representative José Antonio Sangróniz y Castro. It gave
Italy assurances of Francoist Spain's benevolent neutrality in the event of
a war between Italy and any other power and the guarantee that France
would not be permitted to transport colonial troops from North Africa to
Europe via Spanish territory.[50] However, Franco was promising things
that were not yet in his power to give merely in order to secure, as
Anfuso reported on 3 December, a massive infusion of much-needed
Italian forces.[51] By now Mussolini's sense of his own prestige was
engaged and, needing a Fascist Spain to put pressure on France, he could
not contemplate defeat for the Caudillo. He insisted – as did the
Germans – on certain conditions. The most important was an undertaking 'to conduct future Spanish policy in the Mediterranean in
harmony with that of Italy'.[52] However, this was too little too late after
having recognized Franco so precipitately.[53] In the assessment of Sir
Robert Vansittart, 'The two dictator States are creating a third; and, by
recognising General Franco's government before he is sure of winning,
they have committed themselves irretrievably to making a successs of his
venture, thus limiting niceties as to means.'[54]

Mussolini was now a substantial way down the road to a commitment which would soon be barely distinguishable from war against the Spanish Republic. Between the end of July and the end of November, the Duce had moved gradually from the relative caution of his initial decision to supply limited aid in the form of the original 12 Savoia-Marchetti bombers, via the delivery of substantial numbers of Fiat C.R.23 aircraft and of light tanks, artillery and other vehicles throughout August, September and October, to formal recognition.[55] After that romantic gesture of Fascist comradeship, there could be no turning back. Henceforth, there could be only a humiliating withdrawal from the Spanish adventure or an unconditional commitment to Franco's cause. As Ciano bitterly remarked to Hitler in 1940, 'Franco had declared that if he received 12 transport planes or bombers, he would have the war won in a few days. These 12 airplanes became more than 1,000 airplanes, 6,000 dead and 14 billion lire.'[56] The British ambassador, Sir Eric Drummond, saw Ciano on 5 December. Ciano not only claimed that Italy had tried to have volunteers banned but also declared, rather more truthfully, that he and Mussolini did not intend to stand aside while Spain was divided into a Francoist zone and a communist Catalonia.[57]

In the light of Franco's reverse at Madrid, the Germans had little doubt that the stark choice was to withdraw or else throw in greater force. In the German Foreign Office, the Director of the Political Department, Ernst von Weizsäcker, was fearful that the dispatch of substantial assistance would provoke a reaction from London. He believed that Italy should assume the burden of saving Franco from defeat: 'Italy must get so deeply involved that she cannot withdraw without us. Her stronger interest must be reflected in a disproportionate effort.'[58] Mussolini was happy to oblige. Immediately after signing the secret Italo-Spanish agreement on 28 November, the Duce called a staff conference to evaluate the implications of intensifying Italian military aid to Franco and asked Hitler to send a representative. In consequence, on 6 December, Mussolini, Ciano and Roatta were joined by Canaris at the Palazzo Venezia. The Duce's opening proposals revealed his hope that there could be a massive joint operation by the two virile Fascist nations. He suggested that Germany and Italy each prepare a division for Spain, that German and Italian instructors be sent to train the Nationalist forces and that a joint Italo-German general staff guide Franco's staff in the command and coordination of operations. Canaris was empowered only to agree to the coordination of future deliveries of military aircraft and of naval and submarine support for Franco in the Mediterranean. In explanation of this caution, he reiterated the views of the Führer, the *Wehrmacht* and of the *Auswärtiges Amt* (German Foreign Office) that the possible international reaction to the dispatch of large contingents of troops to Spain could seriously jeopardize her rearmament plans. This was disturbing for several reasons, suggesting as it did that the Führer was not as carried away as the Duce with the idea of an all-out crusade against communism and that bailing out Franco would be all the more difficult and that the costs would fall disproportionately on Italy. Yet Mussolini did not take the opportunity to retreat from his opening offer to commit substantial Italian ground forces. Canaris's response gave him the perfect excuse. Unless this was a joint operation with equal commitments on both sides, it was too risky for Italy. However, he nonchalantly maintained his readiness to send an Italian division to Spain.[59] It was the great leap forward in Mussolini's commitment to Franco.

In fact, Canaris's statement did not come as news to the Duce. He had been fully informed in the first days of December by the Italian military attaché in Berlin of the line that the Admiral would follow. Colonel Efisio Marras had informed Rome on 1 December that Canaris regarded any increase of Italo-German intervention as imprudent. At the same time, the Italian chargé d'affaires in Berlin, Massimo Magistrati, had two important meetings at which he saw what he called 'the two faces of the new Germany: the adventurous and imprudent one of the Nazi leaders and the prudent and cautious one of the army and the bureaucracy'. At his spectacular residence in the Leipziger Platz, Hermann Göring told Magistrati that he despaired of Franco's organizational and leadership capacity. Göring said that time was running in favour of the Republic. He was so infuriated by the slowness of Franco's progress that he was prepared to contemplate the dispatch of 10,000 German volunteers from the SS and an equal number of Italian Blackshirts. Field Marshal Werner von Blomberg, the Minister of War, was altogether more cautious. He made it quite clear to Magistrati that Germany could not risk being seen to send volunteers or large-scale deliveries of military equipment to Franco. Colonel Marras was convinced that Hitler inclined to the views of von Blomberg and Canaris.[60]

The minutes of the meeting at the Palazzo Venezia on 6 December show that, without any particular pressure from Canaris, Mussolini, in a flush of arrogance and contempt for Franco, had decided to take responsibility for the fate of the Spanish Nationalists. In doing so, he had been influenced by the reports of Roatta and by the favourable opinions of Ciano and Pariani. Like General Federico Baistrocchi, the Under-Secretary of the Ministry of War, Pariani had initially opposed massive intervention in Spain on the grounds that, in the aftermath of the Ethiopian exertions, to risk confrontation with the Western powers was madness. However, ambitious, and pro-German, he had thrown in his lot with Ciano. His reward had come in October 1936 when he was chosen to replace Baistrocchi, who had fallen victim to a vendetta carried on by Field Marshal Pietro Badoglio.[61] It is likely also that, given a curious personal rivalry with Göring, he wished to outdo him in daring. On 7 December, he wrote to General Roatta appointing him commander-in-chief of all Italian land and air forces already in Spain and soon to be sent.[62] On 8 December, the Duce was deeply impressed by a letter from Luigi Barzini, correspondent in Spain for *Il Popolo d'Italia*. Barzini claimed that a rapid war would see the Nationalists go through the Republicans 'like knives through butter'. Echoing Göring's fear, Barzini expressed the view that time was of the essence, that the Republic had to be destroyed before it got stronger. The Duce was so impressed that he sent copies to the King, to Ciano, to the under-secretaries of War, the Navy and the Air Force, to the Chief of Staff of the *Milizia* and to Ambassador Bernardo Attolico in Berlin.[63]

On that same day, Mussolini gave concrete form to the bravado he had expressed at the meeting two days earlier, setting up, within the *Ministero degli Affari Esteri*, a special office with extraordinary powers, the *Ufficio Spagna*, to coordinate the various ministerial contributions to Italian aid for Franco. Formally directed by Conte Luca Pietromarchi, the *Ufficio Spagna* was under the general authority of Ciano, and enjoyed virtual autonomy in decisions concerning the requisitioning of military resources for Spain.[64] Part of the army general staff effectively came under Ciano's orders, and neither Badoglio as Chief of Staff nor Alberto Pariani as Under-Secretary of the Ministry of War did anything to impede the process. The consequence was that the direction of Italian policy in Spain became the personal concern of Mussolini and Ciano, free from the caution of the permanent officials of the *Ministero degli Affari Esteri* and of the senior officers of the General Staff. Ciano kept a large map of Spain in his office with the military units represented by flags which he and Anfuso would move around like children playing war games as they planned Franco's campaigns.[65]

With his columns defeated at the gates of Madrid, Franco was anxious for all the help that he could get. He had met General Wilhelm Faupel, the German chargé d'affaires, in Salamanca on 8 December and requested an Italian and a German division. Faupel irresponsibly gave the *Generalísimo* the impression that German forces would be forthcoming if he agreed to their being under German command.[66] When he received a copy of Faupel's dispatch, Field Marshal von Blomberg was furious. Attolico reported to Rome that von Blomberg had no intention of sending German troops to Spain and stood by the Palazzo Venezia agreement of 6 December.[67] If anything, this seemed to embolden the Duce's determination to take the fate of the Spanish military rebels into his own hands. Franco was informed on 9 December that Italy was going to be sending officers, NCOs, specialist tank crews, radio operators, artillery-men and engineers, to be incorporated into mixed brigades of Spanish and Italian troops. Rome offered uniforms, arms and equipment for as many of these brigades as Franco could organize. Franco was delighted and immediately made arrangements for the creation of two such mixed brigades. The necessary regular Italian army officers, specialists and ordinary ground troops would begin to arrive in mid-January.[68]

Despite the increase in Italian assistance in the wake of the 6 December meeting, the German commander in Spain, General Hugo von Sperrle, was not even officially informed by Berlin of the agreements made at the Palazzo Venezia.[69] The Germans remained deeply conscious of the need not to antagonize Britain prematurely.[70] In fact, Hitler and his military high command had definitively decided against sending troops to Spain for fear of prematurely risking a general war. They were happy to see Italy drawn into the German orbit, although it was not a question of direct pressure on Mussolini. The Germans seem to have believed that the Duce's impetuousness would do the job for them. In the meanwhile, German aircraft, arms and equipment would be sent, for combat evaluation and to guarantee that Franco was not defeated pre-maturely.[71] The German assessment was accurate. Mussolini deliberated further on what he considered to be 'the unsatisfactory situation', although the position of the Nationalists had not deteriorated. He made the momentous decision to formalize the substantial aeronautical assistance being given to Franco. Hitherto, aircraft and pilots had been incorporated loosely into the Spanish Foreign Legion or *Tercio de Extranjeros*. Now the *Aviazione Legionaria* was created, and would provide the Spanish Nationalists with a 300-aircraft-strong air force.[72] The Duce also decided to send two contingents of 3,000 Blackshirts, each in self-contained units with their own officers, artillery and transport. It is likely that he was anxious to win glory for the Militia (*Milizia Volontaria per la Sicurezza Nazionale*, founded 1923) of which he was commander-in-chief. The consequence of his enthusiasm was that the numbers of Italian 'volunteers' were artificially swollen by the obligatory drawing of lots among the *Milizia* and thus included large numbers of untrained soldiers. One general described his men as 'mostly scum'. In fact, some had been forcibly drafted from convicts and the unemployed in southern Italy. They were told that they would lose their unemployment benefit if they did not volunteer and many were left with the impression that they would be used as labourers in Ethiopia. There were some genuine volunteers from within the armed forces but many were *squadristi* from the early 1920s who had no real military experience and were now advancing in years.[73] An important factor for the 'volunteers', at a time of high unemployment in Italy, was the generous pay offered.[74]

On 14 December Roatta's assistant, Lieutenant-Colonel Emilio Faldella, informed Franco that Mussolini wished the Italian volunteers to be organized separately in autonomous Italian companies with Italian officers in addition to the proposed mixed brigades.[75] Despite his desperate need for assistance, Franco could not conceal his fury at this demonstration of Mussolini's determination to run the Nationalist war effort on his own terms.[76] To emphasize the blatant lack of Italian concern for Franco's opinions, the scale of the 'volunteer' contingents that arrived in late December and early January was 'determined not by previous agreement with Franco but according to independent Italian estimates'.[77] Nevertheless, Franco was only too pleased to be able to press them into front-line action as soon as they disembarked. On 12 January, he hastened to request another 9,000 Blackshirts.[78]

Between mid-December 1936 and mid-February 1937, nearly 50,000 'volunteers' were shipped to Spain. They consisted of Fascist militiamen, hastily recruited workers and some regular troops. For Franco, unaware of their deficiencies in morale and training, the new arrivals were of crucial importance. Given that they had little immediate impact on the stalemate around Madrid, Mussolini quickly grew impatient. In late December, he asked Hitler to send a representative 'with full powers' to a meeting in Rome in mid-January to discuss Italo-German cooperation to bring about 'a real decision in Spain'.[79] In fact, it was becoming ever more apparent that the Italians were going to be left by Hitler to make the decisive contribution to Franco's success.[80]

When Mussolini, Ciano and the under-secretaries of the three military ministries met in the Palazzo Venezia on the evening of 14 January 1937, Hitler's representative was Hermann Göring. His presence was a symbolic affirmation of the growing warmth between the Nazi and Fascist regimes.[81] Mussolini instantly revealed his intense irritation with Franco's sluggish progress. Given that, three weeks earlier, Hitler had definitively discounted large-scale German assistance to Franco, Göring did not go beyond enthusiastic declarations of solidarity with Italy, repeating the now familiar German lament, which Roatta had already heard from Canaris and Magistrati had heard from Field Marshal von Blomberg, that fear of international complications prevented Berlin sending a German division to Spain.[82] Faced with Göring's expressions of regret, Mussolini had either to assume the burden of preventing Nationalist defeat or else to contemplate a humiliating withdrawal. Mussolini was irritated by Göring's reticence but was not displeased to be able to make a bold gesture where his rival was inhibited. Accordingly, driven by his overpowering vanity, Mussolini embraced with relish the task of ensuring Franco's victory, disappointed at the lack of solidarity from his Nazi partners, but satisfied to be the senior partner in Spain. Declaring that Franco must win, he said that there were no longer any restraints on his actions in Spain and he would send massive additional aid to Spain by the end of January.[83] Great effort went into maintaining the secret of the decisions taken at the meeting, although rumours abounded of Mussolini's irritation.[84]

On the next day, the chiefs of staff of the three Italian military ministries met at the Palazzo Chigi with the staff of the *Ufficio Spagna* and Ciano's secretary, Filippo Anfuso, to discuss the minimum aid necessary to ensure victory for Franco. In part because of serious doubts about Franco's military skills, but rather more because of a hope of being able to claim victory in Spain as a triumph of Fascism, it was decided that the Italian troops must be used as an independent force under the command of an Italian general who formally would be under Franco's overall command but in practice would be responsible only to the Duce. Discussion ensued on three strategic possibilities by which the Italian forces would win the Spanish Civil War. Mussolini was keen on a huge assault from Teruel to Valencia to split Republican Spain and cut off Catalonia. The campaign should be preceded, in the Duce's opinion, by the terror bombing of Valencia, the Republican capital. Realizing that such an operation would be difficult without the full cooperation of Franco, other possibilities were discussed. A second option was a thrust from Sigüenza to Guadalajara to complete the Nationalist circle around Madrid. The third, and least ambitious, initiative was an assault on Málaga in order to secure a seaport near to Italy which could also serve as the base for a further attack on Valencia from the south-west.[85] A joint statement to Franco was drawn up after the Mussolini–Göring meeting to inform him of the determination of the Italian and German governments to provide him with 'the maximum possible assistance'. The document was handed to him officially by Anfuso on 23 January. Its insistence that a German–Italian general staff would direct the activities of the forces about to arrive in Spain was a bitter blow.[86] However, he accepted the offer with alacrity.[87]

As a result of the meetings of 6 December 1936 and 14 January 1937, Italian aid was stepped up massively. Between mid-December and mid-February, nearly 50,000 Italian troops arrived in Spain (over 29,000 from the MVSN and nearly 20,000 from the *Regio Esercito*). Three hundred aircraft, together with pilots and maintenance staff, as well as considerable naval assistance, were also provided.[88] The Duce's commitment to

Franco's cause could hardly have been greater considering that substantial Italian forces were still tied down in a major 'pacification' process in Abyssinia. The scale of his support for the Caudillo was such that Mussolini could withdraw from Spain before his final victory only at the cost of considerable humiliation. Indeed, sensing that the Duce was now irretrievably embroiled in Spain, Franco would gradually feel able to make efforts to bring Italian forces on the Nationalist side under his own, rather than Roman, control.

Understandably, Franco, who had long-term political ambitions and was deeply suspicious of any Italian schemes to produce an immediate and spectacular victory, was not attracted by either of the two more ambitious projects and opted for the more limited idea of an attack on Málaga. A somewhat fragmented campaign was turned into a spectacular success by Roatta's use of *guerra celere* (*Blitzkrieg*) tactics against the poorly defended city.[89] Roatta conducted the operations with considerable autonomy and scant regard for Franco's sensibilities. On 8 February 1937, he sent a telegram to the *Generalísimo*: 'Troops under my command have the honour to hand over the city of Málaga to Your Excellency.'[90] Although deriving little satisfaction from a triumph trumpeted by the world's press as the work of Mussolini, Franco was deeply impressed by Italian military prowess. Precisely for that reason, he wanted the Italians to be scattered among his own troops who were now being deployed in the Jarama Valley in an effort to cut off Madrid from Valencia.[91] Relations with the Italians were growing tense and Roatta returned to Rome for consultations with Mussolini. The Duce had no intention of letting his forces be used as piecemeal reinforcements for the Nationalists in the Jarama. With his own troops meeting fierce Republican resistance, Franco had to accept the continued autonomy of the Italians. The Italians proposed an attack from Sigüenza on Guadalajara to close the circle around Madrid. Franco was sufficiently desperate to accept this as a diversionary attack to relieve the pressure on his troops. However, the Italians were considering it as a decisive joint attack.[92]

Franco was torn between his real need for Italian aid and concern that an unstoppable *guerra celere* mounted by the Italians and directed from Rome would put him in the humiliating position of having to accept victories benevolently handed to him by Mussolini. That state of mind, which Mussolini and Ciano permitted to fester, would have deeply damaging consequences for the Duce, if not nearly so much for Franco during the imminent battle of Guadalajara. In complex and confused circumstances, Franco chose to act as if the Italians were acting as a diversion for his beleaguered troops in the Jarama. Accordingly, he failed to provide the support expected by the Italians for what they perceived as a major joint operation. Given the unexpected strength of the Republican defence and the poor quality of the *Corpo di Truppe Volontarie* (CTV), which had been masked by the victory at Málaga, the consequence was the defeat of the CTV at the battle of Guadalajara.[93]

Cantalupo, along with his German counterpart General Faupel, was appalled by what he saw as an irresponsible squandering of the material superiority given to Franco.[94] However, his depressingly realistic assessment that there was no prospect of an early victory was not welcome, given the Duce's mood. Cantalupo's pessimism led to his recall to Rome in early April after barely two months in Spain to be replaced later by the Conte Guido Viola di Campalto. On his return, Ciano gave him a disturbing account of the 'Duce's negative judgement' and claimed that the Fascist Party, the *Ministero degli Affari Esteri* and the army were all opposed to him. He alleged that all were equally determined to continue the war until the end and not accept a defeat at the hands of the Russians. It was made clear that a tortured Mussolini was not interested in hearing Cantalupo's doubts lest they influence him in favour of abandoning his Spanish enterprise. Ciano spoke threateningly of suspicions that Cantalupo's caution regarding Spain made him an anti-Fascist traitor. His words reflected Mussolini's current thinking: 'Understand that this is not a lark – this is war. Perhaps we didn't realize soon enough but now we are convinced that it is a war like any other.'[95]

Although he knew that he had been cynically used by Franco, the disaster of Guadalajara impelled Mussolini to decide irrevocably to pursue victory in Spain no matter what the cost. That cost involved ordering Roatta to obey the orders of Franco and distribute Italian forces as the *Generalísimo* wished.[96] The Duce was particularly enraged by references in the British and French press to a second Caporetto. In May 1937, Guido Manacorda, an intimate friend of the prominent Fascist, Giuseppe Bottai, and occasional intermediary between the Duce and Hitler, told a British MP, Kenneth de Courcy, that Mussolini was contemplating an official declaration of war against the Spanish Republic in order to be able to throw the full resources of Italy into the balance. He was confident that neither France nor Britain would try to stop him but was prepared to go ahead even if they tried to do so.[97] Effectively Mussolini would no longer maintain any pretence or restraint about Italian belligerence in Spain.[98] The Duce gave vent to his bitterness about Guadalajara in an unsigned article entitled 'Guadalajara' on 17 June in *Il Popolo d'Italia* which was ordered to be read out to all sections of the *Milizia*. It did not mention Franco's deficiencies but ended with the words 'Our men who died at Guadalajara will also be avenged.'[99] Six months later, Monsignor Pizzardo, the Vatican Secretary of State, reported that Mussolini 'was too deeply involved in Spain to be able to withdraw' and 'could not contemplate or tolerate a defeat of Franco'.[100] Ironically, at the same time, Ciano was going to great lengths to convince the British and French that Italy had no territorial ambitions in Spain or the Balearics.[101]

After Guadalajara, Roatta was subjected to ferocious criticism and replaced in April 1937 by Lieutenant-General Ettore Bastico, who masterminded thoroughgoing changes in the CTV, introducing more regular officers and improving training.[102] The Italian contribution to the Nationalist war effort became more effective. Franco would have said that this was because the Italians were now under his exclusive command. In fact, the Italians added an element of adventure and speed to his operations. The restructured CTV, with motorized infantry, fast, albeit light, tanks and artillery, played a crucial role in the capture of Santander in August 1937. The victory at Santander was greeted with euphoria by the Italian press, and Fascist youth organizations paraded in honour of the victory.[103] Bastico and Franco, both jealous of their prestige and their prerogatives, fell out after the Caudillo ordered the execution of Basques who had been promised evacuation by the Italians.[104] At Franco's request, he was replaced, on 10 October, by General Mario Berti.[105] Under his command, Italian motorized units also played an important part in the great post-Teruel campaign through Aragón in the spring of 1938, contributing to Franco's uncharacteristically rapid advance. They also made an important contribution to the slow slog through the Maestrazgo towards Valencia in July 1938. After the battle of the Ebro, Berti, whose relations with Franco had been as difficult as those experienced by Bastico, was replaced in mid-October 1938 by Colonel Gastone Gambara, the CTV chief of staff. Promoted to Brigadier-General, Gambara showed considerable panache in his conduct of the Italian contribution to the final assault on Catalonia from December 1938 to February 1939. Italian artillery made crucial contributions in the battles of Teruel and the Ebro.[106] The Spaniards, however, did not manifest much gratitude regarding the fact that the Italians had become involved in a full-scale war effort on their behalf.[107]

Despite the fiction that the Italians in Spain were volunteers, the *Regia Aeronautica* acted as the Nationalist air force. After an initial delay because of a lack of sufficiently high-octane fuel, the 9 Savoia-Marchetti S.81s which arrived safely in late July 1936 had soon gone into action. Lieutenant-Colonel Ruggero Bonomi, their commander, on realizing that there were no Spanish pilots capable of flying them, arranged for the Italians to join the *Tercio de Extranjeros* and the aircraft to become the *Primera Escuadrilla de la Aviación de El Tercio*. They provided cover for the *convoy de la victoria* on 5 August and were soon in regular action, bombing Republican targets. At the same time as the departure of the original 12 S.81s, a *squadriglia* of 12 Fiat C.R.32s and volunteer pilots and mechanics, drawn from different units, was sent by sea, arriving in Melilla on 12 August. The Fiat C.R.32 was a fighter biplane of great manoeuvrability and stability and easy handling. It was the principal fighter of the *Regia Aeronautica* by 1936 and it bore the main burden of air combat for the Nationalists from late August 1936 until the end of the Spanish Civil War. By 21 August, they were established in Seville as the *1ª Escuadrilla de Caza de la Aviación de El Tercio* (the First Fighter Squadron of the Airforce of the Foreign Legion). A further 21 aircraft arrived in late August and early September to permit the formation of a second squadron. Under the overall command of Lieutenant-Colonel Bonomi, they guaranteed air superiority for the Nationalists during the advance on Madrid. Unlike their Republican opponents, the Italian pilots were well trained, were experienced in the use of their aircraft and had full technical back-up. The arrival of Soviet Polikarpov fighter aircraft at the beginning of November 1936 put an end to that superiority.[108] A further group of 12 aircraft, under the command of Comandante Leone Gallo 'Cirelli', were instrumental in repelling the Republican attack on Majorca and securing it as an Italian base.[109] Large quantities of arms and equipment were delivered to Palma. Italian flags flew over the island. Italian servicemen were much in evidence and a reign of terror was instituted against both Spanish leftists and German and other exiled anti-Fascists. Spanish cities were bombed by the *Regia Aeronautica* flying from Majorca, or sometimes from Italy.[110]

The *Regia Marina* (Italian navy) acted similarly as an extension of the Spanish Nationalist Fleet. Italian cruisers contributed decisively to breaking the blockade of Morocco and pushing the Republican navy out of the Straits of Gibraltar. Mussolini's warships bombarded Málaga (and its fleeing population), Valencia and Barcelona. Italian submarines, guided by reconnaissance aircraft of the *Regia Aeronautica*, sank the merchant ships of other nations (particularly the Soviet Union but also Britain) supplying the Spanish Republic.[111]

Because of the relative proximity of Italy to Spain, deliveries of war *matériel* had a much greater impact on immediate operations than those received by Republican Spain from the Soviet Union. According to the official Italian military history of the Spanish Civil War, 'the timeliness of deliveries was often more crucial than their scale given that one side or the other might have had to give in or seek a compromise peace if necessary supplies had not been received in time'.[112] The fact that the Italian air force could protect the Italian merchant ships carrying supplies ensured a rapid and virtually uninterrupted supply. Nearly 80,000 Italians fought in Spain of whom nearly 4,000 were killed. The Italians supplied 759 aircraft, 6,600 cannons, mortars and machine guns, 157 tanks, 7,400 motor vehicles, 1.8 million uniforms, hundreds of thousands of rifles and 7.7 million shells, and 319 million small-arms cartridges. This was costed at 8,500,000,000 lire (£95,000,000 in 1939 terms; £2,375,000,000 in 1995 terms), although the generous payment deal was of 5,000,000,000 lire.[113] By November 1937, the scale of the economic strain was causing Mussolini considerable anxiety.[114]

This cost has to be put into the context of the ongoing Abyssinian war. In Abyssinia, merely to supply troops involved the building of a port at Massawa, a colossal road-building programme and the assembly of a massive fleet of transport vehicles (some of Italian construction but many which had to be bought abroad). The Spanish Civil War saw the Italian forces in Abyssinia stripped of armoured vehicles and artillery. The war became a costly battle of attrition. At an overall cost of 39,000,000,000 lire, and an endless drain in waste and corruption, by 1939 the Italians controlled only the roads and the principal towns of Abyssinia and were engaged in a costly guerrilla war. In general, Italian industry did not supply the necessary transport and armoured vehicles at a rate which could replace what was being used in Spain, with damaging consequences in Abyssinia and later in France.[115] In more general social terms, the costs of the combined Spanish and Abyssinian ventures was an increasing tax burden, a rising cost of living and shortages of both labour and raw materials which had an impact on the efficiency of industry.[116]

It has been claimed that what was lost in Spain made little impact on Italy's subsequent military effectiveness since it was old equipment that needed replacing anyway.[117] In September 1939, Italy had 10 relatively well-equipped divisions and 800 functioning combat aircraft. By May 1940, there were 19 divisions and 1,600 relatively modern aircraft. If what was used up in Spain had been available in September 1939, Italy would have had 30 divisions. The 764 aircraft that were left in Spain included 100 Savoia-Marchetti S.M.79 trimotors – a quarter of those available for bombing, air-torpedoing and reconnaissance. An additional 442 modern artillery pieces and 7,000 vehicles might have made a decisive difference in Albania or in Libya, where Graziani complained that he could not attack Egypt for the lack of 5,200 aircraft. Similarly, had the 373 Fiat C.R.32 fighters left in Spain, condemned as obsolete, been available in North Africa, they could still have dominated the even more antiquated British aircraft in use there.[118]

On 26 January 1939, Mussolini made a speech to celebrate the fall of Barcelona. To a deliriously cheering crowd in the Piazza Venezia, he said:

The splendour of the Barcelona victory is another chapter in the history of the new Europe which we are creating. It is not only the Negrín Government which has been beaten by the magnificent troops of Franco and our intrepid Legionaries; many others amongst our enemies are biting the dust at this moment.

Sections of the crowd, predominantly officers, shouted 'To Paris!'[119]

In the last resort, Mussolini had gained a spectacular victory over communisim, liberalism and the Western democracies. However, the immediate costs in terms of resources and in constraints on his freedom of action would ensure that it was a hollow victory. One of his objectives was to get a reliable ally in the Mediterranean. Franco did clinch his commitment to the Axis, withdrawing Spain from the League of Nations and joining the Anti-Comintern Pact. In fact, in the long term, that never worked to his benefit for two reasons. In the first place, the world war came too early for Franco to be a useful ally. Second, Mussolini had to connive at Spanish neutrality during the Second World War in order to reduce the possibility of a competitor for the French imperial territories that he coveted himself. The greatest cost to Italy was the mortgaging of her foreign policy. Mussolini's medium-term plan of gaining an advantageous agreement with Britain was undermined by the need to move closer to Germany. The real beneficiaries of Italian intervention were Hitler and Franco, certainly not the Duce. Italy was more committed to Hitler yet militarily much weaker. Franco and Mussolini shared a vision of the three Fascist dictators working together to destroy Anglo-French power, but both were dependent on the whims of Hitler.

After the Civil War, Mussolini dealt with Franco in a friendly, albeit noticeably patronizing, manner. Franco put the tensions of 1937 behind him and told Ciano, who visited Spain in July 1939, that he expected from the Duce 'instruction and directives'. Franco gave Ciano the impression of being 'completely dominated by the personality of Mussolini and feels that to face the peace he needs the Duce just as he needed him to win the war'.[120] As passive spectators of the phoney war, Franco and Mussolini were drawn together. The warmth of their relations was underlined by the settlement of Spain's Civil War debts in a lengthy negotiation during the summer of 1939 and the spring of 1940.[121] As a soldier, however, Franco was sufficiently aware of the logistical penury of post-Civil War Spain to refrain from joining the Duce when he went to war on 9 June 1940. Nevertheless, Franco pledged his 'moral solidarity' and as much economic help as Spain could afford. He also delighted Mussolini by following his earlier example and changing Spanish neutrality to non-belligerence.[122] In fact, fearful

perhaps that Hitler would not have enough largesse for two penuri-
ous Mediterranean allies, Mussolini never put any great pressure on
Franco to join the war.[123] By the time that they met face-to-face on 12
February 1941, there was little reason for the Duce to try to cajole Franco
into the war. Spain faced famine and Mussolini had experienced a major
débâcle in Greece and the defeat of Graziani's army by the British at
Bengazi.

Thus, at their inconsequential meeting at Bordighera, Mussolini
encouraged Franco not to go to war on the Axis side. He had written to
the King three days before he was due to meet the Caudillo, 'I regard my
journey to Bordighera as perfectly useless and I would willingly have
avoided it. Franco will not say to me anything different from what he has
already told the Führer.'[124] Filippo Anfuso, acting Minister of Foreign
Affairs in the absence of Ciano, who was fighting in Greece, helped
Mussolini prepare the meeting. The Duce told him, 'I will say to Franco
everything that has to be said but I have no illusions: he will have already
decided before I open my mouth.'[125] At that meeting, after the military
reverses suffered by Italy in the Balkans and in North Africa, the
Caudillo found Mussolini depressed and much aged. He told him of his
faith in Axis victory and admitted, 'Spain wishes to enter the war; her
fear is to enter too late.' Mussolini was inclined to stop trying to persuade Franco to join the Axis war effort in the short term. He said to
Luca Pietromarchi, the one-time head of the *Ufficio Spagna*, 'how can you
push into a war a nation with bread reserves for one day?'[126] According to
General Emilio Faldella, Franco asked him, 'Duce, if you could come out
of the war, would you?' To which Mussolini is alleged to have replied
'Certainly! Certainly!'[127] Such was the understanding with which
Mussolini treated him that, in the after-glow of their meeting, Franco
declared the Duce to be

> the greatest political figure in the world. Whereas Hitler is a mystic,
> a diviner and very close to the mentality of the Slavs, Mussolini in
> contrast is human, clear in his ideas, never far from reality, in a word,
> 'a true Latin genius'.[128]

Throughout his life, Franco – even in the 1940s and 1950s as he was
trying to free himself of his Axis stigma – would always speak warmly of
Mussolini. On Sunday 25 July 1943, when news reached Madrid that, in
the early hours of the morning, the Fascist Grand Council had passed a
motion of no confidence in Mussolini and the King had seized the opportunity to have him arrested and replaced by Marshal Badoglio, there was
panic. Franco ordered a news blackout while frantic efforts were made to
dissociate Falangism from Fascism.[129] Perhaps influenced by his worries

that if the Duce could fall so could the Caudillo, he wept as he recounted the events in Rome to the cabinet.[130] Being of *lágrima fácil*, Franco's grief was not deep-rooted. His relationship with Mussolini had been grounded in a shared resentment of Anglo-French hegemony in the Mediterranean and limited by their mutually incompatible ambitions to take over the French North African Empire. In the last resort, it was one of give and take in which the Duce had given and the Caudillo had taken.

Notes

1 Ismael Saz Campos, *Mussolini contra la II República: hostilidad, conspiraciones, intervención (1931–1936)* (Valencia: Institut Alfons el Magnanim, 1986) *passim*; Antonio Lizarza Iribarren, *Memorias de la conspiración 1931–1936*, 4th edn (Pamplona: Editorial Gómez, 1969), pp. 34–41; Martin Blinkhorn, *Carlism and Crisis in Spain 1931–1939* (Cambridge: Cambridge University Press, 1975), pp. 136–7.
2 Paul Preston, 'Mussolini's Spanish Adventure: From Limited Risk to War', in Paul Preston and Ann Mackenzie (eds), *The Republic Besieged: Civil War in Spain 1936–1939* (Edinburgh: Edinburgh University Press, 1996).
3 Angel Viñas, *La Alemania nazi y el 18 de julio*, 2nd edn (Madrid: Alianza Editorial, 1977), pp. 308–52; Paul Preston, *Franco: A Biography* (London: HarperCollins, 1993), pp. 154–60.
4 Generale Mario Montanari, 'L'impegno italiano nella guerra di Spagna', in *Memorie storiche militari 1980* (Rome: Ufficio Storico dello Stato Maggiore dell'Esercito, 1981), pp. 121–52; Lucio Ceva, 'Influence de la guerre d'Espagne sur l'armement et les conceptions d'emploi de l'aviation de l'Italie Fasciste', in Fondation pour les Études de Défence Nationale, *Adaptation de l'arme aérienne aux conflits contemporains et processus d'indépendance des armées de l'Air des origines à la fin de la Seconde Guerre mondiale* (Paris: Service Historique de l'Armée de l'Air, 1985), pp. 191–9; Lucio Ceva, 'L'evoluzione dei materiali bellici in Italia', in Ennio di Nolfo, Romain H. Rainero and Brunello Vigezzi (eds), *L'Italia e la politica di potenza in Europa (1938–40)* (Milan: Marzorati Editore, 1981), esp. pp. 359–80; Lucio Ceva, 'L'ultima vittoria del fascismo Spagna 1938–1939', in *Italia Contemporanea*, 196; (September 1994); Lucio Ceva, 'Conseguenze politico-militari dell'intervento italo-fascista nella guerra civile spagnola', in Gigliola Sacerdoti Mariani, Arturo Colombo and Antonio Pasinato (eds), *La guerra civile spagnola tra politica e letteratura* (Florence: Shakespeare, 1995), pp. 215–29; Angelo Emiliani, 'Costi e conseguenze dell'intervento italiano nella guerra di Spagna' (unpublished paper); Brian R. Sullivan, 'Fascist Italy's Military Involvement in the Spanish Civil War', in *Journal of Military History* 59: 4 (1995), pp. 697–727.
5 Roberto Cantalupo, *Fu la Spagna. Ambasciata presso Franco: febbraio–aprile 1937* (Milan: Mondadori, 1948), pp. 50–2, 67–8; Renzo de Felice, *Mussolini il duce: lo stato totalitario 1936–1940* (Turin: Einaudi, 1981), p. 340; Felix Gilbert, 'Ciano and His Ambassadors', in Gordon A. Craig and Felix Gilbert (eds), *The Diplomats 1919–1939* (Princeton: Princeton University Press, 1953), pp. 517–18.
6 Luccardi to Ministero della Guerra, 20.7 and 21.7.1936, *I documenti*

diplomatici italiani, 8ª serie, vol. IV (10 maggio – 31 agosto 1936) (Rome: Istituto Poligrafico e Zecca dello Stato/Libreria dello Stato, 1993) (henceforth *DDI*, 8ª, IV) pp. 640–1, 652.

7 Roatta to Luccardi, 21.7.1936, *DDI*, 8ª, IV, p. 651; Alberto Rovighi and Filippo Stefani, *La partecipazione italiana alla guerra civile Spagnola*, 2 vols, each in two parts, *Testi and Allegati* (Rome: Ufficio Storico dello Stato Maggiore dell'Esercito, 1992–3), I, *Testo*, pp. 76–7.

8 Luccardi to Ministero della Guerra, 22.7 and 23.7.1936, *DDI*, 8ª, IV, pp. 659–60, 663.

9 Cerruti to Ciano, 22.7.1936, Archivio Storico e Diplomatica del Ministero degli Affari Esteri (hereafter ASMAE), Spagna Fondo di Guerra (SFG), b. 12, tel. 7131; 23.7.1936, *DDI*, 8ª, IV, pp. 669–70.

10 David Wingeate Pike, *Les français et la guerre d'Espagne 1936–1939* (Paris: Presses Universitaires de France, 1975) pp. 79–93; Clerk to FO, 24.7.1936, FO371/20523, W6881/62/41, 25.7.1936, FO371/20524, W6960/62/41.

11 Cerruti to Ciano, 22.7.1936, Pedrazzi to Ciano, 26 July, *DDI*, 8ª, IV, pp. 656–7, 704; Saz, *Mussolini*, pp. 198–201, 210.

12 Ismael Saz, 'El fracaso del éxito: Italia en la guerra de España' in *Espacio, Tiempo y Forma: Revista de la Facultad de Geografía e Historia de la Universidad Nacional de Educación a Distancia*, Serie V, Historia Contemporánea, tomo V (Madrid: Universidad Nacional de Educación a Distancia 1992), pp. 105–11; Jill Edwards, *The British Government and the Spanish Civil War, 1936–1939* (London: Macmillan, 1979), pp. 16–20, 101–5.

13 Luccardi to Ministero della Guerra, 27.7.1936, *DDI*, 8ª, IV, pp. 706–7.

14 Ingram to Eden, 28.7.1936, *Documents on British Foreign Policy 1919–1939*, second series, vol. XVII, pp. 31–2.

15 He told his wife that 'Bolshevism in Spain means Bolshevism in France, which means Bolshevism next door and in fact a serious threat to bolshevise Europe'; Raquele Mussolini, *My Life with Mussolini* (London, Robert Hale, 1959), p. 91. See also Francesco Belforte (pseudonym of Generale Francesco Biondi Morra), *La guerra civile in Spagna*, 4 vols (Milan: ISPI, 1938–9) II, pp. 303–7.

16 Berardis to Ciano, 23 July 1936, ASMAE, Spagna Fondo di Guerra (SFG), b. 12, tel. 2295/906, reprinted *DDI*, 8ª, IV, pp. 675–77; Saz, *Mussolini*, pp. 206–7.

17 Ferdinando Pedriali, *Guerra di Spagna e aviazione italiana* (Rome: Aeronautica Militare Italiana–Ufficio Storico, 1992) p. 33; Ferdinando Bargoni, *L'impegno navale italiano durante la guerra civile spagnola (1936–1939)* (Rome: Ufficio Storico della Marina Militare – USM, 1992), p. 67.

18 John F. Coverdale, *Italian Intervention in the Spanish Civil War* (Princeton: Princeton University Press, 1975), p. 3; Rovighi and Stefani, *La partecipazione italiana*, I, *Testo*, p. 78; Pedriali, *Guerra di Spagna*, pp. 34–5; Luis Bolín, *Spain: The Vital Years* (Philadelphia: Lippincott, 1967), pp. 170–1; Gerald Howson, *Aircraft of the Spanish Civil War 1936–1939* (London: Putnam, 1990), pp. 273–5.

19 Vitetti to Ciano, 29.7 and 3.8.1936; Ciano to Vitetti, 30 July 1936, *DDI*, 8ª, IV, pp. 711–13, 719–20, 736–7; Saz, *Mussolini*, pp. 204–5.

20 Vitetti to Ciano, 3.8.1936, *DDI*, 8a, IV, p. 739.

21 De Felice, *Mussolini*, p. 367. However, that is not the same as accepting

Grandi's assertion that it was a question of '*aiuti modesti e con una testimonianza di simpatia appena apprezzabile*'; Dino Grandi, *Il mio paese: ricordi autobiografici* (Bologna: Il Mulino, 1985), p. 418.

22 De Rossi to Ciano, 31.7.1936, *DDI*, 8ª, IV, pp. 728–9; Pedriali, *Guerra di Spagna*, pp. 35–6.

23 Cambon to Eden, 2.8.1936; Eden to Cambon, 3.8.1936, FO371/20526, W7504/62/41.

24 Ingram to FO, 1.8.1936, FO371/20526, W7525/62/41.

25 Colloquio di Ciano con Chambrun, 3.8.1936; Mussolini to Ciano, 5.8.1936; Colloquio di Ciano con Chambrun, 5.8.1936; Colloquio di Ciano con Ingram, 6.8.1936, *DDI*, 8ª, IV, pp. 738–9, 750, 757–8; Galeazzo Ciano, *L'Europa verso la catastrofe* (Milan: Mondadori, 1948), pp. 51–2. Cf. Ingram to FO, 4 and 6 August 1936, FO371/20526, W7698/62/41 and FO371/20527, W7921/62/41.

26 Servizio Informazione Militare (SIM) to Ministero degli Affari Esteri (MAE), 5.8.1936, *DDI*, 8ª, IV, pp. 751–2; Angel Viñas, *Guerra, dinero, dictadura: ayuda fascista y autarquía en la España de Franco* (Barcelona, 1984), pp. 51–3; Gerald Howson, *Aircraft of the Spanish Civil War 1936–1939* (London: Putnam, 1990), p. 207; Klaus A.Maier, *Guernica 26.4.1937: Die deutsche Intervention in Spanien und der 'Fall Guernica'* (Freiburg: Rombach, 1975) pp. 24–5; Coverdale, *Italian Intervention*, pp. 87, 103, 106, 119–20.

27 De Rossi to Ciano, 19.8.1936, *DDI*, 8ª, IV, pp. 823–4.

28 De Rossi to Ciano, 20.8 and 22.8.1936; Luccardi to Ministero della Guerra, 21.8.1936, *DDI*, 8ª, IV, pp. 827, 829, 852–3, 861.

29 I am indebted to Brian Sullivan for this information.

30 Colloquio Roatta–Canaris, 28.8.1936, *DDI*, 8ª, IV, pp. 892–5; Coverdale, *Italian Intervention*, pp. 102–4, 119–20; Gerhard L. Weinberg, *The Foreign Policy of Hitler's Germany: Diplomatic Revolution in Europe, 1933–1936* (Chicago: University of Chicago Press, 1970).

31 On the Italian occupation of the Balearics, see Josep Massot i Muntaner, *Guerra civil i repressió a Mallorca* (Barcelona: Publicacions de l'Abadia de Montserrat, 1997), pp. 25–46; Josep Massot i Muntaner, *Vida i miracles del 'Conde Rossi': Mallorca, agost–desembre 1936 – Málaga, gener–febrer 1937* (Barcelona: Publicacions de l'Abadia de Montserrat, 1988), pp. 27–150; Rosaria Quartararo, *Politica fascista nelle Baleari (1936–1939)* (Rome: Quaderni della FIAP, n.d.) *passim*.

32 Colloquio Ciano Canaris, 28.8.1936, *DDI*, 8ª, IV, pp. 895–7.

33 Rovighi and Stefani, *La partecipazione italiana*, I, *Testo*, pp. 128–9; José Luis Alcofar Nassaes, *C.T.V: Los legionarios italianos en la guerra civil española 1936–1939* (Barcelona, 1972), pp. 51–2. For his communications with Rome, Roatta adopted the codename 'Colli' and, for his dealings with the Spanish command, that of 'Mancini'.

34 Luccardi to Ministero della Guerra, 21.8.1936, *DDI*, 8ª, IV, pp. 852–3; De Rossi to Ciano, 3 September 1936, *I documenti diplomatici Italiani, 8ᵉ serie, vol. V (1 settembre – 31 dicembre 1936)* (Rome: Istituto Poligrafico e Zecca dello Stato/Libreria dello Stato, 1994) (henceforth *DDI*, 8ª, V), p. 6. Rovighi and Stefani, *La partecipazione italiana*, I, *Testo*, p. 129, confuses these two documents.

35 De Rossi to Ciano, 22.8.1936, *DDI*, 8ª, IV, p. 861.

36 Luccardi to SIM, 12.9.1936, Rovighi and Stefani, *La partecipazione italiana*, I, *Documenti*, p. 54; *Ibid.*, I, *Testo*, p. 130.

37 Roatta to SIM, 13.9.1936, Rovighi and Stefani, *La partecipazione italiana*, I, *Documenti*, pp. 57–8.
38 Colloquio Roatta–Franco, 16.10.1936, Roatta to SIM, 17.10.1936, Rovighi and Stefani, *La partecipazione italiana*, I, *Documenti*, pp. 117–22; *Ibid.*, I, *Testo*, pp. 133–5.
39 Ingram to Eden, 3.8.1936, R4830/341/22, in *British Documents on Foreign Affairs* (Washington, DC: University Publications of America, 1992) (hereafter *BDFA*), Series F, vol.II, p. 67.
40 The most outspoken allegation of German malice in this regard may be found in Grandi, *Il mio paese*, pp. 418–19. Cf. Brian Sullivan, 'The Italian Armed Forces, 1918–40', in Allan R. Millett and Williamson Murray (eds), *Military Effectiveness*, 3 vols (London: George Allen & Unwin, 1988), vol. 2, p. 185; Denis Mack Smith, *Mussolini's Roman Empire* (London: Longman, 1976), pp. 102–3; Ernst von Weizsäcker, *Memoirs of Ernst von Weizsäcker* (London, 1951), p. 113; Enno von Rintelen, *Mussolini l'alleato: ricordi dell'addetto militare tedesco a Roma (1936–1943)* (Rome: Corso, 1952), pp. 29–30; Joachim Fest, *Hitler* (Harmondsworth: Penguin, 1977), pp. 743, 800–2; Militärgeschichtliches Forschungsamt, *Germany and the Second World War*, (Oxford: Oxford University Press, 1990), vol. 1, pp. 620–3; Weinberg, *Diplomatic Revolution*, pp. 288–98.
41 Drummond to Eden, 26.10.1936, FO371/20417, R6331/341/22; Phipps to Eden, 26.10.1936, R6335/341/22, in *BDFA*, F, II, pp. 87–8; Hassell to Wilhelmstrasse, 6 November 1936, *Documents on German Foreign Policy 1918–1945* (hereafter *DGFP*), Series C, vol. VI (London: HMSO, 1983), pp. 31–3; Elizabeth Wiskemann, *The Rome–Berlin Axis*, 2nd edn (London: Fontana, 1966), pp. 87–90.
42 Von Neurath memoranda, 21.10, 22.10 and 23.10.1936, German–Italian Protocol, 23.10.1936, *DGFP*, C, V (London: HMSO, 1966), pp. 1125–38; Phipps to FO, 27.10.1936, FO371/20418, R6341/341/22. Cf. Grandi, *Il mio paese*, pp. 418–19.
43 Ciano, *L'Europa*, p. 89.
44 No German account of the Hitler–Ciano conversations has been found; *DGFP*, D, III, p. 117; Ciano, *L'Europa*, pp. 94–5; Grandi, *Il mio paese*, pp. 418–20. Grandi implies that Ciano was tricked into the agreement.
45 *Opera omnia di Benito Mussolini*, 36 vols, ed. Edoardo and Duilio Susmel (Florence: La Fenice, 1951–63), vol. 28, pp. 69–70.
46 Von Hassell to Wilhelmstrasse, 18.12.1936, *DGFP*, D, III, pp. 170–3; Weinberg, *Diplomatic Revolution*, p. 298.
47 Paul Preston, *Franco: A Biography* (London: HarperCollins, 1993), pp. 176–85.
48 Azcárate to FO, 5.11.1936, FO371/20584, W1596/9549/41.
49 'Le Baleari sono in nostro possesso. Gli spagnoli imbelli e crudeli. Irrilevanti il numero dei caduti nelle battaglie; enorme, nelle stragi'. 'Nelle vene degli spagnoli ci sono 99 goccie di sangue negro [*sic*]'. La Catalogna non sarà dura a vincere. E una terra di mercanti; e i mercanti non si battono.' Giuseppe Bottai, *Diario 1935–1944* (Milan: Rizzoli, 1989) p. 115.
50 Anfuso to Ciano, 28.11.1936, Protocollo segreto Italo Spagnolo, 28.11.1936, *DDI*, 8*a*, V, pp. 553, 557–8.
51 Anfuso to Ciano, 3 December 1936, *DDI*, 8ª, V, pp. 593–5; Ismael Saz and Javier Tusell (eds), *Fascistas en España: la intervención italiana en la guerra civil*

a través de los telegramas de la 'Missione Militare Italiana in Spagna' (15 diciembre 1936 – 31 marzo 1937) (Madrid/Rome, 1981), p. 25 (henceforth cited as MMIS, *Telegramas*); Cantalupo, *Fu la Spagna*, p. 75 (full text of agreement is on pp. 78–80); also in Ciano, *L'Europa*, pp. 120–1.

52 *DGFP*, D, III, pp. 139–40, 143–4, 147–8; Coverdale, *Italian Intervention*, pp. 122–3, 157–8.

53 *Foreign Relations of the United States 1936* (Washington, DC: Government Printing Office, 1954), II, p. 561.

54 Vansittart memorandum, 'The World Situation and British Rearmament', 31.12.1936, *Documents on British Foreign Policy*, 2nd series, vol. XVII (London: HMSO, 1979), p. 779.

55 Rovighi and Stefani, *La partecipazione italiana*, I, *Testo*, pp. 110, 130, 139.

56 Record of conversation between the Führer and Ciano in Berlin, *Documents on German Foreign Policy 1918–1945*, Ser. D, vol. XI (London: HMSO, 1961), pp. 211–14.

57 Drummond to FO, 5.12.1936, FO371/20553, W17509/62/41.

58 *DGFP*, D, III, pp. 154–5, 159–62; *Die Weizsäcker-Papiere 1933–1950* (Frankfurt am Main: Propyläen Verlag, 1974), pp. 104–5.

59 Verbale riunione a Palazzo Venezia del 6 dicembre 1936–XV, ASMAE, Gabinetto, Spagna, b.3031; Hassell to Wilhelmstrasse, 28.11, 1.12 and 17.12.1936, Dieckhoff to Hassell, 2.12.1936, Dieckhoff memorandum, 11.12.1936, *DGFP*, D, III, pp. 143–4, 146, 149–50, 165, 169; De Felice, *Mussolini il Duce*, pp. 383–4; MMIS, *Telegramas*, p. 27; Coverdale, *Italian Intervention*, pp. 160–4; Weinberg, *Diplomatic Revolution*, pp. 296–8.

60 Col. Efisio Marras, military attaché to Berlin, to SIM, 2 and 4 December; Magistrati to Ciano, 2.12.1936, *DDI*, 8ª, V, pp. 581–2, 588–91; Rovighi and Stefani, *La partecipazione italiana*, I, *Documenti*, pp. 143–5; Massimo Magistrati, *Il prologo del dramma. Berlino, 1934–1937* (Milan: Mursia, 1971), pp. 152–8.

61 Emilio Canevari, *La guerra italiana: retroscena della disfatta*, 2 vols (Rome: Tosi Editore, 1948), I, pp. 418–19.

62 Mussolini to Roatta, 7.12.1936, Rovighi and Stefani, *La partecipazione italiana*, I, *Documenti*, p. 146.

63 Barzini to Mussolini, 8.12.1936, *DDI*, 8ª, V. p. 618.

64 Rovighi and Stefani, *La partecipazione italiana*, I, *Documenti*, pp. 147–53; *Ibid.*, I, *Testo*, pp. 135, 145–7; Alcofar Nassaes, *C.T.V.*, pp. 32–3, 54; MMIS, *Telegramas*, pp. 20–1; Coverdale, *Italian Intervention*, pp. 165–6.

65 Cantalupo, *Fu la Spagna*, pp. 65–9, 71; Gilbert, 'Ciano', p. 521; Grandi, *Il mio paese*, p. 422.

66 Faupel to Wilhelmstrasse, 10.12.1936, *DGFP*, D, III, pp. 159–62.

67 Attolico to Ciano, 12.12.1936, *DDI*, 8ª, V, p. 653.

68 Rovighi and Stefani, *La partecipazione italiana*, I, *Testo*, pp. 152–3; MMIS, *Telegramas*, pp. 28–9; Coverdale, *Italian Intervention*, pp. 167–8, 170–1.

69 Ciano to Attolico, 19.12.1936, *DDI*, 8ª, V, p. 715.

70 Attolico to Ciano, 22.12.1936, *DDI*, 8ª, V, p. 727.

71 Weizsäcker, *Papiere*, p. 103; 'Hispanicus', *Foreign Intervention in Spain* (London: United Editorial 1937), pp. 138–40; Weinberg, *Diplomatic Revolution*, pp. 297–8.

72 Pedriali, *Guerra di Spagna*, pp. 139–41; José Luis Alcofar Nassaes, *La*

aviación legionaria en la guerra de España (Barcelona: Euros, 1975), pp. 137–41; Howson, *Aircraft of the Spanish Civil War*, p. 16.

73 Drummond to Eden, 30.11.1936, FO371/20587, W17280/9549/41; Drummond to Eden, 11.12.1936, FO371/20588, W18182/9549/41; Drummond to Eden, 17.12.1936, FO371/20589, W18522/9549/41; Cambon to Mounsey, 24.12.1936, FO371/20590, W19014/9549/41; memorandum by British consul, Naples, 19.1.1937, FO371/21322, W2164/7/41; British consul, Milan, to Drummond, 26.1.1937, Ingram to Eden, 29.1.1937, F0371/21322, W2234/7/41; Guariglia, *Ricordi*, pp. 325–6; Mack Smith, *Mussolini's Roman Empire*, p. 100; Giorgio Rochat and Giulio Massobiro, *Breve storia dell'esercito italiano dal 1861 al 1943* (Turin 1978), pp. 256–7; Giordano Bruno Guerri, *Fascisti: gli Italiani di Mussolini, il regime degli Italiani* (Milan: Mondadori, 1995), pp. 217–18.

74 Coverdale, *Italian Intervention*, pp. 181–6; Lucio Ceva, 'Ripensare Guadalajara', in *Italia Contemporanea*, 192 (September 1993), pp. 476–8.

75 Martínez Bande, *La campaña de Andalucía*, pp. 184–6.

76 De Felice, *Mussolini il Duce*, p. 385.

77 This was reported to Berlin by Faupel, presumably on the basis of information from Roatta, *DGFP*, D, III, p. 222.

78 MMIS, *Telegramas*, pp. 29, 67, 94.

79 Mussolini to Ciano, 27.12.1936, Ciano to Attolico, 28.12.1936, *DDI*, 8^a, V, pp. 755–6; Hassell to Wilhelmstrasse, 29.12.1936, *DGFP*, D, III, p. 191.

80 Roatta to Ufficio Spagna, 12.1.1937, MMIS, *Telegramas*, pp. 93–4.

81 On the choreography of the visit, see Ramón Garriga, *Guadalajara y sus consecuencias* (Madrid, 1974), pp. 42–3.

82 MMIS, *Telegramas*, pp. 93–4.

83 Verbale della riunione a Palazzo Venezia del 14 gennaio 1937–XV, ASMAE, Gabinetto, Spagna, b.3031; *DGFP*, D, III, pp. 225–6; De Felice, *Mussolini il Duce*, pp. 389–90; Coverdale, *Italian Intervention*, pp. 171–3. On Mussolini's reactions to Göring, see Ingram to Eden, 29.1.1937, FO371/21174, R863/200/22.

84 Ingram to Eden, 29.1.1937. R863/200/22, *BDFA*, Ser. F, vol. 13, pp. 2–4.

85 Riunione a Palazzo Chigi, 15.1.1937, Rovighi and Stefani, *La partecipazione italiana*, I, *Documenti*, pp. 171–3; De Felice, *Mussolini il Duce*, pp. 389–90.

86 Ciano to Mussolini, 18.1.1937, *I documenti diplomatici italiani, 8^a serie, vol. VI (1 gennaio – 30 giugno 1937)* (Rome: Istituto Poligrafico e Zecca dello Stato/Libreria dello Stato, 1997) (henceforth *DDI*, 8^a, VI), pp. 84–5; communicazione fatta al generale Franco a nome del Governo Italiano e del Governo Tedesco, il 23 gennaio 1937–XV decisa a Roma nella riunione a Palazzo Venezia col Generale Göring il 14 gennaio, ASMAE, Gabinetto, Spagna, b.3031; Rovighi and Stefani, *La partecipazione italiana*, I, *Documenti*, pp. 171–3; De Felice, *Mussolini il Duce*, pp. 389–90.

87 Anfuso to Ciano, 24.1.1937, ASMAE, Gabinetto, Spagna, b.3031; MMIS, *Telegramas*, pp. 112–18.

88 Gabinetto Ministero della Guerra to Mussolini, 7.2.1937, Rovighi and Stefani, *La partecipazione italiana*, I, *Documenti*, pp. 178–85; *Ibid.*, I, *Testo*, p. 157–84.

89 Rovighi and Stefani, *La partecipazione italiana*, I, *Testo*, pp. 193–228; Preston, *Franco*, pp. 216–19.

90 Colli (Roatta) to Ufficio Spagna, 8.2.1937, *MMIS*, p. 130.

91　Cantalupo to Ciano, 17.2.1937, ASMAE, Spagna Fondo di Guerra, b.38, no. 287/137; Cantalupo, *Fu la Spagna*, pp. 108–12.

92　Preston, *Franco*, pp. 219–23.

93　Rovighi and Stefani, *La partecipazione italiana*, I, *Testo*, pp. 238–317; Olao Conforti, *Guadalajara: la prima sconfitta del fascismo* (Milan: Mursia, 1967) pp. 51ff; Preston, *Franco*, pp. 229–36; Servicio Histórico Militar (Coronel José Manuel Martínez Bande), *La lucha en torno a Madrid* (Madrid: Editorial San Martín, 1968), pp. 117–70.

94　Cantalupo to Ciano, 19.3.1937, *DDI*, 8ᵃ, VI, p. 357.

95　'*Capisci che non possiamo scherzare; è le guerra. Forse non lo sapevamo abbastanza prima, ma ora siamo persuasi che è una guerra come le altre*' – Cantalupo, *Fu la Spagna*, pp. 196, 222–8, 246–7; Coverdale, *Italian Intervention*, pp. 272–5.

96　Cantalupo, *Fu la Spagna*, pp. 210–14.

97　De Courcy to Cranbourne, 11.5.1937, F0371/21333, W9624/7/41. De Courcy was Honorary Secretary of the Imperial Policy Group, regularly travelled as their chief observer, was used from time to time as a special emissary to Mussolini, had an extraordinary network of contacts and was regarded as a fount of extremely reliable information by senior figures within the Foreign Office and the Defence establishment.

98　Perth to Eden, 1.11.1937, F0371/21182, R7369/2143/22.

99　*Opera omnia di Benito Mussolini*, XXVIII, pp. 198–201; Conforti, *Guadalajara*, pp. 378–82; Drummond to FO, 18.6.1937, FO371/21295, W11820/1/41.

100　Osborne (Holy See) to Eden, 8.10.1937, F0371/21162, R6746/1/22.

101　Drummond to Eden, 7.7.1937, W13375/7/41, *BDFA*, Ser. F, vol. 13, pp. 49–50.

102　Rovighi and Stefano, *La partecipazione*, I, *Testo*, pp. 347–62. See also correspondence between Bastico and Pariani and Ciano, 16.4–30.9.1937, reprinted in Canevari, *La guerra italiana*, I, pp. 486–502.

103　Ingram to Eden, 26.8 and 30.8.1937, F0371/21299, W16231/1/41, W16399/1/41.

104　Rovighi and Stefani, *La partecipazione*, I, *Testo*, pp. 492–4.

105　Viola to Ciano, 19.9.1937, *ASMAE*, Ufficio Spagna, b.2, t.2975/1181; Franco to García Conde, 21.9.1937, Viola to Basticao, 23.11.1944, Rovighi and Stefani, *La partecipazione*, I, *Documenti*, pp. 635–53.

106　Brian Sullivan, 'The Italian Armed Forces, 1918–40', in Allan R. Millett and Williamson Murray (eds), *Military Effectiveness*, 3 vols (London: Allen and Unwin, 1988), II, p. 187.

107　Hodgson to Eden, 10.2.1938, F0371/22621, W2125/29/41, and Hodgson to Halifax, 24.8.1938, F0371/22629, W11582/29/41.

108　Gerald Howson, *Aircraft of the Spanish Civil War 1936–1939* (London, 1990), pp. 133–8.

109　They consisted of three Savoia-Marchetti S.81s, three Savoia-Marchetti S.55Xs, three Fiat C.R.32s and three Macchi M.41s flying boats – Howson, *Aircraft of the Spanish Civil War*, p. 228; Rear-Admiral (D) to C-in-C Mediterranean, undated (probably 31.8.1936), F0371/20536, W10196/62/41.

110　Maclean to FO, 2.10.1936, F0371/20579, W12760/9549/41; FO Minute on probable infractions of Non-Intervention Agreement, F0371/20581, W14097/9549/41. The Italians posted in Majorca were deeply unpopular because of their boasting, stinginess and the scale on which they had spread venereal diseases around not only brothels but also the daughters of the respectable middle classes; Hillgarth (Palma) to FO, 13.11.1937, F0371/21392, W21719/545/41.

111 Bargoni, *L'impegno navale italiano, passim*; José Luis Alcofar Nassaes, *La marina italiana en la guerra de España* (Barcelona: Euros, 1975), pp. 106ff.

112 Rovighi and Stefani, *La partecipazione italiana*, II, *Testo*, p. 442.

113 Sullivan, 'The Italian Armed Forces', p. 191.

114 Rodd (Morgan Grenfell) to Jebb, 8.11.1937, and Phipps (Paris) to Sargent, 26.11.1937, F0371/21167, R7438/64/22, R7965/64/22.

115 Sullivan, 'The Italian Armed Forces', pp. 185–95.

116 Drummond to Eden, 12.2.1937, R1042/64/22, *BDFA*, ser. F, vol. 13, pp. 5–10; Minute by Vansittart, 21.4.1937, F0371/21332, W7951/7/41; Drummond to Eden, 23.4.1937, R2816/64/22, 14.5.1937, R3437/64/22, *BDFA*, ser. F, vol. 13, pp. 31–4, 37–40; Drummond to Eden, 28.5.1937, F0371/21166, R3812/64/22; Perth to Eden, 22.10 and 17.12.1937, R7089/64/22, R8490/64/22, *BDFA*, ser. F, vol. 13, pp. 71–3, 85–7.

117 Mario Roatta, *Otto milioni di baionette: l'esercito italiano in guerra dal 1940 al 1944* (Milan: Mondadori, 1946), pp. 12–13; Mario Montanari, *L'esercito italiano alla vigilia della 2ª guerra mondiale*, 2nd edn (Rome: Ufficio Storico dello Stato Maggiore dell'Esercito, 1993), p. 260; Coverdale, *Italian Intervention*, pp. 407–10.

118 Ceva, 'Conseguenze politico-militari dell'intervento italo-fascista', pp. 222–6; Mario Montanari, 'L'impegno italiano nella guerra di Spagna', in *Memorie Storico-Militari 1980* (Rome: Ufficio Storico dello Stato Maggiore dell'Esercito, 1980), p. 152; Sullivan, 'Fascist Italy's Military Involvement, pp. 711–12.

119 Perth to Halifax, 27.1.1939, *BDFA*, II, ser. F, vol. 15, p. 10.

120 Mussolini to Franco, 6.7.1939, *I documenti diplomatici italiani, 8ª serie, vol. XII (23 maggio – 11 agosto 1939)* (Rome: La Libreria dello Stato, 1952), p. 368; Ciano, *L'Europa*, pp. 439–46; Xavier Tusell and Genoveva García Queipo de Llano, *Franco y Mussolini* (Barcelona: Planeta, 1985), pp. 38–9.

121 Gambara to Ciano, 13.8, 11.10, 28.10, 21.12, 28.12 and 29.12,1939, 30.1 and 19.3.1940; Ciano to Gambara, 14.8, 27.10 and 31.10.1939, 13.2 and 23.2.1940, *I documenti diplomatici italiani, 8ª serie, vol. XIII (12 agosto – 3 settembre 1939)* (Rome: La Libreria dello Stato, 1953), pp. 17–18, 25; *I documenti diplomatici italiani, 9ª serie, vol. I (1 settembre – 24 ottobre 1939)* (Rome: La Libreria dello Stato, 1954), p. 442; *I documenti diplomatici italiani, 9ª serie, vol, II (25 ottobre – 31 dicembre 1939)* (Rome: Istituto Poligrafico e Zecca dello Stato/Libreria dello Stato, 1957), pp. 20, 28, 41–2, 519–20, 576–7; *I documenti diplomatici italiani, 9ª serie, vol. III (1 gennaio – 8 aprile 1940)* (Rome: La Libreria dello Stato, 1959), pp. 190–1, 253–4, 310, 508.

122 Franco to Mussolini, 10.6.1940, *I documenti diplomatici italiani, 9ª serie, vol. IV (9 aprile – 10 giugno 1940)* (Rome: La Libreria dello Stato, 1960), p. 630; Anfuso to Zoppi, 12.6.1940, *I documenti diplomatici italiani, 9ª serie, vol. V (11 giugno – 28 ottobre 1940)* (Rome: Istituto Poligrafico e Zecca dello Stato/Libreria dello Stato, 1965), p. 6.

123 Preston, *Franco*, pp. 372–3.

124 Mussolini to Vittorio Emanuele, 9.2.1941, *I documenti diplomatici italiani,*

9ᵃ *serie, vol.* VI *(29 ottobre 1940 – 23 aprile 1941)* (Rome: Istituto Poligrafico e Zecca dello Stato/Libreria dello Stato, 1986) (henceforth *DDI*, 9ᵃ, VI), p. 558. Cf. José Antonio Giménez-Arnau, *Memorias de memoria: descifre vuecencia personalmente* (Barcelona: Destino, 1978), p. 126.

125 Filippo Anfuso, *Da Palazzo Venezia al Lago di Garda (1936–1945)*, 3rd edn (Rocca S. Casciano: Editoriale Capelli, 1957), p. 153.

126 Ramón Serrano Suñer, *Entre Hendaya y Gibraltar* (Madrid: Ediciones y Publicaciones Españolas, 1947), pp. 261–4; Mussolini–Franco conversation, 12.2.1941, *DDI*, 9ᵃ, VI, pp. 568–82; Ciano, *L'Europa*, pp. 631–43; Tussell and García Queipo de Llano, *Franco y Mussolini*, pp. 120–2. See also Preston, *Franco*, pp. 422–3; Massimiliano Guderzo, *Madrid e l'arte della diplomazia: l'incognita spagnola nella seconda guerra mondiale* (Florence: Manent, 1995), pp. 129–31.

127 Emilio Faldella, *L'Italia nella seconda guerra mondiale: revisione di giudizi* (Bologna: Cappelli, 1959), p. 319.

128 Lequio to Ciano, 18.2.1941, *DDI*, 9ᵃ, VI, p. 604.

129 *La Vanguardia Española*, 27.10, 28.10 and 29.10.1943; *Arriba*, 27.7, 28.7, 30.7 and 1.8.1943.

130 José María Gil Robles, diary entries for 6 and 11 August 1943, *La monarquía por la que yo luché* (Madrid: Taurus, 1976), pp. 51, 53; testimony of José Antonio Girón de Velasco, María Mérida, *Testigos de Franco: retablo íntimo de una dictadura* (Barcelona: Plaza y Janés, 1977), p. 117.

8 Franco and the Allies in the Second World War

Denis Smyth

For much of the twentieth century Spain was a mere shadow of her former imperial and international self; a dependant of the Anglo-French bloc before the Second World War and a satellite of the Anglo-American bloc after that conflict, she mostly lived on the tolerance of the Great Powers and on the periphery of their concerns and confrontations. True, between 1936 and 1939, Spain attracted unwonted international attention as the cockpit for such warring foreign ideologies as Fascism and Communism. However, the very fact that the Spanish Civil War was hijacked by these external forces, that their intervention and non-intervention determined its course and dictated its conclusion, demonstrates dramatically Spain's inability to control her own fate. When not a mere plaything of the first-rank powers, she became their playground – or at least their battle-ground.

Yet there was a brief critical period between 1940 and 1942 when Spain's sovereign foreign-policy choices, especially that most fundamental one for peace or war, again commanded the rapt attention once automatically accorded the grand strategic decisions of Philip II. Of course, this re-found international significance for Spain was not due to any sudden regeneration of her power. Post-Civil War Spain was, in the professional judgement of a technical German financial journal, the Berlin *Bankerarchiv*, 'economically almost annihilated'.[1] This economic prostration had clear implications for Spain's freedom of foreign-policy manoeuvre, a point pithily made by the Captain-General of Catalonia, General Orgaz, in response to a worried cleric's query about the likelihood of Spain's going to war after the fall of France: 'Father, you have no doubt studied Logic – I will give you a premise: To wage war successfully a nation must have money and food; have we money? have we food?'[2] Indeed, some informed commentators, like the British ambassador to Spain in 1939–40, Sir Maurice Peterson, came to the subsequent conclusion that Spain's parlous economic circumstances were such as to rob Franco of any freedom of choice in the matter of peace or war.[3] The Commercial Counsellor in Britain's embassy in Madrid, during 1940–1, John Lomax, came to an even more specific retrospective judgement over the precise source of Spain's ultimate international immobilism during those critical years: the failure of the Spanish harvest in later 1940. This grave crisis in the nation's food supply made Spain critically reliant on imports from abroad which were either directly (i.e. obtained from stocks within the British Empire) or indirectly (i.e. accessible only through the Royal Navy's blockade of enemy-occupied or -dominated Europe) controlled by London.[4]

Undoubtedly, such economic dearth did cramp Franco's foreign-policy style, a fact not lost upon officials in both Britain and the United States. Indeed, even before the US entry into the Second World War, Washington was cooperating with London in regulating the international trade with Franco's Spain in commodities like wheat and gasoline. The basic idea was to keep Franco on such short rations as would deter Spain from warlike preparations and projects and deny any stockpile of strategic supplies to the Germans should they enter Spanish territory. It was also hoped, however, that the regulated flow of vital supplies to Spain would persuade Franco of the material advantage of continued cooperation with the democracies and the simultaneous disadvantage of active alignment with the Axis.[5]

To this latter end, both British and American diplomatic representatives in Spain repeatedly urged their governments to adopt a generous programme of economic assistance to Spain, not only allowing vital shipments of fuel, food and fertilizer through the Allied naval blockade of the Nazi-dominated European mainland, but also actually helping the Spaniards with loans and other facilities to obtain the necessities of their national life. However, liberal and leftist criticism from political and journalistic circles – especially within the United States – eventually scuppered such schemes; for how could the Anglo-Americans claim to be fighting for freedom the world over if they acted to prop up the Franco dictatorship in Spain?[6] Faced with what the US ambassador to Spain from 1942 to 1945, Carlton J.H. Hayes, termed 'a flood of molten lava from certain readily eruptive journals', American policy-makers – who alone had the resources ample enough to bale the Spanish economy out on an adequately impressive scale – ultimately shied away from such a controversial project.[7] Indeed, instead, American scepticism about Franco's grand strategic intentions coalesced with resentment at the pro-Fascist leanings of his regime to prompt Washington to regard trade with Spain as an occasion for coercion rather than an opportunity for courtship. Admittedly, the Americans did grudgingly provide vital petroleum supplies to Spain for much of the Second World War. However, that flow of oil was strictly rationed and supervised by American officials. Moreover, during protracted periods in later 1941 to early 1942 and later 1943 to mid-1944, the Roosevelt administration first tightened and then turned off completely the tap on the oil lifeline to Spain, to retaliate against Franco's pro-German and pro-Japanese provocations.[8] Each time it took British intervention, at the highest level, to dissuade the US administration from draining the lifeblood from the Spanish economy. Thus, on 5 January 1942, the British Prime Minister, Winston Churchill (who was staying in the White House at the time), successfully urged upon President Franklin D. Roosevelt the prudence of restoring an oil ration to Spain, in view of the Allies' own vested strategic interest in avoiding Spanish belligerency on the side of the Axis.[9] Again, in the spring of 1944, Winston Churchill argued – once more with eventual effect on US policy-makers – that the Grand Alliance's overall 'political and military requirements' necessitated a resumption of oil shipments to Spain, not least because coercion was counter-productive in this case:

> I have no doubt that by increasing economic pressure we can even-tually bring Spain to heel. In fact, with reasonable people the mere threat should be enough. The Spaniards are not, however, reasonable and they have a capacity for tightening their belts in resistance to foreign pressure.[10]

The ostensible purpose of the oil embargo applied to Franco's Spain in 1944 was to force the Caudillo to cease all exports of the raw material wolfram (much employed in armaments manufacture) to the Third Reich, which had lost access to all of the world's producing regions save Iberia. Yet Franco, for all the vulnerability of his country's economy to an Allied squeeze on its oil supplies, refused to bow completely to Anglo-American pressure: in the settlement of issues which he concluded with the Western Allies in May 1944 he reserved the right to continue export-ing wolfram, if at a reduced level, to the German war economy.[11] Moreover, Washington and London found they had got distinctly less in practice than Madrid had conceded in principle. Anxious not only to interdict the wolfram trade between Spain and Germany, but also to force other concessions, such as a purge of enemy spies from Spanish territory, Allied diplomats found their hopes dashed, despite Franco's fine words. This was the studied conclusion of Britain's Madrid embassy in its 'general survey of Spanish affairs and Anglo-Spanish relations dur-ing the year 1944':

As always, it proved to be one thing to reach an agreement with the Spanish Government and quite another to obtain its implementation. . . . On the two main points, namely, wolfram and German agents, little progress was made. In spite of the official limitation of wolfram exports, large quantities continued to be smuggled across the [Pyrenean] frontier, until the moment of the German withdrawal [late August 1944], thanks to the efficient transport system set up by the German State organisation, Sofindus, and the complicity of highly-placed Spanish officials. It was not until the end of the year that the last German agents were expelled from Spanish North Africa. On the other hand, very few agents had left metropolitan Spain by the time the Germans withdrew from the Pyrenees, thus making further expulsions impracticable. The Spanish Government were pressed from that moment to intern agents, but by the end of the year this had been done only in the case of about 20 out of a list of about 150. Meanwhile, further agents continued to enter Spain by the German Lufthansa air service, which at the same time, continued to carry valuable merchandise to Germany.[12]

If Franco determined to resist Allied efforts to bend him to their will with economic pressure in 1944, when Anglo-American power and their fortunes of war were so much in the ascendant, then how much less likely was he to have been constrained by such economic threats in his foreign-policy moves earlier on in the war? True, Spain's economic circumstances during the critical years of 1940 to 1942, when her belligerency in the Axis interest might have done grievous damage to the Allied cause, did range from dire to desperate. Yet Franco was not denied all freedom of diplomatic choice by his country's economic straits, any more than the economic straitjacket in which the Allies sought to confine him deprived the Caudillo of all room for strategic manoeuvre. This was so because the real assistance Franco's Spain could lend to the Axis at war was not an access of martial strength but rather access to wider geopolitical horizons.

Spain's geopolitical location astride maritime, imperial and intercontinental lines of communication made her choice for peace or war a matter of considerable – and, at times, critical – importance for both belligerent camps during the Second World War. This was especially true during the period June 1940 to December 1941, when Britain stood alone, confronting the Axis powers with her overstretched and underarmed forces in Europe and North Africa, in the Atlantic and the Mediterranean. The odds were already stacked against Britain's survival after the fall of France and Italy's entry into the lists; the accession of Franco's Spain to the anti-British bloc might have made them insurmountable. The strategic facilities and opportunities afforded by Spain's Atlantic and Mediterranean coastlines, by her command – from both the Spanish metropolitan and Spanish Moroccan shores – of the Straits of Gibraltar, connecting the Atlantic Ocean and the Mediterranean Sea and its potential role as 'a reliable bridge to North Africa' (a phrase used by Hitler himself on one occasion), made Franco a highly desirable recruit for the Fascist powers.[13]

The British, for their part, of course, recognized the dangers inherent in any Francoist move to join the fray: 'I want Franco to keep neutral as long as possible,' Churchill declared, for only thus could the spectre of a further, and quite possibly decisive, deterioration in Britain's already dangerous strategic situation be exorcized.[14] Much of the concern focused on that very symbol of British imperial strength and solidity, the Rock of Gibraltar. Indeed, the Germans calculated that, with Franco's permission to cross Spanish territory, they could take Gibraltar in an assault of only a few days' duration. Even if the British garrison could have withstood the German siege for longer, a few hours' artillery bombardment aimed from the Spanish shoreline against the Rock's air and naval bases would have made their position untenable.[15] Loss of the strategic commanding height at Gibraltar would have subverted the entire British presence in the Mediterranean basin, an area regarded by the German admiral, Raeder, as 'the pivot of [Britain's] world Empire'.[16] Direct passage to and from Egypt would be interdicted, the Suez Canal with its access to Middle Eastern oil and India threatened, and Italy – the weaker Axis twin – shielded from British attack. No wonder that Churchill should subsequently acknowledge that 'Spain held the key to all British enterprises in the Mediterranean'.[17]

Nor would the disadvantages to Britain's cause consequent upon the loss of the Rock have been confined to the 'Middle Sea'. For if Gibraltar fell into enemy hands, the Royal Navy would also lose its only capital-ship base in the eastern Atlantic between Freetown in West Africa and home waters. As a result, the fleet would be poorly placed to fend off attacks on British merchant vessels by German U-boats and surface raiders operating out of Spanish and, in all likelihood, Portuguese ports too. German aircraft based at Spanish airfields would also have an increased radius of operation within which to track, or attack, British convoys. Conscious of his country's reliance on vital imports from over-seas to sustain the home and military fronts, the strategic commentator Basil Liddell Hart had warned the then Minister for War, Leslie Hore-Belisha, in 1938 that 'a friendly Spain' was 'desirable' and 'a neutral Spain' was 'vital' if and when Britain was at war again.[18]

If the problems posed by potential Spanish belligerency against Britain loomed large for that country's grand strategists during 1940–1 when she faced Germany alone in the West and in North Africa, the dangers did not simply disappear with the entry of the United States into the Grand Alliance in December 1941. Indeed, the precise point chosen for the large-scale injection of US power into the Eurafrican war – the French colonial empire in North-West Africa – with the Anglo-American amphibious operation, Torch, of November 1942, revived the latent Spanish menace to the Allies. For, in concentrating masses of men and *matériel* onto the Rock of Gibraltar in advance of the Torch landings, and in sailing most of the huge invasion convoys through the narrow Straits of Gibraltar under the muzzles of Spanish guns on both shorelines, the Anglo-American high command was gambling too much on Franco's goodwill, in the view of some Allied experts.

Thus, although the British ambassador to Spain, Sir Samuel Hoare, had been a fairly consistent advocate of continued collaboration with the Franco regime during the dark days of 1940–1, he was not so sure the Caudillo could be trusted to leave Torch unmolested: for it represented a rude intrusion of Allied power into the very area – French Morocco and western Algeria – which the Spanish leader had long coveted as his own colonial *Lebensraum.* Thus, Hoare warned the British government in very explicit terms, on 29 August 1942, of the risks it and its American allies were running:

> The temptation to cut our lines of communication will be very great. We shall appear to have put our neck between two Spanish knives and Spanish knives are traditionally treacherous. The Germans will be on General Franco's back, dinning into his ears: 'Now is your time. You can cut the Allied throat, destroy the naval and air bases at Gibraltar and win a dazzling reward for your country in North Africa.' Let no one underrate the power of this temptation, or think that because nine Spaniards out of ten do not want war, General Franco might not risk it for the big stakes that in the circumstances it might offer him. He and his brother-in-law have made no secret of their wish to see Germany win the war. What better chance than this could they have of expediting a German victory? Spanish help might take one of two forms. Spanish guns, manned by Spanish troops, might fire on the harbour and aerodrome of Gibraltar and immobilize them in a few hours, or German bombers might be permitted to operate from Spanish territory. In both cases action might be swift and very damaging.[19]

Operation Torch, of course, had been conceived to achieve far-reaching political and military purposes: to help revive the Allied fortunes of war after a long run of reverses; to fortify the American popular appetite for the war; and to relieve pressure on the Red Army on the Eastern Front.[20] All these important goals could have been frustrated by hostile action on the part of Franco's Spain during the initial implementation of Operation Torch. Churchill publicly acknowledged, later in the war, that 'Spain's power to injure' Anglo-American interests 'was at its very highest' during the days leading up to the launching of Torch.[21] As it happened, Franco neither delivered the *coup de grâce* to Britain in 1940–1 nor disrupted Torch's deployments and debouchments. Churchill, for one, never forgot this seemingly masterly inactivity on Franco's part. So, when the Caudillo sought to effect a *rapprochement* with London, in October 1944, to ensure the survival of his regime in the post-war world without Hitler and Mussolini, the British Prime Minister did not rebuff him outright. Certainly Churchill had no hesitation in refusing alliance with Franco's Spain, at that time, to combat what the Spaniard termed 'the insidious might of Bolshevism'.[22] However, the British Premier also rejected the first draft of a reply to the Caudillo's *démarche*, prepared by the Foreign Office. Churchill did so because, he argued, it failed to acknowledge 'the supreme services' which Franco had rendered the British cause in the Second World War by 'not intervening in 1940, or interfering with the use of the [Gibraltar] airfield and Algeciras Bay in the months before Torch in 1942'.[23]

Yet Churchill's gratitude was misplaced. For, as scholarship in recent decades has proven beyond all doubt, Franco's ultimate non-intervention in the Second World War on Germany's side was the result neither of goodwill nor of good judgement. For a start, despite the Caudillo's emphatic assurance to the new British ambassador to Spain, Sir Vernon Mallet, on 27 July 1945, that 'Spain had never, even during the worst days of 1940, intended to go to war with Britain', that was precisely what he had tried to do at that exact moment.[24] As an *Africanista* officer who had earned his military reputation in the savage campaigns of colonial 'pacification' in Spanish Morocco during the early decades of the twentieth century, Franco seized on France's collapse before the Nazi onslaught in May–June 1940 as a welcome opportunity to expand into French Morocco.[25] The Germans, however, made it clear that any territorial changes in that region could be effected only under their auspices and with their approval.[26] Franco, of course, realized that neither his economically enfeebled country nor his antiquated army could bear the wear and tear of a protracted war effort. So he developed a strategy whereby he sought to reap the rewards of participation in Germany's victory by making no more than the most belated and token of contributions thereto.[27] As Ramón Serrano Suñer, the Caudillo's sometime political confidant and flamboyantly pro-Fascist Foreign Minister (for the period October 1940–September 1942), admitted after the war, Spain's policy was 'to enter the war at [the] end, at the hour of the last cartridges'.[28]

As is explained elsewhere in this volume, Hitler saw no need to meet what Franco claimed were 'Spain's legitimate and natural aspirations with regard to her succession in North Africa to territories that were until now France's'.[29] Why jeopardize relations with a more pliant Vichy France and her North African empire when Spain increasingly appeared to want to offer so little in return for so much? The latter point was grasped by Ernst von Weizsäcker, State Secretary of the German Foreign Ministry, as is evident from his private assessment of the Spaniards' position on belligerency: 'They say they could only enter the war at the last moment before the victory of the Axis – but what further good would they be then as co-diners (i.e. at the victors' banquet)?'[30] In the face of this Nazi unwillingness to guarantee him payment in advance for his belligerent services and in the absence of any material proof that Britain was all but down and out, Franco did refuse, on 7 December 1940, to open his Pyrenean frontier so as to allow German troops to cross his territory early in 1941 to attack Gibraltar.[31] Yet this falling out between Führer and Caudillo was over the profit and practicability, not over the principle and propriety, of Spanish belligerency.

So, Franco in reality hardly deserved Churchill's subsequent expressions of gratitude for maintaining Spanish non-belligerency during the critical years of Allied vulnerability, 1940–2. Yet Churchill's later votes of thanks to Franco do more than gloss over the reality of the latter's serious flirtation with belligerency on Germany's side. They also divert attention from the fact that it was Britain, and not Nazi Germany, which came closest to pushing Spain into the war alongside Hitler. For, determined as the Führer was to invade the Soviet Union at the earliest opportunity following his triumph in the west in the early summer of 1940, he never contemplated a forcible entry into Spain, in defiance of Franco's wishes, to seize Gibraltar. Unwilling to postpone Operation Barbarossa, in order to bring the recalcitrant Caudillo to heel, Hitler ceased to pose any immediate threat to Spanish non-belligerency after the spring of 1941 – and the Red Army ensured that the Führer was never in a position subsequently to take revenge on the 'fat little sergeant' (as he later dubbed Franco) who had frustrated his effort to seal the Western Mediterranean before embarking upon Barbarossa.[32]

If Franco escaped Hitler's wrath because of the very magnitude of the latter's project for a military offensive in 1941, then, ironically, Britain's modest defensive priorities during 1940–1 placed the Caudillo in much more proximate peril. For the sheer scale of the damage which a belligerent Spain could do to Britain's fight for survival at that critical time, merely by opening up her geostrategic facilities to the Germans, meant that London did have to contemplate going over to the offensive to prevent, or pre-empt, a mortal menace arising from that quarter. 'Must we always wait until a disaster has occurred?', was Churchill's plaintive query, on 24 July 1940, to his then Foreign Secretary, Lord Halifax, a question prompted by the Prime Minister's concern 'about the dangers of our ships lying under the Spanish howitzers at Gibraltar'.[33] What Churchill and his grand strategic advisers concluded was essential was an insurance policy against the loss of Gibraltar and its precious capital-ship harbour. A substantial amphibious assault force was organized to allow instant retaliation against or, even better, active anticipation of, an enemy attack on the Rock. At its peak of preparedness, by the late summer of 1941, this expeditionary force consisted of 24,000 troops, Britain's entire fleet of amphibious assault-vessels, along with a naval escort comprising 1 battleship, 3 aircraft carriers, 3 cruisers and 19 destroyers. The object of the exercise was the capture of alternative capital-ship bases to Gibraltar among the Iberian-owned Atlantic islands: the Portuguese Azores and Cape Verdes in 1940, when the British force was too weak to tackle Spain's better-defended islands, and the Spanish Canaries in 1941, when the expeditionary force had been built up to the strength necessary to take on this tougher target.[34]

Moreover, the secret conditions which British grand strategists attached, in July 1940, to their assault on the Atlantic archipelagoes envisaged a pre-emptive strike: the islands (Portuguese ones, initially) would be invaded not only if Spain or Portugal actually entered the fray against Britain but also if London concluded that it was 'clear beyond reasonable doubt that either of these Powers intended' to do so.[35] Actually, even a British move against the Portuguese Islands would have provoked Anglo-Spanish hostilities, as is clear from Franco's assurance to Salazar, on 13 July 1940, that he would employ 'all his forces' to protect Portugal from any action by Britain which endangered Iberian independence.[36] A direct British attack on Spanish territory, such as the Canaries, would have led, even more assuredly, to war with Franco's Spain. Yet Churchill had come to the conclusion, within weeks of the fall of France, that preventive attack, in this critical instance, might be the best form of defence. No wonder, then, that he proved unreceptive to the complaint made by the Minister of War Transport, Lord Leathers, in September 1941, over the 'indefinite immobilization' of scarce troop transports and precious cargo vessels necessitated by holding the Atlantic islands expeditionary force in a constant state of readiness and at very short notice. Churchill dismissed Leathers' protest with this observation:

'We have to pay the price, or be caught unawares.'[37] However, the very state of high alert, on Britain's part, over the threat to Gibraltar proved to be the most serious menace posed to Spanish non-belligerency by any foreign power during the Second World War. With the pistol already pointed, an apprehensive hand might discharge it, given any provocation.

Thanks to Franco's maladroit diplomacy, the provocations came thick and fast. Indeed, the American Secretary of State, Cordell Hull, was sufficiently annoyed by Franco's abrasive and acerbic statecraft to denounce it roundly in conversation with the Spanish ambassador in Washington, Juan de Cárdenas, on 13 September 1941:

> I must state that in all of the relations of the [US] Government with the most backward and ignorant governments in the world, this Government has not experienced such a lack of ordinary courtesy or consideration which customarily prevailed between friendly nations, as it has at the hands of the Spanish Government. Its course has been one of aggravated discourtesy and contempt in the very face of our offers to be of aid. I said, of course, we could not think of embarrassing, not to say humiliating ourselves by further approaches of this nature, bearing in mind the coarse and extremely offensive methods and conduct of Suñer in particular and, in some instances, of General Franco. I said that when I thought back about the details of the conduct of the Spanish Government towards the [US] Government what had happened was really inconceivable.[38]

Certainly, Allied diplomats readily resigned themselves to a hostile press in Spain.[39] However, their eyebrows might have been raised had they known just how many of the most abusively anti-Allied editorials were personally penned by Serrano Suñer and that Hitler was so pleased with the result that he privately declared Spain's press to be 'the best in the world'.[40] Still, it was not Spain's propaganda of the word, *per se*, that came to worry Allied statesmen in late 1940; it was what Franco's brave words might betoken by way of actual deeds during 1940–2 that really preoccupied policy-makers in London and Washington.

The first really ominous signs seemed to come in the weeks from early November to mid-December 1940. During that period the Franco regime proceeded to impose its authority on Tangier (hitherto an internationally ruled enclave within Spanish Morocco, situated some 56 kilometres south-west of Gibraltar), abolishing the main institutions of the International Administration and dismissing its British officials.[41] In the analysis of the German ambassador to Spain, Eberhard von Stohrer,

Franco's action was motivated by a desire to grab 'Tangier at least' from the wreckage of his project to expand territorially in North-West Africa with Hitler's grace and favour.[42] The clumsiness of the Spanish take-over in Tangier, accompanied as it was by pro-Axis actions (like the safe haven given there to two Italian submarines evading Royal Naval pursuit) and anti-British riots (like the attacks on British establishments in that city on 3 December 1940), was not calculated to soothe London's sensibilities and there was a howl of protest in the House of Commons at the Spaniards' high-handedness.[43]

However, it was not the temper of Britain's parliamentary elite but rather the concerns of her grand strategists that Franco should have measured before he moved at Tangier. For, in assuming that his Tangier adventure could be viewed in isolation from the widening and deepening world war, Franco was guilty of the worst kind of strategic parochialism. In reality, Franco moved to absorb Tangier into Spanish Morocco at a moment in the development of the global conflict when his action could not but be viewed with foreboding in London. This was due to the conjucture in late 1940 of two British strategic preoccupations. First, there was the spontaneously revived British fear over the vulnerability of Gibraltar. Rightly discerning that Hitler was contemplating a simultaneous descent on the Portuguese and Spanish Atlantic islands, along with the seizure of Gibraltar (all the better to deny the British alternative deep-water harbours), the British Chiefs of Staff Committee (comprising the commanding officers of Britain's army, navy and air force) recommended, on 9 November 1940, the immediate launching of Operations Brisk (against the Azores) and Shrapnel (against the Cape Verdes).[44] Although Churchill shared his strategic advisers' concern that the Nazis might grab the islands while the British dithered, he agreed in the end, on 25 November, that 'the general situation should be watched, and . . . the matter should be reconsidered after the lapse of ten days or a fortnight'.[45] That postponment, of course, resulted in the issue coming up for review precisely when the Spaniards were making their final unilateral moves to integrate Tangier into their Moroccan zone.

As if that coincidence did not appear threatening enough to London, it joined another strategic apprehension growing in Churchill's mind at that time. Ironically, this prime ministerial concern derived directly from the first great success of British land forces in the Second World War: Operation Compass. This offensive was launched against the Italians in the Western Desert on 9 December 1940 and, although the British attackers were heavily outnumbered, they soon turned their initial victories over the enemy into a full-scale rout of the Italian army in North Africa.[46] For all his delight at this welcome turn of events,

Churchill saw danger in the very dimensions of Britain's triumph in the Egyptian desert, as a fellow cabinet minister recorded at the time: 'The P. M. says that he is quite sure that Hitler cannot lie down under this . . . he must make some violent counter-strike. What will it be? . . . Perhaps a blow through Spain.'[47]

Given his pre-existing fears over the insecurity of the British hold on Gibraltar and his new concern over Hitler's possible riposte to Operation Compass, it was all too easy for Churchill to interpret Franco's provocative actions at Tangier as proof perfect that the Caudillo was about to permit the passage of Nazi forces across Spanish territory to seal the Western Mediterranean. Churchill expounded his logic at an emergency meeting held at Chequers on Saturday 14 December 1940 to consider 'the launching of Brisk and Shrapnel Operations forthwith':

> now . . . we had established ourselves more firmly in the Eastern Mediterranean it seemed more and more likely that Hitler would take some action in the Western end. All he had got to do was to squeeze or push aside the Spaniards; and it seemed very likely that he was preparing a coup of some kind in that direction; the Spanish move at Tangier looked suspiciously as though Franco had sold himself.[48]

However, the British Foreign Office, taking a decidedly less alarmist view of Spain's misbehaviour at Tangier, mobilized all its powers of persuasion to restrain the famously impulsive Prime Minister from stampeding into an unnecessary war with Spain. The Foreign Secretary, Lord Halifax (who was about to lose his post, relic of the Chamberlainite appeasement era that he was, to Anthony Eden), argued emphatically that 'the Spanish move into Tangier' was not 'an Axis plot' and that any British counterstroke 'would put Spain definitely into the Axis camp'.[49] Again, the British naval attaché in Madrid, Captain Alan Hillgarth (a personal acquaintance of Churchill's), visited the Prime Minister and his strategic counsellors in London to debunk the notion that Spanish actions at Tangier portended inevitable and imminent belligerency on the side of the Axis.[50]

However, perhaps the most crucial cautionary counsel came from the Joint Intelligence Committee (JIC), a subcommittee of the Chiefs of Staff Committee (composed of representatives of the various branches of Britain's secret intelligence community and chaired by the Foreign Office's representative, William Cavendish-Bentinck) which attempted to formulate integrated intelligence appreciations drawing on the intelligence services' several resources and separate sources. The JIC reported by the New Year, 1941, its conclusion that Franco would not let German troops into Spain and that Hitler would not attempt to force his way through, in the absence of permission to pass.[51] The primary source inspiring this confident and, as it turned out, entirely correct assessment was the debriefing, in part carried out by Cavendish-Bentinck himself, of a spy by the name of Dusko Popov. Popov, a Yugoslav, had agreed to work for the German Military Intelligence Service, the *Abwehr*, only so as to inflict as much injury as he could on the Third Reich. Popov had revealed his true loyalties to the British even before he was sent to London, in late December 1940, on an espionage mission for his unsuspecting German spymasters. Once he reached the British capital, he was able to prove his true colours by passing to his debriefers a timely item of intelligence he had acquired from *Abwehr* contacts in Lisbon before setting off for London. This information was of Franco's early-December refusal to give Hitler leave to cross Spanish territory and attack Gibraltar in the New Year.[52] In view of the important part played by Popov in defusing the dangerous late-1940 crisis in Anglo-Spanish relations, it is ironical indeed that Franco should later have denounced the role of British spies in allegedly jeopardizing ties between London and Madrid during the Second World War. For, on the occasion of his interview with Ambassador Mallet on 27 July 1945, already mentioned, Franco displayed his incomprehension of the fact that Britain's shadow warriors had largely rescued him from the consequences of his own recklessness over Tangier. Mallet's record of the Caudillo's contentions on this matter reads thus:

> He knew that the British Secret Service had reported that Spain was preparing to attack us, but he wished to assure me that these reports were entirely incorrect. Spain always intended to stay neutral and had indeed in the end, as it were by a miracle, succeeded in doing so.[53]

So, Franco never knew that it was human agency (actually a human agent in the person of Popov!) and not divine intervention which had rescued him from blundering into war with Britain over Tangier. However, the second near miss in Francoist–Allied relations during the Second World War did require critical intervention from on high – at least the topmost level of the British government – to resolve peacefully. Again, Franco's timing was distinctly off, as he chose a season (June–July 1941) rife with strategic turmoil and diplomatic tension to indulge in grand gestures and threatening talk. Even before Franco's provocations of the summer, British reverses in the Eastern Mediterranean and the Desert War had made Britain's warlords fret once more over the fragility of their hold on its Western end. Thus, on 29 April 1941 – the day before British troops had to withdraw from the Peloponnese in the face of the superior German forces invading Greece – Churchill communicated to President Roosevelt his concern over the strategic reverberations of such defeats across the 'Middle Sea':

> [A]t the western end of the Mediterranean I must regard the Spanish situation as most critical. Hitler may easily be able to get control of the batteries which could deny us the use of Gibraltar harbour or even the batteries on the African shore.[54]

However, it still took major mistakes by Franco to crystallize British grand strategists' concerns over the security of Gibraltar into a decision to open hostilities against Spain in the autumn of 1941. It was the official Spanish response to the Nazi invasion of the Soviet Union which ultimately threatened to rend irreparably the delicate fabric of Anglo-Spanish relations in the Second World War. Faced with Francoist sins in word and deed, Churchill and his advisers resolved to strike first, to pre-empt hostile action from Spain.

In the beginning, in this instance, was the deed: the formation of a division of 18,000 Spanish volunteers to fight in the German army on the Russian Front.[55] The decision to dispatch the Blue Division to the Eastern Front did not derive from any re-found Francoist enthusiasm for full-blown belligerency in the Axis interest. For, when the German Foreign Minister, von Ribbentrop, was officially encouraged by means of Franco's dispatch of the Blue Division to suggest that 'a public declaration that Spain was in a state of war with the Soviet Union would be appropriate and desirable', Serrano Suñer rebuffed the Nazi *démarche* with these remarks:

> Personally he was inclined to believe that England and possibly America would react to such an announcement if not by a declaration of war on Spain, then undoubtedly by the imposition of a blockade, which would entail cutting off all supplies now in transit. . . . Complications for Spain would also be detrimental to Germany during the Russian campaign.[56]

Thus, the dispatch of the Blue Division to the Russian Front was not the prelude to, but rather a symbolic substitution for, real Spanish belligerency on Germany's side. Franco and Serrano Suñer both stated this to be the case after the end of the Second World War. The Caudillo admitted to Mallet that the Blue Division was 'a mere drop of water' which 'had amounted to nothing but a small gesture'.[57] Serrano Suñer, similarly, later testified to the fact that the *divisionarios* were pawns in a greater game: 'Their sacrifice would give us a title of legitimacy to participate one day in the dreamed-of victory and [yet] exempt us from the general and terrible sacrifices of the war.'[58] That is to say, Franco was playing the same old game with the Nazis, trying to gain admission to the victors' feast on the cheap. Yet just as that self-interested strategy had failed to impress Hitler in later 1940, it earned Franco no credit or credibility with the Führer as the Wehrmacht and the Red Army locked in lethal embrace in the East. Indeed, meeting with Mussolini on 25 August 1941, only days after the Blue Division had started on the final stage of its journey to the Russian front line, Hitler 'spoke in bitter terms about Spain, expressing his genuine and profound disappointment with that country'.[59] In other words, Franco's symbolic contribution to Operation Barbarossa had not altered the negative judgement on the Caudillo's policy which Hitler had communicated to Mussolini on the eve of the launching of that attack on Russia: 'Spain is irresolute and – I am afraid – will take sides only when the outcome of the war is decided'.[60]

However, if the dispatch of the Blue Division to the Eastern Front turned out to be too cheap a gesture to buy Hitler's favour, it came perilously close to costing Franco very dear in terms of his relations with what would turn out to be the victorious camp in the Second World War: the Grand Alliance of Britain, the United States and the Soviet Union.

For a start, as Paul Preston notes, Franco was very fortunate in militarily engaging the Red Army not to have provoked a formal Soviet declaration of war against Spain, which would have left Britain and the United States – after she entered the Second World War in December 1941 – little choice but to follow suit.[61] However, Serrano Suñer calculated that the Franco regime, in sending this Spanish unit to fight on the Russian front, had done enough to curry favour with the Third Reich without sorely provoking the Allies, as he explained many years later: 'Really with the Blue Division we wanted to go a little way towards fulfilling our obligation to Germany without provoking the Allies.'[62] Although the calculation was clearly a fine one, what upset it dangerously – much to Serrano Suñer's consternation – was that Franco added to his pro-Nazi propaganda of the deed some spectacularly anti-Allied words.

This exacerbation of the already strained relations between Spain, on the one hand, and Britain and her then non-belligerent ally, the United

States, on the other, took the form of what Serrano Suñer himself called an 'aggressive speech', which Franco delivered on 17 July 1941 (the anniversary of the military uprising against the Republic which initiated the Spanish Civil War in 1936).[63] The Caudillo used this official commemoration to denounce 'age-long' enemies of Spain who still practised 'intrigues and treachery' against his country, because they 'never forgave [her] for having been great' – a clear reference to Spain's old imperial rivals, Britain and the United States. Not content with airing historic resentments, he roundly abused recent Anglo-American efforts to attach political strings to economic assistance, commenting that it was 'an illusion to believe that the plutocracies make use of their gold for generous or noble deeds'. Asserting that 'the war was badly started', and that the Allies had 'lost it', he warned against any American 'intervention in Europe' which could only end in 'catastrophe' and also exulted at the 'inevitable' destruction of the 'terrible incubus . . . of Russian communism'. He concluded his harangue thus:

> At this moment, when the German armies lead the battle for which Europe and Christianity have for so many years longed, and in which the blood of our youth is to mingle with that of our comrades of the Axis as an expression of firm solidarity, let us renew our faith in the destiny of our country under the watchful protection of our closely united Army and the Falange.[64]

Sir Samuel Hoare notes in his memoirs that 'it would be hard to imagine a more provocative speech' – 'so provocative' that he wondered how the reputedly cautious Caudillo could have delivered it.[65] Indeed, Hoare's initial conclusion was that the speech could not really have been Franco's own work at all and must have been 'either written by Sr. Serrano Suñer himself or by Sr. Ximénez de San Doval, his new young Falangist "Chef de Cabinet"'.[66] For once, however, Serrano Suñer was not the real culprit. The actual source of the anti-Allied invective the Caudillo poured forth in his speech of 17 July was the naval captain Luis Carrero Blanco, who, until his assassination in the final years of the Franco regime, was one of the most trusted of the *Generalísimo*'s political confidants. Moreover, since Carrero Blanco was able to gain, and maintain, Franco's favour precisely because he was such an uncritical counsellor, the sentiments informing the wanton words Franco uttered against the Allies must have sprung from within the Caudillo's own profoundly anti-democratic and anti-leftist political psyche.[67]

Morover, far from approving, let alone authoring, Franco's diatribe against the embryonic British–American–Soviet bloc, Serrano Suñer audibly exclaimed, 'Is this a bullfight?', as the Caudillo basked in the acclaim of his sycophantic claque.[68] What really concerned Serrano Suñer, as he explained to Ambassador von Stohrer ten days later, was the likely consequence of Franco's irresponsible incitement of the Anglo-Americans:

> The speech had been premature. It suddenly opened the eyes of the English and the Americans about the true position of Spain. Previously, the English government especially kept on believing that only he, the Foreign Minister, was pushing for war, while the 'wise and thoughtful' Caudillo would preserve neutrality unconditionally. That illusion has now been taken from them. They had come to realize that Spain, in understanding with the German government, would enter the war at a suitable moment. . . . He had no doubt that the English and Americans were in consultation with each other on how to meet this new situation; it was evident that our enemies were trying, somewhere at long last, to forestall Germany . . . the Spanish government has been receiving information indicating that plans were being studied for a landing in the Spanish zone of Morocco . . . Tangier, too, was threatened, to say nothing of the Canary Islands, which would surely be attacked as soon as the Azores were occupied.[69]

Serrano Suñer was not too far off in his assessment of the impact of Franco's speech on the Allies and on the likely character of their retaliation. The immediate inclination of the British Foreign Secretary, Anthony Eden, was 'to stiffen up to Franco', since he was 'behaving badly again, making pro-Axis speeches and sending troops against Soviet Russia'.[70] Churchill readily agreed with both the diagnosis and prescription of his Foreign Secretary, as the Prime Minister revealed to a meeting of the Chiefs of Staff (Cabinet) subcommittee, on 23 July 1941:

> The Prime Minister said that the political position in Spain had hardened. He thought that at any moment Spain might go over to the German camp. For these reasons he was in favour of carrying out Operation 'Puma' (destined for the Canaries) at the earliest opportunity.[71]

A day later, Churchill advised his War Cabinet colleagues that it made sense 'to make certain of securing the Canary Islands' before the Germans occupied them.[72]

Renamed 'Pilgrim', the projected British attack on the Canary Islands now assumed such ample proportions as to place a real strain on the Royal Navy's already overextended force of destroyers. This was the main consideration prompting a postponement of the British invasion of the Canaries until September 1941, when the requisite number of destroyers – 19 – could more easily be assembled.[73] However, that interval only allowed Churchill to come up with another good reason for pressing ahead with the expedition against Spain's Atlantic archipelago: its potential usefulness in promoting Anglo-American cooperation. The Prime Minister's meeting with President Roosevelt at Argentia, Newfoundland, from 9 to 12 August 1941, was designed to cement the Anglo-American partnership for the present war and the future peace, even though the United States had not yet formally entered the global conflict. During these discussions, which sought to harmonize Anglo-American strategic and diplomatic policies across the full range of international issues, Churchill was quick to pick up on Roosevelt's warning that, according to American sources, the Germans might well move into the Iberian Peninsula on 15 September.[74] The British leader, in reply, briefed the President on the British plan to launch Pilgrim in September. Roosevelt's response was such as apparently to clinch Churchill's decision to go to war against Franco's Spain. So, the Premier informed the Chiefs of Staff on board the battleship *Prince of Wales* on 11 August that 'in view of the President's favourable reaction to the information that we intended to carry out Operation "PILGRIM", it seemed more than ever important that we should launch the expedition in September'.[75]

Thus, Franco's big talk and 'small gesture' had brought his country to the very brink of war with Britain. That this war was actually avoided was entirely due to the British Prime Minister's capacity for strategic reconsideration. Indeed, even when resolving in principle, on 23 July 1941, to seize the Canaries, Churchill had stipulated that the project could be vetoed 'at the last moment if some insuperable objection' emerged.[76] What is most striking about the grounds which did indeed materialize for calling off the Pilgrim attack in September is that Churchill himself had actually sought them out. For he had taken the precautionary step, on 25 July, of requesting 'the fullest possible text of the translation of Franco's recent speech'. Although he did not get the chance, apparently, to read that text carefully until mid-August, it had a dramatic influence upon his appraisal of the urgency of the notional strategic menace emanating from Franco's Spain. Churchill communicated his radically altered assessment of Franco's speech, and its reliability as a portent of imminent hostility from Spain, to Eden on 16 August 1941:

It does not make so hostile an impression upon me as I have derived from the summaries and extract. I do not think it would be a sound deduction from this speech that Franco had given himself over to the Axis. . . . I do not think that this speech by itself, in the absence of further development [*sic*], could be taken as a basis for . . . PILGRIM . . . such action would have to be justified on other grounds.'[77]

No other *casus belli* did subsequently arise to persuade the Allies to make war on Franco's Spain. They thus kept open the easiest access point – at the Western mouth of the Mediterranean – for American forces to enter the Eurafrican war in November 1942. Churchill's grand strategic foresight concerning Franco's real intentions on participation in the world war did not desert him as the preparations for Operation Torch progressed in late August 1942. He emphatically maintained, in the face of American apprehension of the dangers of Francoist action against Allied assault convoys filing through the narrow Straits of Gibraltar, and of Sir Samuel Hoare's warning to the same effect, that Spain would 'do nothing'.[78]

In a rare instance, however, of the Americans insisting on dictating the course of Allied policy towards Spain during the Second World War, President Roosevelt and the US Joint Chiefs of Staff insisted that the Torch landings include one on the Atlantic coast of Morocco at Casablanca – a dispersal of the attacking forces which ensured that they would not all be concentrated in a perilous passage through the Pillars of Hercules but one which ultimately helped weaken the Allies' drive on Tunisia and allowed Hitler to draw them into a protracted battle of attrition there which would wreck any Anglo-American hopes of opening a second front in North-Western Europe in 1943.[79] Roosevelt also took the lead in assuring the Caudillo – in a message personally communicated to the Spanish leader on the morning of 8 November 1942, Operation Torch's D-Day, by US Ambassador Hayes – that Spain had 'nothing to fear from the United Nations'.[80] As an extra precaution against any sudden Francoist alignment with the Axis camp, as the vulnerable US forces sought to establish themselves on the North-West African shore, American intelligence agents (from the Office of Strategic Services) carried out monthly burglaries on the Spanish embassy in Washington before, during and after Torch. These break-ins yielded information on the regular key changes to the Spanish diplomatic cypher, allowing American cryptanalysts to monitor Spanish secret signal traffic between Madrid and Washington throughout the critical period. No clear signs of Francoist belligerency were detected.[81]

Indeed, although some pro-Axis political and military factions did advocate entry into the war on the Nazis' side at the time of Torch, another, monarchist, military grouping inclined towards the Allies and explicitly warned Franco against intervention. The Caudillo, however, was hardly likely to rush to the aid of the Axis in late 1942 to early 1943 as it staggered under a trio of Allied blows: El Alamein, Torch and Stalingrad.[82] Indeed, Franco privately acknowledged the need for a *rapprochement* with 'the Anglo-Saxon countries' in the aftermath of Operation Torch, a realignment of Spanish foreign policy which should be effected 'with all due prudence and circumspection'.[83] So gradual and grudging was the reorientation of Spain towards the Allied camp, even as Nazi military fortunes declined precipitously in the latter stages of the Second World War, that many journalists and politicians in the Allied countries continued to condemn this Anglo-American 'appeasement' of the Spanish dictator. This was not the least reason why Washington, usually and ultimately, was prepared to defer to London's line on dealings with Franco's Spain during the Second World War.[84] Thus, for example, Secretary of State Hull insisted, over the protests of Ambassador Hayes, that Britain take the primary public credit for concluding the May 1944 agreement, mentioned above, with Franco's Spain, all the better to deflect American domestic condemnation of the deal away from the Roosevelt administration.[85] Franco was extremely fortunate that Roosevelt was generally prepared to concede the decisive say in Allied policy towards Spain in the Second World War to his transatlantic partner; for Churchill had cultivated habits of restraint and reflection in managing Madrid, in the face of all the Caudillo's picador-like provocations of John Bull during 1940–1, which not only saved the Grand Alliance from having to see off yet another enemy power in the global struggle but also rescued Franco from the consequences of his own inept statecraft.

Notes

1 Quoted by *The Times* (London), 3.10.1940.
2 FO 371 (Foreign Office General Correspondence after 1906 Political): UK Public Record Office)/24511, C9159/75/41. In the weeks leading up to France's collapse before the violence of the German invasion in May–June 1940, prominent monarchist generals of Spain's army, urged on their fellow senior commanders, and Franco himself, the unpreparedness of the country's armed forces for war. Javier Tusell, *Franco, España y la II Guerra Mundial: entre el Eje y la neutralidad* (Madrid: Ediciones Temas de Hoy, 1995), pp. 95–8.
3 Sir Maurice Peterson, *Both Sides of the Curtain* (London: Constable, 1950), pp. 229–30. Peterson's espousal of the view that Spain's internal weakness in 1940–2 precluded any external adventurism was not unconnected with his

obvious desire to deny any credit to his successor as British ambassador to Spain, Sir Samuel Hoare, for Franco's ultimate abstention from the fray. Peterson clearly remained bitter over his brusque removal from his ambassadorial post in Spain and he used his subsequent job, in Britain's wartime administration as Controller of Overseas Publicity at the Ministry of Information, to snipe at Hoare's activities in Spain. See, for example, Kenneth Young (ed.), *The Diaries of Sir Robert Bruce Lockhart*, vol. II, *1939–1965* (London: Macmillan, 1980), pp. 134, 180.

4 Sir John Lomax, *The Diplomatic Smuggler* (London: Arthur Barker), pp. 104–5.

5 Denis Smyth, *Diplomacy and Strategy of Survival: British Policy and Franco's Spain, 1940–41* (Cambridge: Cambridge University Press, 1986), pp. 59–64; Carlton J. Hayes, *Wartime Mission in Spain* (New York: Macmillan, 1946), pp. 79–80; Herbert Feis, *The Spanish Story: Franco and the Nations at War* (New York: Knopf, 1948; 1966 edition, New York: Norton, 1966), pp. 27–66.

6 Smyth, *Diplomacy and Strategy*, pp. 40–1, 115–32, 135–9, 154–8, 173–9; Hayes, *Wartime Mission*, pp. 135–48; Feis, *Spanish Story*, pp. 148–57, 196–206 (see note above for full details); Willard L. Beaulac, *Franco: Silent Ally in World War II* (Carbondale and Edwardsville, Southern Illinois University Press, 1986), pp. 25–6, 183–5.

7 Hayes, *Wartime Mission*, p. 238; Smyth, *Diplomacy and Strategy*, pp. 195–7.

8 Smyth, *Diplomacy and Strategy*, pp. 186–93; Hayes, *Wartime Mission*, pp. 79–82, 183–225; Feis, *Spanish Story*, pp. 219–54.

9 Smyth, *Diplomacy and Strategy*, pp. 194–5 (see note 5).

10 Prime Minister to President Roosevelt, No. 631, 30.3.1944, PREM 3 (Files of the Prime Minister's office kept at the War Cabinet Offices, dealing with defence and operational subjects: UK Public Record Office)/405/7.

11 Denis Smyth (ed.), *British Documents on Foreign Affairs: Reports and Papers from the Foreign Office Confidential Print* (hereafter *BDFA*), Part III: *From 1940 through 1945*, Series F: Europe, vol. 16: *Western Europe, October 1943–June 1944* (Bethesda, Md.: University Publications of America, 1998), pp. 281–5; United States Department of State, *Foreign Relations of the United States* (hereafter *FRUS*), *1944*, IV (Washington, DC: Government Printing Office, 1966), pp. 409–14.

12 Smyth (ed.), *BDFA*, (see note above) Part III, Series F, vol. 19: *Western Europe, July 1945–December 1945* (Bethesda, Md.: University Publications of America, 1998), pp. 197–9. On the continuing shelter which the Franco regime gave to German spies, even after faithfully promising the Allies to expel these secret agents, see, for example, Ralph Erskine, 'Eavesdropping on "Bodden": ISOS v. the *Abwehr* in the Straits of Gibraltar', *Intelligence and National Security*, 12: 3 (1997), p. 122.

13 United States, British, French Board of Editors, *Documents on German Foreign Policy, Series D (1937–1945)*, vol. XI: *The War Years (September 1, 1940–January 31, 1941)* (London: HMSO, 1960), p. 104.

14 Dalton Papers (British Library of Economics and Political Science at the London School of Economics and Political Science), Diary 24, 2.3.1941.

15 Charles B. Burdick, *Germany's Military Strategy and Spain in World War II* (Syracuse, NY: Syracuse University Press, 1996), pp. 27–8.

16 H.G. Thursfield (ed.), *Führer Conferences on Naval Affairs* (London, Brassey's Naval Annual, 1948), p. 141.

17 Winston S. Churchill, *The Second World War*, 6 vols (London: Cassell, 1948–54, vol. II: *Their Finest Hour* (American edition, Boston: Houghton Mifflin, 1949), p. 519.

18 B.H. Liddell Hart, *The Defence of Britain* (London: Faber, 1939), p. 68.

19 FO 371/31289, C 10745/10738.G. Hoare had also warned the Joint Intelligence Sub-Committee and the Joint Planning Staff (both sub-committees of the War Cabinet's Chiefs of Staff Committee), on 27 August 1942, of the dangers and difficulties posed by Franco's Spain to Torch: CAB 81 (War Cabinet Chiefs of Staff Committees and Sub-Committees: UK Public Record Office)/90, JIC (42) 41st Meeting (o), Min. 1.

20 See, for example, Arthur Layton Funk, *The Politics of Torch: The Allied Landings and the Algiers Putsch, 1942* (Lawrence/Manhattan/Wichita: University of Kansas Press, 1974), pp. 98–9; Michael Howard, *Grand Strategy*, vol. IV, *August 1942–September 1943* (London: HMSO, 1972), pp. xv–xxv.

21 *Parliamentary Debates (Hansard)*, Fifth Series, vol. 400 (London: HMSO, 1944), col. 770, 24 May 1944. During a plenary session of the Potsdam Conference, on 19.7.1945, Churchill also used Franco's restraint at the time of Torch as one of his arguments to deflect Stalin's desire that the Allies put pressure on Franco to quit office in Spain. Rohan Buter, M.E. Pelly and H.J. Yasamee (eds), *Documents on British Policy Overseas*, Series I, vol. I: *The Conference at Potsdam, July–August 1945* (London: HMSO, 1984), p. 427.

22 Franco to the Duke of Alba, Spanish ambassador in London, 18.10.1944, in Smyth (ed.), *BDFA*, Part III, Series F, vol. 17: *Western Europe, July 1944–December 1944* (Bethesda, Md.: University Publications of America, 1998), pp. 415–17 (see note 11 for full details).

23 Prime Minister's personal minute to Foreign Secretary, 11.12.1944, PREM 8 (Papers, 1944–5: UK Public Record Office)/106.

24 *BDFA*, Part III, Series F, vol. 19, p. 194 (see note 11 for full details).

25 Paul Preston, *Franco: A Biography* (London: HarperCollins, 1993), pp. 14–49; Tusell, *Franco, España y la II Guerra Mundial*, p. 115.

26 Tusell, *Franco, España y la II Guerra Mundial*, pp. 116–19; Norman J.W. Goda, *Tomorrow the World: Hitler, Northwest Africa, and the Path toward America* (College Station: Texas University Press, 1998), pp. 56–112.

27 Smyth, *Diplomacy and Strategy*, pp. 87–8.

28 Serrano Suñer's interview with Charles Favrel, *Paris-Presse*, 26.10.1945, FO 371/49663, Z 13272/11696/41.

29 Franco to Hitler, 30.10.1940, in Ramón Serrano Suñer, *Entre el silencio y la propaganda, la historia como fue: memorias* (Barcelona: Planeta, 1977), p. 304.

30 Note of 13.12.1940, Leonidas Hill (ed.), *Die Weizsäcker-Papiere, 1933–1950* (Frankfurt-am-Main: Propyläen Verlag, 1974), p. 228.

31 Smyth, *Diplomacy and Strategy*, pp. 133–4.

32 *Ibid.*, p. 134; Albert Speer, *Spandauer Tagerbücher* (Frankfurt-am-Main: Propyläen Verlag, 1975), p. 252.

33 Churchill's personal minute to Lord Halifax, 24.7.1940, FO 371/24515, C 7429/113/41.

34 Smyth, *Diplomacy and Strategy*, pp. 66–7, 220–4, 233–4.

35 CAB 65 (War Cabinet Minutes, September 1939–May 1945/: UK PRO)/14, WM 209 (40)7, Confidential Annex.
36 Ministério dos Negócios Estrangeiros, *Dez anos de política externa (1936–1947): A nação portuguesa e a Segunda Guerra Mundial*, vol. VII (Lisbon: Imprensa Nacional, 1971), pp. 250–2.
37 Lord Leathers' personal minute to Churchill, 18.9.1941 and Churchill's written comment thereon, which was communicated to the Minister of War Transport on 20.9.1941, PREM 3/361/1.
38 *FRUS, 1941*, vol. II (Washington, DC: Government Printing Office, 1959), p. 914 (see note 11 for full details).
39 FO 371/24511, C8526/75/41; Hayes, *Wartime Mission*, pp. 69–70, Beaulac, *Franco: Silent Ally*, p. 109.
40 Tusell, *Franco, España y la II Guerra Mundial*, p. 115; Intro., H.R. Trevor-Roper, *Hitler's Table Talk, 1941–44: His Private Conversations*, 2nd edn (London: Weidenfeld & Nicolson, 1973), p. 694. At a public German press exhibition held in Madrid in March 1941, Serrano Suñer actually boasted of the uniformly pro-Nazi line he had forced Spain's newspapers to follow during the previous three years, when he exercised powers of press censorship and control for the Franco regime (*Arriba*, Madrid, 13.3.1941; Templewood, *Ambassador on Special Mission*, pp. 103–4).
41 Smyth, *Diplomacy and Strategy*, pp. 135–6, 139.
42 *DGFP*, Series D, XI, p. 465.
43 Smyth, *Diplomacy and Strategy*, pp. 136–9.
44 CAB 79/7, COS (40) 384th Mtg, Min. 2.
45 DO (Defence Committee, Operations), (40) 46th Mtg, Min. 1, copy in PREM 3, 361/6A.
46 See, for example, Gerhard L. Weinberg, *A World at Arms: A Global History of World War II* (Cambridge: Cambridge University Press, 1994), pp. 210–11.
47 Dalton Papers, Diary 23, 17.12.1940.
48 CAB 79/55, COS (40) 33 (o).
49 *Ibid.*
50 FO371/26904, C 460/46/41; Eden to Hoare, 15.1.1941, Avon Papers (UK PRO), FO 954/27A; CAB 80/56, COS (41) 2 (o).
51 Major-General Sir Kenneth Strong, KBE, CB, *Men of Intelligence: A Study of the Roles and Decisions of Chiefs of Intelligence from World War I to the Present Day* (London: Giniger/Cassell, 1970), p. 119; Noel Annan, *Changing Enemies: The Defeat and Regeneration of Germany* (London: HarperCollins, 1995), p. 61; Patrick Howarth, *Intelligence Chief Extraordinary: The Life of the Ninth Duke of Portland* (London: The Bodley Head, 1986), p. 146.
52 F.H. Hinsley and C.A.G. Simkins, *British Intelligence in the Second World War*, vol. IV, *Security and Counter-Intelligence* (London: HMSO, 1990), p. 95; Dusko Popov, *Spy/Counterspy* (New York: Grosset & Dunlap, 1974), pp. 62–3, 70.
53 *BDFA*, Part III, Series F, vol. 19, pp. 194–5 (see note 11 above).
54 Warren F. Kimball (ed.), *Churchill and Roosevelt: The Complete Correspondence*, 3 vols, vol. I, *Alliance Emerging: October 1933–November 1942* (Princeton, NJ: Princeton University Press, 1984), p. 176.
55 Denis Smyth, 'The Dispatch of the Spanish Blue Division to the Russian Front: Reasons and Repercussions', *European History Quarterly*, vol. 24: 4 (1994), p. 537.

56 *DGFP*, Series D, vol. XIII, *June 23, 1941–December 11, 1941* (London: HMSO, 1964), pp. 16–17.

57 *BDFA*, Part III, Series F, vol. 19, p. 187.

58 Ramón Serrano Suñer, *Entre Hendaya y Gibraltar*, 2nd edn (Barcelona: Ediciones Nauta, 1973), p. 209.

59 *DGFP*, Series D, vol. XIII, p. 385.

60 *DGFP*, Series D, vol. XII, *February 1, 1941–June 22, 1941* (London: HMSO, 1962), p. 1067.

61 Preston, *Franco*, p. 442. Stalin, in refraining from committing the Grand Alliance to a formal declaration of hostilities with Franco's Spain, was doubtless anxious to spare the Allies additional strategic complications which could impede the earliest possible opening of a Second Front in Western Europe.

62 Heleno Saña, *El franquismo sin mitos: conversaciones con Serrano Suñer* (Barcelona: Ediciones Grijalbo, 1982), p. 252.

63 *DGFP*, Series D, XIII, pp. 222–3.

64 Translations of Franco's speech, of 17.7.1941, in PREM 4/21/1; Denis Smyth (ed.), *BDFA*, Part III, Series F, vol. 13: *Spain, Portugal and Switzerland, January 1940–December 1941* (Bethesda, Md.: University Publications of America, 1998), pp. 433–5.

65 Templewood, *Ambassador on Special Mission*, p. 113.

66 *BDFA*, Part III, Series F, vol. 13, p. 435.

67 Preston, *Franco*, pp. 436, 441.

68 *Ibid.*, p. 441; Saña, *El franquismo*, p. 253.

69 *DGFP*, Series D, XIII, pp. 223–4.

70 Lord Harvey of Tasburgh Diaries and Papers (British Library), diary entry for 18.7.1941, Add. 56398. Eden's private secretary, Oliver Harvey also recorded, in this diary entry, the Foreign Secretary's conclusion that Britain should seize the opportunity, with the Nazis otherwise engaged against the Red Army, to teach Franco a lesson: 'He [Eden] has always hated this appeasement policy which incidentally has been contrary to American wishes.'

71 CAB 79/86, COS (41) 259th Mtg, Min. 3.

72 CAB 65/23, WM 74 (41), Confidential Annex.

73 Smyth, *Diplomacy and Strategy of Survival*, pp. 233–4.

74 *Ibid.*, pp. 234–5.

75 COS (R) 6, copy in PREM 3/485/5.

76 CAB 79/86, COS (41) 259th Mtg, Min. 3.

77 Churchill's personal minute to Eden, 16.8.1941, PREM 4/21/1.

78 Quoted by Funk, *Politics of Torch*, p. 95.

79 See, for example, Robert H. Ferrell (ed.), *The Eisenhower Diaries* (New York: Norton, 1981), pp. 76–8; John Barnes and David Nicholson (eds), *The Empire at Bay: The Leo Amery Diaries, 1929–1945* (London: Hutchinson, 1988), p. 841; Howard, *Grand Strategy*, vol. IV, pp. 111–39; Weinberg, *World at Arms*, pp. 432–7.

80 Hayes, *Wartime Mission in Spain*, pp. 90–1.

81 Anthony Cave Brown, *The Last Hero: Wild Bill Donovan*, (New York: Vintage/Random House, 1984), pp. 226–33; Robin Winks, *Cloak and Gown: Scholars in the Secret War, 1939–1961* (New York: William Morrow, 1987), pp. 171–3, 511 note 10.

82 Preston, *Franco*, pp. 477–9. See also Tusell, *Franco, España y la II Guerra Mundial*, pp. 364–6, for the chastening impact of Torch and Soviet successes upon Carrero Blanco and other Axis-leaning members of the Francoist ruling elite.

83 General Jordana (Serrano Suñer's replacement as Spanish Foreign Minister, in September 1942) to the Duke of Alba (Spain's ambassador to the United Kingdom, 1939–45), 27.11.1942, Alba Papers (Palacio de Liria, Madrid), Caja 2ª – No. 4.

84 Other reasons prompting the United States to take a back seat to Britain in the formation of Allied policy towards Spain in the Second World War included the following: (i) the greater proximity of Britain and her imperial outposts to Spain's territory, a geopolitical fact which underscored the primacy of British interests in the Spanish question, within the framework of the Grand Alliance; (ii) the precedence which Britain had established in dealing with Spain during the Second World War, by being the only Allied belligerent in the field in the Iberian Peninsula during the critical period of 1940–1; and (iii) the prestige which Sir Samuel Hoare had garnered at home and abroad by flying the flag for the democracies in Spain during the dark days of 1940–1. Indeed, Carlton J. Hayes, that Columbian professor turned American ambassador, found it hard to play second fiddle to Hoare, resenting the latter's unilateralist tendencies and superior airs. Hayes even suggested that Hull try to persuade the British government to recall Hoare to London; the Secretary of State declined to undertake this indelicate task because, as he explained to Hayes, 'of the strong position which there is reason to believe your British colleague holds with his own Government' (Hayes to Under-Secretary of State Sumner Welles, 29.12.1942; memorandum (jointly prepared by Ambassador Hayes and Counselor Beaulac) on 'British Attitude in Spain', 26.12.1942; Hull to Hayes, 20.1.1943: all in Hayes Papers (Columbia University Library), Box I: Correspondence, November–April, 1943).

The feelings between Hayes and Hoare were mutual. Thus, for example, Sir Samuel denounced the American ambassador, in a letter to Foreign Secretary Eden, as 'a very heavy footed professor from Columbia University' with 'no previous experience of public life', who apparently harboured the sentiment that the British Empire was 'a nuisance and an anomaly that ought to be speedily liquidated' (Hoare to Eden, 31.5.1943, Templewood Papers (Cambridge University Library), XVIII, 23).

85 Hayes, *Wartime Mission in Spain*, pp. 226–7.

9   Spain, Britain and the Cold War[1]

Florentino Portero

Introduction

Relations with Britain have traditionally been a priority of Spanish diplomacy. After the end of the Second World War these relations once again rekindled interest for a variety of reasons. The Franco regime had allied itself and had collaborated with the Axis, although it never fully involved itself in the conflict. The result was that many sections of public opinion throughout the world and numerous governments wanted the regime to come to an end. Britain's international position had been strengthened by the experience of the war to the point that no other superpower in Western Europe was in a position to compete for continental leadership. Germany had been defeated and her future was uncertain. France, though one of the victors, was faced with grave political problems. What is more, the special relationship Britain appeared to have with the United States, the new world superpower, gave her a great deal of influence on international politics and more especially in European affairs. From this privileged position, the policy adopted by Britain's Foreign Office towards the Franco regime was to be of lasting and undeniable importance.

'An unfortunate anomaly'

British politics had been a determining factor in the evolution of the Spanish Civil War and in the stance of the Franco regime in the Second World War. In the first instance, the Foreign Office considered that a Republican victory meant that Spain would become a communist state, an even bigger risk to British interests than the country's alliance with the other nations of fascist inclination. The country's non-interventionist policy thus had a twofold objective. The first was to facilitate Franco's victory and avoid triggering off a second world war arising from the division of Europe over the Spanish crisis.[2] Second, the 'carrot and stick' policy applied by both the United States and Britain used to full advantage the conditions and the dependence of the Spanish economy in order to force Franco gradually to separate himself from Nazi Germany.[3]

When the Second World War was coming to an end, the British political classes were faced with having to define a new policy towards Spain. Reopening the debate that had caused such wide division in British public opinion entailed great risks. However, as part of the cabinet the two main political parties imposed an agreed option. There were clearly three positions held from the outset. The first was that of the Labour Party, expressed by its leader Clement Attlee. In his opinion the Franco regime was corrupt and oppressive, and a large number of political prisoners were still held – and many others had simply been shot. The regime existed thanks to the support of Nazi Germany and Fascist Italy and was not widely accepted by the Spanish people. Also, both British public opinion and that of Europe and North America totally rejected the regime and demanded that it be overthrown. The Labour Party therefore considered that the British cabinet should intervene and force the Franco regime out. If this were not done they and the other Western governments, would face strong lobbying from public opinion to take appropriate measures. In fact, on 4 November 1944 Attlee proposed, together with the United States and France, that economic sanctions should be imposed on Spain. The objective was to destabilize the Franco regime and reinstate the democratic institutions by strangling the Spanish economy.[4] Behind these proposals there was a clear desire on the part of Labour to make right the wrong done to Republican Spaniards as a result of Britain's non-interventionist policy.

The more conservative position was represented by the Prime Minister, Churchill, backed by the more important sectors of the Commons and the bureaucracy, including the Foreign Office. Churchill was faced with a firm Labour proposal which – and this is all the more serious – had the support, or at least in part, of the Foreign Office Secretary, the Conservative Sir Anthony Eden, who had been quick to draft a document outlining the new policy.[5] Churchill saw no reason to justify involvement in Spain's internal affairs. Attlee's proposal, he felt, ignored the state's interests and was based on ideological prejudices that under no circumstances should determine British politics. 'Interference in the internal affairs of a country', he said, 'has long been very dangerous, and the dangers are increased when an interference is on ideological grounds.' Economic sanctions would harm British interests, which he was bound to defend, and would also worsen the already poor living standards in Spain. On the other hand, Franco's dictatorship was no crueller than that of Stalin, no more arbitrary than that of Salazar; it made no sense to try to overthrow all these regimes. 'I am no more in agreement with the internal Government of Russia than I am with that of Spain, but I would certainly rather live in Spain than in Russia.' The application of the sanctions proposed by Attlee might, in his opinion, provoke a blood-bath, in the first instance, and in the second, turn Spain into a communist regime, which would benefit only the Soviet Union.

> You [Eden] need not, I think, suppose that Franco's position will be weakened by our warnings. He and all those associated with him will never consent to be butchered by the Republicans, which is what could happen. It is a life and death matter in Spain and I do not think we should, without careful consideration, make ourselves responsible for starting another revolution in Spain. You begin with oil: you will quickly end in blood.

Churchill's objective was to install a constitutional monarchy, and for this to happen the opposition had to be given time to get organized.[6]

Anthony Eden, the Secretary of State for Foreign Affairs, represented the third position. He agreed with the Labour Party that the Franco regime, after the end of the war, was an anachronism and that if the cabinet did not adopt measures public opinion would hold it against them and would lobby them to do so. He also felt that the policy adopted so far had been against his wishes in many instances, and had given Franco the impression that the British government supported him and had dissuaded moderate opposition. It was Eden's recommendation that Franco should be sent a message expressing Britain's rejection of his regime and insisting that it could never be accepted in the international community. He wanted to convince the Caudillo that the time had come to reinstate the monarchy and also to encourage moderate opposition. Only then if no political changes were perceived could sanctions be imposed.[7]

It was up to the Foreign Office to propose a solution acceptable to all in keeping with an evaluation of the state's interests. These were threefold: strategic, political and economic. The first hinged on the Rock of Gibraltar. Thanks to it, Britain controlled the gateway to the Mediterranean, and had a haven for her ships sailing to western Africa and Latin America. It was also a centre for communications and above all an important position that, with other enclaves, made Britain a Mediterranean power. The Rock's value and the difficulties in defending it led to the consideration that what was needed was a friendly or at least neutral government in Madrid. There were two possible threats: Germany's rearmament, which might make Spain anti-British; or a possible Soviet influence on the existing government. A Red Army invasion was not the worry; more worrying was the possibility of a political development which might end in disorder, radicalization and finally power falling again into the hands of groups sympathetic to Moscow. In this case, and in the event of an armed conflict with the Soviet Union, British presence in Gibraltar would be weaker than ever, and the advantages Britain held would be severely jeopardized.[8] From a political point of view, should Franco's regime survive, there would be permanent internal problems for Britain and for the other Western nations as it would provoke public opinion to demand that measures be enforced to ensure the regime's overthrow. Lastly, from an economic perspective the British civil servants underlined the importance of maintaining and increasing trade with Spain. This had traditionally been a good market for British products, and a supplier of goods that were hard to find elsewhere at the same prices. The application of economic sanctions would damage private interests and would also have repercussions, although mild, on the recovery of the British economy.[9] The evaluation of state interests left the politicians very little room for manoeuvre: it was advisable to bring Franco's regime to an end, and make room for a more liberal government, but without affecting the trade relations between the two states and without thereby enabling the Soviet Union to gain influence in Spain.

On the basis of these premises Eden drafted a new document on Britain's policy on Spain which would serve as the basis for a long-term policy taken on by the two leading parties. This document revealed the breach between himself and his superior by bringing up once again the 'non-interventionist' position held by the Franco government during the Second World War and the harsh reprimand that British diplomacy had to apply, but he undertook to defend the interests described, which implied a policy of caution, allowing no option for a shift towards communism and far less that of imposing economic sanctions. He championed intervention in Spanish politics given that the continuation of the Franco regime after the fall of the Axis powers would be 'an unfortunate anomaly' which would bring about the mobilization of Western public opinion. If in the short term no changes took place, the public at large would demand that harsh measures be taken, thereby jeopardizing British interests in the Peninsula. In order to guarantee these interests, it was imperative that the regime be liberalized.

One immediate measure to be taken was to encourage the organization of a moderate opposition to create a viable alternative, and above all to pressure Franco into standing down. The first step would be to send a harsh word of warning: if he did not stand down then relations between the two countries would be revoked and Spain would be excluded from the new international organizations. The new document was finally approved by the cabinet. The warning was sent in a letter from Churchill to Franco in response to a previous letter from the Caudillo.[10]

Before this new policy actually became a reality it was to pass through a new filter. Although Eden had not mentioned what kind of regime should replace that of Franco, in deference to Attlee, who was sympathetic to the Republican cause, the document which came out of the Foreign Office considered only the possibility of the monarchy of Don Juan, one of the sons of Alfonso XIII. This political change would depend on the strongest political institution of that time, the army, and the latter, a symbol *par excellence* of the victors, would not accept a return to the Republic.

'Order, unity and endure'

The triumph of the liberal powers and the Soviet Union, the states that, to a greater or lesser extent, had supported the Republic, made an international campaign likely against the regime. However, Franco never feared that this campaign could lead to the application of harsh sanctions. The experience of the Civil War, of the Second World War and contacts with well-informed people showed that the Western bloc as a whole, and more specifically Britain, were afraid that a destabilization of Spanish politics could facilitate a victory for Communism. In this situation it seemed highly improbable that a destabilizing campaign would be undertaken by these countries, although the Soviet Union might be a different matter.

> Russia must have created a great number of problems for its allies after their victory for these, and more specially England and the United States, to believe that it was advisable to cause problems for Spain; the only ones who would reap any benefit from the situation would be the reds organising riots and seriously disturbing the peace, maquis etc., which would only benefit communism, in a word, Soviet Imperialism.[11]

It was possible, however, that public opinion lobbies and the left-wing parties as well as the Soviet Union might push the Western governments to take measures against Spain, but not for long. Moscow's politics were imperialist and sooner or later would clash head on with those of Washington and London. The wartime alliance was only temporary and could not last much longer. When this severance came, anti-Communist feeling would rise and Spain would be seen as a bastion of Western values, ahead of the rest in the struggle against communism, and international pressures would disappear. All there was left to do was wait.

Meanwhile, and to reduce pressure from abroad as far as possible, Franco initiated a policy of 'gestures'. He implied he was ready to stand down and give way to the monarchy of Don Juan after a prudent period of transition, which would ensure peace and order, reduce the fascist element of the regime and increase the Catholic component. Thus a face-lift and a few vague promises accompanied the following message to the liberal powers: if they wanted a monarchy then they had to create the right conditions for it to exist, reduce the external pressures and facilitate an orderly restoration.

Franco was convinced that to contain this campaign against his regime he needed the recognition of the Soviet threat and the forging of an alliance against it. So from this perspective he launched a diplomatic operation which proved to be far too ambitious. On 21 November 1944 the Duke of Alba handed Eden a letter from General Franco proposing that they unite their policies in order to face up to Soviet expansionism:

> only three countries of those with a large enough population and enough resources have stood out as being strong and virile: England, Germany and Spain; what is more, Germany destroyed, England is left with only one country on the Continent to which to turn its sights: Spain.[12]

In exchange, Franco demanded of the British government that it bring an end to the campaign against his regime and discourage democratic opposition because this only served to facilitate Soviet interests.[13] Time was to prove that Franco was right in thinking that relations with the Soviet Union were to be a key element in the definition of Spain's new role, but he was wrong about the date and about the tone and content of his proposal. Churchill's reply was drafted by the Foreign Office and was approved on 18 December by the War Cabinet. The letter thanked Spain for her collaboration at such a delicate moment but reminded the General of some fundamental aspects of the policy adopted during the Second World War: the facilities provided to German intelligence, the 'non-intervention', the Blue Division, Tangier, the fascist nature of the Falange and in general the anti-British tone of the official press. All these facts were crucial in the relations between the two states so that as long as no important political changes took place to end the existing regime, 'more friendly and co-operative relations' would not be possible. Until such a time, the British government would not support Spain's presence in peace negotiations or in the future world organization.[14]

Churchill's letter was the first action over the 'Spanish question'. It was to be followed among others by the United Nations Conference for

International Organization held in San Francisco. On 19 June a motion was approved by the votes of Britain and the United States that Franco's Spain should not be accepted within the new organization owing to Germany's and Italy's help in its constitution. A short time afterwards, at the Potsdam Conference of the 'Big Three', the recent 'coordination' of British and North American diplomacy on Spain was put to the test.[15] Stalin proposed a diplomatic and economic blockade to force the fall of Franco. The British delegation strongly opposed this as they considered that Spain did not constitute a threat to international security, as the Soviets were implying, and that intervention would mean intervening in her internal affairs and violating the San Francisco Charter. For the British an action of this nature would reinforce Franco's position, and if successful would pave the way for another civil war. In the end, a communiqué similar to that of San Francisco was issued, condemning the regime for its ideological and diplomatic links with the Axis and denying it entry to the United Nations Organization.[16]

The result was a victory for Franco, proving the validity of his policy. Luis Carrero Blanco, Under-Secretary to the Presidency, expressed at that time the regime's position:

> If you stop to think about it for a moment, it must be recognised that in Potsdam we had been defended energetically by Truman and by Churchill. . . . They defended us for their own *interests* . . . when the last shot was fired in the Pacific, a diplomatic war broke out between the Anglo-Saxons and Russia. . . . Out of this basic *cold interest*, the Anglo-Saxons will not only not support, but will oppose every thing they can which might lead to a situation of Soviet hegemony on the Iberian Peninsula. Their interests here are based on order and anti-communism, but they would prefer to achieve this with a regime other than the existing one. . . . Pressure from the Anglo-Saxons for a change in Spanish politics which would interrupt the normal evolution of the existing regime will ease off the more tangible our *order, unity* and *impassivity* become in the face of orders, threats and impertinences. The only formula left to us is: *order, unity and to endure.*[17] [emphasis in original]

Churchill was right when he warned Eden that Franco's position would not be weakened by warnings and threats and that Franco was well aware that Britain and the United States would not tolerate the imposition of destabilizing measures for fear of sparking off the civil conflict again and giving the Soviet Union another opportunity to increase her influence in an area of great strategic value. All that Spanish diplomats had to do was fend off the pressures and make it clear that the monarchy was on its way and wait for the conflict between the capitalist powers and the Soviet Union to explode. Against this backdrop the regime's fascist sins would pale and become history, and the only interest remaining would be in gaining its collaboration. The only risk for Franco was internal. Some of his regime's political forces and especially the highest echelons of the army and some anti-Falange people might believe the message that the interests of the victors might in the future be best represented by the monarchy reinstated by Franco, who was directly responsible for an unnecessarily close *rapprochement* with the Axis and for the creation of the Falange. Only the army with greater or lesser civil support could carry out a *coup* to dislodge Franco from power. This was the challenge the Foreign Office and the British intelligence forces in coordination with their North American counterparts were faced with.

Waiting for Don Juan

During the summer of 1945 Franco worked on developing his 'policy of gestures'. Two important Bills were passed, '*El Fuero de los Españoles*' (The Charter of Spain), in theory a charter of Spaniards' rights, the application of which lay in the hands of the government and the '*Ley de Bases del Regimen local*', a theoretical first step towards the democratization of local life through organic suffrage. Before the National Council, Franco announced that Spain would once again be a monarchy, although he omitted to mention when. Finally, on 21 June an important change was made in the government, reducing the Falange's representation and increasing that of the Catholics. Most important, though, was the designation of Alberto Martín Artajo as the Minister for Foreign Affairs. Although totally inexperienced as a diplomat, Artajo was the visible leader of Spanish Catholic politics, and represented Franco's efforts to give the regime a new look and gain the support of European Christian Democratic parties. Having Artajo to head Spain's diplomacy was very useful to Franco. His image as a moderate man open to political change and his defence of the monarchy gave the Foreign Office and other Western chancellors hope of change. Franco let Artajo believe he was willing to stand aside and let Don Juan take his place after a controlled process which would culminate in the restoration of the monarchy. This new minister attempted to convince the diplomatic corps, and more especially the North American and British ambassadors, of Franco's good faith in moving towards a monarchy and of the need to facilitate international conditions for this to come to fruition, because under pressure and threats Franco could not proceed.[18]

The election of the Labour government brought no change in British policy *vis-à-vis* Spain, which after all had been agreed by the two parties. The new Foreign Secretary, Bevin, did not hesitate to face down the left-wing faction of his party, which demanded that sanctions be imposed against the Franco regime. The fear of Soviet expansionism and of creating the conditions under which the Soviet Union might influence Spain led Bevin to try to secure a transition towards a moderate monarchy. In the light of Artajo's promises the British government demanded something tangible and maintained a chilly tone in its relations with Spain. It also maintained that pressure from public opinion and sectors of the left wing on the governments of the United States and Western Europe could lead them to impose economic or diplomatic sanctions on Spain. Bevin debated between the need to give time to this hypothetical transition led by Franco and the organization of a divided opposition, on the one hand, and on the other the pressures from his own party to bring the Franco dictatorship, the final vestige of European fascism, to an end.

'The Spanish question'

The internal pressure on the French government proved to be so strong that in December 1945 the Quai d'Orsay proposed to its British and North American equivalents that they should jointly break off relations with Spain. The reply from London was negative, but Washington, less interested in Spanish affairs and very sensitive to internal pressure and to maintaining the West's unity, showed itself to be disposed to apply some form of sanction against the Franco regime. It was only the pressure from Britain that held the Americans back. The French government's situation worsened to the point that it closed France's borders with Spain and announced that it was ready to take the Spanish case before the United Nations, as it felt that it posed a threat to international peace. The authorities responsible for French diplomacy were aware that that would not help the transition to democracy in Spain, but felt that it could stave off a crisis for the French government.[19]

For Britain the French proposal was very dangerous. From a legal point of view Spain posed no threat to anyone, and the discussion before the United Nations would set a terrible precedent of intervention in internal affairs of state. From a political point of view the destabilization of a regime could give rise to a civil war which would benefit only Stalin. The condemnation or the pressures applied from outside could frighten the population, already fearful of a new conflict, and would push the military, already in a permanent state of conspiracy, into Franco's arms because their nationalistic ideals made these pressures intolerable to them.

The Caudillo would surrender power only if he felt it were necessary and under such pressure would never do it; quite the opposite, he would become more obstinate than ever. For these reasons the Foreign Office decided to fend off the French proposal.[20]

The United States shared the British analysis regarding the consequences of the French proposal, but was more willing to help the ally in trouble. Only the firmness of London's position convinced the Department of State. Both powers put pressure on Paris and got the French to back down. Instead, the three countries made a joint declaration reiterating the same old arguments.[21]

However, the Soviet Union had seen the advantages offered by the French proposal. When the Paris government retracted, Stalin took up the initiative once again. At the beginning of April 1946 a Polish delegation submitted to the United Nations what had been the French proposal – a formal complaint that Spain constituted a threat to peace – and submitted a request to the Security Council that it analyse the question and adopt the necessary measures.

The 'Spanish question' became an international problem debated in a public forum. Britain tried to curtail the debate as soon as possible, rejecting its inclusion on the Security Council agenda. The United States recognized that this was the best solution; however, considerations of a political nature prevented the Americans from backing this option. They did not want to cause an all-out confrontation with the Soviet Union in which they might also be seen as the defenders of the last vestige of European fascism. Their interests in Spain were limited and, although they were aware of the harm the Polish initiative might cause, they were not willing to pay such a high price.[22] Britain was left out on her own. Faced with the impossibility of holding back the Soviet initiative, Britain simply followed in Washington's footsteps, continuously lobbying for a firm position to be taken.

The debate in the United Nations was an international trial of Francoism from which it could not emerge innocent. The sentence, the resolution of 12 December 1945, politically condemned the regime and upheld the UN's veto. It recommended that its members withdraw their ambassadors and plenipotentiary ministers from Madrid and established a time limit of one year for political change to take place in Spain before new sanctions were to be applied. The international condemnation of the regime did not weaken it. On the contrary, it gave Franco the final reinforcement he needed, just as the British diplomats had forecast. As in Potsdam, Franco had seen for himself how the Anglo-Saxons reacted against Soviet pressure for intervention, ensuring the stability of his government because they were fearful of sparking off another civil war.

The attacks from the Soviet delegates and other countries under Soviet control or under other left-wing governments enabled the Franco propaganda machine to organize a campaign denouncing communist interventionism, claiming that it posed the risk of a new outbreak of civil war. That other governments should attempt to decide Spanish matters was also denounced as an affront to Spain's national dignity. The use of nationalism and fear was fruitful. Many people who until then had demanded political change swung over to support Franco. This process was evident among the high ranks of the army. It was not the right moment to make moves; Don Juan could wait in the light of the urgent need to guarantee internal order.[23]

Isolation

The British policy had failed. Franco was even stronger than before, and it did not seem likely that he was about to give up power to Don Juan. The government had to choose between trying to destabilize Franco, with all the risks that involved, or accepting him. The first option went against British interests, as has been seen. The second option was thrown out by the members of the ruling Labour Party, and also by the powerful trade unions. Both groups demanded that their cabinet adopt efficient measures to provoke these changes in the Spanish government. The solution adopted was to sit back and await developments and formally maintain the former policy.[24] Meanwhile, in the face of possible approval by the United Nations of economic sanctions, the British government prepared a new evaluation of British investments and commercial activities in Spain as well as the possible alternatives. The outcome was not very encouraging. There was a long history of close relations. In some cases, there just was no alternative market or else the transactions would have to be done in dollars or at a very high price. The sterling areas would feel the pinch and Spain would be unable to honour some of her financial commitments. This constituted a set of adverse conditions which, once presented in an intelligent fashion, became an instrument in Bevin's hand to damp down the pressures of the left wing: what was at stake here was the welfare and the jobs of the British working class.[25]

The isolation of the Franco regime began almost at the same time as the international backdrop that made it possible began to disappear. In March 1947 President Truman declared the beginning of what was to be called the 'Cold War'. Before the US Congress he proclaimed the imperialistic nature of the Soviet Union's politics and his readiness to face down that country whenever it attempted to subvert the internal order of any sovereign state.

The initial premise of Franco's policy had come to be. Moscow's initiative against him already had far less backing from the democratic powers. The possibility of a new world war, which would set the democratic nations against the Soviet Union, would cause the former to value Spain's geostrategic position as well as its firmly anti-communist position.

As of 1947 the American administration began to divide over policy towards Spain, as greater importance was given to the political or strategic component. President Truman and a large section of the State Department were more inclined to encourage the overthrow of Franco. Other government employees of the State Department and most of the Pentagon supported the bringing of isolation to an end, as being unjust and a failure. They were also in favour of a closer relationship with Spain and integrating it as part of the Western bloc, and making use of Spain's strategic importance. It was the contradiction between the overall interests in containing the spread of communism, on the one hand, and the old policy of defence of democracy and the struggle against fascist regimes on the other. In the midst of this dilemma the British government played a fundamental role.

At the end of the year, when the United Nations had once again to rethink its policy on Spain according to the mandate of the resolution passed the previous year, the United States and Britain united once more to prevent economic sanctions from being applied, and reaffirmed the 1946 resolution. This resolution still stood, although it no longer had any political force. Once again the Anglo-Saxon powers had defended the regime against the Soviet Union.

The United Nations vote was clear proof of the absurd stance of the British policy. A few months behind the United States, the Foreign Office was caught up in a serious debate about activities in Spain. The first step came from the Chargé d'Affaires in Madrid. In a long declaration he recognized the contradictory nature of the policy in force, and expressed doubt as to whether the Spanish people had the capacity to coexist under a democracy.

> when I contemplate democracy as practised in those European countries which have 'regained their liberty' and the spectacle presented by democracy in Italy and France, I feel a sickening doubt about the whole thing *as regards Spain* and come to the conclusion that a strong hand – police or army or what have you – is probably *the* only thing for these wild and extravagant people.

He warned that the end of the UN resolution of 1946 was just around the corner, that the opposition had no alternative, that Franco was stronger than ever and that Britain's economic and strategic interests required good relations with Spain. Therefore:

> If there was any chance of a change by all means let us pin our hopes on the Opposition. But in the absence of any practical alternative it seems to me we stand to gain damn all and lose quite a deal by clutching on to our ideological distaste for the régime. I realise of course the political difficulty involved in modifying our attitude towards Spain. But I really do believe that it would be better to do so now with fairly good grace while this is still possible, rather than be obliged to do so with bad grace later on.[26]

The Minister of Defence was to follow the Chargé d'Affaires. In a letter to Bevin, Alexander accepted that for political reasons it was unthinkable for the cabinet to accept the integration of Spain in the new defence organizations. However, the strategic importance of Spain, her firm anti-communist stance, the size of her armed forces and their low operational ability made a *rapprochement* advisable which would facilitate the country's modernization for the good of all.[27] In October it was the British delegate to the Organisation for European Economic Co-operation who called the Foreign Office's attention to the need, felt by the majority of the delegations, to include Spain on the list of bene-ficiaries of the Marshall Plan. If the objective were to plan European economic development, then it was not realistic to ignore a state of the size, population and potential of Spain.[28] Bevin stood his ground. He did not deny the limitations of his policy, but there were two reasons why he was adamant in carrying it through. The first was internal politics. He could not, before the parliamentary majority, members of the Labour Party and the trade unions, defend a policy that could be interpreted as pro-Franco. The other reason was European politics: the new regional institutions had to be constituted on the basis of a firm commitment to democracy.[29] Britain, which had attempted to prevent France and the United States from applying economic sanctions against Spain, for rea-sons of coherence did no more than defend the old policy. The Americans were in favour of bringing isolation to an end and the French opened their borders anew with Spain and rapidly negotiated a commercial and financial agreement which came into being on 18 May 1948, a situation which left the British diplomats in an uncomfortable position.

At the end of 1947 there were three main objectives to Spain's diplo-matic strategy: to benefit from the Marshall Plan funds; to gain access to the North Atlantic Treaty Organization; and to bring the 1946 United Nations resolution to an end. The latter was a stain on the regime's image. These three aims implied a certain degree of conflict between London and Washington.

The North Americans were willing to include Spain as beneficiaries of the Marshall Plan and only harsh opposition from the British and the French prevented this from happening.[30] For the Labour cabinet, participation in such an operation with a regime such as Franco's was unacceptable, for reasons of ideology. Had they done so, they would have been faced with strong opposition from the Party, the trade unions and the voters, as we have already seen. What is more, it would have been in total contradiction with the Labour cabinet's vision of the new European institutions. For these reasons the Foreign Office pressured the State Department, calling its attention to the negative consequences on European public opinion should Spain under the Franco regime be included in the Marshall Plan. In the words of the Under-Secretary of the Western Department:

> On the international level the effect of United States help to Franco would, it seems to us, be little short of disastrous, since even to moderate people all over the world it might well seem to bring confirmation of the Communist charge that United States policy is fundamentally reactionary and antidemocratic. It would certainly be a source of astonishment and embarrassment to most of the 'Marshall plan' countries and particularly of course to His Majesty's Government and the British public.[31]

The concession of Marshall Plan funds to Spain would damage the democratic morale of the Europeans and strengthen Franco's political position, an outcome Washington did not desire.[32] Pressure from the British and the French, seconded by other European states, was not only important in convincing the State Department and Truman himself that Spain should not be 'invited' to participate, but also crucial when the President had to face Congress, which was calling by a large majority for the inclusion of Spain. Truman was thus able to use strategic reasons to back his argument. At a purely European level, Britain prevented Portugal's attempt to propose to the Paris Conference that Spain become a member, an attempt made out of self-interest, to stabilize the Peninsula, and done in coordination with the Spanish government. However, after an interview with the Foreign Secretary, the Lisbon government realized that its proposal would bear no fruit and would only cause friction.[33] Spain remained an outsider; her government felt humiliated and Britain appeared, once again, to have been responsible for this renewed isolation.

The same arguments were used in negotiations to create NATO. From the outset it was considered desirable that Spain be included, but inclusion was postponed until such time as political problems were resolved.[34] Just as in the debate about the Marshall Plan, the Spanish government avoided directly applying for admittance, instead proceeding via the Spanish lobby in the United States and Portugal. The arguments used for the inclusion of Spain were strategic and very closely considered, but the political veto stood.[35]

The third session of the UN General Assembly inherited the contradictory Spanish policy. The 1946 resolution was still formally in force, but had in fact lost much of its power of coercion when in 1947 the application of sanctions against Spain was not approved, even though no substantial political changes had occurred. Once again, Britain, backed by other European states, put pressure on the United States, which was tempted to lessen the isolation of the regime, not to deal with the 'Spanish question'. Britain preferred to uphold a discredited resolution rather than to favour Franco, so as to avoid being accused by the Eastern bloc of complicity with fascism and of being anti-Communist. Their pressure was successful. Once again the cohesion of the Western bloc won, over the strategic advantages of including Spain. Following a Latin American initiative the 'Spanish question' was finally debated in May 1949, but the abstention of the United States and West European countries was crucial to the failure of the supporters of Franco.[36]

Limited recognition

The 'Spanish question' was the product of an international situation already resolved, characterized by the attempt to maintain the war alliance and combat fascism. Following the declaration of the Cold War in 1947, the situation changed dramatically. From then on, it became more of an anachronism than ever. It appeared that Franco's regime was no more dictatorial than that of Moscow or other Popular Republics. During the Second World War Franco had sustained relations with Hitler that went way beyond neutrality, but it would seem these could no more be censured than Soviet behaviour in Poland or enforced Communism in Eastern Europe. Did it make sense, then, to isolate Spain and withdraw ambassadors when normal diplomatic relations were maintained with the Eastern bloc?

The answer to that question had provoked in Britain, and more so in the United States, large pressure groups who clamoured more loudly than ever for a change of policy. Although these feelings were more generalized in the Conservative and anti-Communist groups, even on the left and in the Labour Party itself they were becoming patent. From the Conservative ranks people like Churchill, Lord Salisbury, Lord Halifax and above all Butler were known as ardent proponents of bringing isolation to an end. Shying away from any comment which might be interpreted as a defence of the Franco regime, they underlined the contradiction between having an ambassador in Moscow and not in Madrid, as well as the diminished influence over the defence of British interests that this implied. They too called for Spain's inclusion in NATO because of her high strategic value. In Labour Party ranks the MPs Warbey and Williams demanded that the cabinet resume normal relations and that Spain be incorporated in NATO. Portugal's accession to this organization, in their opinion, rendered invalid the democratic argument, and the imminence of a third world war made it inadvisable for them to be too selective when choosing friends. Newspapers such as *The Times* and the *Daily Telegraph* joined the campaign in favour of the exchange of ambassadors.[37]

The outbreak of war in Korea was a decisive element for the future of the 'Spanish question'. If the development of the Cold War had undermined the isolation of the Franco regime, the new events were to bring it to an end. The Asian conflict led many to believe that a confrontation with the Soviet Union was inevitable and imminent. Under these circumstances military considerations had to be primary. The isolation of Spain and Franco seemed to be all the more absurd as Spain's strategic importance was reassessed. The arguments previously upheld by the State Department became less effective, as the problem was no longer one of ensuring the cohesion of the Western bloc in the medium term but rather winning the possibly imminent third world war. The Spanish lobby asserted itself in Washington; military considerations carried more weight and the United States changed its policy. In spite of pressure from the British, the American delegation successfully backed the repeal of the 1946 United Nations resolution in the fifth session of the General Assembly. Soon after, the ambassadors returned to Spain and the governments of Washington and Madrid began negotiations, culminating in the 1953 agreements. Isolation was over.

British–Spanish relations continued in the same vein as before. From an economic point of view things gradually improved satisfactorily for both sides. Politically, the tension remained. Britain had not managed to force controlled change towards a democratic monarchy because of her limited influence, the lack of support from her allies and international events. Franco knew how to make best use of the situation and was clever enough to turn the international pressures into political strength. For Franco, Britain was responsible for the negative attitude maintained for many years by the United States towards his government, for the survival of the 1946 resolution far beyond 1947, the loss of the Marshall Plan funds and the fact that Spain was not invited to join NATO – and above all, for the permanent smear campaign against the regime in the shape of the veto against Spain's accession to the continental political organizations.

The end of isolation did not mean full recognition.[38] The ambassadors returned, trade relations continued to improve, but the political veto still stood: Spain would not join NATO, the Council of Europe or the European Community.

Proof of the regime's strength was its ability to stir up nationalist sentiment, which had always been a fruitful means of mobilization, around a new bone of contention, Gibraltar. Franco unleashed an anti-British campaign demanding that the Rock of Gibraltar be returned to Spain. The future of this enclave and Britain's refusal to allow Spain into the West's political organizations were to mark the future development of relations between the two countries.

Notes

1 A first version of this chapter was published as 'Las relaciones hispano-británi-cas 1945–1950', *Bulletin d'Histoire Contemporaine de l'Espagne* 8–9 (June 1989), pp. 40–8.
2 For a recent review of Spanish–British relations during the Civil War, see Juan Avilés, *Pasión y farsa: franceses y británicos ante la Guerra Civil española* (Madrid: Eudema, 1994); Enrique Moradiellos, *La perfidia de Albión: el gobierno británico y la Guerra Civil española* (Madrid: Siglo XXI, 1996).
3 Among the most recent works on the subject the most notable are: Rafael García Perez, *Franquismo y Tercer Reich* (Madrid: Centro de Estudios Consti-tucionales, 1994); Javier Tusell, *Franco, España y la II Guerra Mundial: entre el eje y la neutralidad* (Madrid: Temas de Hoy, 1995); Paul Preston, *Franco, A Biography* (London: HarperCollins, 1993).
4 PRO [Public Record Office] PREM 8/106, 'War Cabinet. Policy towards Spain. Note by the Lord President of the Council and Deputy Prime Minister (Clement R. Attlee)', 4.11.1944.
5 PRO PREM 8/106, Draft of telegram from Eden to Halifax, 9.11.44.
6 PRO PREM 8/106, from Churchill to Eden, 10.11.1944; 'War Cabinet. Policy towards Spain. Memorandum by the Minister of Economic Warfare', 15.11.1944.
7 PRO PREM 8/106, Draft of telegram from Eden to Halifax, 9.11.1944
8 PRO FO 371/49.579, 'Security in the Western Mediterranean and the Eastern Atlantic. Report by the Post-Hostilities Planning Staff', 19.5.1944. PRO FO 185/1756, from Hoyer Millar to Mallet, 'Summary of Study of British Post-War Strategic Requirements in the Western Mediterranean and North-Eastern Atlantic', 2.8.1945.
9 For a detailed analysis of the effects the application of economic sanctions on

Spain might have on the British economy, see PRO FO 371/60.351. Minutes of Hoyer Millar, 2.3.46 and 'Probable Effect of Britain's Economic Position of a Rupture of Trade Relations with Spain'. R. Garran, 10.4.1946.

10 PRO PREM 8/106, from Eden to Churchill, 17.11.1944; 'War Cabinet. Policy towards Spain. Memorandum by the Secretary of State for Foreign Affairs', 'The Allied Attitude towards the Franco Government. Memorandum by Lord Templewood', 18.11.44; 'War Cabinet. Conclusions of a Meeting of the War Cabinet held at No. 10, Downing Street, S.W.1 on Monday, 27th. November, 1944 at 5.30 pm'.

11 Comment by Franco to his cousin and collaborator in 1944, quoted in Francisco Franco Salgado-Araujo, *Mi vida junto a Franco* (Barcelona: Planeta, 1977), p. 314.

12 Alberto Lleonart Anselem and Fernando M. Castiella Maiz, *España y la O.N.U. I (1945–46). La 'Cuestión española'. Documentación básica sistematizada y anotada* (Madrid: CSIC, 1978), pp 14–15.

13 *Ibid.*

14 *Ibid.*, pp. 16–17.

15 PRO PREM 8/106, from Halifax to Eden, 7.4.1945; PRO FO 371/49.611, from Halifax to Eden, 7.4.1945; *Foreign Relations of the United States 1945* (hereafter *FRUS*) (Washington, DC: Government Printing Office), V, pp. 672–3.

16 PRO CAB 99/38, 'Terminal'. 'Record of the Proceedings of the Berlin Conference. 17th July to 1st August, 1945'.

17 Archivo Alberto Martín Artajo. Luis Carrero Blanco, 'Notas sobre la situación política', 29.8.1945.

18 Javier Tusell, *Franco y los católicos: La política interior española entre 1945 y 1957* (Madrid: Alianza, 1984), pp. 36ff. PRO FO 371/49.589, from Bowker to Eden, 23.7.1945; PRO FO 371/49.658 A, from Mallet to Eden, 6.8.1945; PRO FO 371/49.589, from Mallet to Bevin; Memorandum, Tom Burns, 6.8.1945; from Mallet to Bevin, 13.8.1945; PRO FO 371/49.590, from Mallet to Bevin, 14.8.1945; from Mallet to Bevin, 22.8.1945; PRO FO 371/49.613, from Mallet to Bevin, 17.9.1945; PRO FO 371/49.590, from Mallet to Bevin, 22.9.1945; PRO FO 371/49.614, from Mallet to Bevin, 1.12.1945.

19 PRO FO 371/60.421, from Cooper to Bevin, 27.2.1946; from Cooper to Bevin, 4.3.1946; *FRUS*, 1946, vol. V, 'The Ambassador in France [Caffery] to the Secretary of State', 27.2.1946, P.1043–44.

20 PRO FO 371/60.352 'Spain', 3.3.1946; PRO FO 371/60.421, from Cooper to Bevin, 4.3.1946; PRO FO 371/60.353, From Foreign Office to United Kingdom Delegation to United Nations, New York, 23.3.1946.

21 PRO FO 371/60.354, from Halifax to Bevin, 28 III 1946; PRO FO 371/60.355, from Halifax to Bevin, 1.4.1946 and 8.4.1946.

22 *FRUS*, 1946, vol. V, 'The Secretary of State to the United States Representative at the United Nations [Stettinius]. Background Information and Guidance for the United States Delegate', 12.4.1946, pp. 1065–9.

23 PRO FO 371/49.629, from Mallet to Bevin, 19.12.1945; PRO FO 371/60.372, from Mallet to Bevin, 18.1.1946; PRO FO 371/60.349, from Mallet to Bevin, 21.1.1946; PRO FO 371/60.421, from Mallet to Bevin, 2.3.1946; PRO FO 371/60.352, 'Spain', 4.3.1946; PRO FO 371/60.446, Minute of O. Harvey, 16.4.1946; PRO FO 371/60.360 'Policy towards Spain', I.P. Garran, 7.6.1946; PRO FO 371/60.377, from Mallet to Bevin, 11.6.1946.

24 PRO FO 371/60.360, 'Policy towards Spain', 7.6.1946; PRO FO371/60.377, from Mallet to Bevin, 11.6.1946; Minute of O. Harvey about the Bevin–Mallet interview, 5.10.1946.

25 PRO FO 371/67.867 'Cabinet. Economic Sanctions against Spain. Memorandum by the Secretary of State for Foreign Affairs, 3.1.1947. Annex. British Imports from Spain'; PRO FO 371/67.897 'Spain: Vulnerability to Import Embargo. Economic Intelligence Department. Foreign Office', 23.4.1947; from Hoyer Millar to Howard, 21.1.1947.

26 PRO FO 371/67.871 from Howard to Crosthwaite, 25.11.1947.

27 PRO FO 371/73.336, from Alexander to Bevin, 11.8.1948.

28 PRO FO 371/73.338, from E. Hall Patch to R. Makins, 21.10.1948.

29 PRO FO 371/73.336, from Bevin to Alexander, 28.9.1948.

30 *FRUS*, 1947, vol. III, 'The Ambassador in France (Caffery) to the Secretary of State', 29.6.1947, p. 300; 'The Ambassador in France (Caffery) to the Secretary of State', 3.7.1947, pp. 308–9; 'The Ambassador in the United Kingdom (Douglas) to the Secretary of State', 4.7.1947, p. 312.

31 PRO FO 371/67.871, from Harvey to Balfour, 24.11.1947.

32 PRO FO 371/73.334, 'Spain' P.M. Crosthwaite, 6.3.1948.

33 PRO FO 371/73.334, from Bevin to the British delegation at the Paris Conference, 13.3.1948; from Bevin to Stirling, 15.3.1948; PRO FO 371/73.335, from Ronald to Bevin, 16.4.1948.

34 *FRUS*, 1948, vol. III, 'The British Embassy to the Department of State. Aide Memoire', 11.3.1948, pp. 46–8; 'Minutes of the Third Meeting of the United States–United Kingdom–Canada Security Conversations, Held in Washington', 24.3.1948, pp. 66–7; 'Memorandum of the Sixth Meeting of the Working Group Participating in the Washington Exploratoty Talks on Security, July 26, 1948', p. 299; *FRUS*, 1949, vol. IV, 'Memorandum by the Joint Chiefs of Staff for the Secretary of Defense [Forrestal]', 5.1.1949, p. 13; Peter Calvocoressi, *Survey of International Affairs, 1949–1950*. (Oxford: Oxford University Press, 1953), p. 295.

35 *FRUS*, 1949, vol. IV, 'The Secretary of State to Certain Diplomatic Missions. Views on Spanish Participation in the North Atlantic Pact', 14.4.1949, p. 739; Antonio Marquina, *España en la política de seguridad occidental, 1939–1986* (Madrid: Ejército, 1986), pp. 231, 245–6.

36 An example in PRO FO 371/73.337, 'Extract from Record of Meeting at the Quai d'Orsay on 4th October, 1948, at 3.30 pm'.

37 AMAE, leg. R. 2.035, exp. 4, debate en la Cámara de los Comunes, 2.2.1949; from Santa Cruz to Artajo, 2.2.1949; from Santa Cruz to Artajo, 10.3.1949; 'Discusión en los Comunes sobre España y el Pacto Atlántico'. Oficina de Información Diplomática, Boletín de Información no. 914, 23.3.1949; debate en la Cámara de los Lores, 6.4.1949; debate en la Cámara de los Comunes, 2.5.1949; debate en la Cámara de los Comunes, 11.5.1949; debate en la Cámara de los Comunes, 12.5.1949; from Santa Cruz to Artajo, 24.3.1949; from Santa Cruz to Artajo, 25.4.1949; from Santa Cruz to Artajo, 10.5.1949; editorial *The Times*, 18.5.1949; AMAE, leg. R. 2.014, exp. 13, from Santa Cruz to Artajo, 9.5.1949.

38 PRO FO 371/73.333, from Howard to Crosthwaite, 11.2.1948; PRO FO 371/73.334, from Harvey to Kirkpatrick, 3.3.1948; PRO FO, 73.337, from Johnson to Bevin, 7.10.1948; from Kirkpatrick to Johnson, 16.10.1948; AMAE, leg. R.3510, exp. 1, Minuta, 13.12.1948.

10 Spain and the United States, 1945–1975

Boris N. Liedtke

The fascinating story of the political and diplomatic relations between the United States and Spain during the Cold War helps to explain the survival of the Franco dictatorship. It also has wide-ranging implications for the development of US Cold War policy. The pivot was the changing attitudes of US policy-makers in Washington after 1945. At the end of the Second World War, the US position towards the Franco dictatorship was hostile. This account shows the slow abandonment of this hostility, the eventual adoption of a more cynical approach by the Republican administration under Eisenhower and the subsequent implementation of US policy towards Franco throughout the administrations of Presidents Kennedy, Johnson, Nixon and Ford. The historic analysis will take us from the early period of ostracism to the signing in 1953 of the military and economic agreements right through the 1960s and early 1970s, a period throughout which the relationship saw no fundamental changes. By 1975 Spain formed an integral part not only of US military planning but also of Western cultural and economic life. Concerns voiced by European nations and the United States in the 1940s about the lack of democratic principles in Spain had given way to the exploitation of Spain's agricultural wealth, raw materials and, most important of all, the sunny coast along the Mediterranean. Foreigners who once flocked to the Iberian nation to risk their life for a cause now entered the country for an enjoyable time during their summer holidays. This transition was made possible by the acceptance of Spain into the Western defence structure following the signing of the Madrid Agreements in 1953.

Ever since these agreements, large sections of the Spanish political establishment and the left-wing opposition have argued that Franco had bought them at the cost of national sovereignty. In return, the Spanish dictator ensured the survival of his regime by eliminating possible foreign support for democratic forces and by obtaining sufficient economic aid to keep the Spanish economy afloat.

On the other side of the Atlantic, the Eisenhower administration was criticized for compromising its democratic values by entering into a superfluous agreement with a fascist dictator. Arguably, global changes in technology, warfare and the geopolitical balance meant that Washington not only had to rise to its global responsibilities but had to abandon its previous idealistic approach to world affairs. In this respect, the American compromise with the Franco dictatorship could be seen as the first in a series of Realpolitical decisions that led the United States to the brink of nuclear war in Cuba, defeat in Vietnam and ultimately to victory against the Soviet system. Throughout this period and as President Kennedy stated in his only inaugural speech, the United States was willing to 'pay any price, bear any burden, meet any hardship, support any friend, oppose any foe to assure the survival and the success of liberty'.[1] It mattered little that to ensure the triumph of American values, successive administrations had to trample upon human rights in Vietnam, endanger world peace in Cuba, or ignore the wrongdoings of a fascist regime in Spain. In the context of Cold War history, the American change of policy towards the Franco dictatorship deserves close scrutiny.

During the spring months of 1945, the war machinery of the Allied powers slowly ground to a halt. The victorious armies of the Americans and the British Commonwealth, with some help from French contingents, had liberated most of Europe. The nightmare of West European fascism belonged to the past. Nevertheless, the Iberian Peninsula was still dominated by a totalitarian regime. Only months before the outbreak of the Second World War, General Franco had consolidated his rule over Spain. However, the Spanish Civil War had drained the country of her national resources, leaving the economy in ruins. As a result, the Spanish dictator seemingly steered his country through the Second World War along a path of neutrality or non-belligerency not because he had chosen to do so, but because Spain's economy dictated it. Franco did, however, continue to maintain close and cordial diplomatic as well as economic relations with Germany throughout the war. The Allies had known this during the world conflict. They knew that Spain had supplied Germany with wolfram and mercury and that Spanish soldiers had fought under German command in Russia. However, they were grateful to Franco for having remained neutral during a vital period of the Allied offensive: the landing in Northern Africa (Operation Torch). Spain's past was controversial and it provided diplomats and politicians with enough material to justify either isolation from or integration into the Western defence structure.

Consequently, two contradictory versions of Spain's recent history were formulated. Those favouring isolation of the Franco regime saw it as another fascist system, created through the help of the Axis and totalitarian in its form. On the other hand, those favouring the integration of Spain into the Western structure tried to prove that Franco's association with Hitler was not what it seemed but really had been a diplomatic *coup* for the Spanish dictator. Francoist myth-makers claimed that the Spanish Caudillo had never been willing to help Hitler in his struggle against the Allies, alleging that the military and economic support which Hitler received from Franco had been wrung out of him. In exchange the Spanish dictator was able to guarantee Spain's neutrality.[2] The meeting at Hendaye in October 1940 between the two dictators had been disappointing for both, but Francoists projected it as a clever success for the Spanish dictator. Franco himself promoted this argument wholeheartedly; after all, his position would have improved considerably if his country had been welcomed by the international community.

However, during the last days of the war, President Franklin D. Roosevelt made his antipathy towards the Spanish regime known. Liberals across Western Europe and the United States had good reasons to expect that following the defeat of the Fascist powers in Italy and Germany, General Francisco Franco would meet a similar fate. Initially, the Roosevelt and later the Truman administration seemed eager to demonstrate their disapproval of the political structure of the Spanish regime, as well as its cordial relations with Nazi Germany. In various press conferences, President Truman reiterated his dislike of Franco. He publicly acknowledged that Spain's government had been founded with the help of Nazi Germany and Fascist Italy during one of the bloodiest civil wars of this century.[3] As a result, it came as no surprise that the three major Western powers, France, Britain and the United States, condemned Spain in a tripartite statement issued in early 1946. Nor was it surprising that Spain was excluded from the United Nations. After some discussions in the UN, which were initiated and strongly supported by Communist countries, the General Assembly recommended to all nations the immediate withdrawal of their ambassadors to Spain.[4] From then onwards and during the following four years, most countries maintained only limited diplomatic relations with Spain.

As the international community in general and Truman in particular publicly voiced their opposition to Franco, military planners in the US armed services identified Spain as a useful ally. Her strategic geographic position at the south-western tip of the European continent, guarding the entrance to the Mediterranean, as well as the Pyrenees, a natural protection against an invading army from the north, made her a valuable potential partner in a future European conflict. The raw materials that can be found on the Iberian Peninsula and Spain's relatively large standing army further enhanced her geopolitical importance. From the military point of view, Spain had too many assets to be ignored or isolated, let alone alienated. As a result, study after study restated the military importance of Spain and encouraged successive administrations to enter into close relations. However, during the years immediately after the Second World War, little attention was being paid to these military interests. Only as time went by and relations with the Soviet Union deteriorated did these gain in importance.

Already at the Yalta conference in February 1945, it became obvious that the Atlantic Charter was representative of Western war aims only. The Soviet Union was pursuing other goals. Despite several attempts by Western diplomats and politicians to find a compromise, the trend towards a permanently divided Europe became unavoidable. Churchill's famous speech at Fulton, Missouri,[5] George Kennan's 'long telegram' from Moscow[6] and the chilly atmosphere throughout the Paris Conference of 1946 were clear indications that the two superpowers were pursuing different aims that were impossible to reconcile.

Throughout 1947, the European situation deteriorated considerably. Apart from the economic hardship and the increasing dollar gap, the Soviet Union moved from a defensive creation of satellite states to an aggressive challenge to countries outside Central Europe. When Britain announced that she could no longer support the Greek government and had to withdraw her occupying forces, alarm bells went off in Washington. The crisis culminated in Truman's message to Congress on 12 March 1947.[7] The division of the world into a bipolar order could no longer be denied, and Truman outlined his doctrine in a vague and indeterminate commitment to the free part of the world. The same year this commitment was expanded into the Marshall Plan to save Europe from economic and political disaster. If Spain were to receive any aid under these programmes, Franco had either to go or to make far-reaching changes to his regime.

At the time, neither the United States nor the British government saw any alternative to Franco. The monarchists had been divided by the law of succession, which transformed Spain into a monarchy without a monarch. The Republican government in exile was divided internally over a number of issues, including its relation towards the far left. Most important of all, though, was the unwillingness of London and Washington to risk instability in Spain out of fear that this might lead to an increase of communist activities in France and Italy.[8]

In the meantime, the Joint Chiefs of Staff decided that it was time to change American foreign policy towards Spain and to initiate cordial military relations with Franco. Nowhere was this more apparent than in a study concluded in August 1947 titled 'Drumbeat'. Even though it was not the first of its nature, it was the clearest indication of US military interests in Spain. It concluded that from a military point of view, the United States should furnish economic aid to Spain as soon as feasible.[9] Shortly afterwards, and on the basis of military recommendations, the Policy Planning Staff, headed by George Kennan, decided that it was in the national interest to modify US policy towards Spain.[10]

Before the end of the year the National Security Council, headed by President Truman with representatives from the Department of Defense and State Department, acted on Kennan's recommendation.[11] The previous policy of isolating Franco was not only abandoned but severely criticized. Washington gave instructions to work towards a normalization of US–Spanish relations, both political and economic. As a direct result, the United States relaxed restrictive measures on commerce, eliminated tariffs on a variety of exports and generally encouraged private trade with and financial assistance for Spain. At the same time, US delegates at the UN were instructed to oppose any further measures that could adversely affect Spain. Officially, the change of policy was justified by the failure of ostracism to weaken the Franco regime. However, with hindsight and given the context of the military studies, it should be clear that in reality the deteriorating relationship with the Soviet Union was the cause.

The years 1948 and 1949 confirmed that a bipolar balance of power had become reality. Czechoslovakia, one of the most advanced industrial states in Eastern Europe, fell to a Communist coup. The Soviet delegates decided to walk out of the Allied Control Council, the body officially charged with governing Germany, causing that country to remain divided for over forty years. Even more shocking for Washington was the success of the Communist revolution in China. In the same year US military strategists detected, to their horror, that the Soviet Union had successfully detonated an atomic bomb, breaking the US monopoly on nuclear arms.

Throughout this period, Spain relentlessly tried to exploit the deteriorating relations between the two superpowers by lobbying for military and economic assistance and against the UN recommendation. Essential for these efforts was the appointment of José Lequerica as inspector of the Spanish Embassy in Washington. Under his guidance a Spanish Lobby was formed in Congress that was supported by Catholics, commercially orientated Representatives, warmongers, anti-communists, and those who simply wanted to exploit the issue for political reasons.[12] The influence of this lobby on US relations with Spain should not be underestimated. Again and again it brought up the Spanish issue, and on several occasions it came close to forcing the administration to allocate funds to Spain against the wishes of the White House. In the end, though, it was only in the context of an overall change of policy towards the Soviet Union that the Truman administration considered a revision of its attitude towards the Franco dictatorship.

During the first half of 1950, a series of discussions were conducted at the highest level in Washington concerning relations with Spain. As these went on, a consensus emerged that the necessary steps should be taken to ensure the full cooperation of the Spanish regime in case of war with the Soviet Union.[13] It was feared that during a conflict in Europe, Franco might decide to remain neutral, or that the price he would demand for his participation would be too high. Throughout these discussions, the necessity to invest in Spain's infrastructure was highlighted. If the US military wanted to make use of installations in Spain, these had to be improved urgently. New roads, airfields, port facilities and pipelines had to be constructed. A joke in Congress suggested that Spain's best defence was her appalling infrastructure, which was bound to slow down any advancing army. As a result of the urgent need to make use of Spain's resources, relations with Madrid had to improve. While it was acknowledged that possible objections by France and Britain could not be ignored, every effort was to be made to overcome these and to help Spain improve her relations with other European countries.

With the outbreak of the Korean War in 1950, the need to exploit Spain's military potential became even more pressing. For the first time since the end of the Spanish Civil War, the US Export and Import Bank earmarked specific funds for projects in Spain. The UN decided to withdraw its 1946 recommendation and promptly Britain and the United States appointed ambassadors to Madrid. At the same time, discussions were initiated by the Department of Defense on a further revision of relations with Spain. For twelve months, the State Department and the Pentagon engaged in talks over the Spanish question. The latter saw no point in further delaying military agreements. The State Department, on the other hand, was concerned about negative repercussions this might have on relations with other allies in Europe. Above all, France felt that any US–Spanish military agreement would be proof that US troops planned to withdraw from Central Europe in the event of Soviet attack. The United States had to make it clear that a defence of Europe was not only possible but strategically desirable. The remilitarization of Germany supported the US commitment and ability to defend NATO against a Soviet invasion.

As these diplomatic concerns were discussed, the National Security Council finally issued another policy paper, in June 1951, on relations towards Spain.[14] The changes were dramatic. Diplomatic and political considerations were no longer to hinder the development of Spain's military potential. While it was recognized that it would be advantageous to integrate Spain into NATO, opposition by France and Britain to direct US military agreements with Spain was bluntly ignored. The previously idealistic approach by the United States towards foreign affairs was abandoned for a classical Realpolitical policy. Despite Franco's dictatorship and the repression of liberty and fundamental freedoms under his regime, Washington did not even attempt to explain or justify its new approach in words other than those previously used by European statesmen of the nineteenth century. Political or military concerns by other NATO countries were insufficient to delay military negotiations.

In a press conference, Truman stated that his disapproval of Spain's human rights record should not override the conviction of US military planners.[15] Without delay, the President authorized a mission by Admiral Sherman, the Chief of Naval Operations, to hold preliminary talks with General Franco and high-level Spanish officers in Madrid. These talks went extremely well and the press speculated that agreements could be signed within months. Above all, Sherman established cordial relations with Franco and his Chief of Staff, General Juan Vigón. However, shortly after leaving Madrid, Admiral Sherman suffered a heart attack and died. Even though this delayed the talks somewhat, the United States was able to send two study teams in order to establish the requirements of the Spanish economy and to decide which locations were the most appropriate for US military installations.

The economic mission under Dr Sidney Sufrin, an academic at Syracuse University, was a disaster. Sufrin failed to free his team from the influence of Franco's state holding company, the INI (Instituto Nacional de Industria). The Spanish bureaucrats followed him everywhere, making it impossible to gather independent economic material. As a result he had to rely heavily on previously compiled studies by the State Department. At the same time he handled the complicated situation clumsily, causing several conflicts between his team and the American Embassy. On a more humorous side, he caused great laughter at a reception given in honour of the Duke of Alba at the US Embassy. Upon arrival, the Duke greeted Sufrin with a friendly slap on the back. When Sufrin wanted to return the friendly gesture, his hand got caught in his pocket. As he forced it out, he lost control and hit the Duke in his more delicate private parts.[16]

The military mission, on the other hand, was more successful. It was clearly established that the Pyrenees provided a useful natural defence against an invading Red Army, allowing the United States to maintain a foothold on the continent from which to liberate Europe. While it was already accepted that the Iberian Peninsula was extremely useful for air force and naval bases, the exact location of these had not been established. The military mission under Air Force General James Spry had received instructions to survey existing facilities that might meet US requirements. After inspecting a series of sites, the group decided that it was more beneficial to construct new facilities at strategic locations than to compromise by expanding existing airfields and ports. Given the appalling infrastructure of Spain at the time and the enormous supply requirements of a modern air force, it became clear that the sites were determined above all by logistical considerations. As a result, a large number of bases were located near the coast or communication hubs. Unfortunately this meant that in many cases they were situated near major Spanish cities. Naturally, these bases were strategic bombing targets for an enemy air force and their proximity to population centres endangered civilian life. While the study group acknowledged this, the issue was not considered important enough for facilities to be based elsewhere.[17]

Once the two reports had been received in Washington, they were analysed by a number of governmental agencies, and shortly afterwards two negotiation teams were sent to Spain to meet their counterparts. The more important one was a military team under General A.W. Kissner, who had previously been involved in the base negotiations with Portugal. The economic mission, headed by George Train, included a number of officials from the State Department. The Spanish military team was headed by General Juan Vigón. The economic team reported to the Spanish Minister of Commerce, Manuel Arburúa.

Over the following 18 months, the two sides were engaged in negotiations. The development of these can be divided into three phases. During the initial phase, from April to December 1952, the two sides familiarized themselves with each other's demands. The US team wanted to obtain several air force bases in Spain, notably at Torrejon, near Madrid, in the southern area of Cádiz–Seville–Málaga, and near Zaragoza, as well as a naval base at Rota, near Cádiz. The air force bases were strategically situated to support an attack on the Soviet Union while remaining outside the reach of the Red Army. The naval base was to become the headquarters of the Sixth Fleet, operating in the Mediterranean and of enormous strategic importance. In return the United States was willing to grant military and economic aid.[18] Generally speaking, Spain was willing to grant these bases but wanted to be assured that, in case of war, sufficient forces together with the necessary equipment were under

Spanish command to guarantee the defence of the country against an invading force. This implied that the United States had to rebuild the Spanish armed forces into a modern army – a task that would have put considerable strain on US military stockpiles. Alternatively, the United States could guarantee Spain's defence by way of a treaty similar to the commitment given to NATO. As it turned out, the US administration decided to do the latter. By the end of 1952, it appeared that the two sides would come to an agreement. Then, almost out of the blue, Franco decided to withdraw concessions made by the Spanish negotiators earlier.

In a note, the Spanish dictator inextricably linked the utilization of military facilities on Spanish soil with sufficient military equipment for Spain's armed forces to guarantee an independent national defence. This concept became known as 'parallel development' of the military facilities and Spain's national defence capabilities. At the same time it was made clear that under no circumstances was Spain willing to allow the United States to use military bases without prior consultation.

During the second phase of the negotiations, from December 1952 to June of the following year, the two sides engaged in a diplomatic bluff and counter-bluff. Neither of the two was willing to give in to demands made by the other, and several times the talks were on the brink of breaking up.[19]

In the final phase of the negotiations, the two sides decided to find an acceptable compromise. Spain's demand for a 'parallel development' was partly met by a US guarantee to defend Spain against an attack by any foreign power. Even though such a commitment requires approval by Congress, Truman and his legal advisers considered that the permanent stationing of troops in Spain was sufficient to guarantee a defence of the bases, of the infrastructure necessary to maintain them and, implicitly, of Spain herself.[20] On the other issue, it was decided that prior consultation would take place in all circumstances apart from a Soviet sneak attack on Europe. Under such circumstances the facilities could be used immediately and Spain merely had to be informed. It is highly questionable whether Spain had the choice of remaining neutral in such a conflict even without the agreements. In order to avoid domestic criticism against the Franco dictatorship, the United States was willing to sign a secret agreement that guaranteed Spain this right. This was in the interest of the Spanish regime, which thus hoped to maintain the perception of full sovereign control over its foreign policy.

These compromises were sufficient for the Spanish regime to go ahead with the agreements. On 26 September 1953 the two sides signed three official agreements and one secret one. In return for granting facilities, Spain obtained military aid worth around US$600 million and economic aid of almost US$500 million. However, the actual figures are less important than the fact that through these agreements Spain was welcomed back to the international community. Before the end of the year, France, Germany, Italy and Britain had resumed military cooperation with Spain. At the same time, financial institutions felt comfortable enough to grant credits to Spain's industry. Over the next ten years more than US$1 billion worth of credits were approved by private credit institutions in the United States alone. Additionally, US$500 million came from the US Export Import Bank. These credits together with growing commercial activities and foreign investments help to explain the economic growth Spain experienced during the following years.[21] This was in direct contrast to the stagnating economic activities during the late 1940s and early 1950s.

Clearly, the Franco regime benefited both economically and politically through these agreements, thus helping the dictatorship to remain in power for another 22 years. At the same time, though, it was one of the first measures taken by the dictatorship that loosened its grip on power and thus marked the beginning of the end of the nationalist state.

For the United States it was the first of a series of far-reaching compromises justified by the necessities of the Cold War. From the present point of view it is irrelevant and mere hypothetical speculation whether these compromises were unavoidable to ensure victory in the Cold War. What is of importance is the present implications for US foreign policy. By abandoning its traditional idealistic approach towards global affairs, the United States entered uncharted territory.

Despite this change of policy, the United States did not rush through a base construction programme as she had done several years earlier in Morocco. Opposition by Congress and the public to such wasteful programmes resulted in a long delay. In order to minimize costs, the builders decided to use construction equipment and dismantled military hardware from the military bases in Morocco. Finally, after a period of five years, the main military bases and port facilities at Rota, near Cádiz, became operational in the late 1950s. Tactical and strategic functions of other bases, above all in Morocco, were transferred to those in Spain.

However, the progress of technology influenced warfare and shifted the strategic aims for military planners in the post-war period. From 1945 to 1953 the United States had to rely on B-29s for the delivery of nuclear bombs. Their comparatively short range meant that they had to make far-reaching use of overseas bases. By 1953, the United States had developed a long-range strike capability through the B-36 and B-47 bombers, reducing the strategic value of overseas bases.

By 1957 the United States had developed the delivery capability of the Stratofortress B-52. The bomber had a range of 10,000 miles and a capacity of 60,000 lb of bombs. At the same time the United States developed tactical and strategic missiles such as the Pershing missile. With the development of these new weapon delivery systems overseas bases lost further strategic importance.

As the American base system was once more streamlined in the early 1960s, Spain's military bases became useful for tactical air and naval operations. In order to fulfil this role, the 16th Air Force was established, the largest overseas Strategic Air Command of the United States. It operated in Spain and Morocco and reported directly to the headquarters of Strategic Air Command at Offutt, Nebraska. The strategic role of other overseas military bases, such as the ones in Morocco, were transferred to troops based in Spain. This made them vital for naval planning in the Mediterranean and the Atlantic, as well as for USAF strategic war plans in Europe.

While military strategists made the best use of these facilities, from Franco's point of view the link-up with the United States reduced pressure on his regime. On the one hand, it made Spain an acceptable ally for other European nations and limited international ostracism to a few Communist states. On the other, it eliminated any chances of success for a domestic opposition movement to introduce democratic reforms. With the signing of the agreements and the subsequent relationship between the two countries, Franco had transformed his regime into an acceptable foreign ally. The extent of this development became obvious in December 1959 when President Eisenhower, as part of a world tour and to discuss the management of the military basis, decided to make a whistle stop in Madrid. Landing at the Torrejón air base, Eisenhower shook the hand of the Spanish dictator and proceeded to make a brief and rather unemotional statement. Franco, aware of the press opportunity, decided to respond with a long discourse. During the one-day visit, the crowds who turned up to greet the American, and friendly meetings between the two heads of state, caused the President to warm to the Spanish cause.[22] By the end of the visit, the understanding between the two had improved to such an extent that they gave each other a friendly farewell embrace at the Madrid airport. Franco was so overcome with joy that for some weeks he spoke of little else but the relationship between the two countries.[23]

This close relationship between the two countries did not continue during the administration of President Kennedy. When the negotiations for the renewal of the Madrid agreements came up in 1963, the two countries did not see eye to eye. The Spanish negotiators asked for a guarantee by the Americans for nuclear protection against any nation attacking Spain. At the same time they requested US$300 million worth of military equipment. The arguments put forward echoed those made ten years earlier. Spain remained vulnerable to a Soviet attack because of the American bases and had no proper capability of defending herself against the invasion by modern armed forces.

Yet technological advances, reducing the usefulness of overseas bases, and the overall budget cuts for the global defence programmes meant that the American negotiators were not going to give in to Spanish demands. Following Spain's proposal, the Americans offered US military end-items worth US$75 million, with Spain being allowed to purchase another US$175 million worth. Furthermore, the Export Import Bank would earmark additional funds for Spain.

The American counter-proposal was received and discussed during several cabinet sessions. Following these discussions at the highest level in early 1963, Spain threatened not to renew the base agreements unless the conditions set by the Americans were improved considerably. This was nothing more than a diplomatic bluff to gain access to more military aid. However, the Americans correctly analysed the situation and decided not to give in. Initiallly the United States tried to solve the deadlock with a visit by the Deputy Secretary of Defence. This attempt was rebuffed, and despite efforts by the Spanish ambassador in Washington to find a solution, Franco decided to wait for an improvement of the conditions set by the Americans.

However, the balance of strength between the two sides had shifted. The fact that the bases themselves had little military value to Spain without an American military presence and the necessity for further military hardware put the Americans in a strong position. Franco, having overestimated the importance of his position, had to back down and accept a mildly improved counter-offer. Under this compromise Spain received US$100 million in credits from the Export Import Bank and US$100 million worth of military end-items, and was allowed to purchase an additional US$50 million worth of US equipment. In return, the agreements were extended for another five years, and the United States was allowed officially to station a squadron of Polaris nuclear submarines at Rota. Several submarines had already been stationed at the US port prior to the signing of the renewed agreements. The United States also agreed to issue a joint declaration stating that 'a threat to either country would be a matter of common concern to both countries'. However, the United States had always understood that the Madrid agreements and their military presence had forced US troops *de facto* to defend Spain in case of war. As a result, the joint declaration added little to the previous agreements. It clearly fell short of the nuclear commitment given to NATO countries which Spain had demanded at the outset of the negotiations. Naturally, this did not discourage Franco's regime from hailing the declaration as a full-scale alliance between the two nations.[24]

Five years later, when the agreements once more came up for negotiation, the Spanish cabinet, encouraged by Franco, issued a statement calling for the removal of the US air base at Torrejón. This decision to invoke the termination of the agreements ushered in a procedure whereby the two sides entered a sixth-month consultation period. Again the move was nothing but a vain attempt to put pressure on Washington in the hope of obtaining further military aid and assurance of a full military commitment by the United States to Spain's defence.

With the military conflict in Vietnam having escalated to a full-scale war, the Nixon adminstration showed little interest in granting Spain generous terms. The domestic mood in the United States had turned strongly against military commitments abroad. As a result of this, Washington assumed an uncompromising stance towards Spain. The foreign policy-makers in Washington, influenced largely by National Security Adviser Henry Kissinger, threatened to cause a complete breakdown of Spanish–American relations. In the wake of the United States' unwillingness to give way, Spain's request for military aid was rapidly scaled back from US$1 billion to US$300 million and finally to US$50 million worth of military aid and US$25 million worth of credits.[25] While Spain remained of strategic interest to the United States, the continuous haggling by the Spanish dictatorship for additional military aid had caused the relationship between the two countries to deteriorate. By the late 1960s, Spain was still seen as a place worth having military bases in but not at any price. The relationship had become purely based on a quid pro quo deal.

In 1970, Richard Nixon together with Henry Kissinger visited Spain. The two had been briefed that US military planners remained interested in the strategic advantages Spain had to offer. However, aware of the deteriorating health of Franco, it was US policy to maintain a working relationship with the regime without upsetting the more moderate leaders who were expected to assume the responsibility of running Spain after Franco's death. There was no serious attempt to persuade Franco to step down early or to make wide-ranging democratic changes. Washington had been willing to live with the Spanish dictatorship for over 25 years and was unwilling to jeopardize the stability of the Iberian Peninsula for the unlikely benefits of liberating Spain from the dictatorship a few years before natural events would bring about a transition to democracy.

During the visit of President Nixon, the Spanish crowds turned out in even greater numbers than before. This time both Nixon and Franco played to the multitudes from the very beginning of their meetings. The talks between the two were unfocused and carried much less importance than the friendly show put on for public consumption. There was little to talk about; Nixon was unwilling to make any lasting concessions to Franco, who in turn had little bargaining power left with the Americans.

Despite the deteriorating health of the Spanish dictator, Franco was able to remain in power longer than his American counterpart. Plagued by the Watergate scandal, Nixon was forced to step down and his Vice-President assumed the presidency. Gerald Ford took the opportunity in May–June 1975 to visit Franco, becoming the third and last US president to do so. During his two-day visit, the US President made it clear that he had more interest in meeting Juan Carlos than in posing for photo opportunities with General Franco. The ailing health of the Spanish dictator was a good enough excuse to justify the fact that the American dignitary spent more time with the young Bourbon than with the ageing head of state.

Relations between the two countries had been on hold for over seven years, while Washington awaited the death of Franco and hoped for a transition towards a more democratic system. In the last days of the dictatorship, the State Department was careful not to upset any political force that might emerge after the death of Franco. When he finally passed away, on 20 November 1975, it freed the two countries to reopen their relationship and plan for a closer alliance.

However, during this last phase of the Spanish dictatorship, there had been no noteworthy attempts by Washington to ensure that the next regime in Spain would be one based on democratic principles. As with the compromise made almost thirty years earlier in a joint declaration between the United States, France and Britain, Washington was more interested in preserving the political stability in Spain than in advancing democratic principles. This stability was crucial for the United States to make best use of Spain's strategic as well as economic resources. From the Spanish point of view, the dictatorship had throughout three decades bargained for an improvement in conditions. Never, during all negotiations concerning the bases, did the regime back down once it had secured what it believed to be the best American counter-offer. There was no question that Franco was willing to give up Spain's sovereign control over her foreign and defence policy in return for military and economic aid that allowed him to remain in power. The basis of the relationship between the two countries had emerged after the 1953 agreements and changed little over the following 22 years. Only with the death of Franco were Madrid and Washington free to reconsider their foreign policy towards each other. As it turned out, the governments that followed Franco were able to integrate Spain fully into the Western defence community. However, none could reverse the concessions made by Franco concerning the military bases until the Cold War came to an end, drastically reducing the usefulness of these facilities for US military planners.

Notes

1 *Public Papers of the Presidents of the United States of America: Containing the Public Messages, Speeches and Statements of the President: John F. Kennedy 1961* (Washington, DC:, Government Printing Office), 1962, p. 1.

2 *Report on Spain* (Washington, DC: Spanish Embassy Washington), 1946, p. 1.

3 *Public Papers of the Presidents of the United States of America: Containing the Public Messages, Speeches and Statements of the President: Harry S. Truman 1945* (Washington, DC: Government Printing Office, 1961), Doc. 107.

4 J. Lleonart y Amselem, 'España y la ONU: la cuestión española 1945–1950', *Revista de Política Internacional*, 152 (July/August 1977).

5 Churchill speech, 'The Sinews of Peace', 5 March 1946, at Westminster College, Fulton, Mo., in James Robert Rodes, (ed.), *Winston S. Churchill: His Complete Speeches 1897–1963* (New York: Chelsea House, 1974), pp. 7285ff.

6 George Kennan, 'Long Telegram' from Moscow, 22 February 1946, in *Foreign Relations of the United States 1946* (Washington, DC: Government Printing Office), 1969, volume VI, p. 687.

7 *Public Papers of the Presidents of the United States of America: Containing the Public Messages, Speeches and Statements of the President: Harry S. Truman 1947* (Washington, DC: Government Printing Office, 1963), p. 178.

8 National Archives, Military Branch, US Joint Chiefs of Staff, CCS 092, Spain (4-19-46), Sec. 1–8, 15.3.1946, Possible Developments, JIC Memo 242.

9 Steven T. Ross and David A. Rosenberg, (eds), *American Plans for War against the Soviet Union 1945–1950* (New York: New York Publishing Inc., 1990), vol. 1947, pp. 3–39.

10 National Archives, Military Branch, CCS092, Spain (4–19–46), Sec. 1–8, PPS/12, US Policy toward Spain, 24.10.1947.

11 National Archives, Civil Branch, NSC-3, United States Policy toward Spain, 5.12.1947.

12 Lowi, Theodore J., 'Bases in Spain', in Harold Stein (ed.), *American Civil–Military Decisions* (Alabama: University of Alabama Press), 1963, pp. 679ff.

13 National Archives, Civil Branch, NSC72, Secretary of State, 8.6.1950.

14 National Archives, Civil Branch, NSC72/6, Revision by Senior NSC Staff of NSC 72/5, 27.6.1951.

15 *Public Papers of the Presidents of the United States of America: Containing the Public Messages, Speeches and Statements of the President: Harry S. Truman 1951* (Washington, DC: Government Printing Office, 1963), 19.7.1951.

16 National Archives, Civil Branch, Lot Files 59D108, 25.10.1951, Sufrin Diary, Part 6.
17 National Archives, Military Branch, US Joint Chiefs of Staff, CCS 092, Spain (4-19-46), Sec. 1–8, 31.10.1951, Report by the JMST (Spain); and National Archives, Civil Branch, Lot Files 64D563, 2.11.1951, US Embassy, Madrid, to Department of State.
18 National Archives, Military Branch, CD 091.3 Spain 1952, 22.3.1952, Term of Reference for the Joint US Military Group (Spain).
19 *Foreign Relations of the United States 1952–1954*, vol. VI, (Washington, DC: Government Printing Office, 1988), 27.3.1953, Chargé Jones to Department of State, p. 1923.
20 *Ibid.*, 25.9.1953, Memo Secretary of State to Bonbright, p. 1959.
21 Stanford Research Institute, *Las inversiones norteamericanas en España* (Barcelona: Cámera de Comercio Americana en España, 1972).
22 Benjamin Welles, *Spain: The Gentle Anarchy* (London: Pall Mall, 1965), pp. 247–52.
23 Paul Preston, *Franco: A Biography* (London: HarperCollins, 1993), p. 681.
24 R. Rubottom and J. Carter Murphy, *Spain and the US since World War 2* (New York: Praeger, 1984), pp. 80–4.
25 A. Marquina, *España en la política de seguridad occidental, 1939–1986* (Madrid: Ediciones Ejército 1986), pp. 820–36.

11 Breaking the shackles from the past:

Spanish foreign policy from Franco to Felipe González

Angel Viñas

When General Francisco Franco died on 20 November 1975, Spain's position in the international system was well established but also heavily shackled. This chapter attempts to highlight some of the major developments in Spanish foreign policy since his death. The cumulative effects of those developments enabled Spain to cast off two of the most important inherited shackles: her absence from Europe's economic, political and military organizations and the maintenance of an extremely unequal security relationship with the United States.

The legacy of Francoism

Following the 1953 concordat with the Holy See and the executive agreements with the United States, the Franco regime had been increasingly successful in its quest for international respectability. The US link had been adjusted several times and the Spanish dictatorship had also achieved some success in eroding the deep disequilibria that it had accepted at its inception.[1] The linkage with Washington had made the regime presentable in the Western world and had facilitated Spain's membership in the network of global international organizations (the UN and the Bretton Woods institutions, essentially). US support had also been vital in securing IMF and Organization for European Economic Co-operation (OEEC) assistance for a major overhaul of economic strategies which took place in 1959.[2] It never overcame, however, European resistance to the idea of Spain's becoming a member of NATO.

Giving up Franco's dreams of self-sufficiency had enabled Spain to share in the wave of Western economic prosperity during the golden 1960s to such an extent that, when he died, it could safely be asserted that the Spanish economy had overcome its secular underdevelopment.

Economic modernization had increased Spain's attractiveness for foreign goods, know-how, technology and, last but not least, direct investment. Bilateral relationships with most of the Western countries had improved. Even the European Community had concluded in 1970 a carefully crafted preferential trade agreement with Spain. In no way was it meant to open 'Europe's' doors to the dictatorship.

Economic success not only had paid handsome foreign policy dividends, but had also contributed to a larger acceptance of the regime's institutions. This had allowed for a well-controlled and agonizingly slow political liberalization. The propaganda apparatus changed Franco's image. He was portrayed as Spain's great modernizer, although his original contempt for political pluralism, liberalism, social democracy and human rights remained unchanged.[3]

Political dissent had surfaced time and again and had led, time and again, to furious waves of unmitigated repression. This brutality had added to the shackles that constrained Spain's international position. Large sectors of public opinion in a great number of Western countries were still resolutely hostile to the Spanish regime. In fact, Franco's 'original sin', i.e. the recollection of Axis assistance in the establishment of his dictatorship and of his own leanings towards the Fascist powers during the Second World War, was to accompany him until his death. Although able to cultivate special relationships – always of an almost exclusively rhetorical content – with Latin American and Arab countries, the regime was never considered a fully fledged partner by many of the Western powers.[4]

Some of the deep feelings which the Franco regime inspired in Western public opinion erupted suddenly in September 1975, when death sentences were carried out on five alleged terrorists who had been tried by military courts in highly suspicious circumstances. An international outcry ensued. Several ambassadors to Madrid, the majority from the European Community member states, were recalled to their capitals for consultations. Pope Paul VI openly expressed his bitterness. Mexico's President suggested that, *inter alia*, Spanish UN membership should be suspended. Sweden's Olof Palme openly collected money in Stockholm's streets to provide financial support for political prisoners in Spain. The embassy in Lisbon was burned down and sacked.

This crisis was put to good advantage by King Hassan of Morocco (not without some support from France and the United States) in order to advance his claims on the last remaining Spanish colony in Africa, the Western Sahara, whose decolonization Madrid had been considering. For a few tense days it appeared as if the dictatorship would end with a major crisis on its hands. However, an arrangement, which was somewhat humiliating for the regime's self-image, was reached with Morocco and

Mauritania. It was subsequently subject to continuous waves of domestic criticism. When General Franco's funeral took place some days later, another international pariah, General Pinochet of Chile, was the only significant head of state willing to pay his last respects.

Fortunately, Spain could by then count on a wide spectrum of political, economic and intellectual forces ready to embark upon a perilous but also exhilarating transition. During the 1960s, two of the major sources of its economic success had been emigration to Western European countries, and an astonishing tourist and foreign investment boom. Spaniards had learned both outside and inside their country that there was more to life than immutable nationalistic rhetoric and immutable political institutions.

In sum, by the early 1970s the critical question was for how long the regime would be able to maintain its political and institutional differentials after Franco's death. When this happened, the evolution towards another kind of political system could be stopped only by brute force. This transition became a success story in its own right and remains so even in the wake of the dramatic changes in Central and Eastern Europe after the collapse of Communism and the break-up of the Soviet Union.[5]

A democracy with excellent international behaviour

The transition aimed at creating a fully fledged, Western-type pluralistic democratic system.[6] This at least implied the establishment of fundamental freedoms and respect for and development of human rights, a thorough institutional modernization, regional devolution, the modernization of relations with the Holy See and the Roman Catholic Church and, last but not least, the introduction of a high degree of civilian control over a military establishment and security apparatus where pro-Francoist and anti-democratic sentiments were widespread.

While all this was being accomplished, nothing remotely similar to the major questions raised internationally in the case of Portugal ever arose in the case of Spain. Quite the contrary; from the outset, Spain's political class interacted with the international environment so as to elicit from it support for the domestic transformation process. This environment was favourable. There were, however, differences of interest and tactics that soon became apparent. On the one hand the United States was essentially concerned with maintaining military bases in Spain. On the other hand, most of the Western European countries were more sensitive to long-term developments and stringent democratization requirements.[7]

Between 1976 and 1980 the transition agenda dealt mainly with domestic issues. It was plagued by recurrent waves of home-grown terrorism. On 23 February 1981, a *coup* was attempted by a disgruntled group of army officers and soldiers who, together with members of the paramilitary civil guard, seized the lower house of Parliament and took the entire government hostage. This hare-brained action was grounded in the traditional political theory of the Spanish armed forces: when politicians no longer appeared to represent the national will and seemed too weak to tackle major problems like terrorism (which was running high at the time) or separatism (which some military men equated with territorial devolution), it was the patriotic duty of nationally minded officers simply to oust them.

After the attempted *coup* Spain joined the Atlantic Alliance. The importance of this step cannot be overestimated. One of the major doors that had been kept stubbornly closed to the Franco regime had opened. A whole set of shackles was thus simply cast off.

Eventually, domestic political developments raised the curtain for a new act. This happened once the Spanish Socialist Party (PSOE), harshly persecuted under Franco and legalized only in February 1977, took office at the end of 1982.[8] If Spain had lived until then under the primacy of domestic reform, it was to undergo from 1983 an immensely complex experience of new transformations where political, economic, social and foreign policy strategies became intimately intertwined.

Building upon the foundations laid during the transition proper, the years after 1983 were also a period in which foreign policy developments multiplied at dizzying speed. Spain joined the European Community, confirmed her membership of NATO, subjected the security relationship with the United States to a substantial revision, enhanced her capabilities for influence projection both in the Community and internationally, Europeanized strategic options, and diligently worked towards the creation of a certain margin of international manoeuvre while maintaining excellent relations with Washington.[9] In sum, Spain proved that her transformation into a fully fledged and stable democracy could be carried through in a highly civilized manner and without disrupting existing international equilibria. Furthermore, foreign policy was implemented with a view to enhancing modernizing trends at home.

Thus, in no way can Spanish foreign policy after 1975 be considered in its international and domestic ambitions as a mere extension of the strategies pursued during the Franco regime.[10]

Looking for international support

Franco's successor as head of state, King Juan Carlos, embarked on the transition well aware of the regime's strengths and weaknesses. Carlos

Arias Navarro, Prime Minister under Franco, stayed on. An old hand of the Francoist foreign policy establishment, a former ambassador to Buenos Aires, Washington and Paris, and a convert to moderate reform, Jose Maria de Areilza, was appointed in December 1975 to be the King's first Foreign Minister.

Areilza saw as his main challenge the need to ensure the largest possible measure of international support for the efforts yet to be undertaken to democratize Spain. This was not an easy task. Although Franco's death was widely perceived as opening the door to major domestic political changes, concerns about Spain's future stability were barely disguised. The Spanish equivalent of the coronation on 27 November 1975 was attended by, among others, Germany's Walter Scheel and France's Valéry Giscard d'Estaing.[11] This was the first visit to Spain by a French President in many decades. Giscard expressed his hope for the restoration of friendly relations between the two countries and, perhaps more significantly, his wish that Spain could soon join Europe.

The new Foreign Minister was sensitive to French and indeed European support for the impending domestic changes but he understood very well the crucial need for the Spanish reform process to be seen to be firmly endorsed by Washington.[12] He was helped by circumstances. The US–Spanish agreement was in a process of renegotiation that had started under Franco. Areilza suggested to Henry Kissinger that it should be upgraded to a fully fledged treaty, which implied approval by the US Senate. This, in his view, would serve a twofold purpose: it would convince Washington of Spain's unswerving alignment in the defence of the West and would, simultaneously, demonstrate both internationally and domestically that the new Spanish monarchy was able to secure a degree of commitment from the US such as the Franco regime had never been able to attain.

The new treaty of friendship and cooperation was concluded in January 1976.[13] In early June, the King and Queen made an official visit to the United States. Juan Carlos formally addressed the US Congress to great acclaim and made no bones about his own commitment to installing a true democratic system. Areilza also managed to lay the foundations for an improvement in relations with the Holy See by starting the process for revision of the 1953 concordat. However, in the six and half months for which he served as Foreign Minister, he could scarcely achieve much more of substance. In particular, the possibility of establishing relations with Israel was not accepted by the Prime Minister. Arias Navarro was later reported to have been described by the King as an 'unmitigated disaster'.[14] In July 1976 Juan Carlos gambled on an obscure but promising young politician from the moderate wing of the Francoist establishment: Adolfo Suárez was to become the emblematic Prime Minister of the transition proper.

The search for outside support was not limited to the government. The left-wing opposition, particularly the Socialist Workers' Party (PSOE), also needed it. Foreign assistance, particularly by the Socialist International and Germany, was given in such a way that it helped develop not only the fledgling party and trade union structures but also policy orientations.[15] This support for the still illegal parties finally became a litmus test of the democratic credibility of the reform process. In December 1976 the PSOE held its 27th congress. It was the first time since 1932 that such an event had taken place in Spain. It was attended by, among other luminaries, Willy Brandt, Olof Palme, Bruno Kreisky and Pietro Nenni.

A new foreign policy is implemented

Suárez chose as Foreign Minister a well-known diplomat of impeccable Christian Democratic credentials, Marcelino Oreja, previously undersecretary to Areilza. Between July 1976 and September 1980 Oreja made an outstanding contribution to the design and implementation of a new Spanish foreign policy. This was a period of relative consensus[16] in terms of activities in the international arena, although this fact was frequently obscured by ideological discussion. The reasons for the consensus are not difficult to identify. It did not take long for the major political actors in Spain to realize that foreign policy had to be predicated upon a clearly identified range of widely shared democracy-enhancing objectives and values. It was also clear that the nascent political system needed to free itself from the constraints inherited from the Franco regime, not only domestically but also internationally.

The first test of these beliefs was the alacrity with which the government took the necessary measures to establish full diplomatic relationships with almost all the countries from which diplomatic recognition had been withheld. Among them were Romania, Yugoslavia, Bulgaria, Poland, Czechoslovakia, Hungary, the Soviet Union and Mexico. These last two cases had, needless to say, the greatest political significance. The Soviet Union had been the only great power that had substantially helped the besieged Republic during the Civil War and had subsequently become one of Franco's *bêtes noires*. Mexico had adamantly refused to give diplomatic recognition to the Franco regime, giving recognition instead to the notional Spanish Republic in exile. The only significant country with which diplomatic relationships were to remain in abeyance for a long time after that period was Israel.

The rationale for some sort of consensual foreign policy gathered momentum after the first democratic elections of 15 June 1977. The mixed bag of centre and reformist parties which had come together under the banner of the Union of the Democratic Centre (UCD), led by Adolfo Suárez, won easily, although they fell short of an absolute parliamentary majority. The PSOE came second. Much to its chagrin and surprise, popular support for the Communist Party did not materialize to any substantial degree. The right was perceived as being still too much associated with the previous dictatorship and did very poorly. A few regional and minuscule leftist parties filled in the remaining parliamentary landscape.

The Parliament that emerged from the June 1977 elections was ultimately to be endowed with constitution-making powers and to oversee the final break with the institutions of the Franco regime. This was achieved after considerable wheeling and dealing among political elites and not without difficulties. The new constitution was approved in a referendum on 6 December 1978. Consensus was also maintained in foreign policy implementation, although ideological debates about principles and the role of Spain in the world were fierce. This consensus was positively reflected in four areas: the aspiration to join the European organizations; the need to neutralize the domestic consequences of external developments that might put the transition process under duress; the normalization of relations with the Holy See; and the belief that the nascent Spanish democracy had to craft a special relationship with Latin America. It was negatively reflected in the government's reluctance to take major decisions that would not be supported by the new legal opposition.

In the first area, the government flagged its intentions in July 1977 almost immediately after taking office. Spain wanted to join the Community itself, as Portugal had similarly indicated four months earlier and Greece had done in June 1975. The long and arduous accession negotiations were officially opened in February 1979. They were to drag on until 1985.

That clear signal towards the Europe that had most consistently and stubbornly kept its doors closed to the Franco regime was rapidly enhanced by a request for membership of the Council of Europe. The importance of this second step cannot be overemphasized. Spain became its 20th member in November 1977, more than a year before the constitution was approved. This meant that the international community was serious in accepting that the political and institutional transformation was already so advanced that Spain could become a partner in the common endeavour to preserve human rights and the rule of law in concert with the older and more established European democracies.[17] This operation was flanked by Spain's accession to a wide range of multilateral agreements on the protection of human rights and fundamental freedoms, something which, for obvious reasons, the Francoist dictatorship had never contemplated. Here the role of the new foreign policy in liberating the incipient political system from the shackles of the past shone through clearly as never before.

The second area was more complicated. It involved the need to ensure a high degree of international cooperation against terrorism and the problem of how to deal with the aftermath of the West Saharan crisis.

Terrorism took three forms: ETA (Basque) independentist terrorism had grown during the Franco regime and was to prove the most durable of all, feeding as it did on a social base; ideological, extreme left-wing terrorism carried out by minuscule groups such as GRAPO and FRAP; and, at a much lower level, agitation for the independence of the Canary Islands by a grouplet (MPAIAC) relying on Algerian support. This support, given by the great loser in the West Saharan arrangement, was obviously meant to put pressure on Madrid. Only ETA and MPAIAC activities gave rise to the need for foreign policy action.

The fight against ETA implied cooperating with France, where the terrorists had built a dense network of support. This cooperation started in 1976 and was difficult to develop. It involved contacts at the highest levels, reciprocal visits by the two heads of state and government, the establishment of a specific framework between the police and security services, the reinterpretation of French legislation and much more. In January 1979, Oreja was able to achieve a breakthrough when France gave up her practice of granting the status of political refugee to Basque extremists. Asylum policy remained unaffected, however.[18] The need to convince French politicians and professionals in the police and the judiciary that ETA members were plain terrorists and not freedom-fighters operating within a non-democratic system continued well into the 1980s.

In comparison to these issues, offsetting the international implications of MPAIAC activities was not difficult. Certainly, for the Spanish political class events seemed to take a ludicrous turn, when Algerian-supported approaches were made to the Organization of African Unity, calling on it to consider the 'African character' of the Canary Islands. Counteracting this development took some effort but it fairly soon became possible to convince the African countries of the inanity of such claims.

Dealing more directly with the sequels of the West Saharan crisis was not easy since it involved devising specific policies towards the two rivals for regional hegemony in Northern Africa, Morocco and Algeria (the latter having been one of the major supporters of the Saharan independence movement in the fight against the annexation by Morocco). Relations with the North African countries had always been complicated for Spain, and their centre of gravity had traditionally alternated between Algiers and Rabat. The balancing act of placating Algeria while retaining Moroccan friendship became even more difficult when the cause of the independence movement was taken up by the parties on the left in Spain. In the spirit of the times, the government had to take care that bilateral relations and the defence of the Spanish position at the United Nations did not become too heavy a burden on domestic political developments.[19]

In the third area, relations with the Holy See were put on new foundations. In January 1979, after arduous negotiations coinciding with the crafting of the constitution, the 1953 concordat was replaced by a set of new agreements reflecting the domestic cultural and institutional changes that had taken place in Spain. The government gave up its time-honoured prerogatives to meddle in some of the Roman Catholic Church's internal affairs and the Church in effect accepted being placed on a level of comparative equality with other denominations.[20] Here again the shackles of the past were cleanly broken.

Finally, in the fourth area, consensus was also achieved on the need to devise a new policy towards Latin America, where the Francoist dictatorship had found one of its major sources of international support and prestige. While paying lip-service to common Hispanic values, the Franco regime had tended to identify that source among the most conservative and even reactionary political and social circles in the Western Hemisphere. During the transition, the gamble was how to put such support and prestige to the service of the young Spanish democracy. This gamble was not exempt from difficulties and Madrid had to combine the gravitation towards modernizing and liberal forces with the need to avoid alienating official support in many countries in turmoil.[21]

Consensus was retained when approaching the long-stagnating Gibraltar issue. In March 1980, Parliament unanimously supported a PSOE resolution intended to give Oreja a strong hand in his negotiations with Britain which led, the following month, to the Lisbon agreement.[22]

There was no lack of consensus either for another ambitious diplomatic offensive: the aspiration to host one of the meetings of the Conference on Security and Cooperation in Europe (CSCE). Important diplomatic gatherings in Spain could be counted on the fingers of one's hand during the almost 40 years of the Franco regime. With the CSCE starting its operations after the Helsinki Final Act, it was deemed that it would give a certain fillip to the new political system in Spain if both Eastern- and Western-bloc countries were to agree to hold one of their periodic gatherings in Madrid within the new framework. With this in mind, Spain played an important role in the Belgrade meeting in 1977, bridging positions between the blocs. After hard negotiations it was agreed that the follow-up meeting should indeed take place in Madrid in September 1980.[23]

The CSCE experience enabled Spanish foreign policy to take on a less inhibited profile. Suárez paid a highly publicized visit to Fidel Castro, and Spain became an observer of the Non-Aligned Movement at its conference in Havana. In September 1979 the fact that Suárez was the first European Prime Minister to receive Yasser Arafat caused a minor sensation. However, at the time, some of these steps seemed to many, particularly among the right but also within the cabinet, an indication of a loss of direction and energy. Suárez was seen as trying to steer a somewhat neutral course between the blocs. Little by little, bickering and infighting about foreign policy became the order of the day.

It did not help that domestic political developments gradually eroded the consensual basis upon which the foreign policies of the incipient democratic system had been implemented. The general elections of 1 March 1979 did not change the relative positions of the UCD and the PSOE much. The Socialists subsequently became more critical and active in convincing the electorate that they would be able to take office without the help of the Communists, although this had not been the case in the local government elections. In September 1979, an extraordinary congress did away with the Marxist self-definition of the PSOE. An implicit redefinition of the party's foreign policy stance had already occurred.

By then, domestic political changes were in the air. Within the cabinet a wide range of frequently incompatible aspirations provided a fertile ground for centrifugal tendencies to break loose. The Socialists went on the offensive and in May 1980 subjected Suárez to a vote of no confidence. He was able to surmount it but the decomposition of the UCD had already begun. In September 1980, José Pedro Pérez-Llorca took over as Foreign Minister one day before the CSCE preparatory meeting was to convene. In January 1981, tired, exhausted, bereft of new ideas, Suárez abruptly resigned.

His successor, Leopoldo Calvo Sotelo, was to remain in office little more than a year and a half. However, he gave Spanish foreign policy a new twist which was to irretrievably shatter whatever consensus still survived.

The NATO file

Calvo Sotelo's intentions were stated in the speech he made before Parliament on 18 February 1981. Under the assumption that he would be accepted as Prime Minister to head a minority UCD government, he referred to the need for strengthening the political dialogue with other parties and the trade unions so as to tackle critical problems in economic and regional policies. Then he dropped a bomb: his cabinet would begin negotiations to achieve a parliamentary majority that would allow Spain to join the Atlantic Alliance.

The NATO connection had by then become a major subject of contention in Spain. Arias Navarro had mentioned it briefly in January 1976. After the first democratic elections in June 1977 Suárez had indicated that the political forces should discuss the appropriateness of Spain's joining the Alliance. In October 1978 the first UCD congress had gone a little further and endorsed NATO membership. On 30 March 1979 Suárez had underscored the need for wide parliamentary support in order to take such a measure. Oreja had gradually clarified the government's position while the debate about what was perceived as lack of strategic direction in Suárez's foreign policy intensified. In June 1980, Oreja went on to say that the government was utterly in favour of early NATO membership. Two conditions needed to be fulfilled: the process of integration into the Community should continue, and Spanish–British conversations about the transfer of sovereignty over Gibraltar should be under way (following obviously the recently concluded but still unimplemented Lisbon agreement). He added that membership could be effected before the general elections due in 1983 and that a decision might be taken in 1981. It seems that Suárez himself had been considering such a step before he resigned. However, no UCD government had really launched the wide national debate so often mentioned.

After the attempted *coup* of 23 February 1981, Calvo Sotelo remained true to his word. The government did not lose much time in starting the parliamentary proceedings to take Spain into NATO. By then the feeling had also become widespread that the Alliance would help the Spanish military to be less obsessed with domestic developments. The NATO issue overshadowed foreign policy during the last UCD government and greatly contributed to the further polarization of political life. The cabinet's decision enraged the Socialists, Communists (who were by then tearing themselves to pieces) and the whole of the extreme left. This opposition found fertile ground in public opinion, which was unprepared for such a step.[24] Slowly but surely, opinion polls began to lean heavily against NATO membership while the internal difficulties of the government, at that time a mere coalition of frequently warring factions, considerably increased.

The cabinet, however, remained united on the NATO issue and moved on swiftly and surely. On 31 August 1981 Parliament was formally apprised of the matter. Immediately afterwards, the Socialists called for a referendum. Some additional diversionary moves came to nothing. At the end of October a slim majority of just 10 votes in the lower house gave the government the green light for Spain to join the Alliance. Compared with the 186 votes in favour of membership, 146 were cast against. There were 18 absentees. The UCD could count on the right, the Basque and Catalan nationalists and one small party. The whole of the left voted against membership.[25] There could not have been a clearer polarization.

The parliamentary decision contained some interesting provisions. Once adhesion had been effected, it was stated, the Spanish government should not accept, in the subsequent negotiations within the Alliance, any commitments that would imply the storage or the installation of nuclear weapons on Spanish soil. The government had also to take into account the need to guarantee the security of the Peninsular and extra-Peninsular territories. The government was also requested, in line with Oreja's intimation the previous year, to recover sovereignty over Gibraltar and to accelerate the political and economic negotiations with the Community.

On 26 November 1981 the Senate followed the lower house, although by a larger margin: 106 against 60 votes. Two days later, Pérez-Llorca wrote to the NATO Secretary-General stating the government's willingness to receive an invitation to adhere to the North Atlantic Treaty. On Sunday 30 May 1982, the Spanish chargé d'affaires deposited in Washington the instrument of adhesion. All diversionary manoeuvres carried out by the opposition parties met with complete failure. Spain had become the Alliance's 16th member.

Throughout the same period, negotiations were carried out to renew the 1976 treaty with the United States. It was downgraded again to the level of agreement, but Spain's accession to NATO allowed the Spanish negotiators to rebalance some aspects. Thus a strict regulation was agreed concerning the movement of US ships and aircraft in Spanish waters, air space and national territory. The distinction between the use of military facilities within the bilateral connection and the multilateral NATO framework was secured. Much more remained to be done before a complete rebalancing could take place, but any detailed analysis of the 1976 treaty and the 1982 agreement shows to what extent the disequilibria had been reduced in comparison with those accepted by the Franco regime.

Nevertheless, the political life of the government was more than precarious. In October 1981, the Deputy Prime Minister advised Calvo Sotelo to go to the country. He refused. Calvo Sotelo believed that the Socialists would win and break off the NATO accession process that had just started. Before this process ended, regional elections almost obliterated the UCD in Andalucía and gave the PSOE a resounding victory. There was literally no time to guarantee the fulfilment of the parliamentary provisions. In July 1982, Suárez himself left the UCD. In August, the Prime Minister finally decided to dissolve Parliament.[26] When, in September, formal contacts were established with NATO to define the forms of Spanish participation, the dice were rolling heavily for the PSOE.

Seen from the viewpoint of the last UCD government – and certainly from the US perspective – the NATO decision was Spain's definitive anchorage in the Western world and, possibly, a brake on military unruliness. It ended the contradiction between Suárez's flexibility, or lack of inhibition, in certain foreign policy areas and the more orthodox and ideological orientations approved by the UCD congresses. This contradiction had been magnified by the media and enhanced by dissension within the ruling coalition. Suárez was castigated for his alleged ambivalence about rigidly following what could be considered as a conventional Western alignment.[27]

The Calvo Sotelo decision was tactically encouraged by two major additional considerations. First and foremost was the realization that if his government did not apply for, and obtain, Alliance membership for Spain, a Socialist successor government, or one with Socialist participation, would be unlikely to do so. In this sense, Calvo Sotelo was more than willing to incur the ire of the left, particularly when, in the wake of the attempted *coup*, it was inhibited by its desire to avoid rocking the boat of the still fragile democratic system.

Second, some members of the last UCD government, particularly in the economic sector, may have seen the NATO option as a way of showing Spanish solidarity with Western Europe. Such solidarity could perhaps break the deadlock into which the negotiations with the European Community had by then run.[28] Calvo Sotelo, who had been minister in charge of the negotiations, knew all too well the difficulties caused by President Giscard d'Estaing, calling in June 1980 for a pause in the run-up to the second enlargement so that the Community could sort out its agricultural and budgetary problems. Since that time, the negotiations had slowed down and French resistance had gone on solidifying. While the NATO process continued, Spanish diplomacy feverishly multiplied contacts with some of the major powers in the Community and tried to overcome the difficulties by encouraging negotiations on the less conflictive aspects. Nevertheless, in July 1981 the lowest point of the whole process was reached.

In his memoirs Calvo Sotelo underscores the ideological motivation of congruence: Spain wanted to join the European Community and Europe.

It therefore followed that it had also to join the defence network of the Western European democracies. When the first approach turned out to be fraught with difficulties, the only way to show solidarity with Europe was to join in the common defence.[29] This argument was unlikely to find much favour with the Spanish left at that time. The Socialists, in particular, had defended NATO in the 1950s. Since then, the new generation that had come to power in the party was more attuned to the fact that the Atlantic Alliance had accommodated both the Portuguese dictatorship and the scarcely democratic regime of the Greek colonels. The Alliance was not perceived as freedom-loving but as a *mal mineur* which Spain could do without. The Spanish contribution to Western defence was based on the bilateral security relationship with the United States, which had attained the dignity of a treaty.

In December 1976, the 27th Socialist congress had condemned the relationship with the United States, which indisputably lacked democratic credentials. It had also called for Spain to remain independent *vis-à-vis* the blocs. However, by the time of the 1979 general elections the Socialist policy line had dramatically changed. The US security link was no longer questioned. Accepting this was considered more than enough. For the Socialists the strategic priority for Spain was not the Alliance but the Community and the corresponding tightening of relationships with its member states.

However, other political formations, particularly on the extreme left, had clearly neutralist leanings and were certainly able to make mischief for the Socialist party. To the extent that with regard to the NATO dossier the UCD government had not appeared actually to break the prevailing consensus, the debate had remained mostly ideological. It became seriously political when Calvo Sotelo went much further than his predecessor. Opposition to NATO membership then became a rallying cry, a means of identification, for most of the Spanish left. It also found nourishment in a diffuse but potent and specifically Spanish anti-Americanism that flared up during the early years of the Reagan administration, partly in response to its heavy-handedness in Central America.

Circumstantially, this feeling was further encouraged in the critical year of 1981 when the then US Secretary of State Alexander Haig was reported to have described the attempted *coup* as 'an internal matter'. The subsequent indignation contributed to the belief that the security policy readjustment on the left, particularly among the Socialists, which had been necessary for full participation in the consensual transition towards the building and consolidation of the democratic system, did not require any further concessions.

Nevertheless, to explain the opposition to NATO two further factors must be mentioned. The Spanish decision did not match the historical experience of those Western European countries which all political forces in Spain, including the left, wanted to join. Western Europe had experienced the GIs as liberators from the shackles of Fascism. It had seen the United States as the unique provider of economic assistance through the Marshall Plan, and of military security against the threat from the East. Influenced by the collective memory of the Civil War and the Franco regime, many people did not see in the Soviet Union an evil empire. More importantly perhaps, the GIs, or rather the US Air Force, had been experienced as the incarnation of USA political support for the Franco regime.[30] The 1981 decision therefore jumped the gun for the Spanish left. Still unexposed to the benefits of economic and political comradeship in the Community, they were asked to swallow a crumbling government's ideas of ideological congruence.

The second factor has been highlighted by Maxwell. It has to do with possibly the most important intellectual shackle inherited from the past: that is, the limitation of Spanish elites in terms of international exposure as a result of the severely constricted role of Spain in international affairs during the Franco years. Spain 'did not share in the formative influences and common experience of the modern industrialized nations such as victory or defeat in World War II, post-war reconciliation and economic reconstruction, and the building of European transnational institutions'.[31] This was the case with the government and *a fortiori* with the left-wing opposition, which had remained underground until 1977.

The two factors interacted powerfully. The Socialists, however, kept the outcome within limits. The PSOE saw itself in office in the not too distant future. During its 29th congress in October 1981, it unambiguously announced that it would ask the Spanish people to decide, in a referendum, whether Spain should be a NATO member or not. Its opposition gained new strength in anticipation of the 1982 general elections. Later on, in a cautiously and thoughtfully crafted electoral manifesto, the PSOE highlighted its commitment to the referendum and promised that it would stop the negotiations to integrate Spain into the Alliance's military structure. However, it did not promise to take Spain out of NATO. This was an implicit acknowledgement that the future could not be simply a return to the past.

The Socialists accused the UCD governments of lacking coherence in their foreign and security policies and promised highly structured remedial action with a view to strengthening Spain's role in the international arena. Joining Europe was given pride of place and the PSOE committed itself to further rebalancing the military aspects of the relationship with the United States. In their view, they were the best-placed political party in Spain to consign to the dustbin of history the last remaining shackles of the Francoist heritage.

The NATO issue was presented during the campaign in a fighting spirit whose effects went beyond the limits of the manifesto. It undoubtedly contributed to the landslide in favour of the Socialists and added to the utter collapse of the UCD. Nor were the PSOE's chances harmed by the fact that before the elections the security services identified clandestine preparations among extreme-right military circles for yet another attempt at a *coup*. The Socialists received almost twice as many votes as those gained by the right wing. It was the first time in Spain's parliamentary history that such an ovewhelming majority had been secured by any party.

Enter Felipe González

The new Prime Minister, Felipe González, assembled the foreign policy team which, under his uncontested leadership, was to prepare for the final and definitive break with the sequels of the Francoist past. In the first purely Socialist government in all of Spanish history, Fernando Morán became Foreign Minister. Manuel Marín as junior minister was put in charge of the negotiations with the European Community. Luis Yañez took over cooperation activities with Latin America.[32]

Between 1983 and 1986, one of the most critical periods for Spanish foreign policy, the new government's stance was defined by four imperatives. Spain, as host country, had to contribute towards the unblocking of the CSCE meeting in Madrid that had been languishing over the past two years. This was no minor problem, because the East–West environment had by then considerably deteriorated. Second, relations had to be strengthened with governments of neighbouring countries and others whose weight was decisive for speeding up the negotiating process with the Community. Third, integration into the Community had to be achieved as soon as possible. And lastly, the ground had to be prepared for fundamental decisions on how to shape Spanish contributions to international security.

These imperatives compounded a daunting task. Although the prevailing *Zeitgeist* in the West had been very supportive of the Spanish democratic transition and consolidation, some question marks arose in 1982–3 about how the new government would navigate a profoundly changed international environment. Obviously these issues did not all have the same weight. The CSCE meeting had a circumstantial importance and its conclusion, which took place in September 1983, clearly did not depend on Spanish good offices alone.

From the outset, González and Morán[33] worked indefatigably to inject a new spirit into relations with France, Portugal and Britain. Under Mitterrand's first presidency, advances were made in cooperation against ETA terrorism and in circumventing some of the French concerns about the crucial chapters in the accession negotiations to the Community. Periodic ministerial meetings strengthened this *rapprochement*. By 1985 the political impulse led to the establishment of bilateral summits such as those France maintained with Germany or Italy. With Morán, a convinced Lusophile, in the driving seat, the complex relationship with Portugal also grew warmer.

In December 1982, the new government took the plunge and opened to pedestrians the frontier with Gibraltar, which Spain had kept closed for 13 years. After a difficult beginning, the conversations with London led to the Brussels declaration of November 1984, by which the previous Lisbon agreement would be implemented. Spain committed herself to lifting restrictions, which happened in February 1985, and Britain agreed to discuss the question of sovereignty.

The relationship with Germany took on a new quality. González supported the new German government's attitude during the 'Euromissile crisis'. At the European Council in Stuttgart in June 1983 Chancellor Kohl succeeded in establishing a formal link between Community enlargement and intra-Community discussions on financial reform. The negotiations thus received a powerful encouragement. Some additional difficulties were finally overcome and the accession of both Spain and Portugal was solemnly signed on 12 June 1985. It took place on 1 January 1986, a pivotal date in Spanish history.

Two weeks later, after several rounds of secret contacts, the establishment of full diplomatic relations between Spain and Israel was announced.

On the security front, integration into the Alliance's military structure was frozen but no time was lost in assuaging US and Western fears about the Spanish role in the security field. The government was concerned not to tamper with Spain's agreed international alignment or to upset the European scene at a time of increasing tensions between the superpowers. A protocol was negotiated indicating that the 1982 agreement itself should not affect the nature or form of Spanish participation in NATO. The agreement was then ratified by a Socialist-dominated Parliament, a first in Spanish history, with only the four Communist members and a few others opposing.

Morán also sought to develop a more global approach towards North Africa. Rather than continue the tradition of making alternate overtures to Algeria or Morocco, the government decided on a wider-ranging strategy that would allow for more fruitful cooperation between Spain and the Maghreb. Finally, the Socialists attempted to enhance Spain's influence in Latin America, where they believed they could have an influence on regional developments. The handling of policy towards Central America required some finesse in view of the Reagan administration's obsession with that part of the world.

Nevertheless, during the years 1983–5, it was the NATO issue which remained firmly at the forefront of Spanish and Western preoccupations. González unveiled his strategy gradually. In October 1984 a ten-point programme highlighted the basic principles of Spanish security policy and was endorsed by Parliament. It acknowledged that it was in Spain's interest to stay in NATO, although this should not involve integration into the military structure or allow for the deployment of nuclear weapons on Spanish territory. US military presence should be reduced. The possibility of Western European Union (WEU) membership was raised. However, the divisions within the PSOE deepened. In the 30th congress in December 1984, it was only after great personal effort that González succeeded in winning a majority over to his position. In a sense, EC and NATO memberships became psychologically and even politically linked, as the long-serving German Foreign Minister Hans-Dietrich Genscher recognized from the outset.[34]

During 1985, domestic politics critically affected the NATO issue. The referendum commitment split the political parties and polarized all political activity. González vainly tried to re-establish some degree of consensus with the right-wing opposition. On the other hand, the government could not give up on its promise since, for its new security policy to become fully effective, it desperately needed to receive the acquiescence of the majority of Spanish citizens, the first time such support would have been obtained in Spanish history.

The referendum was held on 12 March 1986, slightly over two months after accession to the Community. Spanish NATO membership was subject to some restrictive conditions. Out of an electorate of 29 million people, 17.25 million went to the polls. Of the votes cast, over 9 million (52.5 per cent) supported the government's position. Almost 7 million (about 40 per cent) were opposed. The right had recommended abstention. The referendum was a personal success for Felipe González and marked the end of Spain's intense domestic debate about membership in the Atlantic Alliance.

In November 1988, after having negotiated the forms of participation in NATO, Spain signed the accession protocol to the WEU. On 1 December the US–Spanish security relationship was put, after arduous negotiations, on a new basis. This was the first time the Spanish side had succeeded in getting its viewpoint largely accepted by the Americans. The aim was to pattern the relation along the lines prevailing between the United States and her European allies and gradually to reduce US military presence in Spain. This fundamental re-equilibrium in the US–Spanish relationship and the Spanish anchorage in the European organizations laid the foundations for Spain to return to the mainstream of European economic, political and security developments.

Subsequent policies ensured that this was the case. In a very short period of time, a number of major decisions led to the clear-headed Europeanization of Spanish strategic options. It may seem peculiar, but this process also led to a drastic improvement in the US–Spanish relationship. In time, the political climate in which this relationship evolved became excellent. This is something that the planners in the Department of State had been aiming at since the late 1950s. Only under conditions of democracy and deep integration into the European mainstream, not in a more or less isolated dictatorship, could that aim be achieved. Two further developments showed the warmth of the new relationship with the United States. In 1995, thanks to US support, Javier Solana, González's third Foreign Minister, became NATO Secretary-General. In 1997 Carlos Westendorp, González's fourth and last Foreign Minister, also thanks to US support, became High Representative for Bosnia-Herzegovina.

When, after the 9 November 1989 collapse of the Berlin Wall, the resulting turbulence shattered the international environment, Spain was in a rather comfortable position to meet the challenges to come. Furthermore, González was the first leader of a Western European country to give unequivocal support to Helmut Kohl.[35] This was more than fitting: back in the 1930s, Adolf Hitler had substantially assisted General Franco on his way to power. Half a century later, democratic Spain was to provide political and diplomatic support to democratic Germany when the latter, and Europe, were confronted with the dawn of a truly new era.

No better illustration could be devised to exemplify the break with the substance, ambitions, priorities, strategies and style of Spanish foreign policy during the Franco regime. That break was now complete. No shackles remained.

Notes

1 For a full analysis of those initial disequilibria, see Angel Viñas, *Los pactos secretos de Franco con Estados Unidos: bases, ayuda económico, recortes de soberania* (Barcelona: Grijalbo, 1981). For a highly detailed account of the historical evolution of Spanish security policies, see Antonio Marquina, 'España en la

politica de seguridad occidental' (Madrid: Ediciones Ejército, 1986).

2   Angel Viñas, 'Franco's Dreams of Autarky Shattered', in Christian Leitz (ed.), *Spain in an International Context* (New York: Berghahn Books, forthcoming), examines this critical volte face from a foreign policy viewpoint.

3   Paul Preston, *Franco: A Biography* (London: HarperCollins, 1993), has drawn an excellent portrait of Franco's evolving image.

4   A former ambassador and one of the key men for the relationships with Washington, gives a very distorting picture of Francoist foreign policy as one of the major historical achievements of the dictatorship: Juan José Rovira, 'Franco y la política exterior', in *El legado de Franco* (Madrid: Fundación Nacional Francisco Franco, 1992).

5   Eric Solsten and Sandra W. Meditz, in *Spain: A Country Study* (Washington, DC: Government Printing Office), state that 'the democratization that Franco's chosen heir, Juan Carlos, and his collaborators peacefully and legally brought to Spain over a three-year period was unprecedented. Never before had a dictatorial regime been transformed into a pluralistic, parliamentary democracy without civil war, revolutionary overthrow, or defeat by a foreign power' (pp. 54–5).

6   For useful examples of an abundant body of literature in English dealing with the Spanish transition, see José Maravall, *The Transition to Democracy in Spain* (London: Croom Helm, 1982); Paul Preston, *The Triumph of Democracy in Spain* (London: Methuen, 1986); and Edward Moxon-Browne, *Political Change in Spain* (London: Routledge, 1989).

7   A useful analytical framework is provided by Laurence Whitehead, 'International Aspects of Democratization', in Guillermo O'Donnell, Philippe C. Schmitter and Laurence Whitehead (eds), *Transitions from Authoritarian Rule: Comparative Perspectives* (Baltimore: Johns Hopkins University Press), pp. 000–00. See also Charles T. Powell, 'La dimensión exterior de la transición política española', *Revista del Centro de Estudios Constitutionales*, May–August 1994, pp. 79–116. Helmut Schmidt, *Die Deutschen und ihre Nachbarn: Menschen und Mächte II* (Berlin: Siedler, 1990), gives a useful view of German preoccupations.

8   Juan J. Linz and Alfred Stepan, in *Problems of Democratic Transition and Consolidation: Southern Europe, South America, and Post-Communist Europe* (Baltimore: Johns Hopkins University Press, 1996), p. 108, indicate that 'there is broad scholarly consensus that Spanish democracy was consolidated no later than the peaceful transfer of power to the socialist opposition after the October 1982 general elections'. However, other interpretations are easily found. From a purely foreign policy point of view the case could be made that the transition ended in 1986 when Spain joined the Community and decided to remain in NATO.

9   Kenneth Maxwell and Steven Spiegel, in *The New Spain: From Isolation to Influence* (New York: Council on Foreign Relations Press, 1994), p. 251, refer to the period since 1982 as the years when 'Spanish democracy was firmly consolidated, major economic reforms were implemented, the military was modernized and placed under civilian control, the relationship with the United States was made more equitable, and Spain joined the EC. . . . Spain moved dramatically to assert a new role in Europe and on the world stage.'

10 In the English-speaking world a somewhat contrary view was developed by Benny Pollack and Graham Hunter, *The Paradox of Spanish Foreign Policy:*

Spain's International Relations from Franco to Democracy (London: Pinter, 1987). The break with the Francoist past is exhaustively analysed by Gerlinde Freia Niehus, *Aussenpolitik im Wandel: Die Aussenpolitik Spaniens von der Diktatur Francos zur parlamentarischen Demokratie* (Frankfurt am Main: Vervuert, 1989). A useful summary by the same author is 'Die Aussenpolitik Spaniens nach Franco', in Walther L. Bernecker and Josef Oehrlein (eds), *Spanien heute: Politik, Wirtschaft, Kultur* (Frankfurt am Main: Vervuert, 1991), pp. 225–63.

11 The Duke of Edinburgh and US Vice-President Nelson Rockefeller also attended. The latter had already attended Franco's funeral.

12 José María de Areilza, *Diario de un ministro de la Monarquía* (Barcelona: Planeta, 1977), pp. 24, 43, 57, 64, 187–7. Emilio Menendez del Valle, 'Política exterior y transición democrático en España', in José Felix Tezanos, Ramón Cotaelo and Andres de Blas (eds), *La transición democrático española* (Madrid: Sistema, 1989), p. 717, has rightly highlighted the importance of Areilza's tenure of office as the necessary foundation for what would be done under his successor in terms of foreign policy.

13 On that occasion, according to Areilza, the Secretary of State advised him to resist European pressures that were not compatible with Spanish requirements and to implement reform gradually and cautiously. Kissinger speculated that Spain would join the Community first and the Atlantic Alliance second.

14 Arias Navarro had made a name for himself during the Civil War as an unremittingly harsh military prosecutor. Later he was a tough Interior Minister. Areilza drew an unflattering portrait: utterly ignorant and contemptuous of the outside world, mistrustful in the extreme, addicted to thinking in mere clichés, shaped by his experiences in repression, endowed with a police mentality and hooked on the gossip provided by the intelligence service.

15 Santos Juliá, *Los socialistas en la política española* (Madrid: Taurus, 1997), is probably the best historical account to date of the PSOE's political manoeuvring in the 1970s.

16 Pedro A. Martínez Lillo, 'Consenso y política exterior en la transición española', in Tusell and Soto (eds), *Historia de la transición*, pp. 159–81, recently underlined this important aspect, which has been downplayed by Jonathan Story, 'Spain's External Relations Redefined: 1975–1989', in Richard Gillespie, Fernando Rodrigo and Jonathan Story (eds), *Democratic Spain: Reshaping External Relations in a Changing World* (London: Routledge), pp. 30–49, and Fernando Rodrigo, 'Western Alignment: Spain's Security Policy', ibid., pp. 50–66. Obviously, the consensus process had its ups and downs, but it remains a central analytical framework.

17 This admission has been described by Emilio Muñoz Alemany, *El proceso de integración de España en el Consejo de Europa* (Granada: Universidad de Granada, 1989), and José Luis Messia, *Por palabra de honor: la entrada de España en el Consejo de Europa* (Madrid: Parteluz, 1995). Messia was the Spanish observer at the Council of Europe. Areilza was to become president of the Council's parliamentary Assembly. Oreja later became the Council's Secretary-General.

18 Sagrario Morán, *ETA entre España y Francia* (Madrid: Editorial Complutense, 1997), provides a comprehensive treatment of the difficult relationship with France from the angle of the fight against ETA terrorism.

19 Marquina, 'La política exterior de los gobiernos de la Unión de Centro Democrático', in Javier Tusell and Alvaro Soto (eds), *Historia de la transición, 1975–1986* (Madrid: Alcànza Universidad, 1986), pp. 208–9, gives a clear picture of these convoluted relationships. For the Saharan conflict itself, see Tony Hodges, *Western Sahara: The Roots of Desert War* (Westport: Lawrence Hill, 1983), pp. 167, 185, 215, 350, 355.

20 José Mario Armero, *Política exterior de España en democracia* (Madrid: Espasa, 1989), pp. 28–31, 104–7.

21 Celestino del Arenal, *La política experior de España hacia Iberoamérica* (Madrid: Universidad Complutense, 1994), offers a lucid and highly sophisticated analysis of this critical angle of Spanish foreign policy.

22 Peter Gold, *A Stone in Spain's Shoe: The Search for a Solution to the Problem of Gibraltar* (Liverpool: Liverpool University Press, 1994), pp. 22–4.

23 Armero, *Política exterior*, pp. 114–15.

24 The best treatment available on perceptions and reactions of Spanish public opinion to actions by the political parties in relation to the NATO dossier is Consuelo del Val Cid, *Opinión pública y opinion públicada: los españoles y el referéndum de la OTAN* (Madrid: CIS,1996).

25 Just a year before, an influential work had appeared which heavily coloured the perceptions and many of the arguments not only of the socialists but of the whole Spanish left: Fernando Morán, *Una política exterior para España* (Barcelona: Planeta, 1980).

26 Leopoldo Calvo Sotelo, *Memoria viva de la transición* (Barcelona: Plaza y Janés, 1990), pp. 73–4, 76–7, 123–41, gives a highly personal account with scathing attacks on the PSOE and Felipe González in view of their later volte face.

27 Calvo Sotelo, ibid., pp. 126–7, has drawn a rather negative portrait of Suárez's dabbling in foreign affairs: he had travelled abroad very little, did not speak any foreign language, had a certain reticence towards Western-type democracies, was bothered by the highly technical details of EC negotiations, felt more at ease in Latin America, nurtured a certain anti-American feeling, etc.

28 Raimundo Bassols, ambassador to the Community and later in charge of negotiations as junior minister, provides an insider's account of the *rapprochement* with the EC up until the Socialist landslide: *España en Europa: historia de la adhesion a la CE, 1957–85* (Madrid: Política exterior, 1995). He charges the French Socialist administration with wilfully slowing down the negotiations so as not to give any card to the mortally wounded UCD government which had just completed the NATO accession.

29 Gregory F. Treverton, 'Spain, the United States, and NATO: Strategic Facts and Political Realities', in Federico G. Gil and Joseph S. Tulchin (eds), *Spain's Entry into NATO: Conflicting Political and Strategic Perspectives* (Boulder: Lynne Rienner, 1988), pp. 122–39, however, gives a completely different interpretation of the NATO decision as seen from an American specialist's perspective: 'It was almost an act of desperation by a failing government that was unable to end the impasse in the EC negotiations and was searching for surrogates for a foreign policy it did not really have' (p. 124).

30 This last point was made many times by Felipe González, both as Prime Minister and after having left office. Suffice it to mention three examples, all in the United States: the Wilson Center conference on Spain (September

1985), the eighth annual Paul-Henri Spaak Lecture (Harvard University, April 1988) and the New York University lecture (September 1996).

31 Kenneth Maxwell, 'Spain, from isolation to influence', in Kenneth Maxwell (ed.) *Spanish Foreign and Defence Policy* (Boulder: Westview Press, 1991), p. 3.

32 Juan Antonio Yáñez and Angel Viñas, 'Diez años de política exterior del gobierno socialista', in Alfonso Guerra and José Felix Tezanos (eds), *La decada del cambio: diez años de gobierno socialista, 1982–1992* (Madrid: Sistema, 1992), pp. 85–133, have given a glimpse of the changes and orientations in Spanish foreign policy from the government's perspective; Yáñez is a former Director for International Affairs in the Prime Minister's office.

33 Fernando Morán wrote extensively about his tenure of office: *España en su sitio* (Barcelona: Plaza y Janes, 1990). He left the cabinet at the beginning of July 1985 in González's first government reshuffle. His successor was Francisco Fernández Ordóñez. Angel Viñas, 'Dos hombres para la transición externa: Fernando Morán y Francisco Fernández Ordóñez', *Historia Contemporánea*, vol. 15 (1996), pp. 257–88, makes an attempt to identify the specific input of both ministers to the design and outcomes of Spanish foreign policy during the 1980s.

34 Hans-Dieter Genscher, *Erinnerungen* (Berlin: Siedler, 1995), p. 371.

35 Horst Teltschik, *329 Tage: Innenansichten der Einigung* (Berlin: Siedler, 1991), p. 29. In his memoirs, Helmut Kohl has underlined this aspect: Helmut Kohl, with Kai Diekmann and Ralf Georg Reuth, *Ich wollte Deutschlands Einheit* (Berlin: Propyläen, 1996), pp. 143, 197, 360. González phoned him on 11 November. Previously, Kohl had spoken to Mrs Thatcher, Presidents Bush and Mitterrand and Mr Gorbachev. González 'gave me assurance that I could count on his assistance at any time, particularly when the need arose to work out a solution in a pan-European framework'. In the German Chancellor's view, among the leaders of the Community member states, only Felipe González and the Irish Prime Minister were from the outset in favour of German unification.

Index

Note: Page numbers followed by 'n' refer to notes